GOVERNING

ACADEMIC

ORGANIZATIONS

New Problems
New Perspectives

Edited by

Gary L. Riley

Graduate School of Education
University of California, Los Angeles

J. Victor Baldridge

Higher Education Research Institute, and
University of California, Los Angeles

McCutchan Publishing Corporation
2526 Grove Street
Berkeley, California 94704

© 1977 by McCutchan Publishing Corporation
All rights reserved

Library of Congress Catalog Card no. 76-56995
ISBN 0-8211-1715-7

Printed in the United States of America

To
Garth James, Jennifer Lynn, and Molly Jo

Contents

Acknowledgments

No book is written in isolation, and this is particularly true in the case of *Governing Academic Organizations.* Numerous persons—contributors, research methodologists, critics, and sponsors—helped us decide what needed to be said and find the best way to say it. In particular:

Allan M. Cartter—advocate, friend, and mentor, whose untimely death impoverished higher education policy research and analysis.

Lewis B. Mayhew and James G. March—from whom we learned how to ask the right questions, and from whom we continue to learn how to answer them.

Alexander W. Astin, C. Robert Pace, Lewis Solmon, and James W. Trent—colleagues and sounding boards in the higher education community at UCLA.

Joyce and Harold Prairie, John Schlotfeldt, and Janet Smart—infidels on the educational firing line, whose reliable judgments have helped us to make sense out of it all.

Finally, Kathleen M. Erickson and Patty Miller—tireless readers who pressed us to quit making speeches and put it all into writing.

Introduction

In the spring of 1976, while most colleges were holding graduation, the massive City University of New York closed its doors, sent its students home, and pushed its faculty and staff into the unemployment lines. Frantic meetings with state officials, city leaders, and university officials produced no money for the strife-torn university. The City of New York was flat broke and the State of New York could not (or would not) help. Governor Hugh Carey and Mayor Abe Beame were forced to go to the White House for help, although President Ford was reluctant to give it. Higher education had come to a new stage. The trend toward off-campus control of the universities was now a front-page reality. The students, faculty, and university administrators waited while political leaders determined the fate of the university.

CUNY survived—at least for the time being. Mr. Ford finally helped bail out the tottering city finances and the university reopened its doors. But it will never be the same again. The bareknuckled fight over the university forced CUNY to abandon many of its almost sacred goals and educational policies. The changes were enormous:

- —The 126-year-old policy of free tuition for city residents was dropped, and some of the highest fees for public education in the nation were imposed.
- —The controversial "open admissions" policy for all city high school graduates was abandoned.

—A massive 17 percent budget cut sliced about 4,500 employees, including 2,900 faculty and administrators.

—The governing board was revamped so the state government had more control over the university.

The interesting thing about all these critical educational changes was that they occurred without any of the normal trappings of "academic governance": no university senate "task forces" decreed the changes, no faculty committees pondered late into the night, no administrators locked horns with faculty spokesmen, no students gave "input" into the decision process. Was this good or bad? Perhaps we should not judge, but one thing is clear: it is certainly different.

In 1971, we published a collection of articles on academic decision making entitled *Academic Governance* (Berkeley: McCutchan). In the period since, the roof caved in around the issue of college and university governance. Although the perspective is short, the few years since 1971 look like times of major change. To be sure, the changes were already coming; but in 1971 most of us were too busy watching the last throes of the "student revolution" to get a sense of the deeper changes.

This book tries to catalog and study the major trends in academic governance. Some of the trends persist from earlier times, but new issues have emerged, from cases like CUNY and from events like the financial collapse of New York City. What have we seen?

1. *The importance of external forces continues to grow.* In 1971, the focus was primarily on the *internal* operation of colleges and universities. Since then forces in the larger society have impinged on the academic world to an unprecedented degree. The CUNY experience, to a lesser degree, has affected many colleges. The surrounding social, economic, and political environments permeate all colleges and universities today. Issues which seem to be the most troublesome are not only local, but regional and national in scope. Mayor Beame went to Washington for a solution.

The lowering of public trust has launched us into an age of accountability. It is, oddly enough considering the enrollment figures, a time when higher education has been cast into a "steady-state." There are no-growth mandates and shrinking resources, but there are also greater and greater public demands for services. Ten years ago these issues were considered local; today they are clearly national matters.

2. *State control continues to grow.* In response to all these social changes there has been increased centralization of college and univer-

sity systems at the state level. This has accentuated a feeling of local helplessness, and has reduced the power and autonomy of the local administrator to that of a middle-level manager. The net result of this phenomenon has been to force people to take a much broader view of college and university governance than was believed appropriate during the early 1970's. This broad view is not only essential to understanding *national* trends, it is also fundamental for understanding the operations of *local campuses*. They are being swept along in the mainstream of national and state politics and economics, and have very little control over the forces which set the direction of academic change. The events at CUNY underscore vividly these processes.

3. *Faculty unionism has made strong inroads.* In 1971, faculty unionism was in its infancy. In the few short years that followed, the infant became a giant! Today over 400 campuses are unionized, over half the states have laws allowing collective bargaining for state employees, 20 to 25 percent of all faculty are union members, and permissive legislation is being developed in most other states. In many ways the growth of faculty unions is a response to the conditions listed above: external control and state centralization. The economic crisis also had its influence. Today, a book on academic governance would be seriously limited without an analysis of unionism's impact on governance, personnel practices, and administration.

4. *The student revolution died a quiet death.* In 1971, the war in Vietnam, the trashings on the campuses, and the new role of students in governance were matters of general concern. Unfortunately, the students are now quiet. At CUNY, students complained but no one really listened and no riots paralyzed the campus.

Several factors contributed to the reduction of student influence in academic governance. First, the general apathy following the hot times of the 1960's sent students back to the study halls, beer parlors, and football games—and away from the barricades, senate committees, and rallies. Second, the rising interest in careers, partly due to the economic recession, propelled students back to their books and back to worrying about jobs. Third, increased state control removed many decisions from the campus, farther and farther away from the arenas where students had even meager influence. Finally, the rapid pace of faculty unionization was almost viciously against student influence. When the faculty wrested influence away from reluctant administrations they certainly were not going to share their hard-won advantages with students—contrary to all union rhetoric.

Research on Higher Education

The changing conditions listed above—plus many others—dictate a different treatment of governance today than half a decade ago. In addition, new research activities suggest some changes. In the past few years researchers have made vast improvements in the designs and methodologies used to study higher education. In *Academic Governance,* we wrote that the existing literature was descriptive and highly speculative. Today, however, a review of the professional literature reveals that there has been a significant increase in theory-based studies, in large-scale survey research efforts, and in multidisciplinary approaches. Moreover, there now exist data bases which are sufficiently comprehensive and uniform from one year to the next to allow researchers to conduct longitudinal investigations. These improvements make it possible to deal empirically with a number of factors which previously were dealt with only conceptually.

Other changes in the literature on higher education reflect new awareness, too. Perhaps best illustrated by the nearly completed series of Carnegie Reports on Higher Education, researchers in a number of disciplines have investigated college and universities. Even the literature of practicing administrators and college trustees includes discussions of "organizational centralization," "environmental relations," and "models of academic governance." The appearance of these terms and concepts reflects the influence of conceptual developments and empirical findings by organization theorists, sociologists, political scientists, management specialists, and economists. Therefore, in this volume we are able to discuss academic operations within a much broader conceptual framework and with greater focus upon related policy outcomes than previously was the case.

Organization of the Book

We have identified the major thrust of this volume. The "new problems" are national in scope. The "new perspectives" are defined in terms of the macrosystem of American higher education. Just as the challenge of the late sixties and the early seventies was to develop improved local governance in response to local conflict, the challenge of the next decade is to develop improved linkages between local campuses and the larger social and institutional systems.

Governing Academic Organizations discusses internal governance, but places it within the context of environmental policies, issues, and trends. Many of the articles included in this volume do not appear elsewhere in published form; several were written specially for this book. Others are considered to be classics in the field of academic governance and, although a few years older than other selections, they are fundamental to understanding the characteristics of academic organizations.

Many of the selections are data-based. Their discussions grow out of empirical findings from research projects in higher education. In some cases, a contributor utilizes an informal descriptive—almost conversational—style of presentation. Nevertheless, these discussions are usually based upon research results and experience with comparative organizational data. The book is organized into five parts, each part representing an important dimension of academic governance.

Part I: Colleges and Universities as Complex Organizations

This section serves two purposes. First, it argues that colleges and universities are unique organizations. Second, it addresses the controversial issue of institutional diversity in higher education. Much of the current literature argues that American higher education is becoming less diverse and more homogeneous. A number of factors have contributed to this alleged trend. Systemwide centralization reduces local autonomy and local options in program development, staffing patterns, and even institutional structures. With increased centralization has come a higher degree of bureaucratization. Systemwide routine procedures are one method of ensuring uniformity of resources throughout the system. Some people argue that institutions have been more reluctant to innovate recently. Fewer dollars account for part of this reluctance, but increased accountability also poses a potential threat to campuses wishing to try something a little out of the ordinary.

However, there are several indications that diversity is still thriving. Colleges and universities have many differences: governance patterns, organizational structures, client characteristics, and faculty characteristics, among others. Part I deals with the organizational features of academic organizations, and shows some of the enormous diversity in academic governance patterns.

Part II: Innovation and Change

With scarce resources and increased public pressure to serve the needs of diverse student populations, colleges and universities are faced with the complex problem of having to do more with less. History reveals that American higher education has been most

responsive to the need for educational reform during times of affluence; but the 1970's are not affluent times. Under these circumstances, what is the future of educational reform, innovation, and
change? There are two schools of thought: one school holds that
higher education cannot be responsive without sustained financial
support; the other argues that the financial cutback will act as an
incentive for change.

If higher education must expand to be responsive to new student
needs, and if this expansion is dependent upon increased financial
support, then higher education will be less innovative in the seventies, and the mix of institutions will be less diverse. However, if
higher education is forced to make budget allocations on the basis of
clearly established priorities, and if these priorities reflect the desire
to innovate in responsive ways, then higher education might become
more diverse as each institution determines its priorities based upon
local needs and preferences. Part II offers arguments on both sides of
this innovation issue, and authors identify several factors that are
empirically related to innovation, academic reform, and institutional
change.

Part III: The Environmental Context

This section includes chapters on the public and the law as they
relate to higher education, as well as a chapter on systemwide coordination. Leaders in these areas offer data-based descriptions of the
present situation in higher education. They share a substantial
amount of "informed speculation" about where higher education
seems to be heading. Part III shows the boundaries and constraints
imposed by legislation and multicampus administration. Authors do
not uniformly agree that state systems are taking over and that local
campus autonomy is dead. But it is nevertheless clear that local options are significantly influenced by external, system-related constraints.

Part IV: The "Estates" and Their Role

Neil J. Smelser and Gabriel Almond (*Public Higher Education in
California,* Berkeley: University of California Press, 1974) define the
"estates" in higher education as the students, administrators, faculty,
and trustees. All have vested interests in institutional policies and
practices. More frequently than not, these interests are in direct conflict with each other. This has been called the "endemic conflict
among the estates."

Part IV makes use of new information that has become available since 1971. Moreover, the roles of the estates have undergone considerable change in the past several years, change that is having an impact upon governance practices and decision structures. External associations and influences have served to accentuate certain forms of "endemic conflict" among the estates, while actually helping to resolve other kinds of conflict endemic to the early 1970's. In Part IV we focus on several important groups, including faculty, administrators, trustees, and students. Several chapters are reviews designed to summarize current trends.

Part V: Collective Bargaining

Of the many topics which are currently of interest to students and practitioners in higher education, few attract as much attention as collective bargaining. The reasons are several, but include the fact that faculty unionization introduces an entirely new conceptual framework of administration and management into the professionalized academic environment. Collective bargaining has an impact upon governance structures and institutional processes. We can expect changes in academic senates, committee structures, and departmental arrangements. Furthermore, collective bargaining influences the "estates" in higher education, their roles and relationships. In short, bargaining has an impact upon all of the topics described in the previous four parts of the book.

Unlike many contemporary discussions of collective bargaining in higher education, the selections included in this book are largely data-based. Discussions cross institutional boundaries, and include implications of collective bargaining in both the public and the private sectors. They also address the impact on both the local and system levels of the higher education network.

PART I

Colleges and Universities as
Complex Organizations

1

Alternative Models of Governance in Higher Education

J. Victor Baldridge, David V. Curtis, George P. Ecker, and Gary L. Riley

Organizations vary in a number of important ways: they have different types of clients, they work with different technologies, they employ workers with different skills, they develop different structures and coordinating styles, and they have different relationships to their external environments. Of course, there are elements common to the operation of colleges and universities, hospitals, prisons, business firms, government bureaus, and so on, but no two organizations are the same. Any adequate model of decision making and governance in an organization must take its distinctive characteristics into account.

This chapter deals with the organizational characteristics and decision processes of colleges and universities. Colleges and universities are unique organizations, differing in major respects from industrial organizations, government bureaus, and business firms.

Distinguishing Characteristics of Academic Organizations

Colleges and universities are complex organizations. Like other organizations they have goals, hierarchical systems and structures,

The research reported in this paper was supported by the Stanford Center for Research and Development in Teaching, by funds from the National Institute of Education (contract no. NE-C-00-3-0062).

2

officials who carry out specified duties, decision-making processes that set institutional policy, and a bureaucratic administration that handles routine business. But they also exhibit some critical distinguishing characteristics that affect their decision processes.

Goal Ambiguity

Most organizations are goal-oriented, and as a consequence they can build decision structures to reach their objectives. Business firms want to make a profit, government bureaus have tasks specified by law, hospitals are trying to cure sick people, prisons are in the business of "rehabilitation."

By contrast, colleges and universities have vague, ambiguous goals and they must build decision processes to grapple with a higher degree of uncertainty and conflict. What is the goal of a university? This is a difficult question, for the list of possible answers is long: teaching, research, service to the local community, administration of scientific installations, support of the arts, solutions to social problems. In their book *Leadership and Ambiguity*, Cohen and March comment:

Almost any educated person could deliver a lecture entitled "The Goals of the University." Almost no one will listen to the lecture voluntarily. For the most part, such lectures and their companion essays are well-intentioned exercises in social rhetoric, with little operational content. Efforts to generate normative statements of the goals of the university tend to produce goals that are either meaningless or dubious [Cohen and March, 1974, page 195].

Goal ambiguity, then, is one of the chief characteristics of academic organizations. They rarely have a single mission. On the contrary, they often try to be all things to all people. Because their existing goals are unclear, they also find it hard to reject new goals. Edward Gross (1968) analyzed the goals of faculty and administrators in a large number of American universities and obtained some remarkable results. To be sure, some goals were ranked higher than others, with academic freedom consistently near the the top. But both administrators and faculty marked as important almost every one of forty-seven goals listed by Gross!

Not only are academic goals unclear, they are also highly contested. As long as goals are left ambiguous and abstract, they are readily agreed on. As soon as they are concretely specified and put into operation, conflict erupts. The link between clarity and conflict may help explain the prevalence of meaningless rhetoric in academic policy statements and speeches. It is tempting to resort to rhetoric when serious content produces conflict.

Client Service

Like schools, hospitals, and welfare agencies, academic organizations are "people-processing" institutions. Clients with specific needs are fed into the institution from the environment, the institution acts upon them, and the clients are returned to the larger society. This is an extremely important characteristic, for the clients demand and often obtain significant input into institutional decision-making processes. Even powerless clients such as schoolchildren usually have protectors, such as parents, who demand a voice in the operation of the organization. In higher education, of course, the clients are quite capable of speaking for themselves—and they often do.

Problematic Technology

Because they serve clients with disparate, complicated needs, client-serving organizations frequently have problematic technologies. A manufacturing organization develops a specific technology that can be segmented and routinized. Unskilled, semiskilled, and white collar workers can be productively used without relying heavily on professional expertise. But it is hard to construct a simple technology for an organization dealing with people. Serving clients is difficult to accomplish, and the results are difficult to evaluate, especially on a short-term basis. The entire person must be considered; people cannot be separated easily into small, routine, and technical segments. If at times colleges and universities do not know clearly *what* they are trying to do, they often do not know *how* to do it either.

Professionalism

How does an organization work when its goals are unclear, its service is directed to clients, and its technology is problematic? Most organizations attempt to deal with these problems by hiring expertly trained professionals. Hospitals require doctors and nurses, social welfare agencies hire social workers, public schools hire teachers, and colleges and universities hire faculty members. These professionals use a broad repertoire of skills to deal with the complex and often unpredictable problems of clients. Instead of subdividing a complicated task into a routine set of procedures, professional work requires that a broad range of tasks be performed by a single employee.

Sociologists have made a number of important general observations about professional employees, wherever they may work:

1. Professionals demand *autonomy* in their work. Having acquired considerable skill and expertise in their field, they demand freedom from supervision in applying them.

2. Professionals have *divided loyalties.* They have "cosmopolitan" tendencies and loyalty to their peers at the national level may sometimes interfere with loyalty to their local organization.
3. There are strong tensions between *professional values* and *bureaucratic expectations* in an organization. This can intensify conflict between professional employees and organizational managers.
4. Professionals demand *peer evaluation* of their work. They believe that only their colleagues can judge their performance, and they reject the evaluations of others, even those who are technically their superiors in the organizational hierarchy.

All of these characteristics undercut the traditional norms of a bureaucracy, rejecting its hierarchy, control structure, and management procedures. As a consequence, we can expect a distinct management style in a professional organization.

Finally, colleges and universities tend to have *fragmented* professional staffs. In some organizations there is one dominant professional group. For example, doctors are the dominant group in hospitals. In other organizations the professional staff is fragmented into subgroups, none of which predominates. The faculty in a university provides a clear example. Burton R. Clark comments on the fragmented professionalism in academic organizations:

The internal controls of the medical profession are strong and are substituted for those of the organization. But in the college or university this situation does not obtain; there are twelve, twenty-five, or fifty clusters of experts. The experts are prone to identify with their own disciplines, and the "academic profession" overall comes off a poor second. We have wheels within wheels, many professions within a profession. No one of the disciplines on a campus is likely to dominate the others. . . . The campus is not a closely knit group of professionals who see the world from one perspective. As a collection of professionals, it is decentralized, loose, and flabby.

The principle is this: where professional influence is high and there is one dominant professional group, the organization will be integrated by the imposition of professional standards. Where professional influence is high and there are a number of professional groups, the organization will be split by professionalism. The university and the large college are fractured by expertness, not unified by it. The sheer variety supports the tendency for authority to diffuse toward quasi-autonomous clusters [Clark, 1963, pages 37, 51].

Environmental Vulnerability

Another characteristic that sets colleges and universities apart from many other complex organizations is environmental vulnerability. Almost all organizations interact with their social environment to some extent. But though no organization is completely autonomous, some have considerably greater freedom of action than others. The degree of autonomy an organization has vis-à-vis its environment is one of the critical determinants of how it will be managed.

For example, in a free market economy, business firms and industries have a substantial degree of autonomy. Although they are regulated by countless government agencies and constrained by their customers, essentially they are free agents responsive to market demands rather than to government control. At the other extreme, a number of organizations are virtually "captured" by their environments. Public school districts, for example, are constantly scrutinized and pressured by the communities they serve.

Colleges and universities are somewhere in the middle on a continuum from "independent" to "captured." In many respects they are insulated from their environment. Recently, however, powerful external forces have been applied to academic institutions. Interest groups holding conflicting values have made their wishes, demands, and threats well known to the administrations and faculties of academic organizations in the 1970's.

What impact does environmental pressure have on the governance of colleges and universities? When professional organizations are well insulated from the pressures of the outside environment, then professional values, norms, and work definitions play a dominant role in shaping the character of the organization. On the other hand, when strong external pressure is applied to colleges and universities, the operating autonomy of the academic professionals is seriously reduced. The faculty and administrators lose some control over the curriculum, the goals, and the daily operation of the institution. Under these circumstances, the academic professionals are frequently reduced to the role of hired employees doing the bidding of bureaucratic managers.

Although colleges and universities are not entirely captured by their environments, they are steadily losing ground. As their vulnerability increases, their governance patterns change significantly.

"Organized Anarchy"

To summarize, academic organizations have several unique organizational characteristics. They have *ambiguous goals* that are often strongly contested. They serve *clients* who demand a voice in the decision-making process. They have a *problematic technology*, for in order to serve clients their technology must be holistic and adaptable to individual needs. They are *professionalized organizations* in which employees demand a large measure of control over institutional decision processes. Finally, they are becoming more and more *vulnerable to their environments.*

The character of such a complex organizational system is not satisfactorily conveyed by the standard term "bureaucracy." Bureaucracy carries the connotation of stability or even rigidity; academic organizations seem more fluid. Bureaucracy implies distinct lines of authority and strict hierarchical command; academic organizations have blurred lines of authority and professional employees who demand autonomy in their work. Bureaucracy suggests a cohesive organization with clear goals; academic organizations are characteristically fragmented with ambiguous and contested goals. Bureaucracy does adequately describe certain aspects of colleges and universities, such as business administration, plant management, capital outlay, and auxiliary services. But the processes at the heart of an academic organization—academic policy making, professional teaching, and research—do not resemble the processes one finds in a bureaucracy. Table 1-1 summarizes the differences between the two types of organizations.

TABLE 1-1

Organizational Characteristics of Academic Organizations and More
Traditional Bureaucracies

	Academic organizations (colleges and universities)	Traditional bureaucracies (government agency, industry)
Goals	Ambiguous, contested, inconsistent	Clearer goals, less disagreement
Client service	Client-serving	Material-processing, commercial
Technology	Unclear, nonroutine, holistic	Clearer, routinized, segmented
Staffing	Predominantly professional	Predominantly nonprofessional
Environmental relations	Very vulnerable	Less vulnerable
Summary image	"Organized anarchy"	"Bureaucracy"

Perhaps a better term for academic organizations has been suggested by Cohen and March. They describe the academic organization as an "organized anarchy"—a system with little central coordination or control:

In a university anarchy each individual in the university is seen as making autonomous decisions. Teachers decide if, when, and what to teach. Students decide if, when, and what to learn. Legislators and donors decide if, when, and what to support. Neither coordination . . . nor control [is] practiced. Resources are allocated by whatever process emerges but without explicit accommodation and without explicit reference to some superordinate goal. The "decisions" of the system are a consequence produced by the system but intended by no one and decisively controlled by no one [Cohen and March, 1974, pages 33-34].

The organized anarchy differs radically from the well-organized bureaucracy or the consensus-bound collegium. It is an organization in which generous resources allow people to go in different directions without coordination by a central authority. Leaders are relatively weak and decisions are made by individual action. Since the organization's goals are ambiguous, decisions are often by-products of unintended and unplanned activity. In such fluid circumstances, presidents and other institutional leaders serve primarily as catalysts or facilitators of an ongoing process. They do not so much lead the institution as channel its activities in subtle ways. They do not command, but negotiate. They do not plan comprehensively, but try to apply preexisting solutions to problems.

Decisions are not so much "made" as they "happen." Problems, choices, and decision makers happen to come together in temporary solutions. Cohen and March have described decision processes in an organized anarchy as

sets of procedures through which organizational participants arrive at an interpretation of what they are doing and what they have done while they are doing it. From this point of view an organization is a collection of choices looking for problems, issues and feelings looking for decision situations in which they might be aired, solutions looking for issues for which they might be the answer, and decision makers looking for work [Cohen and March, 1974, page 81].

The imagery of organized anarchy helps capture the spirit of the confused organizational dynamics in academic institutions: unclear goals, unclear technologies, and environmental vulnerability.

Some may regard "organized anarchy" as an exaggerated term, suggesting more confusion and conflict than really exist in academic organizations. This is probably a legitimate criticism. The term may also carry negative connotations to those unaware that it applies to specific organizational characteristics rather than to the entire campus community. Nevertheless, "organized anarchy" has some strong points in its favor. It breaks through the traditional formality that often surrounds discussions of decision making, challenges our existing conceptions, and suggests a looser, more fluid kind of organization. For these reasons we will join Cohen and March in using "organized anarchy" to summarize some of the unique organizational characteristics of colleges and universities: (1) unclear goals, (2) client service, (3) unclear technology, (4) professionalism, and (5) environmental vulnerability.[1]

1. Our list of characteristics of an organized anarchy extends Cohen and March's, which contains (1) and (3), plus a characteristic called "fluid participation."

Models of Academic Governance

Administrators and organization theorists concerned with academic governance have often developed images to summarize the complex decision process: collegial system, bureaucratic network, political activity, or participatory democracy. Such models organize the way we perceive the process, determine how we analyze it, and help determine our actions. For example, if we regard a system as political, then we form coalitions to pressure decision makers. If we regard it as collegial, then we seek to persuade people by appealing to reason. If we regard it as bureaucratic, then we use legalistic maneuvers to gain our ends.

In the past few years, as research on higher education has increased, models for academic governance have also proliferated. Three models have received widespread attention, more or less dominating the thinking of people who study academic governance. We will examine briefly each of these models in turn: (1) the bureaucracy, (2) the collegium, and (3) the political system. Each of these models has certain points in its favor. They can be used jointly to examine different aspects of the governance process.

The Academic Bureaucracy

One of the most influential descriptions of complex organizations is Max Weber's (1947) monumental work on bureaucracies. Weber discussed the characteristics of bureaucracies that distinguish them from less formal work organizations. In skeleton form he suggested that bureaucracies are networks of social groups dedicated to limited goals and organized for maximum efficiency. Moreover, the regulation of a bureaucratic system is based on the principle of "legal rationality," as contrasted with informal regulation based on friendship, loyalty to family, or personal allegiance to a charismatic leader. The hierarchical structure is held together by formal chains of command and systems of communication. The bureaucracy as Weber described it includes such elements as tenure, appointment to office, salaries as a rational form of payment, and competency as the basis of promotion.

Bureaucratic characteristics of colleges and universities. Several authors have suggested that university governance may be more fully understood by applying the bureaucratic model. For example, Herbert Stroup (1966) has pointed out some characteristics of colleges and universities that fit Weber's original description of a bureaucracy. They include the following:

1. Competence is the criterion used for appointment.

2. Officials are appointed, not elected.
3. Salaries are fixed and paid directly by the organization, rather than determined in "free-fee" style.
4. Rank is recognized and respected.
5. The career is exclusive; no other work is done.
6. The style of life of the organization's members centers on the organization.
7. Security is present in a tenure system.
8. Personal and organizational property are separated.

Stroup is undoubtedly correct in believing that Weber's paradigm can be applied to universities, and most observers are well aware of the bureaucratic factors involved in university administration. Among the more prominent are the following.

1. The university is a complex organization under *state charter*, like most other bureaucracies. This seemingly innocent fact has major consequences, especially as states increasingly seek to exercise control.
2. The university has a *formal hierarchy*, with offices and a set of bylaws that specify the relations between those offices. Professors, instructors, and research assistants may be considered bureaucratic officers in the same sense as deans, chancellors, and presidents.
3. There are *formal channels of communication* that must be respected.
4. There are definite *bureaucratic authority relations*, with certain officials exercising authority over others. In a university the authority relations are often vague and shifting, but no one would deny that they exist.
5. There are *formal policies and rules* that govern much of the institution's work, such as library regulations, budgetary guidelines, and procedures of the university senate.
6. The bureaucratic elements of the university are most vividly apparent in its *"people-processing" aspects*: record keeping, registration, graduation requirements, and a multitude of other routine, day-to-day activities designed to help the modern university handle its masses of students.
7. *Bureaucratic decision-making processes* are used, most often by officials assigned the responsibility for making routine decisions by the formal administrative structure. Examples are admissions procedures, handled by the dean of admissions; procedures for graduation, routinely administered by designated officials; research policies, supervised by specified officials; and financial

matters, usually handled in a bureaucratic manner by the finance office.

Weaknesses in the bureaucratic model. In many ways the bureaucratic model falls short of encompassing university governance, especially if one is primarily concerned with decision-making processes. First, the bureaucratic model tells us much about authority—that is, legitimate, formalized power—but not much about informal types of power and influence, which may take the form of mass movements or appeals to emotion and sentiment. Second, it explains much about the organization's formal *structure* but little about the dynamic *processes* that characterize the organization in action. Third, it describes the formal structure at one particular time, but it does not explain changes over time. Fourth, it explains how policies may be carried out most efficiently, but it says little about the critical process by which policy is established in the first place. Finally, it also ignores political issues, such as the struggles of various interest groups within the university.

The University Collegium

Many writers have rejected the bureaucratic model of the university. They seek to replace it with the model of the "collegium" or "community of scholars." When this literature is closely examined, there seem to be at least three different threads running through it.

A description of collegial decision making. This approach argues that academic decision making should not be like the hierarchical process in a bureaucracy. Instead there should be full participation of the academic community, especially the faculty. Under this concept the community of scholars would administer its own affairs, and bureaucratic officials would have little influence (see Goodman, 1962). John Millett, one of the foremost proponents of this model, has succinctly stated his view:

I do not believe that the concept of hierarchy is a realistic representation of the interpersonal relationships which exist within a college or university. Nor do I believe that a structure of hierarchy is a desirable prescription for the organization of a college or university. . . .

I would argue that there is another concept of organization just as valuable as a tool of analysis and even more useful as a generalized observation of group and interpersonal behavior. This is the concept of community. . . .

The concept of community presupposes an organization in which functions are differentiated and in which specialization must be brought together, or coordination, if you will, is achieved not through a structure of superordination and subordination of persons and groups but through a *dynamic of consensus* [Millett, 1962, pages 234-235].

A discussion of the faculty's professional authority. Talcott Parsons (1947) was one of the first to call attention to the difference between "official competence," derived from one's office in a bureaucracy, and "technical competence," derived from one's ability to perform a given task. Parsons concentrated on the technical competence of the physician, but others have extended this logic to other professionals whose authority is based on what they *know* and can *do*, rather than on their official position. Some examples are the scientist in industry, the military adviser, the expert in government, the physician in the hospital, and the professor in the university.

The literature on professionalism strongly supports the argument for collegial organization. It emphasizes the professional's ability to make his own decisions and his need for freedom from organizational restraints. Consequently, the collegium is seen as the most reasonable method of organizing the university. Parsons, for example, notes (page 60) that when professionals are organized in a bureaucracy, "there are strong tendencies for them to develop a different sort of structure from that characteristic of the administrative hierarchy . . . of bureaucracy. Instead of a rigid hierarchy of status and authority there tends to be what is roughly, in formal status, a company of equals."

A utopian prescription for operating the educational system. There is a third strand in the collegial image. In recent years there has been a growing discontent with our impersonal contemporary society. The multiversity, with its thousands of students and its huge bureaucracy, is a case in point. The student revolts of the 1960's and perhaps even the widespread apathy of the 1970's are symptoms of deeply felt alienation between students and massive educational establishments. The discontent and anxiety this alienation has produced are aptly expressed in the now-famous sign worn by a Berkeley student: "I am a human being—do not fold, spindle, or mutilate."

As an alternative to this impersonal, bureaucratized educational system, many critics are calling for a return to the "academic community." In their conception such a community would offer personal attention, humane education, and "relevant confrontation with life." Paul Goodman's *The Community of Scholars* (1962) still appeals to many who seek to reform the university. Goodman cites the need for more personal interaction between faculty and students, for more relevant courses, and for educational innovations to bring the student into existential dialogue with the subject matter of his discipline. The number of articles on this subject, in both the mass media and the professional journals, is astonishingly large. Indeed, this concept of the collegial academic community is now widely proposed as one answer to the impersonality and meaninglessness of today's large multiversity. Thus conceived, the collegial model functions more as a revolutionary ideology and a utopian projection than a description of actual governance processes at any university.

Weaknesses in the collegial model. Three themes are incorporated in the collegial model: (1) decision making by consensus, (2) the professional authority of faculty members, and (3) the call for more humane education. These are all legitimate and appealing. Few would deny that our universities would be better centers of learning if we could somehow implement these objectives. There is a misleading simplicity about the collegial model, however, that glosses over many realities.

For one thing, the *descriptive* and *normative* visions are often confused. In the literature dealing with the collegial model it is often difficult to tell whether a writer is saying that the university is a collegium or that it ought to be a collegium. Discussions of the collegium are frequently more a lament for paradise lost than a description of reality. Indeed, the collegial image of round-table decision making is not an accurate description of the processes in most institutions.

Although at the department level there are many examples of collegial decision making, at higher levels it usually exists only in some aspects of the committee system. Of course, the proponents may be advocating a collegial model as a desirable goal or reform strategy. This is helpful, but it does not allow us to understand the actual workings of universities.

In addition, the collegial model fails to deal adequately with the problem of *conflict.* When Millett emphasizes the "dynamic of consensus," he neglects the prolonged battles that precede consensus, as well as decisions that actually represent the victory of one group over another. Proponents of the collegial model are correct in declaring that simple bureaucratic rule making is not the essence of decision making. But in making this point they take the equally indefensible position that major decisions are reached primarily by consensus. Neither extreme is correct, for decisions are rarely made by either bureaucratic fiat or simple consensus.

The University as a Political System

In *Power and Conflict in the University* (1971), Baldridge proposed a "political" model of university governance. Although the other major models of governance—the collegial and the bureaucratic

—have valuable insights to offer, we believe that further insights can be gained from this model. It grapples with the power plays, conflicts, and rough-and-tumble politics to be found in many academic institutions.

Basic assumptions of a political model. The political model assumes that complex organizations can be studied as miniature political systems. There are interest group dynamics and conflicts similar to those in cities, states, or other political entities. The political model focuses on policy-forming processes, because major policies commit an organization to definite goals and set the strategies for reaching those goals. Policy decisions are critical decisions. They have a major impact on an organization's future. Of course, in any practical situation it may be difficult to separate the routine from the critical, for issues that seem minor at one point may later be decisive, or vice versa. In general, however, policy decisions bind an organization to important courses of action.

Since policies are so important, people throughout an organization try to influence them to reflect their own interests and values. Policy making becomes a vital target of interest group activity that permeates the organization. Owing to its central importance, then, the organization theorist may select policy formation as the key for studying organizational conflict and change, just as the political scientist often selects legislative acts as the focal point for his analysis of a state's political processes. With policy formation as its key issue, the political model operates on a series of assumptions about the political process.

1. To say that policy making is a political process is not to say that everyone is involved. On the contrary, *inactivity* prevails. Most people most of the time find the policy-making process an uninteresting, unrewarding activity. Policy making is therefore left to the administrators. This is characteristic not only of policy making in universities but of political processes in society at large. Voters do not vote; citizens do not attend city council meetings; parents often permit school boards to do what they please. By and large, decisions that may have a profound effect on our society are made by small groups of elites.

2. Even people who are active engage in *fluid participation.* They move in and out of the decision-making process. Rarely do people spend much time on any given issue. Decisions, therefore, are usually made by those who persist. This normally means that small groups of political elites govern most major decisions, for they invest the necessary time in the process.

3. Colleges and universities, like most other social organizations,

are characterized by fragmentation into *interest groups* with different goals and values. When resources are plentiful and the organization is prospering, these interest groups engage in only minimal conflict. But they are likely to mobilize and try to influence decisions when resources are tight, outside pressure groups attack, or internal groups try to assume command.

4. In a fragmented, dynamic social system *conflict* is natural. It is not necessarily a symptom of breakdown in the academic community. In fact, conflict is a significant factor in promoting healthy organizational change.

5. The pressure that groups can exert places severe *limitations on formal authority* in the bureaucratic sense. Decisions are not simply bureaucratic orders but are often negotiated compromises between competing groups. Officials are not free simply to issue a decision. Instead they must attempt to find a viable course acceptable to several powerful blocs.

6. *External interest groups* exert a strong influence over the policy-making process. External pressures and formal control by outside agencies—especially in public institutions—are powerful shapers of internal governance processes.

The political decision model versus the rational decision model. The bureaucratic model of organizational structure is accompanied by a rational model of decision making. It is usually assumed that in a bureaucracy the structure is hierarchical and well organized, and that decisions are made through clear-cut, predetermined steps. Moreover, a definite, rational approach is expected to lead to the optimal decision. Graham T. Allison has summarized the rational decision-making process as follows:

1. *Goals and objectives.* The goals and objectives of the agent are translated into a "payoff" or "utility" or "preference" function, which represents the "value" or "utility" of alternative sets of consequences. At the outset of the decision problem the agent has a payoff function which ranks all possible sets of consequences in terms of his values and objectives. Each bundle of consequences will contain a number of side effects. Nevertheless, at a minimum, the agent must be able to rank in order of preference each possible set of consequences that might result from a particular action.

2. *Alternatives.* The rational agent must choose among a set of alternatives displayed before him in a particular situation. In decision theory these alternatives are represented as a decision tree. The alternative courses of action may include more than a simple act, but the specification of a course of action must be sufficiently precise to differentiate it from other alternatives.

3. *Consequences.* To each alternative is attached a set of consequences or outcomes of choice that will ensue if that particular alternative is chosen. Variations are generated at this point by making different assumptions about the

accuracy of the decision maker's knowledge of the consequences that follow from the choice of each alternative.

4. *Choice.* Rational choice consists simply of selecting that alternative whose consequences rank highest in the decision maker's payoff function [Allison, 1971, pages 29-30].

The rational model appeals to those who regard their actions as essentially goal-directed and rational. Realistically, however, we should realize that the rational model is more an ideal than an actual description of how people act. In fact, in the confused organizational setting of the university, political constraints often undermine the force of rationality. A political model of decision making requires us to answer some new questions about the decision process:

The first new question posed by the political model is *why* a given decision is made at all. The formalists have already indicated that "recognition of the problem" is one element in the process, but too little attention has been paid to the activities that bring a particular issue to the forefront. Why is *this* decision being considered at *this* particular time? The political model insists that interest groups, powerful individuals, and bureaucratic processes are critical in drawing attention to some decisions rather than to others. A study of "attention cues" by which issues are called to the community's attention is a vital part of any analysis.

Second, a question must be raised about the right of any person or group to make the decisions. Previously the *who* question was seldom raised, chiefly because the decision literature was developed for hierarchical organizations in which the focus of authority could be easily defined. In a more loosely coordinated system however, we must ask a prior question: Why was the legitimacy to make the decision vested in a particular person or group? Why is Dean Smith making the decision instead of Dean Jones or why is the University Senate dealing with the problem instead of the central administration? Establishing the right of authority over a decision is a political question, subject to conflict, power manipulation, and struggles between interest groups. Thus the political model always asks tough questions: Who has the right to make the decision? What are the conflict-ridden processes by which the decision was located at this point rather than at another? The crucial point is that often the issue of *who* makes the decision has already limited, structured, and pre-formed *how* it will be made.

The third new issue raised by a political interpretation concerns the development of complex decision networks. As a result of the fragmentation of the university, decision making is rarely located in one official; instead it is dependent on the advice and authority of numerous people. Again the importance of the committee system is evident. It is necessary to understand that the committee network is the legitimate reflection of the need for professional influence to intermingle with bureaucratic influence. The decision process, then, is taken out of the hands of individuals (although there are still many who are powerful) and placed into a network that allows a *cumulative buildup* of expertise and advice. When the very life of the organization clusters around expertise, *decision making is likely to be diffused, segmentalized, and decentralized.* A complex network of committees, councils, and advisory bodies grows to handle the task of assembling the expertise necessary for reasonable decisions. Decision making by the individual bureaucrat is replaced with decision making by committee, council, and cabinet. Centralized decision making is replaced with diffuse decision making. The process becomes a far-flung network for gathering expertise from every corner of the organization and translating it into policy [Baldridge, 1971, page 190].

The fourth new question raised by the political model concerns alternative solutions to the problem at hand. The rational decision model suggests that all possible options are open and within easy reach of the decision maker. A realistic appraisal of decision dynamics in most organizations, however, suggests that by no means are all options open. The political dynamics of interest groups, the force of external power blocs, and the opposition of powerful professional constituencies may leave only a handful of viable options. The range of alternatives is often sharply limited by political considerations. Just as important, there is often little time and energy available for seeking new solutions. Although all possible solutions should be identified under the rational model, in the real world administrators have little time to grope for solutions before their deadlines.

In *Power and Conflict in the University*, Baldridge summed up the political model of decision making as follows:

First, powerful political forces—interest groups, bureaucratic officials, influential individuals, organizational subunits—cause a given issue to emerge from the limbo of on-going problems and certain "attention cues" force the political community to consider the problem. Second, there is a struggle over locating the decision with a particular person or group, for the location of the right to make the decision often determines the outcome. Third, decisions are usually "preformed" to a great extent by the time one person or group is given the legitimacy to make the decision; not all options are open and the choices have been severely limited by the previous conflicts. Fourth, such political struggles are more likely to occur in reference to "critical" decisions than to "routine" decisions. Fifth, a complex decision network is developed to gather the necessary information and supply the critical expertise. Sixth, during the process of making the decision political controversy is likely to continue and compromises, deals, and plain head cracking are often necessary to get any decision made. Finally, the controversy is not likely to end easily. In fact, it is difficult even to know when a decision *is* made, for the political processes have a habit of unmaking, confusing, and muddling whatever agreements are hammered out.

This may be a better way of grappling with the complexity that surrounds decision processes within a loosely coordinated, fragmented political system. The formal decision models seem to have been asking very limited questions about the decision process and more insight can be gained by asking a new set of political questions. Thus the decision model that emerges from the university's political dynamics is more open, more dependent on conflict and political action. It is not so systematic or formalistic as most decision theory, but it is

probably closer to the truth. Decision making, then, is not an isolated technique
but another critical process that must be integrated into a larger political image
[Baldridge, 1971, pages 191-192].

It is clear that a political analysis emphasizes certain factors over
others. First, it is concerned primarily with problems of goal setting
and conflicts over values, rather than with efficiency in achieving
goals. Second, analysis of the organization's change processes and
adaptation to its environment is critically important. Second, analysis of the organization's change processes and adaptation to its environment is critically important. The political dynamics of a university are constantly changing, pressuring the university in many
directions, and forcing change throughout the academic system.
Third, the analysis of conflict is an essential component. Fourth,
there is the role of interest groups in pressuring decision makers to
formulate policy. Finally, much attention is given to the legislative
and decision-making phases—the processes by which pressures and
power are transformed into policy. Taken together these points constitute the bare outline for a political analysis of academic governance.

*The revised political model: an environmental and structuralist
approach.* Since the political model of academic governance originally appeared in *Power and Conflict in the University*, we have
become aware that it has several shortcomings. For this reason we
offer a few observations about some changes in emphasis, a few cor-
rections in focus.

First, the original political model probably underestimated the
impact of routine bureaucratic processes. Many, perhaps most, decisions are made not in the heat of political controversy but according
to standard operating procedures. The political description in *Power
and Conflict in the University* was based on a study of New York
University. The research occurred at a time of extremely high conflict when the university was confronted with two crises, a student
revolution and a financial disaster. The political model developed
from that study probably overstresses the role of conflict and negotiation as elements in standard decision making, since those were the
processes apparent at the time. Now we would stress that it is important to consider routine procedures of the governance process.

Second, the original political model, based on a single case study,
did not do justice to the broad range of political activity that occurs
in different kinds of institutions. For example, NYU is quite different from Oberlin College, and both are distinctive institutions

compared to local community colleges. Many of the intense political dynamics observed in the NYU study may have been exaggerated in a troubled institution such as NYU, particularly during the heated conflicts of the late 1960's.

Third, we want to stress even more strongly the central role of environmental factors. The NYU analysis showed that conflict and political processes within the university were linked to environmental factors. But even more stress on the environmental context is needed.

Finally, as developed in *Power and Conflict in the University*, the political model suffered from an "episodic" character. That is, the model did not give enough emphasis to long-term decision-making patterns, and it failed to consider the way institutional structure may shape and channel political efforts. Centralization of power, the development of decision councils, long-term patterns of professional autonomy, the dynamics of departmental power, and the growth of unionization were all slighted by the original model. There are other important questions concerning long-term patterns: What groups tend to dominate decision making over long periods of time? Do some groups seem to be systematically excluded from the decision-making process? Do different kinds of institutions have different political patterns? Do institutional characteristics affect the morale of participants in such a way that they engage in particular decision-influencing activities? Do different kinds of institutions have systematic patterns of faculty participation in decision making? Are decision processes highly centralized in certain kinds of institutions?

Finally, we are not substituting the political model for the bureaucratic or collegial model of academic decision making. In a sense, they each address a separate set of problems and, taken together, they often yield complementary interpretations. We believe, however, that the political model has many strengths, and we offer it as a useful tool for understanding academic governance. See Table 1-2 for a comparison of the three decision-making models.

Images of Leadership and Management Strategies

Thus far we have made two basic arguments: (1) colleges and universities are unique in many of their organizational characteristics and, as a consequence, it is necessary to create new models to help explain organizational structure, governance, and decision making; and (2) a political model of academic governance offers useful insights in addition to those offered by the bureaucratic and collegial

TABLE 1-2
Three Models of Decision Making and Governance

	Bureaucratic	Collegial	Political
Assumptions about structure	Hierarchical bureaucracy	Community of peers	Fragmented, complex professional federation
Social	Unitary: integrated by formal system	Unitary: integrated by peer consensus	Pluralistic: encompasses different interest groups with divergent values
Basic theoretical foundations	Weberian bureaucracy, classic studies of formal systems	Professionalism literature, human-relations approach to organization	Conflict analysis, interest group theory, community power literature
View of decision-making process	"Rational" decision making; standard operating procedures	Shared collegial decision: consensus, community participation	Negotiation, bargaining, political influence, political brokerage, external influence
Cycle of decision making	Problem definition; search for alternatives; evaluation of alternatives; calculus; choice; implementation	As in bureaucratic model, but in addition stresses the involvement of professional peers in the process	Emergence of issue out of social context; interest articulation; conflict; legislative process; implementation of policy; feedback

models. In this section we will suggest that some alternative images of leadership and management style are needed to accommodate the unique characteristics of academic organizations.

Leadership Under the Bureaucratic Model

Under the bureaucratic model the leader is seen as a hero who stands at the top of a complex pyramid of power. The hero's job is to assess problems, propose alternatives, and make rational choices. Much of the organization's power is held by the hero. Great expectations are raised because people trust the hero to solve their problems and to fend off threats from the environment. The image of the authoritarian hero is deeply ingrained in most societies and in the philosophy of most organization theorists.

We expect leaders to possess a unique set of skills with emphasis on problem-solving ability and technical knowledge about the organization. The principles of "scientific management," such as Planning, Programming, Budgeting Systems (PPBS) and Management by Objectives, are often proposed as the methods for rational problem solving. Generally, schools of management, business, and educational administration teach such courses to develop the technical skills that the hero-planner will need in leading the organization.

The hero image is deeply imbedded in our cultural beliefs about leadership. But in organizations such as colleges and universities it is out of place. Power is more diffuse in these organizations; it is lodged with professional experts and fragmented into many departments and subdivisions. Under these circumstances, high expectations about leadership performance often cannot be met. The leader has neither the power nor the information necessary to consistently make heroic decisions. Moreover, the scientific management procedures prescribed for organizational leaders quickly break down under conditions of goal ambiguity, professional dominance, and environmental vulnerability—precisely the organizational characteristics of colleges and universities. Scientific management theories make several basic assumptions: (1) the organization's goals are clear; (2) the organization is a closed system insulated from environmental penetration; and (3) the planners have the power to execute their decisions. These assumptions seem unrealistic in the confused and fluid world of the organized anarchy.

Leadership Under the Collegial Model

The collegial leader presents a stark contrast to the heroic bureaucratic leader. The collegial leader is above all the "first among equals" in an organization run by professional experts. Essentially, the collegial model proposes what John Millett calls the "dynamic of consensus in a community of scholars." The basic role of the collegial leader is not so much to command as to listen, not so much to lead as to gather expert judgments, not so much to manage as to facilitate, not so much to order but to persuade and negotiate.

Obviously, the skills of a collegial leader differ from those required by the scientific management principles employed by the heroic bureaucrat. Instead of technical problem-solving skills, the collegial leader needs professional expertise to ensure that he is held in high esteem by his colleagues. Talent in interpersonal dynamics is also needed to achieve consensus in organizational decision making. The collegial leader's role is more modest and more realistic. He does not stand alone, since other professionals share the burden of decision making with him. Negotiation and compromise are the bywords of the collegial leader; authoritarian strategies are clearly inappropriate.

Leadership Under the Political Model

Under the political model the leader is a mediator or negotiator between power blocs. Unlike the autocratic academic president of the past, who ruled with an iron hand, the contemporary president must play a political role by pulling coalitions together to fight for desired changes. The academic monarch of yesteryear has almost vanished. In his place is not the academic hero but the academic statesman. Robert Dahl has painted an amusing picture of the political maneuvers of Mayor Richard Lee of New Haven, and the same description applies to academic political leaders:

The mayor was not at the peak of a pyramid but rather at the center of intersecting circles. He rarely commanded. He negotiated, cajoled, exhorted, beguiled, charmed, pressed, appealed, reasoned, promised, insisted, demanded, even threatened, but he most needed support and acquiescence from other leaders who simply could not be commanded. Because the mayor could not command, he had to bargain [Dahl, 1961, page 204].

The political interpretation of leadership can be pressed even further, for the governance of the university more and more comes to look like a "cabinet" form of administration. The key figure today is not the president, the solitary giant, but the political leader surrounded by his staff, the prime minister who gathers the information and expertise to construct policy. It is the "staff," the network of key administrators, that makes most of the critical decisions. The university has become much too complicated for any one man, regardless of his stature. Cadres of vice-presidents, research men, budget officials, public relations men, and experts of various stripes surround the president, sit on the cabinet, and help reach collective decisions. Expertise becomes more critical than ever and leadership becomes even more the ability to assemble, lead, and facilitate the activities of knowledgeable experts.

Therefore, the president must be seen as a "statesman" as well as a "hero-bureaucrat." The bureaucratic image might be appropriate for the man who assembles data to churn out routine decisions with a computer's help. In fact, this image is fitting for many middle-echelon officials in the university. The statesman's image is much more accurate for the top administrators, for here the influx of data and information gives real power and possibilities for creative action. The statesman is the innovative actor who uses information, expertise, and the combined wisdom of the cabinet to plan the institution's future; the bureaucrat may only be a number manipulator, a user of routine information for routine ends. The use of the cabinet, the assembly of expertise, and the exercise of political judgment in the service of institutional goals—all this is part of the new image of the statesman leader which must complement both the hero leader and the collegial leader.

Table 1-3 presents a summary and comparison of the three basic images of leadership and management we have just described.

Summary

Colleges and universities are different from most other kinds of complex organizations. Their goals are more ambiguous and contested, they serve clients instead of seeking to make a profit, their technologies are unclear and problematic, and professionals dominate the work force and decision-making process. Thus colleges and universities are not standard bureaucracies, but can best be described as "organized anarchies" (see Cohen and March, 1947).

What decision and governance processes are to be found in an organized anarchy? Does the decision process resemble a bureaucratic system, with rational problem solving and standard operating procedures? Does it resemble a collegial system in which the professional faculty participate as members of a "community of scholars"? Or does it appear to be a political process with various interest groups struggling for influence over organizational policy? Each image is valid in some sense; each image helps complete the picture. Finally, we question the standard image of leadership and manage-

TABLE 1-3
Images of Leadership and Management Under Three Models of Governance

	Bureaucratic	Collegial	Political
Basic leadership image Leadership skills	Hero Technical problem-solving skills	"First among equals" Interpersonal dynamics	Statesman Political strategy, interpersonal dynamics, coalition management
Management	"Scientific management"	Management by consensus	Strategic decision making
Expectation	Very high: people believe the hero-leader can solve problems and he tries to play the role	Modest: leader is developer of consensus among professionals	Modest: leader marshals political action, but is constrained by the counter efforts of other groups

ment. Classic leadership theory, based on a bureaucratic model, suggests the image of the organizational leader as a hero who uses principles of scientific management as the basis for his decisions. We have suggested that the leader's image should be that of the academic statesman, and that management should be considered a process of strategic decision making.

References

Allison, Graham T. *Essence of Decision.* Boston: Little, Brown, 1971.

Baldridge, J. Victor. *Power and Conflict in the University.* New York: John Wiley, 1971.

Clark, Burton R. "Faculty Organization and Authority." *The Study of Academic Administration,* edited by Terry Lunsford. Boulder, Colo.: Western Interstate Commission for Higher Education, 1963. Reprinted as chapter 4 in this volume.

Cohen, Michael D., and March, James G. *Leadership and Ambiguity: The American College President.* New York: McGraw-Hill, 1974.

Dahl, Robert. *Who Governs?* New Haven, Conn.: Yale University Press, 1961.

Goodman, Paul. *The Community of Scholars.* New York: Random House, 1962.

Gross, Edward, and Grambsch, Paul V. *Changes in University Organization, 1964-1971.* New York: McGraw-Hill, 1974.

Gross, Edward. *University Goals and Academic Power.* Washington, D.C.: Office of Education, 1968.

Millett, John. *The Academic Community.* New York: McGraw-Hill, 1962.

Parsons, Talcott. "Introduction." *The Theory of Social and Economic Organization,* by Max Weber. New York: Free Press, 1947.

Stroup, Herbert. *Bureaucracy in Higher Education.* New York: Free Press, 1966.

Weber, Max. *The Theory of Social and Economic Organization.* New York: Free Press, 1947.

2

Power Structures in Universities and Colleges

Edward Gross and Paul V. Grambsch

Given our commitment to look upon universities as organizations, the concern with the identification and ordering of goals is understandable. Yet, merely to present a description of those goals and the changes in them would be to leave us with a view of universities from the outside. We would be able to discern the general direction of the organization, but little of its internal dynamics. We would not be in a position to make predictions for the future nor even to understand the shape of goal structures themselves.

It seemed essential that we should turn our attention to those persons who *define the goals and move the organization toward attaining them*. Theoretically, one could imagine a situation of power equalization in which *all* concerned participants would influence goals equally, through a town meeting arrangement or through some set of organized message transmission in the manner of sealed bids on a municipal contract. Even the least hierarchical of organizations seems to be far from such a model, though some, of course, wish to move in that direction. Nevertheless, we thought we would begin by identifying those who would likely play at least a small role in goal definition and attainment. Then we would ask our respondents whether some were more important than others, and to what extent.

Reprinted in an abridged version from *Changes in University Organization, 1964-1971* (New York: McGraw-Hill, 1974).

As might have been expected, we found a definite power structure in existence, with some persons and groups perceived as having far more influence than others.

Identification of such a power structure seemed not merely of interest in itself. Rather, we were interested in it for the light it might shed on goals. We assumed that power holders would have a causal impact, in the sense that they would affect or even determine goals and the manner of their attainment. Such is not an obvious assumption, for it is quite possible that the causal direction is just the reverse. For example, it is possible that universities with a certain type of goal structure (perhaps as a consequence of historical factors) attract certain kinds of persons into positions of high influence, or the goal structure facilitates the accretion of power to those persons. If so, instead of assuming that "power holders cause goals," we could say that goals "cause" certain kinds of power structures to emerge. . . .

In the case of universities, goals are difficult to modify directly. They characterize general directions for the university which, over time, become traditional and even sanctified. A service orientation, for example, is often justified (if questioned at all) by its relationship to the traditional American values of egalitarianism and helping one's neighbor. The "ivory tower" goals associated with the intellect or the classical disciplines are not even felt to require justification. A frontal attack on goals is likely, therefore, to be met with powerful resistance. But if there is a causal relationship between goals and power holders, one may be able to proceed indirectly to change goals by changing power holders. Note that this approach might bear fruit whatever the direction of causation. If power holders "cause" goals, then a change in power holders would presumably result in changes in goals. On the other hand, if certain goals attract a particular type of power holder or make it easy for certain kinds of persons to assume power, then changing the power holders might again, in time, cause the goals to languish for lack of persons likely to implement them. Although such an indirect approach will likely produce only small goal changes, those changes may well be larger than would result from a direct attack on goals themselves.

Our procedure was simply to identify persons and categories of persons who might play some role in the definition of goals as well as in their achievement. . . . These were not, of course, necessarily comparable, e.g., asking a person to compare "federal government" with the president of the university, but we found that our respondents had no difficulty with this question. These persons or categories were all recognized as centers of power which do affect goals.

The form of the question asked the respondent "how much say" each of these persons or categories of persons had about university goals. Respondents were reminded that a person might have "a lot of say" in his own department, for example, but little about the goals of the university as a whole. In this way, we hoped to avoid the practice of simply asking for "power holders" without specifying the area or scope of the power. The overall power structure of the sixty-eight universities, for both 1964 and 1971, is presented in Table 2-1.

TABLE 2-1
The Overall Power Structure of American Universities, 1964-71

Power holder rank order	1971			1964		
	Rank	Mean	Standard deviation	Rank	Mean	Standard deviation
President	1	4.52	.69	1	4.65	.62
Regents or trustees	2	4.36	.81	2	4.37	.82
Vice-presidents	3	4.06	.81	3	4.12	.82
Deans of professional schools	4	3.50	.80	4	3.62	.84
Dean of liberal arts	5	3.41	.83	6	3.56	.89
Dean of graduate school	6	3.35	.89	5	3.59	.89
Faculty	7	3.35	.92	7	3.31	.97
Legislators	8	3.20	1.35	9	2.94	1.37
Chairmen	9	3.10	.88	8	3.19	.93
Federal government	10	2.89	.95	10	2.79	1.06
State government	11	2.80	1.09	11	2.72	1.21
Students	12	2.77	.79	14	2.37	.82
Grants	13	2.68	.93	12	2.69	1.06
Alumni	14	2.58	.79	13	2.61	.90
Citizens	15	2.11	.94	15	2.08	1.02
Parents	16	1.94	.73	16	1.91	.87

The mean scores for each power holder have been ordered from 1 through 16 in both 1964 and 1971. These averages are, of course, affected by variations among universities, but there are not so many of those variations as might be expected. Inspection of the standard deviations reveals relatively little variation, with the size of the larger ones (legislators, federal government, state government, grants, and citizens) largely attributable to the "public-private" distinction, as we shall note below.

Turning then to the rank order in the table, we note first the striking correspondence between the rank order in 1964 and in 1971.

Particularly noteworthy is the fact that students, felt by so many to have increased their power, are perceived as having done no more than move up two positions, remaining in the bottom set of power holders. We will return to this finding presently. For the moment, the correspondence in rank order in the two years makes it easy for us to examine the rank order in the two years without having to jump back and forth in our discussion.

In American universities, then, the person perceived by our respondents as having the most say about university goals was, and still is, the president. To some, this will not seem surprising. After all, he (and it is, overwhelmingly, a "he") is the chief executive, identified in the public mind with the university, and perhaps the single person whose decisions carry most weight. Radicals or those taking a Machiavellian view of power might dismiss this finding as a mere artifact of the perceptual process. After all, we did not measure "power," only persons' perceptions of power. Hence, persons pick out the "front man," who is only an agent of "interests" who are the real power. This controversy rages in studies of power, and we do not claim to have resolved it here. We do think, however, that a stronger case can be made for the validity of this finding than can be made in most studies of community or societal power. When one asks a member of a complex society, such as the United States, or even a modestly sized local community to identify the "key" power holders, it is understandable that he will name the more prominent or those in official positions. What else can he do? He can hardly have access to the meetings of the boards of corporations, the strategy conferences of military commanders, or the executive sessions of city councils. So he will do the best he can with whatever information is provided by the mass media. But we are dealing with the perceptions of seventy respondents in the circumscribed ambience of the university in which they work full-time. Further, our population included *all* persons at dean level and above, from one-fourth to all chairmen and directors, plus 3 to 10 percent of faculty. We have strong assurance that some of them do indeed have access to secret meetings and other behind-the-scenes activities. In fact, we would guess that the perceptions of power are based, for this group, far less than usual on public statements or assumptions about official position and more upon actual observations of these persons making decisions, justifying courses of action, or actually seeking to bring influence to bear on others (including the respondents). One may, of course, still ask whether they are being honest in their replies, but we hope that the fears of a few might be offset by the courage of others—this being one of the benefits of using large numbers. All things considered, we feel confident that the president belongs at the top of the list. Note also that the mean score in both years is above 4.5, meaning that on a scale in which the maximum score assignable was 5, a mean of such magnitude could only result if a high proportion of persons assigned him a score of 5.

Our respondents' assignment of regents to second position (and, like the president, with mean scores over 4.00) was not anticipated and runs contrary to the tendency of regents to assign to themselves a relatively low power position. Some part of this tendency may be characteristic of all power holders in organizations. They feel relatively powerless in view of the need to secure the cooperation of others in the attainment of planned personal ends. But, in any case, regents are perceived as second in power only to the president. Objective assessments of the power of regents in the United States take note of three areas in which regents make major decisions: selection of the president, overall management of university funds, especially investments, and general approval of major changes in educational policy (e.g., approval of black studies programs, or addition of a new professional school). In the case of presidential selection, the regents often preside over the decision rather than make the actual choice, since a representative committee is influential in producing the "short list." In any case, selection of a president is a rare event (perhaps less so in recent years), and some members of the regents at a given university may never experience it during their terms of office. Overall fund management and major changes in educational policy also are relatively rare events: some members of the faculty who move on to another university after a stay of three or four years may also not experience any such change. Yet, it remains true that though these involve relatively infrequent actions, they are of obvious importance when they do occur and are highly publicized.

In American universities the regents or trustees often make up the legal government of the university, but this fact may not itself be of major significance in accounting for the high position they are perceived to have on the list of power holders. Our own observation is that many of our colleagues are unaware of the regents' legal position. It seems, however, to be a case of potential power, and it may be that, precisely for that reason (plus ignorance of the fact that such potential power exists), the occasional exercise of such power comes as a shock and leads to an elevated perception of the power of the regents. The faculty is likely to be peculiarly sensitive to this potential power, for it has been used in recent years to fire members of the faculty, occasionally including even tenured persons. Over the period of our study, particular prominence has been given to the political aspects of such firings. Politically motivated firings by a group of laymen who exercise potential power occasionally provide support for the Machiavellian theories referred to earlier.

The third and last of the power holders with a mean score above 4.00 is the vice-president. There seems little surprise in his position. He shares directly in the power assigned to the president; he is the person that often acts as the "inside president" while the president faces outward (making speeches, representing the university, seeking legitimation and money), and he usually shares an office in the part of the campus or building occupied by "central administration." Perhaps more important is the increasing tendency for universities to functionalize the role, with larger universities having as many as five or six vice-presidents. Some of these officers will have clear responsibility for strictly academic functions (one, for example, may be in charge of health sciences, another of all professional schools, another of research) and hence will usually be persons with impeccable academic credentials. Such persons cannot be brushed aside by faculty as "mere paper shufflers."

That deans come next in the rank order would seem to follow from their official position in the administrative hierarchy. Although little significance can be attached to small rank differences, it is interesting that deans of professional schools head the list in both years. This finding is less a confirmation of faculty fears of growth of "dean power" than it appears, as we shall note below. For the time being, such a primary position may be more properly attributed to the interactional network of the deans of professional schools in comparison to the two other kinds of academic deans. Deans of professional schools experience fewer of the legitimation problems of the other deans—their schools are obviously engaged in activities of value to the community. Hence, they often mingle freely with local business and industrial leaders, with representatives of professional organizations, and with labor union leaders. On campus, their "power" is suggested by the large size of professional schools, in teaching, research, and service staff, as well as by enrollment of students in both regular day classes and evening or extension classes.

The assignment of parents, citizens of the state, alumni, and grant donors to bottom positions suggests that the fears that these persons maneuver behind the scenes are not shared by faculty and administration. The assignment of the more obviously influential legislators and state government to middle positions appears to be a consequence of averaging public and private institutions, as we shall see presently.

Faculty are found just below the deans but above chairmen (and federal government) in both years. Apart from providing some assurance that our respondents were not merely recording persons according to official position (which would have placed chairmen above faculty), the finding has important implications. Some part of the reason for this position is due to the "working faculty," that is, those who serve as chairmen of campuswide administrative committees with important missions related to university goals, such as introduction of new curricula, shifts in admission standards, examining cases of threatened violations of academic freedom, or proposing mergers of two divisions of the university. Surely also, the ranking of faculty at about the same position as federal government is not accidental but related to the fact that particular faculty have acquired power as heads of research institutes as a consequence of receiving large amounts of federal money.

The data in Table 2-1 represent averaging over sixty-eight universities. In both 1964 and 1971 we were next concerned with whether such averaging concealed internal variations by type of university that might affect the overall findings. To that end, in 1964 we performed multivariate analysis on the rank order of power holders, making use of the variables of size, productivity (number of Ph.D.'s produced per year), type of control (public-private), quality (prestige, and number of volumes in library), graduate emphasis, and region of the country. The result was that the overall relationships were found to hold up strongly with little change for all variables with the main exception of type of control. Since the multivariate analysis was so unproductive, we repeated it in 1971 only for the type of control variable and for prestige (which had proved to be an important control variable for other parts of our analysis, especially those on goals). The breakdown by prestige into four levels was again unproductive. The comparison of power structures in private and public institutions is provided in Tables 2-2 and 2-3.

As can be seen, the main effect of separating universities by type of control in both 1964 and 1971 is that legislators and state government rise in rank in public universities (and fall in private universities), whereas grants rise slightly in private universities. It is interesting to note, however, that though the standard deviations of these categories drop, they remain relatively high. In other words, even in public universities there is variation in how legislators and state government are perceived and variation in private universities with

TABLE 2-2
A Comparison of the Power Structure of Private and of Public Universities, 1964

Private			Public		
Power holder rank order	Mean score	Standard deviation	Power holder rank order	Mean score	Standard deviation
President	4.70	.58	President	4.62	.63
Regents or trustees	4.24	.88	Regents or trustees	4.41	.78
Vice-presidents	4.10	.82	Vice-presidents	4.07	.83
Deans of professional schools	3.64	.80	Deans of professional schools	3.53	.79
Dean of liberal arts	3.57	.83	Dean of graduate school	3.53	.85
Dean of graduate school	3.54	.87	Legislators	3.45	1.07
Faculty	3.29	.96	Dean of liberal arts	3.43	.83
Chairmen	3.16	.90	Faculty	3.27	.93
Grants	2.84	1.03	Chairmen	3.13	.87
Alumni	2.53	.84	State government	2.91	1.02
Federal government	2.53	.99	Federal government	2.79	.94
Students	2.25	.69	Alumni	2.57	.80
State government	1.86	.90	Grants	2.49	.89
Parents	1.70	.68	Students	2.34	.73
Legislators	1.63	.92	Citizens	2.28	.88
Citizens	1.43	.63	Parents	1.90	.72

TABLE 2-3
A Comparison of the Power Structure of Private and of Public Universities, 1971

Private			Public		
Power holder rank order	Mean score	Standard deviation	Power holder rank order	Mean score	Standard deviation
President	4.60	.66	President	4.48	.70
Vice-presidents	4.15	.78	Regents or trustees	4.45	.75
Regents or trustees	4.15	.89	Vice-presidents	4.02	.82
Deans of professional schools	3.69	.84	Legislators	3.80	1.00
Dean of liberal arts	3.63	.82	Deans of professional schools	3.42	.77
Faculty	3.50	.93	Dean of liberal arts	3.31	.82
Dean of graduate school	3.46	.95	Dean of graduate school	3.31	.86
Chairmen	3.30	.88	Faculty	3.28	.91
Grants	2.94	.98	State government	3.13	.99
Students	2.84	.77	Chairmen	3.00	.86
Federal government	2.84	.98	Federal government	2.91	.93
Alumni	2.59	.81	Students	2.74	.80
State government	2.06	.93	Alumni	2.57	.78
Legislators	1.81	.98	Grants	2.56	.88
Parents	1.81	.68	Citizens	2.39	.92
Citizens	1.49	.64	Parents	2.00	.75

reference to grants. We would guess that such variation reflects actual differences in the behavior of these power holders. For example, it is only in some states that legislators have taken highly publicized punitive actions toward universities in their states.

Looking back over these first findings on power distribution, one is left with the impression that the power structure in universities is not so different as might have been believed. The most important source of variation appears to be type of control and even that is not a simple distinction, for there remain variations among universities, probably attributable to local conditions. Our data lead us to conclude that the power structure of American universities is remarkably uniform, at least among the sixty-eight under study here.

Perceived Changes in Power, 1964-71

The lack of any noticeable change in rank order between 1964 and 1971 was a surprise to the writers. Since we expected some changes, we had included a new question in the 1971 questionnaire. Immediately following the question we have just discussed (that is, the respondent's perception of how much say each power holder has over university goals), we asked the following question:

In reviewing the above list of positions and agencies how has the influence of each on major university policies changed during the past seven or eight years? Has it increased, decreased, or remained about the same?

	Increased markedly	Increased moderately	Remained about the same	Decreased moderately	Decreased markedly
The regents (or trustees)	_____	_____	_____	_____	_____
Legislators	_____	_____	_____	_____	_____
*					
*					
*					
Parents	_____	_____	_____	_____	_____

Our findings on this question are presented in Table 2-4.

We were quite unprepared for the picture presented in Table 2-4. It offers a ranking quite out of order with that presented in Table 2-1. When we break out the data by type of control (Table 2-5), the picture is again quite different from Tables 2-2 and 2-3, though with

TABLE 2-4
Changes in Power During the Past Eight Years

Power holder by change in power	Mean score	Standard deviation
Students	4.06	.68
Legislators	3.64	.81
Faculty	3.42	.83
Regents or trustees	3.41	.87
State government	3.34	.67
Federal government	3.34	.83
Vice-presidents	3.33	.82
President	3.21	.92
Deans of professional schools	3.12	.63
Citizens	3.09	.54
Grants	3.05	.59
Dean of liberal arts	3.00	.65
Dean of graduate school	2.99	.68
Chairmen	2.97	.61
Alumni	2.96	.54
Parents	2.89	.49

the expected elevation of legislators and state government to higher positions in public universities, and grants to a somewhat higher position in private universities.

We may, therefore, confine our attention to Table 2-4.

Although the power holders in Table 2-4 have been arranged in order ranging from those who are believed to have increased power the most (students) to those who have actually lost power (parents), this table is one case where assigning ranks to the scores would be misleading. The question itself asked the respondent to score the change in power "over the last seven or eight years" by checking one of: "increased markedly," "increased moderately," "remained about the same," "decreased moderately," and "decreased markedly." A score of 5 was assigned for "increased markedly," a score of 4 for "increased moderately," and so forth. Hence, we can assume that any average score substantially above 3 (for "remained about the same") implies an increase, and a score substantially below 3 implies an actual decrease.

The first thing to note about Table 2-4, then, is that the scores range *above* 3.00, implying a general tendency to believe that the power of *most* of the named power holders has risen. Since our list of power holders is, if anything, too broad, it seems hardly likely that there is a power holder whom we omitted to name whose power has dropped substantially. The phenomenon of an increase in control

TABLE 2-5

Changes in Power at Public and Private Universities During the Past Eight Years

Private			Public		
Power holder by change in power	Mean score	Standard deviation	Power holder by change in power	Mean score	Standard deviation
Students	4.14	.66	Students	4.03	.69
Faculty	3.52	.82	Legislators	3.81	.81
Federal government	3.40	.85	Regents or trustees	3.57	.88
Vice-presidents	3.35	.82	State government	3.41	.70
President	3.33	.93	Faculty	3.37	.83
Legislators	3.19	.59	Vice-presidents	3.32	.82
Deans of professional			Federal government	3.31	.81
schools	3.15	.62	President	3.15	.90
State government	3.15	.57	Citizens	3.14	.59
Grants	3.15	.65	Deans of professional		
Dean of liberal arts	3.08	.65	schools	3.11	.63
Regents or trustees	3.03	.70	Grants	3.00	.55
Chairmen	3.02	.61	Dean of graduate		
Dean of graduate			school	2.98	.68
school	3.01	.66	Alumni	2.97	.53
Citizens	2.97	.38	Dean of liberal arts	2.96	.65
Alumni	2.95	.58	Chairmen	2.95	.61
Parents	2.88	.45	Parents	2.89	.51

by all levels is not so strange as it first might seem. . . . It suggests a situation in which more resources become available to a wider spectrum of power holders who are now able to influence each other to a greater extent than previously. For our respondents, who are included in the power holders listed, there is apparently a sense that everyone, including themselves, has either held onto his former ability to control others or has increased his control (the chairmen are an exception, to be noted presently).

But even though there seems to be a general rise in ability to control what happens in universities, it is important to note the substantial differences in such control reflected in Table 2-4. Of those who are believed to have lost power—chairmen, alumni, and parents—the finding for alumni and parents, who were perceived as having very little power in both 1964 and 1971 anyhow, indicates that their position near or at the bottom is becoming ever more secure. For chairmen, who occupied a position in the middle (9th in 1971 and 8th in 1964), the implications are more serious, but before examining them, let us look at the other power holders. . . .

Those whose power is believed to have increased considerably include: a set of "outsiders" (legislators, regents, state and federal government) plus students and faculty, whereas those whose power is believed to have remained about the same include administrators of the university, plus citizens and grants. In discussing these groups, we can pass quickly by citizens and grants, since they were both judged to be of low power anyhow (see Table 2-1), and since the diminution of grant funds from private donors would have led us to expect either that they would do no more than maintain their previous ranking as power holders or even drop in rank.

What we have then is a situation where a group of outsiders (legislators, regents, state and federal government) and students and faculty are believed to have increased their power considerably, whereas administrators in the university are believed either to have retained their power (but not increased it) or, in the case of the lowest level of administrator, the chairmen, have actually lost power. The position of outsiders is not surprising, since their actions are publicized, and it is easy for even small increments to be evaluated as large shifts in power. Such at least seems to be the judgment of our respondents. We must bear in mind that these same respondents indicated that they felt there had been substantially *no* change in the ranking of these power holders, relative to one another, between 1964 and 1971. Thus, while students are perceived to have changed the most, their relative position remains near the bottom, but the little change that is evident (from 14th in 1964 to 12th in 1971) is perceived as a very large change.

A somewhat similar argument can be made for state government and legislators, categories which have risen slightly in relative position[1] but are believed to have risen considerably above many others. Particularly impressive is the strong showing of regents, because they also scored so high in relative ranking among all power holders (Table 2-1). Here then we have a group which shows just the opposite effect we observed for alumni and parents, who, we said, were securing their place at the bottom. Regents or trustees, already very high, are believed to have increased their power considerably. Although they still rank below the president (Table 2-1), one cannot help wondering whether their strong comparative showing in increased power does not imply some reduction of the power difference between them and the president.

1. The changes are better viewed by comparing Tables 2-2 and 2-3 where type of control is held constant. Among public universities, legislators rose from 6th to 4th rank, and state government from 10th to 9th. Among private universities, legislators rose from 15th to 14th, and state government remained the same (13th) in both years.

Administrators showed no such increase in power and just held their own or, in the case of chairmen, actually lost power. This finding surely reflects their handling of student and "outsider" criticism and agitation over the past seven years. The sight of students' occupying the president's or dean's office leaves a vivid impression, even though relatively little of enduring quality changes. Even though administrators do not rise in perception of change in power, they do retain their relative rank in middle or higher positions as power holders. In this case, there is no drop in relative rank (see Table 2-1) between 1964 and 1971, but the decline in absolute amount of power is perceived as large.

In sum, the power structure of universities has not changed, if by "structure" we refer to the pattern of relative distribution of power. Presidents still sit firmly at the top; other central administrators are not far behind; and students are near the bottom. But the little gain made by students is felt to be very impressive, especially because no comparable gain is shown by top and central administration. If anything, this conclusion reflects a perception by administrators and faculty that the power of top and central administration is so large that the failure to increase it is something that is impressive (perhaps because no one thought they could not do so if they wished). So too, the power of students to make any change in their relative power was considered so slight that even a tiny increment is felt to be an enormous achievement beyond what was expected.

In looking for a metaphor to illuminate this finding, we might think of the powerful political establishment in Rome near the height of its power in ancient days contemplating the slave revolt of Spartacus—marveling that mere slaves could accomplish so much, but never for a moment doubting that its military power could suppress the revolt. It would not be surprising to hear patricians mocking the administration or top army leaders because slaves were giving them so much trouble. We are not implying that administrators are military leaders or that students are slaves, but—well, we will drop the metaphor.

Finally, the perception that the power of the faculty has risen deserves special mention. To some it appears to be a "deviant" finding. Since the attack on universities—from legislators, citizens, and students—is perceived as having reduced the power of administrators, how can it not be perceived as also having reduced the power of the faculty? Some of the attack has been clearly against particular members of the faculty, as in the most publicized attempts to fire radical professors. Yet, we must remember that our respondents include the very persons who are presumably the target of such attacks (the professors). How then can they, and their administrators, conclude that faculty power has increased absolutely? Some part of this assessment surely results from the improvement over the last few years in faculty salaries and working conditions, which have, after a long lean period, finally begun to approach decent levels and for some (the entrepreneurial researchers) have become enough at last to provide a thundering answer to a mother-in-law's repeated reminder that her daughter might have married a doctor (a real one, that is). Professors are mostly not yet rich, but they live better than most of them ever have before and better than their peers in the most prestigious of European or British Commonwealth universities. Another factor influencing the evaluation of change in power of the faculty may well be that they have lost comparatively less than members of the administration, who have often suffered public humiliation, as well as being forced to resign. Perhaps a smaller relative loss is perceived as a gain. . . .

Clusters of Power Holders

When we examined the relationship of power holders to one another, we found two clusters. One cluster we termed *external*, for it consists of legislators, state government, citizens, regents, federal government, and parents; a second cluster we called *internal*, for it embraces chairmen, deans (including deans of professional schools), and faculty. The alignment of deans of professional schools with deans of liberal arts and faculty was striking and suggested a different coalition than many faculty think is the case. In turn, the clustering strongly suggested that power in universities is not a zero-sum variable. That is, because one group has more, it does not follow that another group has less. Powerful deans are not found in universities with weak faculties: quite the reverse. A powerful set of deans is usually found along with a powerful faculty, as a powerful dean of liberal arts is found along with a powerful set of departmental chairmen. One conclusion is that faculties may well maintain their power only when deans and chairmen have the power to provide proper conditions, and that may require that deans and chairmen have a great deal of power indeed. Lest faculty draw too much comfort from this finding, it should be pointed out that power is not a zero-sum for external power holders either: having strong regents or trustees does not necessarily deprive the federal government of power.

The relationship of power to goals produced important findings. When we examined the relationship of power to goals across all universities, we found there was a considerable drop in the sheer number of relationships since 1964. Goals seem to be more complex and hence more difficult to achieve, or else they provide less opportunity than they used to as an avenue by which potential power seekers may accumulate power. A major reason seems to be a decline in frills and a need for all power holders (external and internal) to give their energies to bread-and-butter goals. But there remains a major variation in goals between the two kinds of power holders. *Those universities falling in the top part of the distribution of external power holders are also those found stratified in such a way as to emphasize the practical, land-grant type of goals.* In turn, where one examines the stratification by internal power holders, a wholly different set of system goals emerges—those associated with the liberal arts, with protecting academic freedom, and with protecting the quality and prestige of the university.

The examination of power and goals within universities produced a similar set of contrasts, along with goals which emphasize the need to placate citizens and other "outsiders," on the one hand, and the need to placate students (through providing the right to inquire and rights of political action) and faculty (through providing opportunities for them to pursue their professional careers), on the other hand. We suggest that power has shifted from the system level to the local level. Legislators, regents, and citizens were engaged in struggles with deans, chairmen, and faculty which had major effects on the structure of goals within each university. Hence, there was more variability among universities in that impact and possibly the beginnings of a fragmenting of the whole system of universities.

In the end, an examination of further findings led us to the conclusion that *a shift in the power of external power holders was likely to have a greater effect on goals than would a corresponding shift in power of internal power holders.* For example, if regents were to increase their power over deans, the effect on goals would be considerable. To have a similar effect, deans would have to increase their power not simply over the local regents but increase it to the point where they were among the most powerful deans in the whole system of universities. When we note that the set of goals associated with external power holders is strongly opposed to the set of goals associated with internal power holders, the implications of this finding are serious. The power of deans, chairmen, and faculty are found associated with practically the same set of goals, and those are quite different from those associated with regents, legislators, and state government.

3

Diversity in Higher Education: Professional Autonomy

J. Victor Baldridge, David V. Curtis,
George P. Ecker, and Gary L. Riley

This paper argues that, contrary to the views of several contemporary observers, American higher education is not becoming more homogeneous but more diverse. Higher educational institutions vary widely in their organizational structure, purposes and goals, and governance patterns. In order to compare these diverse institutions systematically, the Stanford Project on Academic Governance established a typology consisting of eight broad categories. These categories are shown to vary systematically on many important organizational features: environmental relations, complexity of professional task, and institutional size and complexity. It is also demonstrated that the different categories of institutions, reflecting different organizational features, have different patterns of professional autonomy for the faculty.

An analysis of academic governance in the United States shows the bewildering diversity of institutional patterns. There are many different institutional forms, different sets of environmental pressures, different professional configurations, and different goals. There is star-

Research supported by the Stanford Center for Research and Development in Teaching, by funds from the National Institute of Education, U.S. Department of Health, Education, and Welfare (contract no. NE-C-00-3-0062). The opinions expressed in this publication do not necessarily reflect the position, policy, or endorsement of the National Institute of Education.

tling diversity in the range from major universities to community colleges, medical schools to technical schools, institutions with graduate schools to liberal arts colleges, massive multiversities to proprietary business schools. It is virtually impossible to make reasonable statements about institutional patterns that apply universally.

Not only do institutions have widely different structures and purposes, but they also have widely different forms of professional autonomy for their faculties. In some instances the faculties are highly professional, determining their own work processes and controlling personnel practices. In other situations the faculty are merely hired employees, and have very little professional autonomy.

The decision processes also vary substantially. Some institutions are dominated by strong presidents. Some have strong faculty and collegial participation. Some allow students a strong voice in the decision-making process. Some are bound by state system regulations and have little decision-making latitude. Some are virtually dominated by the local communities that they serve. Any adequate understanding of American higher education must take this hodgepodge of institutional styles into account.

These major differences between institutions seem obvious even to the most naive observer. Nevertheless, most studies of academic governance have been extremely narrow in scope, often ignoring the complexity of the system. Research on academic governance has characteristically fallen into two patterns: (1) case studies of a single institution and its decision-making processes, and (2) studies based on small, nonrepresentative samples covering only a small segment of higher education. Of course, focusing on a single segment permits one to investigate it in depth. But the data provided by narrowly focused studies should be supplemented by studies based on samples that cover the whole spectrum of American higher education. For this purpose the Stanford Project on Academic Governance, a project supported under the Stanford Research and Development Center in Teaching, surveyed the entire higher educational spectrum, from community colleges through the elite institutions with graduate schools. This paper reports some of the findings.

The Debate over Diversity

The assertion that American higher education is extremely diverse and complex is being challenged by several contemporary observers and national commissions. These critics suggest that there is now a tendency toward increasing homogeneity. It may be useful to summarize the pros and cons of the argument, since in addition to their theoretical interest they have important *policy implications*.

Arguments for Homogeneity

At least three factors have been identified as promoting more homogeneity in higher education: (1) "institutional imitation," a process by which institutions lower on the academic pecking order try to imitate those above; (2) the shift from private education to public; and (3) the movement into the mainstream of previously unique institutions that have served specialized clienteles, and the opening of their doors to a broader spectrum of students.

Institutional imitation. In *The Academic Revolution* (1968) Christopher Jencks and David Riesman argue that there is a strong pattern of imitation in higher education. Institutions with less prestige tend to imitate those with more prestige. Community colleges frequently expand their programs to offer a bachelor's degree; four-year colleges expand to offer a master's degree; and colleges with master's degree programs look forward to the day they can offer the doctorate.

Riesman and Jencks suggest that until recently there were many forces promoting diversity, including religious, political, ethnic, social class, and geographic differences in institutions and their clienteles. However, they believe that today there are strong economic and professional pressures that have gradually obscured the diversity. In order to prepare people to enter the economic mainstream, colleges have tended to imitate each other, gradually developing similar programs and similar clienteles. Observing the history of higher education, Jencks and Riesman argue:

The local college was local first and a college second; the Catholic college was Catholic first and a college second; the Negro college was Negro first and a college second, and so forth. But as time went on these disparate institutions took on lives and purposes of their own. Undergraduates thought of themselves less as future women, Baptists, or teachers and more often simply as students, having a common interest with students in all sorts of other places called colleges rather than with girls, Baptists, or teachers who were not students. Similar changes have taken place at the faculty level. Even the college president of today often thinks of himself less as the president of a college in San Jose, a college catering to the rich, or a college for Irish Catholics than as president of an academically first-rate, second-rate, or third-rate college. Such a man's reference group is no longer the traditional clientele and patrons of his institution or the trustees who will speak for them, but the presidents of other colleges, many of which had historically different origins and aims. The result is convergence of aims, methods, and, probably, results [Jencks and Riesman, 1968, page 25].

Jencks and Riesman summarize their point by saying, "Our overall

feeling is that homogenization is proceeding faster than differentiation" (page 154).

The Newman Reports (Newman et al., 1971, 1973) agree that because of institutional imitation and other factors, American higher
education is growing more homogeneous. The report argues that the
options for American students are being closed, that academic programs are growing more similar all the time, and that new students
with new interests cannot find a unique home in the increasingly
similar American institutions:

American higher education is renowned for its diversity. Yet, in fact, our colleges and universities have become extraordinarily similar. Nearly all 2,500 institutions have adopted the same mode of teaching and learning. Nearly all strive to
perform the same generalized educational mission. The traditional sources of
differentiation—between public and private, large and small, secular and sectarian, male and female—are disappearing. Even the differences in character of
individual institutions are fading. It is no longer true that most students have real
choices among differing institutions in which to seek a higher education.
    Colleges and universities are, to be sure, not the only American institutions
which have become homogenized; changes in American society have dramatically altered the mission, size, and character of many important institutions. But
the growing uniformity of higher education institutions should command special
attention [Newman et al., 1971, pages 12, 16].

The shift from private to public. Many observers also argue that
homogeneity may also be promoted by the shift from private to public institutions. Over the last fifty years there has been a steady
movement of students from the private into the public sector. In
1900 the majority of students in higher education were enrolled in
private institutions; today about two-thirds are enrolled in public
institutions. Many observers argue that the diversity of American
higher education is being correspondingly reduced, that the unique
programs offered by private institutions are gradually being obliter-
ated, and that state schools display disconcerting similarity. Thus the
shift toward state dominance of higher education may reinforce the
trend toward homogeneity that institutional imitation has already
started.

*The movement of distinctive colleges into the academic main-
stream.* In his book *The Demise of Diversity* (1974), C. Robert Pace
compared a group of people who had graduated from college in 1950
with a group who had graduated in 1970. He concluded that the
1970 group had had a more homogeneous education than the 1950
group. He also examined several different types of colleges and suggested that many of them have lost their unique character and moved

into the mainstream of American higher education. In particular, he noted that the elite liberal arts colleges and the state colleges have grown less distinctive in their missions and programs.

Some of Pace's findings seem debatable, however. First, his sample totally excluded community colleges, thus eliminating a very diverse student population. Second, he admits that, although students' *experiences* had become more homogeneous, the *outcomes* in terms of student attitudes and skills had become more diverse. It is hard to see how an argument for increased homogeneity can be made if the outcomes are actually more heterogeneous. Pace himself suggests that "the case for arguing that there has been a general decline in diversity and distinctiveness does not on the surface appear to be strongly convincing. But beneath the surface there is reason for believing that the case is more convincing" (page 130). In general, we find the former part of Pace's statement to be more convincing than the latter. It appears that his own data indicate a strong element of complexity and diversity in American higher education.

Arguments Against Homogeneity

The argument that educational homogeneity is increasing may seem persuasive. There is, indeed, much institutional imitation; state institutions are increasingly displacing private ones; and many distinctive types of institutions have now moved into the academic mainstream. In spite of these facts, however, we believe there are strong counterarguments.

Historical trends. In the history of higher education, as some institutions have moved up the ladder of academic prestige there has always been a proliferation of other institutions below. The widespread growth of community and junior colleges in this country over the last two decades is hardly a sign of increasing homogeneity. In addition, there are many new kinds of technical institutions, expanding education into industrial settings, and an upsurge of proprietary institutions. These developments are simply not consonant with a trend toward educational homogeneity. Thus, in spite of imitation and state control, we believe the differences between institutions are *increasing* rather than decreasing.

It was because of the obvious difference between colleges that the Carnegie Commission on Higher Education (1969-72) felt compelled to commission in-depth studies of unique segments of American academic life. In that effort Pace developed a profile of Protestant colleges; Astin and Lee examined small, private institutions with limited resources, which they called the "invisible colleges"; Bowles and

DeCosta examined higher education for blacks; Fein and Weber examined medical education; Dunham compiled a profile of state colleges and regional universities; and Greeley focused on Catholic higher education. To be sure, there were some signs of increased homogeneity (e.g., the Catholic colleges were losing some of their distinctiveness), but on the whole there were plenty of signs of a dynamic institutional diversity.

Of course, as we enter a period of steady enrollments and diminished resources, the proliferation of new institutions may slow down. However, the thrust toward diversity still seems strong, especially in the proprietary institutions and the community colleges. The future may bring more homogeneity, as critics are predicting. However, the historical trends have moved in the opposite direction.

Diversity within institutions. Not only has there been substantial diversity *between* institutions, but there has also been a growing diversity *within* institutions. In fact, since World War II there has been an astonishing proliferation of technical training efforts, academic subjects, research efforts, and degree-granting programs within institutions. Increased size has been a major factor in this internal differentiation, for a large enrollment makes it possible to support specialized programs. Those who speak of institutional homogeneity have been short-sighted in failing to examine the proliferation of options *within* the multiversity campuses. We do not agree that program and career options have been decreased within institutions. On the contrary, any systematic examination of college catalogs from twenty years ago and today would suggest just the opposite.

International comparisons. In this debate we must constantly ask the critical question: Is the American higher educational system more or less diverse, *compared to what?* We have already suggested that compared to higher education in earlier historical periods, the current system is more diverse. In addition, the American higher educational system is more diverse compared to systems elsewhere in the world. No other system has so large a percentage of students from as diverse socioeconomic, racial, and academic backgrounds as the United States. No other system approaches the institutional diversity to be found in the American system, which is supported by federal, state, foundation, tuition, and church money combined. In short, by any reasonable measure the American higher educational system is more complex, diverse, and fragmented than any other higher educational system in the world.

The effects of public control. The critics say that more public control over higher educational institutions will lead to more homogeneity, but this is not necessarily true. Surely there is enormous diversity in both the public and the private sector, and the mere bookkeeping fact that more students are attending publicly supported institutions does not necessarily imply that those institutions will exhibit less diversity. *In fact, there is strong reason to suspect that increasing public control may actually lead to more diversity.*

The phenomenon of institutional imitation is more apparent in the private universities. By contrast, as state systems have developed, they have generally tried to formulate policies that enforce some degree of diversity among public institutions. For example, the California Master Plan defines the unique role of the community colleges, the state colleges and universities, and the University of California system. In other states with strong system management, such as Illinois and Wisconsin, the state central management has played an important role in promoting diversity among its institutions. In many ways the state systems are major *promoters* of diversity, for the private institutions have been more susceptible to the imitation phenomenon.

Of course, we are not so naive as to believe that the on-paper versions of state master plans are sufficient to enforce diversity. We are well aware that there is great pressure for imitation in the state systems—everybody in California wants to be Berkeley and UCLA. And, of course, some California state colleges recently changed their names to "universities." In spite of those obvious tensions, we still believe that the statewide planning efforts encourage much more diversity than the private sector would have generated. For example, the huge state colleges in California still do not offer the doctorate (with one minor exception). Private institutions of similar size and complexity almost universally do—they are able to imitate more readily.

Factors on which diversity is measured. One of the biggest problems presented by the literature is a confusion over what factors are being measured. Do the critics mean that higher education has a more homogeneous clientele than it once did—that students are drawn from a narrower segment of society? Obviously not, for the clientele is clearly more diverse than it has ever been. Do the critics mean that the programs offered within institutions have become more homogeneous—that is, more limited? This interpretation does not seem reasonable either. Do the critics mean that the outcomes of education all seem the same—that graduates now have a narrower range of skills and job opportunities than they once did? Again, this is surely not the case. Do the critics mean that the governance patterns in education have grown similar—that decision-making processes and formal control systems are all alike? Clearly, this is not the case, as our research and many other studies have strongly demonstrated.

We do not believe that the system has grown less diverse on any of these factors or on any other important factors that we can identify. Part of the problem seems to be a slippage of terminology. For example, some observers (e.g., Jencks and Riesman, 1968) have pointed to the phenomenon of institutional imitation as evidence of increasing homogeneity. If one looks at the total system of higher education, however, it seems apparent that there is a strong proliferation of new institutions as others move up in the system. To say that an individual institution has become more like other institutions is not necessarily to say that the whole system has become more homogeneous. We believe that this confusion is at the heart of the debate. Certainly we have seen individual institutions change missions in imitation of others. On the whole, however, the system has still retained a remarkably vigorous ability to spawn new institutions and to generate new options.

Policy and Research Implications of the Debate

It is important to note that almost everyone entering the debate over diversity has an important policy implication at the back of his mind. Those arguing that the system is becoming more homogeneous may see themselves as the liberal vanguard, demanding more diversity in order to meet the needs of more students, create more job opportunities, and achieve new social goals. They see themselves fighting against an entrenched, conservative academic system that tends to force everyone into a similar academic mold. This point of view is implicit in, for example, the Newman Reports and the Carnegie Commission studies. The cry that the system is becoming more homogeneous is basically a plea for more diversity in order to accommodate more students with new interests and needs—a worthy goal, indeed. Coupled with these concerns there is also the implicit—and often explicit—call for more federal money to promote that diversity.

In that sense, the complaint that the American system is becoming more homogeneous is primarily a plea for planning, federal money, and support for the diversity needed to accommodate new students from different racial and socioeconomic backgrounds, and with different job aspirations. In view of these policy goals, we agree with these powerful social critics that increasing diversity is necessary, and should be supported by whatever means are consonant with academic values.

But we also believe that the supporting argument should be phrased differently. Let us not base the demand for more diversity on the empirically incorrect statement that homogeneity is increasing. Instead, we should take a completely different tack. We should argue that, historically and internationally, the American educational system has been the most diverse in the world. Given that kind of development, it is logical to argue that we should maintain that momentum and even increase it. "We've got a good thing going"— and let's support it.

Diversity and public policy about governance. The debate over diversity in higher education, which we have discussed at length, is an issue that at first may not seem to have much to do with academic governance. We believe it is critical, however. If American higher education has become as homogeneous as many critics would have us believe, then decision making and policy planning could change substantially. If higher education is really homogeneous, then it is theoretically possible to impose uniform management and decision-making systems on it. For example, a master planner in state government could propose faculty work patterns, evaluation procedures, decision processes, mechanisms of faculty participation, and patterns of student involvement in governance without regard to particular institutional settings and circumstances.

This possibility illustrates the danger in the debate over diversity. Those who argue that the American system has become homogeneous are trying to maximize the opportunities offered for new kinds of students. But their efforts could have the unfortunate side effect of convincing policy planners in state and federal government that homogeneous management and budgetary policies are appropriate for homogeneous institutions. By placing so much emphasis on the development of homogeneity, many leading critics in the educational field may have unwittingly created an atmosphere in which policy planners can begin to enforce even more homogeneity through their management policies, evaluation systems, and accounting processes.

Diversity and the conduct of research. The debate over diversity also has critical research implications. If researchers believe that higher education is homogeneous, they will look for one basic pattern of professional behavior, faculty work patterns, and academic governance. This is, unfortunately, what most researchers have done. On the other hand, if researchers believe that there is broad diversity in higher education, then they will be sensitive to the complexity of their subject and will plan for systematic comparisons across different types of institutions. Because we believe that the system is diverse, we have taken the latter course.

Contemporary Diversity: Establishing a Typology of Institutions

One major task of the Stanford Project on Academic Governance was to establish a meaningful typology that would aid in comparing diverse kinds of institutions. The task was a perplexing one. Where does one draw the line between various kinds of institutions? Obviously, the answer to that question depends on one's interests and the issues that are being explored. One category system makes sense for one purpose; another makes sense for another purpose. We wanted a category system that would serve two functions. First, it had to be intuitively meaningful to those who work in American higher education. Second, we wanted it to make theoretical sense to the organizational researcher.

The Carnegie Commission on Higher Education had already established a typology based on the clustering of similar institutional characteristics: degree offerings, financial support, features of the student body, size, and prestige of research. The Carnegie typology covers the range of American higher education institutions, from elite multiversities with doctoral programs to small, specialized, proprietary colleges. It is relatively complex, consisting of twelve categories with many minor subdivisions and further distinctions between public and private. There is a total of thirty-two distinct categories.

In the Stanford Project on Academic Governance we thought that there would be a great advantage in using the Carnegie typology, since adopting this standard would allow comparative work by other researchers. But we found that the very complex Carnegie typology with its fine nuances did not serve our purpose. As a result, we collapsed the twelve Carnegie categories down to eight. In general, the Stanford Project's revision maintains the overall outline of the Carnegie typology while reducing its categories to a more manageable number. Every higher educational institution in the United States had been categorized by the Carnegie Commission, and using their data we could easily place each institution in our enlarged categories. Each category is described below.

1. *Private multiversity*. Among the most elite institutions in the country, the private multiversities are large, highly prestigious institutions that, by the Carnegie definition, awarded at least 20 Ph.D.'s (or

M.D.'s, if the medical school is on the same campus) and received at least $3,000,000 in federal financial support in 1970-71. These institutions have an elite faculty with complex research and teaching responsibilities. Their graduate programs are the leading ones in the country, and their extensive research programs are highly regarded. Some examples are Cornell, Harvard, Princeton, Stanford, and Yale universities.

2. *Public multiversity.* At the apex of the state systems stand the giant and prestigious public multiversities—the University of California, the Universities of Illinois, Michigan, Minnesota, Washington, Wisconsin, and so on. They are extremely large, they receive enormous amounts of federal research money, they have highly prestigious graduate programs and elite faculties.

3. *Elite liberal arts college.* In American higher education there have always been some small private liberal arts colleges that are outstanding, with highly trained faculties and high-quality degree programs. Although they do not receive as much federal research money as the multiversities, they nevertheless are strong scholarship and research centers. Usually, they are best known for their bachelor's programs, but most of them offer some master's degrees and even a few doctor's degrees. Examples of institutions in this category are Dartmouth, Reed, Smith, Swarthmore, and Vassar colleges.

4. *Public comprehensive.* We established two categories for the middle-range public institutions. The "public comprehensives" constitute the upper level of this middle group. These are the solid, middle-quality state institutions that are to be found throughout the United States. In general, their strong point is their bachelor's program, but almost all of them offer some master's or professional programs, and many offer a few doctor's degrees as well.

5. *Public college.* In the middle range of public institutions, the public colleges are on the lower level in terms of faculty quality, student selectivity, and strength of degree programs. Little research is carried out in these institutions, for their chief mission is to provide undergraduate programs for the average American college student. In addition, most of these colleges do offer at least one professional or occupational program such as nursing or teaching. We used this category as a catchall for public institutions above the community-college level but not qualifying for the category of public comprehensive.

6. *Private liberal arts college.* The best of the private institutions were included in category 3. All the remaining liberal arts colleges offering at least a bachelor's degree were included in this category.

There are more institutions of this kind in the country than any other.

7. *Community college.* Although they are relative newcomers, the public "open-door" community colleges are the fastest growing segment of American higher education. These institutions offer associate of arts degrees, with both transfer programs into other colleges and technical programs for terminating students. The funding for these institutions is provided by local districts, by the state, or by a combination of both. Usually, no more than a fourth of the faculty at these institutions have Ph.D.'s; teaching, not research, is their exclusive occupation.

8. *Private junior college.* Once a thriving segment of higher education, in the last few decades these institutions, which offer A.A. degrees, have been dying out or expanding to offer four-year programs. Most are either church-sponsored institutions serving a church-based clientele, or so-called finishing schools. The formal training of the faculty in these institutions is the lowest in the whole spectrum of American higher education; about 10 percent of the faculty have Ph.D.'s.

Basic Diversity: Some Measures

Are the differences between institutions in the various categories substantial? Of course, this is a matter of perspective. Whether a glass is half full or half empty depends on the viewer's perspective, not the glass. Whether colleges in these categories are significantly different is a question of judgment and point of view. We believe they are really different.

What organizational features are most important in influencing the diverse patterns of governance that emerge in American higher education? The potential list is long, but three features stand out as particularly important. First, we must understand the *environment* in which an institution exists. The environmental context of financial support, formal control, and relations with other social institutions is an extremely important determinant of institutional decision-making processes. Second, the nature of the *professional task* often shapes the degree of professional autonomy. Institutions with a limited range of tasks, such as colleges that concentrate on undergraduate teaching, have radically different professional work patterns and governance processes than institutions with an extremely diverse and complicated range of tasks. Third, the *size* and administrative *complexity* of an institution greatly affect its patterns of activity. Small, homogeneous colleges have significantly different governance and professional work patterns than huge multiversities.

Are the eight types of institutions identified above really diverse in their environmental relations, professional task, and complexity? Or are they, as so many have insisted, really homogeneous? We believe the facts clearly support the diversity argument. Table 3-1 shows scores for different types of institutions on a wide variety of institutional characteristics, derived from the College Entrance Examination Board's data files, and from a national survey of faculty we conducted in 1971. Let us look briefly at these differences.

Environmental Relations

It is increasingly obvious that many of the most critical decisions for colleges and universities around the nation are being made outside the institutions themselves. The halls of Congress, the governor's office, the state system office, the foundation director's office—these are only a few of the powerful external forces impinging on the academic community from all sides. The student revolution and subsequent public reaction in the mid-1960's weakened the fabric of many academic institutions. The financial crises and faculty unions of the 1970's raised new challenges. Growing state system networks are currently looming large on the environmental horizon. In short, any useful study of higher education today must take environmental factors into account. It is obvious from an examination of Table 3-1 that the different types of institutions in the Stanford typology vary significantly on most of the environmental variables. When we examine *funding sources*, there is systematic variation in different types of institutions. First, there is a fairly sharp distinction between the public and private institutions, as might be expected. In general, public institutions get somewhat over half their funds from the state, while private institutions depend much more on tuition and foundation money. The private multiversities are almost unique in their dependence on federal research money. Only a handful of institutions receive much support from the churches, even among those that are formally controlled by religious denominations.

In general, the institutions at the upper end of the typology obtain their funds from a wider variety of sources (they have a higher "dispersed cash" rating), they are more affluent, they pay their faculties better, and they are more selective in their student admissions. The institutions vary considerably in age and endowment, the private multiversities and elite liberal arts colleges being the oldest and most heavily endowed. All of these different characteristics have been drawn together in the combined factor, "institutional heritage."

TABLE 3-1
Environmental Characteristics: Breakdown by Institutional Types

	N	Funding Sources				Institutional heritage							Local funds	Church/foundation funds		External/internal influence ratio‡
		% state money	Public/private	% tuition money	Dispersed cash*	Affluence: $ per student	AAUP salary scale†	AAUP mean salary ($1,000s)	CEEB selectivity scale	Age of institution	% federal research money	% endowment	% local money	% church money	% foundation money	
Institutional type average for all institutions	300	31		41	.10	2,428	6.1	11.0	2.6	60	1.9	3.5	9.5	3.4	1.4	.62
Private multiversity	6	2	Pri	35	1.00	9,997	2.5	15.0	4.5	142	27.0	21.0	.2	2.5	6.1	.54
Public multiversity	13	51	Pub	21	.70	4,914	3.3	13.2	3.8	101	10.0	2.3	.3	0	1.6	.68
Elite liberal arts college	25	1	Pri	70	.30	4,907	3.4	11.8	4.5	104	2.1	13.5	0	1.4	2.5	.49
Public comprehensive	40	65	Pub	26	.27	2,530	3.8	11.1	2.9	69	1.5	.8	1.7	.1	.1	.66
Public college	16	76	Pub	20	.18	3,273	3.8	11.7	3.6	55	1.3	.3	.1	0	.3	.52
Private liberal arts college	85	1	Pri	63	.09	2,894	6.4	9.8	3.1	74	.3	4.8	.2	7.2	3.1	.61
Community college	96	50	Pub	15	.02	1,771	8.2	11.5	1.3	24	.9	.4	28.5	.3	0	.68
Private junior college	19	1	Pri	68	.00	2,183	8.8	8.4	2.6	64	.7	4.1	0	16.6	1.0	.65

*0 = highly concentrated
†1 = highest salaries (AAUP Bulletin, 1971 Salary Scale)
‡1 = highly dispersed

Finally, the last column in Table 3-1 shows the "external/internal influence ratio," a measure of the influence of outsiders versus that of insiders. This measure is a scale constructed from several questions on our faculty questionnaire. A higher score indicates more external influence. In general the figures in this column suggest two patterns: (1) state-related institutions were subject to more outside influence than others; and (2) institutions at the lower end of the typology were subject to more outside influence than those at the higher end. Once again, we find that the environmental characteristics vary systematically with the different types of institutions.

Characteristics of the Professional Task

We assume that one of the critical differences among higher educational institutions is the nature of their professional tasks. In the academic world there are many different professional tasks, including teaching, research, and community service. It is difficult to measure the variety of activities a college or university might incorporate. In general, however, they can be classified according to their academic degree programs and the professional qualifications of their faculties. Clearly, this is not the only way to classify the different tasks of a college or university, but it is an appropriate and significant one. Institutions that offer doctoral programs and have a very high percentage of faculty members with doctoral degrees are generally carrying out complex research, graduate training, and policy analysis, as well as undergraduate teaching. At the other extreme, community colleges offering A.A. degrees have an entirely different role and activity pattern, confined almost exclusively to undergraduate teaching.

Different types of institutions vary systematically in terms of professional task, as Table 3-2 shows. The institutions at the upper end of the typology offer doctoral degrees; over three-fourths of their faculty members have Ph.D. degrees; their entering freshmen have extremely high SAT scores; and their faculties have high publication rates. Those at the lower end of the typology—the community colleges and private junior colleges—offer only the A.A. degree; few of their faculty members have Ph.D. degrees; their students have low SAT scores; and there is very little publication by their faculties. Between these two extremes the complexity of the professional task usually increases with every step up the typology. There is a strong correlation between an institution's place in the typology and its professional task expertise indicators.

TABLE 3-2
Some Characteristics of Different Types of Institutions

		Professional task expertise					Institutional size and complexity				
	N	Highest degree offered*	% faculty with Ph.D.	Combined student SAT scores	% faculty with published book	% faculty with published article	No. faculty	No. students	No. depart-ments	No. schools and colleges	No. structural units
	300	2.0	39	929	16	12	193	3,010	21	7	27
Private multiversity	6	4.0	82	1,223	48	49	1,248	11,710	61	9	60
Public multiversity	13	4.0	77	1,010	33	38	1,110	17,920	65	10	82
Elite liberal arts college	25	2.7	69	1,185	26	18	143	1,880	22	5	23
Public comprehensive	40	3.0	53	917	19	13	272	5,100	25	5	31
Public college	16	2.6	55	999	20	13	204	2,220	20	3	19
Private liberal arts college	85	2.2	44	937	15	12	84	1,130	17	3	17
Community college	96	1.0	15	828	10	5	111	2,200	17	0	30
Private junior college	19	1.0	12	889	61	7	39	600	9	0	7

*1 = A.A.; 2 = B.A.; 3 = M.A.; 4 = Ph.D.

Institutional Size and Complexity

Organization theorists in recent years have intensively studied the impact of an organization's size on its decision-making processes and structural features (see Blau, 1970; Baldridge et al., 1973). It is now well established that the larger the organization, the more complex its decision-making processes and its departmental and administrative structure. The amount of decentralization, the degree of conflict between subunits, the development of complex decision-making networks, and other aspects of decision-making processes are highly dependent on the organization's size and complexity.

The institutions in the various categories vary fairly systematically with measures of size and complexity, as Table 3-2 indicates. In general, institutions at the higher end of the typology are larger, though the elite liberal arts colleges tend to be somewhat smaller than the public institutions just below them. Aside from that one exception, there is a strong correlation between an institution's place in the typology and its size and complexity.

Diversity in Professional Autonomy

We have been discussing some basic aspects of diversity in academic institutions, in terms of environmental relations, professional task, and size and complexity. Our interest for the rest of this paper will focus on "professional autonomy," the degree of freedom the faculty has in controlling central educational tasks and professional activities. The literature on faculty as professionals is extensive (for a review, see Baldridge, 1971; Thompson, 1967). It is sufficient to say here that, in a strong professional organization, the professionals demand the right to control their work, to determine central professional objectives, to judge the performance of professional peers, and to select the professional staff. We consider these the marks of true professional autonomy. Organizations that are strong on these aspects are generally recognized as "professional," while ones that seem weak are more "bureaucratic" in character. Are there significant differences among the colleges? There certainly are, as Table 3-3 clearly shows.

Regulation of Work Activities

It is generally assumed that professionals control their own work activities, that they are not supervised extensively, and that the institution assumes a "hands off" attitude. We tried to measure autonomy in the work realm by asking three questions: Are your contracts

TABLE 3-3
Diversity in Professional Autonomy

		Regulation			Personnel			Departmental autonomy		Decision making	
		1	2	3	4	5	6	7	8	9	10
		Contracts very specific	Courses assigned in contract	Strong regulation of travel	Department controls faculty promotions	Department controls faculty hiring	Work evaluated by peers	Department controls course offerings	Department controls its budget	Department run by consensus	Decisions very centralized
Institutional typology (N = 300)	r =	-.43	-.41	-.55	.43	.51	.44	.31	.09	.22	-.12
Private multiversity (N = 6)	x̄	14	15	25	49	76	64	84	40	22	51
Public multiversity (N = 15)	x̄	17	27	62	44	82	43	69	38	25	44
Elite liberal arts (N = 24)	x̄	25	15	39	49	66	58	73	40	14	21
Public comprehensive (N = 41)	x̄	31	46	85	30	64	29	54	31	28	50
Public college (N = 21)	x̄	34	34	78	23	52	38	55	27	18	42
Private liberal arts (N = 84)	x̄	57	34	73	13	37	25	62	43	20	41
Community college (N = 90)	x̄	48	52	92	18	44	23	48	29	18	48
Private junior college (N = 19)	x̄	56	53	83	08	21	09	55	33	08	48

*Numbers in each cell indicate the average percent of respondents who agreed with statement.

very specific about your work assignments? Are your courses arbitrarily assigned by your contract? Does the institution have many rules and regulations about professional travel?

The differences between institutions are enormous. There is a consistent pattern: the higher up the institutional scale, the lower the institution's control of work activities. There is less specification in the contracts, courses are selected by individual professors rather than administrative directive, and there are fewer controls over professional travel. At the other end of the scale, administrators control the terms of work, write them into contracts, and develop elaborate rules for behavior.

Control over Personnel Matters

The essence of professionalism is expert knowledge. Thus, the essence of professional autonomy is control over personnel. Experts demand—and usually obtain—the right to hire, evaluate, promote, and control their peers. Professionals argue that only they can reasonably evaluate the professional knowledge and expertise of other professionals.

Again, the pattern is strong. At the lower end of the scale, faculties have very little control over hiring, promotion, or evaluation of work (see columns 4, 5, and 6, Table 3-3). Administrative superiors make most of these critical decisions. In the institutions at the higher end of the scale, there is more professional autonomy. In issues of faculty hiring and evaluation, the faculty has very strong influence. On the issue of promotion the influence seems divided between faculty and administration. But this division is in sharp contrast to the two-year colleges where faculty seem almost excluded from the process. Only 8 percent of the private junior college faculties report control over promotions, while in prestige multiversities almost one-half of the faculty report such influence.

Departmental Autonomy

In a college or university a department is not just a convenient administrative unit, it is the home base of an academic discipline, a unit of intellectual identification and professional expertise. Consequently, professional freedom is dependent on a strong departmental unit, and enough freedom for the department to determine its work. We asked two questions: Does the department have control over course offerings? Does the department have control over its budget?

The results were consistent with our other findings, as columns 7 and 8 in Table 3-3 show. In the institutions at the higher end of the scale, 84 percent of the faculty said the department controlled courses. At the other extreme, only 48 percent of the faculty in the community colleges reported such control. The differences on budget control were not so strong, but still significant. The pattern was for more control at the higher end of the scale. However, the results were mixed: private liberal arts colleges, which seemed to have little faculty influence on most of our other measures, had a surprisingly strong degree of faculty influence on budget issues—stronger than any other type of school (43 percent).

Decision-Making Activities

Participation in decision making is often discussed as a desirable feature of a strong professional faculty. Faculty are the experts, and should be allowed to apply their expertise to the institution's decision process. We asked two questions: Is your department run by consensus or does a small clique dominate? Is decision making in your institution highly centralized, or is it more democratic?

On the issue of departmental decision making, most faculty report that the department is not run by a small, undemocratic clique of senior people (column 9, Table 3-3). However, differences do emerge; in higher prestige institutions, more people report that "the department is run by consensus." On the matter of institutional-level decision processes, we were surprised that the differences are not great (column 10, Table 3-3). Roughly half the respondents in all institutions said the institution was dominated by the administration, while roughly half said it was more democratic. Perhaps this is more a reflection of the individual's own biases and position in the institution than a reflection of the institution's processes. The one exception to the rule is interesting: in elite liberal arts colleges only 21 percent felt the administration dominated. Perhaps the "collegial" image lives—but only in these rare instances!

Summary

We have argued that there are significant differences among higher educational institutions, especially on the three key factors of *environmental relations, professional task,* and *institutional size and complexity.* Some institutions are heavily dependent on their environment, while others have a great deal of autonomy. Some seek to accomplish relatively simple tasks, while others grapple with a kaleidoscope of objectives. Some are small and simple, while others are massive and complex. We believe, contrary to many other current observers, that the American system is extremely complex and diverse and, in particular, that academic governance processes are and should be different in different institutions. Because of the enormous differences in academic organizations, it is necessary to group them meaningfully for purposes of study. For that reason we developed a typology of higher educational institutions comprising eight categories distilled from the more complex typology previously developed by the Carnegie Commission. The institutions in these categories vary systematically on almost all of our measures of environmental relations, professional task, and institutional size and complexity.

In addition, "professional autonomy," the ability of the faculty to control their work environment, is very different in different institutions. A consistent pattern emerges. In the higher prestige institutions there is much more freedom from bureaucratic regulation and supervision, and there is more control by the professionals over personnel issues. There is greater autonomy for the academic department to manage its affairs, and there is more participation by the faculty in decision making (at least at the departmental level). The opposite tendencies hold true at the lower end of the scale. Interestingly enough, there is a strong, regular variation as we look up and down the different types of institutions. In short, on this critical issue of professional autonomy there is certainly real diversity in American higher education.

References

Baldridge, J. Victor. *Power and Conflict in the University*. New York: John Wiley & Sons, 1971.

Baldridge, J. Victor, et al. "The Adoption of Innovations: The Effect of Organizational Size, Differentiation, and Environment," Research and Development Memorandum no. 108. Stanford, Calif.: School of Education, Stanford University, 1973.

Blau, Peter M. "A Formal Theory of Differentiation in Organizations." *American Sociological Review* 35, no. 2: 201-218.

Carnegie Commission on Higher Education. *Reports*. New York: McGraw-Hill, 1969-72.

Jencks, Christopher, and Riesman, David. *The Academic Revolution*. Garden City, N.Y.: Doubleday, 1968.

Newman, Frank, et al. *Report on Higher Education*. Washington, D.C.: Department of Health, Education, and Welfare, 1971.

Newman, Frank, et al. *The Second Newman Report: National Policy and Higher Education Report of a Special Task Force to the HEW*. Cambridge, Mass.: MIT Press, 1973.

Pace, C. Robert. *The Demise of Diversity: A Comparative Profile of Eight Types of Institutions.* Berkeley, Calif.: Carnegie Foundation for the Advancement of Teaching, 1974.
Thompson, James D. *Organizations in Action.* New York: McGraw-Hill, 1967.

4

Faculty Organization and Authority

Burton R. Clark

As we participate in or study various faculties in American higher
education, we observe decisions being made through informal interaction among a group of peers and through collective action of the
faculty as a whole. Formal hierarchy plays little part, and we have
reason to characterize the faculty as a collegium.[1] At the same time
we sense that what we now observe is not a counterpart of the collegiality of the days of old. The modern faculty in the United States is
not a body to be likened to the guilds of the medieval European university (Rashdall, 1936), or to the self-government of a dozen dons
in a residential college at Oxford or Cambridge (Snow, 1951), or to
the meager self-rule that was allowed the faculty in the small liberal
arts college that dominated American higher education until the end
of the last century (Hofstadter and Metzger, 1955; Schmidt, 1957).
The old-time collegium has modern reflections, as in the Fellowships
of the colleges at Yale, but for the most part it is no longer winningly
with us, and the kind of collegiality we now find needs different con-
ceptualization. We also observe on the modern campus that informa-

Reprinted from *The Study of Academic Administration* (Berkeley, Calif.: Center
for the Study of Higher Education, 1963).

1. A major type of collegiality is that involving collegial decision: "In such
cases an administrative act is only legitimate when it has been produced by the
cooperation of a plurality of people according to the principle of unanimity or
of majority." (Weber, 1947, p. 400.)

tion is communicated through formal channels, responsibility is fixed in formally-designated positions, interaction is arranged in relations between superiors and subordinates, and decisions are based on written rules. Thus we have reason to characterize the campus as a bureaucracy. But, at the same time, we sense that this characterization overlooks so much that it becomes misleading. Though the elements of bureaucracy are strong, they do not dominate the campus; and though they grow, their growth does not mean future dominance if other forms of organization and authority are expanding more rapidly.

The major form of organization and authority found in the faculties of the larger American colleges and universities, and toward which many small campuses are now moving, is now neither predominantly collegial nor bureaucratic. Difficult to characterize, it may be seen as largely "professional," but professional in a way that is critically different from the authority of professional men in other organizations such as the business corporation, the government agency, and the hospital. To approach this unusual pattern, we will first discuss trends in the organization and culture of the campus as a whole and then turn to the related trends in the organization and authority of the faculty.

We begin with broad changes in the nature of the campus because they condition the structure of authority. Authority is conditioned, for example, by the nature of work, the technology of an organization. The mass assembly of automobiles does not allow much personal discretion on the part of the worker; surgery in the hospital operating room requires on-the-spot judgment and autonomous decision by the surgeon and one or two colleagues. To understand faculty authority, we need some comprehension of what academic work has in common with work in other settings and how it differs from work elsewhere. Authority is also conditioned by patterns of status. Status comes in part from formal assignment, hence men called deans usually have much of it, but status is also derived in academia from one's standing in a discipline, and this important source of status is independent of the official scheme (Wilson, 1942; Caplow and McGee, 1958). Authority is also conditioned by traditional sentiments. Legends and ideologies have a force of their own. Conceptions of what should be are formed by what has been or by ideals handed down through the generations. The stirring ideologies of the community of scholars and academic freedom are forces to be reckoned with when one is dealing with faculties and in understanding their organization. Thus, the work itself, the status system, the traditional sentiments, all affect authority.

Trends in the Social Organization of the Campus

Four trends in the campus, closely related, are as follows: unitary to composite or federal structure; single to multiple value systems; nonprofessional to professional work; consensus to bureaucratic coordination.

Unitary to Federal Structure

The history of American higher education is a history of movement from unitary liberal arts colleges to multistructured colleges and universities. The American college of 1840 contained a half dozen professors and fifty to a hundred students (Hofstadter and Metzger, 1955, pages 222-223); in 1870, average size was still less than ten faculty and a hundred students. All students in a college took the same curriculum, a "program of classical-mathematical studies inherited from Renaissance education" (Hofstadter and Metzger, 1955, page 226). There was no need for subunits such as division and department; this truly was a unitary structure. In comparison, the modern university and college is multistructured. The University of California at Berkeley in 1962-63, with over 23,000 students and 1,600 "officers of instruction," was divided into some fifteen colleges or schools (e.g., College of Engineering, School of Public Health); over fifty institutes, centers, and laboratories; and some seventy-five departments (including Poultry Husbandry, Romance Philology, Food Technology, and Naval Architecture). In three departments and three schools, the subunit itself contained over fifty faculty members. Such complexity is not only characteristic of the university: a large California state college contains forty or so disciplines, grouped in a number of divisions; and even a small liberal arts college today may have twenty departments and three or four divisions.

The multiplication of subunits stems in part from increasing size. The large college cannot remain as unitary as the small one, since authority must be extensively delegated and subsidiary units formed around the many centers of authority. The subunits also stem from plurality of purpose; we have moved from single- to multi-purpose colleges. Goals are not only more numerous but also broadly defined and ambiguous. Those who would define the goals of the modern university speak in such terms as "preserving truth, creating new knowledge, and serving the needs of man through truth and knowledge" (Kerr, 1963). The service goal has a serviceable ambiguity that covers anything from home economics for marriage to research and development for space. A tightly integrated structure could not be established around these goals. Organizational structure accommodates to the multiplicity of goals by dividing into segments with different primary functions, such as liberal arts and professional training, scientific research and humanistic education. The structure accommodates to ambiguity of goals with its own ambiguity, overlap, and discontinuity. We find some liberal arts disciplines scattered all over the campus (e.g., statistics, psychology), residing as components of professional schools and of "other" departments as well as in the appropriately named department. No neat consistent structure is possible; the multiple units form and reform around functions in a catch-as-catch-can fashion. Needless to say, with a multiplicity of ambiguous goals and a variety of subunits, authority is extensively decentralized. The structure is federal rather than unitary, and even takes on some likeness to a loosely-joined federation.

Single to Multiple Value System

Most colleges before the turn of the century and perhaps as late as the 1920's possessed a unified culture that extended across the campus (Hofstadter and Metzger, 1955; Schmidt, 1957), and this condition still obtains in some small colleges of today. But the number of colleges so characterized continues to decline and the long-run trend is clear: the campuswide culture splits into subcultures located in a variety of social groups and organizational units. As we opened the doors of American higher education, we admitted more orientations to college—college as fun, college as marriage, college as preparation for graduate school, college as certificate to go to work tomorrow, college as place to rebel against the Establishment, and even college as a place to think. These orientations have diverse social locations on campus, from fraternity house to cafe espresso shop to Mrs. Murphy's desegregated rooming house. The value systems of the students are numerous.

The faculty is equally if not more prone to diversity in orientation, as men cleave to their specialized lines of work and their different perspectives and vocabularies. Faculty orientations differ between those who commit themselves primarily to the local campus and those who commit themselves primarily to their far-flung discipline or profession; between those who are scientists and those who are humanists; between those who think of themselves as pure researchers or pure scholars and those who engage in a professional practice and train recruits. The value systems of the faculty particularly cluster around the individual disciplines and hence at one level of analysis there are as many value systems as there are departments.

Nonprofessional to Professional Work

Intense specialization characterizes the modern campus; academic man has moved from general to specific knowledge. The old-time teacher—Mr. Chips—was a generalist. He covered a wide range of subject matter, with less intensity in any one area than would be true today, and he was engaged in pure transmission of knowledge. In the American college of a century ago, the college teacher had only a bachelor's degree (in the fixed classical curriculum), plus "a modest amount of more advanced training, perhaps in theology . . ." (Hofstadter and Metzger, 1955, page 230). There was no system of graduate education, no reward for distinction in scholarship, and the professor settled down into the groove of classroom recitation and the monitoring of student conduct. We have moved from this kind of professor, the teacher generalist, to the teacher of physics, of engineering, of microbiology, of abnormal psychology, and to the professor as researcher, as consultant, as professional-school demonstrator. We have moved from transmission of knowledge to innovation of knowledge, which has meant specialization in research. Taking the long view, perhaps *the* great change in the role of academic man is the ascendance of research and scholarship—the rise of the commitment to create knowledge. This change in the academic role interacts with rapid social change: research causes change, as in the case of change in technology and industrial processes; and such changes, in turn, encourage the research attitude, as in the case of competition between industrial firms, competition between nations, competition between universities. In short, the research component of the academic role is intimately related to major modern social trends.

In his specialization, modern academic man is a case of professional man. We define "profession" to mean a specialized competence with a high degree of intellectual content, a specialty heavily based on or involved with knowledge. Specialized competence based on involvement in knowledge is the hallmark of the modern professor. He is preeminently an expert. Having special knowledge at his command, the professional worker needs and seeks a large degree of autonomy from lay control and normal organizational control. Who is the best judge of surgical procedure—laymen, hospital administrators, or surgeons? Who is the best judge of theories in chemistry—laymen, university administrators, or professors of chemistry? As work becomes professionalized—specialized around esoteric knowledge and technique—the organization of work must create room for expert judgment, and autonomy of decision making and practice become a hallmark of the advanced profession.

Not all professional groups need the same degree of autonomy, however. Professionals who largely give advice or follow the guidelines of a received body of knowledge require extensive but not great autonomy for the individual and the group. They need sufficient leeway to give an honest expert opinion or to apply the canons of judgment of their field. Those requiring great autonomy are those who wish to crawl along the frontiers of knowledge, with flashlight or floodlight in hand, searching for the new—the new scientific finding, the new reinterpretation of history, the new criticism in literature or art. Academic man is a special kind of professional man, a type characterized by a particularly high need for autonomy. To be innovative, to be critical of established ways, these are the commitments of the academy and the impulses of scientific and scholarly roles that press for unusual autonomy.

Consensual to Bureaucratic Coordination

As the campus has moved from unitary to composite structure, from single to multiple systems of values, from general to specialized work, it has moved away from the characteristics of community, away from the "community of scholars." A faculty member does not interact with most other members of the faculty. In the larger places, he may know less than a fifth, less than a tenth. Paths do not cross. The faculty lounge is no more, but is replaced by coffee pots in dozens of locations. The professor retains a few interests in common with all others, such as higher salaries, but he has an increasing number of interests that diverge. Even salary is a matter on which interests may diverge, as men bargain for themselves, as departments compete for funds, as scientists are paid more, through various devices, than the men of the humanities.

In short, looking at the total faculty, interaction is down, commonality of interest is down, commonality of sentiments is down. With this, coordination of work and policy within the faculty is not so much now as in the past achieved by easy interaction of community members, by the informal give-and-take that characterizes the true community—the community of the small town where everyone knows nearly everyone else, or the community of the old small college where the professors saw much of everyone else in the group. The modern campus can no longer be coordinated across its length and breadth by informal interaction and by the coming together of the whole. Informal consulting back and forth is still important; the administration and the faculty still use the lunch table for important business. But campuswide coordination increasingly moves toward the means normal to the large-scale organization, to bureaucratic means. We appoint specialists to various areas of administration, give them authority, and they write rules to apply across the system. They communicate by correspondence, they attempt to make decisions fairly and impartially by judging the case before them against the criteria of the rulebook. Thus we move toward bureaucratic coordination, as the admissions officer decides on admissions, the registrar decides on the recording of grades, the business officer decides proper purchasing procedures, and various faculty committees decide on a wide range of matters, from tenure to travel funds to the rules of order for meetings of an academic senate.

In sum: the campus tends toward composite structure, toward a multiplicity of subcultures, toward intense professionalism, and toward some bureaucratic coordination.

Change in Faculty Organization and Authority

The organization and authority of the faculty accommodate to these trends in at least three ways: by segmentation, by a federated professionalism, and by the growth of individual power centers.

Segmentation

As campuses increase in size, complexity, and internal specialization, there is less chance that the faculty will be able to operate effectively as a total faculty in college affairs, or as the governmental body we have in mind when we speak of a community of scholars. The decision-making power and influence of the faculty is now more segmented—segmented by subcollege, by division, and particularly by department. Since the interests of the faculty cluster around the departments, faculty participation in government tends to move out to these centers of commitment. Who selects personnel, decides on courses, and judges students? The faculty as a whole cannot, any more than the administration. Indeed, as departments and professional schools grow in size and complexity, even they often do not; it is a wing of the department or a part of the professional school that has most influence. A liberal arts department that numbers forty to eighty faculty members may contain six or eight or a dozen specialties. The day has arrived when a department chairman may not even know the name, let alone the face and the person of the new instructors in "his" department.

What happens to the governmental organs designed for the faculty as a whole? They move in form from Town Hall to representative government, with men elected from the various "states" coming together in a federal center to legislate general rules, which are then executed by the administration or the faculty committees that constitute an administrative component of the faculty. With the move to representative government, there is greater differentiation in participation; a few "actives" participate a great deal; a considerably larger group constitutes an alert and informed public and participates a modest amount; the largest group consists of those who are not very interested or informed and who participate very little. The structure of participation parallels that found in the larger democratic society, and apparently is normal to a representative mass democracy. The situation is, of course, vexing to those who care about faculty government.

Professionalization

The authority of the faculty which flows out toward the departments and other units of the campus becomes located in the hands of highly specialized experts; and, as suggested earlier, takes on some characteristics of professional authority. Almost everywhere in modern large-scale organizations, we find a tug-of-war going on between administrative and professional orientations. In the hospital, the basic conflict in authority lies between the control of the nonmedical hospital administrator and the authority of the doctors. In industry, a fascinating clash is occurring between management and the scientist in the research and development laboratory. (See Kornhauser, 1962; Marcson, 1960.) The fantastic expansion of research and development has brought over 400,000 scientists and engineers into industry, there to be committed to innovation and to the development of new inventions to the point of practical utility. Many of these technologists have a high degree of expertise, a strong interest in research —often "pure" research—and they press for a large degree of freedom. Their fondest wish is to be left alone; they make the point that in scientific work it seems rational to do just that, that basic discoveries stem not from managerial direction but from the scientist following up his own initial hunches and the leads he develops as he proceeds. Management has found such men difficult to deal with; their morale suffers easily from traditional forms of management, and they present unusual demands on management to change and accommodate. In this situation, professional authority and bureaucratic authority are both necessary, for each performs an essential function: professional authority protects the exercise of the special expertise of the technologist, allowing his judgment to be preeminent in many matters. Bureaucratic authority functions to provide coordination of the work of the technologists with the other major elements of the firm. Bureaucratic direction is not capable of providing certain expert judgments; professional direction is not capable of providing the overall coordination. The problem presented by the scientist in industry is how to serve simultaneously the requirements of autonomy and the requirements of coordination, and how to accommodate the authority of the professional man and his group of peers to the authority of management and vice versa (Kornhauser, 1962).

The professional-in-the-organization presents everywhere his special kind of problem. He gains authority, compared to most employees, by virtue of his special knowledge and skills; he loses authority, compared to a man working on his own, by virtue of the fact that organizations locate much authority in administrative positions. The problem of allocation of authority between professionals and bureaucrats does, however, vary in intensity and form in different kinds of organizations. As mentioned earlier, advisers and practitioners need a modest degree of authority, while scientists and academics have perhaps the highest requirements for the autonomy to engage in research, in unfettered teaching, and in scholarship that follows the rules of consistency and proof that develop within a discipline.

The segmentation of the faculty into clusters of experts gives professional authority a special form in academic organizations. In other situations, there usually are one or two major professional groups within the organization who, if they are influential, substitute professional control for administrative control. This occurs in the case of medical personnel in the hospital who often dominate decision making. The internal controls of the medical profession are strong and are substituted for those of the organization. But in the college or university this situation does not obtain; there are twelve, twenty-five, or fifty clusters of experts. The experts are prone to identify with their own disciplines, and the "academic profession" overall comes off a poor second. We have wheels within wheels, many professions within a profession. No one of the disciplines on a campus is likely to dominate the others; at a minimum, it usually takes an alliance of disciplines, such as "the natural sciences" or "the humanities," to put together a bloc that might dominate others. The point is that with a variety of experts—chemists, educationists, linguists, professors of marketing—the collective control of the professionals over one another will not be strong. The campus is not a closely knit group of professionals who see the world from one perspective. As a collection of professionals, it is decentralized, loose, and flabby.

The principle is this: where professional influence is high and there is one dominant professional group, the organization will be integrated by the imposition of professional standards. Where professional influence is high and there are a number of professional groups, the organization will be split by professionalism. The university and the large college are fractured by expertness, not unified by it. The sheer variety supports the tendency for authority to diffuse toward quasi-autonomous clusters. Thus, faculty authority has in common with professional authority in other places the protection of individual and group autonomy. It is different from professional authority in other places in the extremity of the need for autonomy and in the fragmentation of authority around the interest of a large variety of groups of roughly equal status and power. The campus is a holding company for professional groups rather than a single association of professionals.

Individualization

When we speak of professional authority we often lump together the authority that resides with the individual expert and the authority that resides with a collegial group of experts. Both the individual and the group gain influence at the expense of laymen and the general administrator. But what is the division of authority between the individual and the group? Sometimes group controls can be very tight and quite hierarchical, informally if not formally, as young doctors learn in many hospitals, and as assistant professors learn in many departments. The personal authority of the expert varies widely with the kind of establishment, and often with rank and seniority. The campus is a place where strong forces cause the growth of some individuals into centers of power. We will review several of these sources of personal authority.

First, we have noted the expertise of the modern academy. The intense specialization alone makes many a man into king of a sector in which few others are able to exercise much judgment. Thus, *within* a department, men increasingly feel unable to judge the merits of men in specialties they know nothing about. The technical nature of the specialized lines of work of most academic men, then, is a source of personal authority. If we want to provide a course on Thomas Hardy, we are likely to defer on its content to the judgment of the man in the English Department who has been knee-deep in Hardy for a decade. The idea of such a course would really have been his in the first place; Hardy falls within his domain within the English Department, and his judgment on the need for the course will weigh more than the judgment of others.

Second, some professional experts now have their personal authority greatly enhanced by money. Despite his location within an organization, the professor in our time is becoming an entrepreneur. It used to be that the college president was the only one on campus, other than an enterprising and dedicated member of the board of trustees, who was capable of being an entrepreneur. Many of the great presidents were great because they were great at coming home with the loot—adventurers who conquered the hearts and pocketbooks of captains of industry and then with money in hand raided wholesale the faculties of other institutions. Presidents who can raise money and steal faculty are still with us, but they have been joined by professors. Kerr (1963) has suggested that the power of the individual faculty member is going up while the power of the collective faculty is going down because the individual as researcher, as scholar, and as consultant relates increasingly to the grant-giving agencies of the federal government and to the foundations. He has direct ties to these major sources of funds and influence; indeed, he participates in their awarding of grants and even has problems of conflict of interest. A professor-entrepreneur, by correspondence and telephone and airplane trips, lines up money for projects. He sometimes arranges for the financing of an entire laboratory; occasionally he even brings back a new building. Even when the professor does little of the arranging, it is *his* presence that attracts these resources. He represents competence, and the grant givers pursue competence.

The entrepreneurial activity and resources-gaining influence of professors, which extends down to assistant professors in the social as well as the natural sciences, has had remarkable growth since World War II, and the personal autonomy and power thus achieved in relation to others in the university is considerable. A professor does not have to beg postage stamps from a departmental secretary nor a two hundred dollar raise from the department chairman nor travel money to go to a meeting from a dean or a committee if he has monies assigned to him to the tune of $37,000, or $175,000, or $400,000. His funds from outside sources may be called "soft" funds, in the jargon of finance, but they are hard enough to hire additional faculty members and assistants, to cover summer salaries, and to provide for travel to distant, delightful places.

The following principle obtains: a *direct* relation of faculty members to external sources of support affects the distribution of influence within the campus, redistributing influence from those who do not have such contacts to those who do, and moving power from the faculty as a whole and as smaller collectivities to individual professors. In the university of old, members of the faculty achieved a high degree of influence by occupying the few professorial positions available in a structure that narrowed at the top. Their source of influence was structural and internal. The source of great influence in the modern American university is less internal and less tied to particular positions; it is more external and more tied to national and international prestige in a discipline, and to contact with the sources of support for research and scholarship that are multiplying and growing so rapidly.

This individualization in faculty organization and authority excites impulses in the faculty and the administration to establish some collective control, for much is at stake in the balance of the curriculum, the equality of rewards in the faculty, and even the character of the institution. But the efforts at control do not have easy going. Collective bodies of the faculty and the administration are hardly in a position, or inclined, to tell the faculty member he can have this contract but not that one, since the faculty member will define the project as part of his pursuit of his own scholarly interests. When the faculty member feels that this sensitive right is infringed, he will run up the banners of academic freedom and inquiry, or he will fret and become a festering sore in the body politic of the campus, or he will retreat to apathy and his country house, or he will make it known in other and greener pastures that he will listen to the siren call of a good offer.

Third, personal authority of the professorial expert is increased in our time by the competitiveness of the job market. The expansion of higher education means a high demand for professors, and the job market runs very much in the professor's favor in bargaining with the administration. His favorable position *in* the market enhances his position *on* campus. He can demand more and get it; he can even become courageous. In the world of work, having another job to go to is perhaps the most important source of courage.

To recapitulate: Faculty organization and authority tend in modern times to become more segmented, more professional in character, and somewhat more individualized. We are witnessing a strong trend toward a federated structure in colleges and especially in universities —with the campus more like a United Nations and less like a small town—and this trend affects faculty authority by weakening the faculty as a whole and strengthening the faculty in its many parts. Faculty authority becomes less of a case of self-government by a total collegium, and more of a case of authority exercised department by department, subcollege by subcollege. The *role* of faculty authority is shifting from protecting the rights of the entire guild, the rights of the collective faculty, to protecting the autonomy of the separate disciplines and the autonomy of the individual faculty member.

Faculty authority in our time tends to become professional authority in a federated form. We have a loose alliance of professional men. The combination of professional authority and loosely joined structure has the imposing function of protecting the autonomy of the work of experts amidst extensive divergence of interests and commitments. The qualities of federation are important here. The federation is a structure that gives reign to the quasi-autonomous, simultaneous development of the interests of a variety of groups. Within an academic federation, a number of departments, divisions, colleges, professional schools, institutes, and the like can coexist, each pushing its own interests and going its own way to a rather considerable extent. Professional authority structured as a federation is a form of authority particularly adaptive to a need for a high degree of autonomous judgment by individuals and subgroups.

This trend toward a federation of professionals is only part of the story. To hold the separate components of the campus together, we have a superimposed coordination by the administration, and, as Kerr (1963) has suggested, this coordination increasingly takes on the attributes of mediation. The administration attempts to keep the peace and to inch the entire enterprise another foot ahead. The faculty, too, in its own organization, also counters this divisive trend with a machinery of coordination. The very fact of diffusion of authority makes the faculty politician more necessary than ever, for the skills of politics and diplomacy are needed. There must be faculty mediators; men who serve on central committees, men with cast iron stomachs for lunch table discussions and cocktail parties, men who know how to get things done that must be done for the faculty as a whole or for part of the faculty. There must be machinery for setting rules and carrying them out impartially across the faculty. The modern campus is, or is becoming, too large and complicated for collegial or professional arrangements to provide the overall coordination, and coordination is performed largely by bureaucratic arrangements—e.g., the rulebook, and definite administrative domains.

Federated professionalism within an organization, like many other trends, thus promotes countertrends. Specialization and individualization seriously weaken the integration of the whole. The weakness of collegiality or professionalism in the large organization, as suggested earlier in the case of industry, is that it cannot handle the problem of order, it cannot provide sufficient integration. Thus the above trends in faculty organization and authority open the door to bureaucracy—more bureaucracy in the administration, more within the faculty itself. The modern large faculty, therefore, combines professionalism, federated structure, and bureaucracy—perhaps in a mixture never before evidenced in human history.

This combination of what seem contradictory forms of organization perplexes observers of academia. Is the faculty collegial? Yes, somewhat. Is it split into fragments? Yes, somewhat. Is it professional? Yes, somewhat. Is it unitary? Yes, somewhat. Is it bureaucratic? Yes, somewhat. Different features of the faculty strike us according to the occurrences of the week or the events we chance to observe. The ever-mounting paperwork firmly convinces us that the campus is doomed to bureaucratic stagnation. The fact that the president often gets what the president wants convinces us that he really has all the authority. The inability of a campus to change a department that is twenty years behind in its field convinces us that departmental autonomy has run amok and the campus is lacking in leadership and in capacity to keep up with the times. One observer will see the campus as a tight ship, the next will speak of the same campus as a lawless place where power lies around loose. No wonder we are confused and no wonder that outsiders are so often even more confused or more irrelevant in giving advice.

But in the combination of forms of organization and forms of authority that we find today within the campus and within the faculty itself, there are certain trends that are stronger than others and certain features that tend toward dominance. The society at large is tending to become a society of experts, and the campus has already arrived at this state. Expertise is a dominant characteristic of the campus, and organization and authority cluster around it. Because of its expertness, together with its ever-growing size, the faculty moves away from community, moves away from collegiality of the whole. The faculty moves toward decentralized or federated structure, and authority moves toward clusters of experts and the individual expert. Thus professional authority tends to become the dominant form of authority, and collegial and bureaucratic features fall into a subsidiary place. In short, when we say college, we say expert. When we say expert, we say professional authority.

References

Caplow, Theodore, and McGee, Reece J. *The Academic Marketplace.* New York: Basic Books, 1958.

Hofstadter, Richard, and Metzger, Walter P. *The Development of Academic Freedom in the United States.* New York: Columbia University Press, 1955.

Kerr, Clark. *The Uses of the University.* Cambridge, Mass.: Harvard University Press, 1963.

Kornhauser, William. *Scientists in Industry: Conflict and Accommodation.* Berkeley: University of California Press, 1962.

Marcson, Simon. *The Scientist in American Industry.* New York: Harper & Brothers, 1960.

Rashdall, Hastings. *The Universities in Europe in the Middle Ages,* edited by T. M. Powicke and A. B. Emden. New York: Oxford University Press, 1936.

Schmidt, George P. *The Liberal Arts College.* New Brunswick, N.J.: Rutgers University Press, 1957.

Snow, C. P. *The Masters.* New York: Macmillan, 1951.

Weber, Max. *The Theory of Social and Economic Organization.* New York: Free Press, 1947.

Wilson, Logan. *The Academic Man.* New York: Oxford University Press, 1942.

PART II

Innovation and Change

5

Change Processes in Educational Organizations

J. Victor Baldridge and Terrence E. Deal

Change or innovation is a topic constantly discussed in the educational world. Colleges and universities are always changing, either by deliberate design or by whim or fate. Students, faculty members, administrators, and the general public are concerned about the ability of educational organizations to adapt in the face of new demands, and, as a consequence, the careers of educational administrators reflect their ability to stimulate and manage change. Being known as an "innovative" administrator often assures promotion within an organization and movement from one organization to another. Most change management is largely based on intuition and seat-of-the-pants strategy. Certainly there are no valid, tested scientific principles of change. Stimulating and managing change could, however, be less an intuitive process if knowledge based on social science research and the experience of practicing change agents were applied. At least three things are needed to understand change processes in educational organizations: a comprehensive *organizational perspective,* that is, an understanding of crucial organizational subsystems and processes involved in innovation; familiarity with *strategies* that

Adapted from R&D Memorandum no. 126, "An Organizational View of Educational Innovation," published by the Stanford Center for Research and Development in Teaching. This research was conducted at the Center pursuant to contract NE-C-003-3-0062 with the National Institute of Education, Department of Health, Education, and Welfare.

can be used to cause and support educational changes, such as leadership dynamics, the role of change agents, the dynamics of organizational politics, and the use of program evaluation processes; and *practical experience* with the dynamics of educational change, either from actually administering a changing institution or from gaining vicarious experience through case studies of actual attempts to change educational organizations.

Difficulties in Applying Research to Administrative Practice

The prevailing climate in education favors innovation over maintaining the status quo. This climate nudges even the most conservative educational administrator, whether motivated by job satisfaction, career enhancement, or job security, toward changing any aspect of an institution in order to claim the title "innovator." As such efforts often cause unavoidable problems or give rise to formidable obstacles, the question often asked is, "What do I do now?"

There is unlimited opportunity to locate books, monographs, articles, and essays—all dealing in some way with adoption, implementation, or support of innovation. In fact, there is a long and distinguished history of such research done by anthropologists, psychologists, sociologists, economists, and social psychologists. This history, coupled with a continuing interest in innovation on the part of social scientists, has produced an enormous body of literature that continues to grow at a staggering rate. Everett Rogers reviewed over five hundred articles in the area of innovation diffusion in 1962. Nine years later, over fifteen hundred articles were examined in a revised edition (Rogers and Shoemaker, 1971).

As changing social and economic circumstances press nearly all social institutions to change policies and programs, the body of innovation studies continues to grow not only in size but in scope. The attention of the social scientist has expanded from factors that *promote or discourage* innovation to include factors that *maintain* innovation and *evaluate* whether social inventions are accomplishing their intended purpose. Schools, particularly, have been studied as they have integrated the races, modified curricula and instruction, or altered the work arrangements of teachers. The entire range of the innovation process, from invention to implementation and assessment, is presently being scrutinized by representatives of the various social science disciplines. Indeed, for the administrator seeking solutions to perplexing problems of how to produce change or support new programs, there is an abundance of scholarly literature.

In spite of the sheer volume of material, however, there is a general consensus, particularly among educational administrators, that research has not produced practical assistance in proportion to its enormous volume. They feel that much innovation research is not applicable to the important problems of administering change for several reasons.

Individualistic bias. Until recently most of the research on innovation diffusion has been individualistic. Studies have focused on a single technical invention (a new fertilizer, a new medicine, a new curriculum), and the factors that cause an individual user (farmer, physician, teacher) to adopt or reject it. Quite often, the individual characteristics of the adopter receive most of the attention: What type of farmer will adopt a new fertilizer? What kind of physician will start using a new drug? What personal characteristics cause teachers to accept or reject a new approach to instruction?

In these studies, the factors that produce innovative outlooks or behaviors are typically individualistic. For example, are the adopters young or old, rich or poor, leaders or followers? Is their social status high or low? Are they at the center of a communications network or isolated? Do they have a traditional or a modern outlook? (See Rogers and Shoemaker, 1971.)

Neglect of organizational features. Despite the fact that most major social inventions are used by organizations rather than by individuals, complex organizations and their innovation problems are rarely treated in the literature. Educational innovations are examples of social inventions adopted primarily by complex organizations, not by individuals. Even when an individual instructor might be considered the adopter, the fact that an instructor is firmly enmeshed in the social system of the college carries strong organizational implications for both the adoption and maintenance of new instructional techniques. Unfortunately, the literature on innovation provides little help for administrators who must confront innovation in its organizational context. In fact, Rogers' monumental study of innovation (1962) summarized the conclusions of the research in fifty-two major propositions, *not one of which referred to a complex organization as the innovation adopter or to organizational features as affecting the process.* The revised version (1971) is no better in dealing with organizational factors.

Stress on nonmanipulable factors. Another characteristic of innovation research that has weakened its usefulness for administrators is that it has not stressed manipulable factors. The individualistic bias has emphasized individuals and personal characteristics as important determinants of the spread and adoption of important social inventions. A result of this emphasis has been to conclude, for example, that young, inexperienced teachers from middle-class families are more likely to adopt new instructional practices.

It is readily apparent that none of these characteristics is directly manipulable. Administrators cannot make instructors younger or control their social origins. They can give them opportunities to gain more experience, but this is an expensive, time-consuming process. Research and past experience both stress the difficulties involved in changing people—their outlooks, values, or habits. Through hiring and firing practices, administrators can control the kinds of individuals who participate in an organization. But professors—tenured or otherwise—are almost impossible to fire, and decreasing enrollments reduce the possibility that new people with "innovative" characteristics can be selected into the organization.

In short, the social psychological bias in innovation research has produced conclusions that point to administrative efforts to change *individuals* as being a way of stimulating the adoption of new practices. Because colleges are particularly limited in terms of adding new teachers or firing old ones, innovation research has encouraged the development of people-changing strategies such as T-groups, sensitivity training, and laboratory groups. But, as a recent article by Bowers (1973) points out, these strategies have not been particularly effective. The administrator is, therefore, still in the almost impossible position of trying to manipulate *people* to bring about *structural* changes.

Neglect of policy implications. Another weakness of innovation literature is that many social scientists have not focused sharply enough on policy questions or developed policy implications from their studies. The problems selected for inquiry are largely disciplinary in origin. Psychologists have studied the personality characteristics of innovators; anthropologists, the kinship patterns of innovators; sociologists, the position of innovators in social networks. The goal of such discipline-based research is not to solve the practical problems of innovation; rather, it is to advance the development of the discipline. Administrators looking for solutions to problems of managing innovation find, instead, scholarly treatises written in the appropriate academic jargon with the popular conclusion: "More research is needed." The research has an academic- rather than a problem-oriented focus.

In the field of education, research and development centers were established expressly for the purpose of doing problem-oriented or policy research. There is, however, a significant gap between the reach and grasp of the centers (Baldridge, 1973). Many have continued to sponsor academic-oriented research under the guise of the problem-oriented banner. Others have sponsored problem-oriented research without appropriate roots in disciplines, adequate research design, or appropriate methodological considerations. Either practical implications have not been developed from important research studies, or unimportant research has unduly influenced the development of administrative guidelines and policy. Very few policy documents on innovation have been placed in the hands of administrators to help them as they labor to change institutions. Where guidelines have been available, as we pointed out previously, they invariably provide the administrator with recommendations for action that are outside his or her span of control.

Overcommitment to a specific strategy: the "black bag" problem. Innovation research has again fallen short of administrative expectations because it has failed to test alternative strategies for causing or controlling educational innovation. Instead, there has been a regrettable tendency to seize on a few narrow perspectives and then to apply them willy-nilly regardless of the organization's real need. The narrow perspectives of the "human relations-organizational development" school have been seized on by most educational consultants and "change agents" and developed into specific strategies for producing change. Once developed, the strategies are placed in a consultant's black bag, endowed with magical powers, and sold at a premium to administrators who need assistance.

To be sure, some narrow perspectives may produce the intended effects and may indeed result in the adoption and successful implementation of new curricula, instructional techniques, work patterns, or new approaches to decision making. However, innovation research has seldom carried the process of inquiry to the stage of experimentally testing several change strategies. Thus, we can never be sure whether it is the consultant, the strategy, or the "Hawthorne effects" that produced changes. Without careful testing of a variety of approaches, administrators can become wedded to simplistic, narrow strategies of change.

In a sense we are suggesting a shift in overall orientation to the problem of innovation in *organizations.* The terminology alone pulls us in the wrong direction, for the "adoption of innovations" induces thoughts of a commercial distribution of products from a manufacturer to a potential buyer. With that perspective, the research and development community may be tempted to huckster particular products. In the urgency to sell, they may overlook the need to build *problem-solving capacity* into the organizations they are serving. Researchers, developers, administrators, and educators have seldom created an innovative environment where alternatives could be considered and options explored.

Donald Campbell has perceptively commented that the tradition of social innovation that ties it to particular products and techniques has led to social waste, forcing the defense of innovations that did not deserve defending. Campbell argues, instead, for a risk-taking approach to solving social problems, where a variety of innovations and techniques can be explored.

If the political and administrative system has committed itself in advance to the correctness and efficacy of its reforms, it cannot tolerate learning of failure. To be truly scientific we must be able to experiment. We must be able to advocate without that excess of commitment that blinds us to reality testing. . . .

One simple shift in political posture which would reduce the problem is the shift from the advocacy of a specific reform to the advocacy of the seriousness of the problem, and hence to the advocacy of persistence in alternative reform efforts should the first one fail. The political stance would become: "This is a serious problem. We propose to initiate Policy A on an experimental basis. If after five years there has been no significant improvement, we will shift to Policy B." By making explicit that a given problem solution was only one of several that the administrator or party could in good conscience advocate, and by having ready a plausible alternative, the administrator could afford honest evaluation of outcomes. Negative results, a failure of the first program, would not jeopardize his job, for his job would be to keep after the problem until something was found that worked [Campbell, 1972, page 189].

We must not be in the business of disseminating a particularly exciting new product. We must be in the business of creating organizations with built-in capacities for assessing needs and creating viable alternatives. The adoption of any specific innovation is a sideline activity that must not consume our energies. *Our continuing enterprise should be the building of flexible organizations responsive to environments, organizations with reserves of expertise and resources to sustain long-range problem solving.*

Problems with Using Research for Change: A Summary

The profusion of innovation research has not been particularly useful for administrators as they are changing, reforming, or installing new ideas in educational organizations. This gap between the research and administrative action stems from several characteristics of the innovation research: an individualistic perspective tends to ignore the fact that most social inventions are adopted by organizations, not individuals. There has been a focus on factors that are difficult or impossible for an administrator to control. The policy implications of much innovation research are not spelled out. Alternative strategies for change that result from the research are not adequately tested. Consultants have discouraged an experimental problem-solving approach by promising simple solutions from their "black bag" of tricks. Let us turn now from the problems in the literature to some perspectives we believe can be helpful.

Goal One: Broadening Perspectives on Educational Innovation

Our first objective is to question some common assumptions about educational change. This allows one to develop a broader perspective from which to view the issue.

Two Common Perspectives on Change: Invention and Diffusion

There are several problems in discussing change or innovation. First, the topic lends itself to easy trivialization; the most insignificant changes sometimes become objects of serious research. Thus, the literature is filled with minute details about small-scale projects, many of which failed—often a good thing! We wish to concentrate on changes that have major impact for the organization, that involve significant numbers of participants, that seriously affect how the organization achieves its goals, and that require large investments in terms of personnel, time, and money. There are other kinds of changes, but we have chosen to focus on what we consider to be serious organizational developments. This immediately eliminates a considerable block of literature.

A second problem arises from the complex and slippery terminology that is used in discussing the subject. Progress can be made simply by showing some of the different approaches to the problem. It is useful to divide the literature into three categories: invention, innovation and diffusion, and basic organizational change.

The invention process. Invention is the process of developing new technologies and procedures for an organization. In the educational world this means new curriculum ideas, new procedures for teaching, or new methods of organization. The essence of invention is that a new procedure has been developed that was not previously available. One major source of new inventions in the educational world is the research and development activities of various federal laboratories and centers. In addition, local university, college, and public school systems work to invent procedures. One example of an educational invention would be a new computerized method of teaching mathematical skills. Invention is probably the least common of the various types of organizational change; it is rare, indeed, to develop really new products or procedures.

The diffusion process. Social scientists have been interested in the diffusion processes of technological and social inventions, an interest readily apparent from the many publications on the subject. The innovations studied cover a broad spectrum of social life: smallpox inoculations, educational innovations, agricultural inventions, child-rearing practices among American mothers, medical inventions, the introduction of modern machinery into underdeveloped nations.

Much of the literature has concentrated on limited kinds of technological innovations—a new vaccine or fertilizer, for example. Often such innovations are highly technical, and effectiveness can be proved before dissemination. The payoff time is relatively short so the person adopting the innovation can decide whether or not to continue using it. Also, the innovation's technical efficiency can be readily evaluated. Finally, the decision maker is usually an individual or a small group, not a complex organization.

Most major educational innovations are not so technically narrow or so easily put into effect. The decision base of a farmer is simpler than that of a university. The farmer judges his innovation by the grain that grows. But how does a college judge whether its students have learned social studies better under a new system? How does a university evaluate its success at doing better research? The adopter of most educational innovation is a complex organization, which increases the complexity of the decision process and the multiple chains of command necessary to carry out a decision. Different analytic tools must be developed to understand the complex process of educational innovation.

Another Perspective on Change: Organizational Subsystems

Apart from invention and diffusion, there is a third and even more fascinating case of change that deals with basic transformations in the organization itself. It is a much more significant, far-reaching kind of change. Although a new technology or procedure may bring change in an organization, changes in basic authority structure, goals, and programs represent even more fundamental transformations.

As has been noted, one of the limitations of innovation research has been its individualistic bias. This individualistic view has had an important influence on administrators' conceptions of the change process, mainly through its contribution to the human relations approach to organizational innovation. The human relations approach has emphasized the importance of individual leadership in promoting change and has singled out the attitudes, characteristics, and outlooks of individuals as forces to be overcome if educational change is to be successful.

In contrast, our perspective on educational change and innovation is based on changing *organizational factors.* We resist the human relations tendency to place the burden for changing people on the administrator. Instead, we emphasize that educational change engages all the subsystems that together comprise complex educational organizations. These include the goals, the environment, the formal system or structure, and the technology of the organization, as well as individuals and groups in an informal system of relationships. These various organizational subsystems are related in systematic ways. Any subsystem can pressure another subsystem to change. A changing environment, for example, affects educational goals, technology, and the formal structure. A changing formal structure interacts with informal relationships.

A systemic map of organizational change is far more complex than the popular individualistic model. An educational administrator must be aware of a variety of organizational elements. These must be balanced, controlled, and changed to assure the success of an educational innovation.

Organizations are complex networks. It is almost impossible to study change processes without first examining the various subsystems. One of the most widely used taxonomies of organizational subsystems, proposed by Stanley Udy, Jr. (1965), is shown in Figure 5-1. It is composed of a number of parts: goals, environment, technology, formal structure, group and individual processes.

Goals. Organizations are social systems set up to achieve specific goals. Often the goals are contradictory, opposed by various participants in the organization, and rather vaguely articulated. Neverthe-

FIGURE 5-1
Organizational Subsystems (from Udy, 1965)

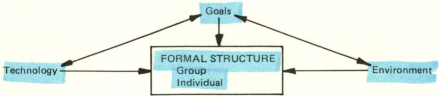

less, it is true that institutional missions, goals, and objectives are critical starting points for many organizational changes.

Environment. Organizational theorists are gradually realizing that many significant changes come from the environment. The environment consists of a broad collection of clients, suppliers, customers, government regulatory agencies, and a host of other organizations. No analysis of change can afford to neglect the strong influence of the environment for both promoting, supporting, or hindering change, as the case may be.

Technology. Every organization has procedures for carrying out its work. In industrial organizations there can be a great deal of technological hardware, including processes for production and assembly lines. Other kinds of organizations also have complicated technologies, although they may not involve such large amounts of hardware. In client-serving organizations such as hospitals and schools the technology consists of "treatment" activities for clients or patients. Research on organizational change in this area has typically looked at "sociotechnical" relations, that is, the social consequences of introducing some new work technology.

For educational organizations the "technology" is generally the instructional program. The main message for us is that the structure of an educational system is at least partly shaped by its technology—a deterministic argument very similar to that of the environmentalists. Educational technology has undergone rapid change in the past decade, both because of changed societal needs and because of the large amount of resources devoted to curricular and instructional improvement. The administrative implication of this line of research is that, when instructional changes occur, changes must also be made in the structure of the organization, or the program will not function well.

Formal structure. Every organization has a system for regulating its operation. A formal authority structure, a hierarchy of command, systematic decision processes, and reward processes are all part of the formal structure. Organizations frequently try to manipulate these characteristics in order to achieve their goals. Structure is the prime administrative handle that provides leverage both for producing and adjusting to educational innovation.

Group-Individual. One of the major traditions of organizational research, called the "human relations school," has concentrated on informal relationships within an organization. Researchers within this tradition, usually schooled in social psychology, have studied individual attitudes, the informal structure of the organization, group processes, and group norms. Much of the literature on organizational change falls within this human relations school.

Subsystems and the Process of Change

It is important to realize several things about organizational subsystems and the change process:

Almost all of the major traditions of research on organizational change have focused on one subsystem at a time. Researchers who examine individual and group behavior are likely to ignore most of the other subsystems. Each study tends to overemphasize or accentuate the importance of a single perspective. Generally, social scientists conducting research on educational innovation narrow their focus to the relationship between no more than two or three organizational subsystems. This reduced scope is essential when establishing scientific criteria for judging scientific, scholarly work.

Implementing an educational innovation, on the other hand, requires a broader outlook. An administrator must take all the organization's subsystems seriously. The primary goal is not an academic understanding of the relationships but the manipulation of goals, formal structure, or environment to allow the desired educational change. The administrator needs a broad organizational perspective and a general understanding of how the various organizational subsystems relate.

Each of the subsystems may be seen as an impetus for change, or as the unit that is being changed. The subsystems may be studied as either an independent or a dependent variable. For example, we might examine a change in educational goals to determine what impact that change had (independent variable). Or, on the other hand, we might examine changes in goals (dependent variable) that are being produced by some other subsystem, such as a rapid change in the environment surrounding a college. In short, each subsystem can be viewed as either the thing *being changed* or the thing that is *causing the change.* It is important to keep these distinctions in mind.

A particular organizational subsystem is usually the beginning of practical change. Rarely does an organization try to change many activities at once. An organization trying to improve its activities will generally concentrate on one subsystem as a starting point for change, and improvement is usually piecemeal and gradual. For example, a college may try to make limited improvements in its teaching technology without having to deal with accompanying changes in authority structures and morale problems. Or it may focus on faculty morale and attitudes without dealing with the environment or the formal authority system. The normal practice is to begin making marginal improvements in one area and to adjust for the repercussions in other subsystems later. This brings up a final important point—the interconnectedness of the different subsystems.

Any change in an organization is likely to involve more than one subsystem. Organizational changes are complex, and the effects are interwoven throughout various subsystems. Goals cannot be changed without affecting group attitudes and technology; the environment cannot shift substantially without formal authority structures being seriously affected; major upheavals in individual or group morale certainly have repercussions on decision processes and other formal systems. In short, a change in one subsystem almost surely results in changes in other subsystems. Any strategy of research or any active program of organizational change must carefully analyze possible interconnections.

Each of these perspectives is a research tradition. Each focuses on certain organizational characteristics and relationships and tends to ignore or exclude others. In reality, however, the perspectives overlap, and all deserve the attention of the educational administrator concerned with innovation.

Goal Two: Studying Strategies of Innovation

There are administrative strategies designed to produce and manage educational innovation. Such strategies include leadership, evaluation, change agents, politics, and the use of research staff as a means of promoting organizational change. Which of these strategies is effective in a change situation is contingent on a variety of factors. The selection of an administrative strategy in innovation should reflect what is changing and what is being changed. Program changes may require one strategy; environmental or structural changes, another. Beyond these general considerations, however, there are some specific "rules" about a good change strategy.

Rule One: A Serious Assessment of Needs Is Necessary

To mention the requirement for careful needs assessment seems ridiculous. After all, is not all change preceded by such analysis? Unfortunately, this is not always the case. Various problems obscure the needs assessment stage of organizational change.

The "captured" administrator. All too often administrators develop their own pat diagnosis of what they think an organization needs, and, with the best of intentions, they apply that solution to every problem that arises. People often have axes to grind, and the old saying holds: "Give a little boy a hammer and suddenly the whole world needs to be hammered." Usually administrators adopt some preconceived solution that is very near to their own center of control and to the levers of power they can pull. This is not necessarily bad, for we all have a tendency to specialize and to concentrate our change efforts in our own sphere of activity. It may, however, lead to a persistant bias or the persistent neglect of the needs of the whole organization if an administrator can see no other solutions.

Consultants and their bags of tricks. The process of diagnosis is often circumvented by outside consultants who have preconceived solutions. We have already mentioned that many organizational consultants come with "black bags" filled with special techniques for resolving organizational problems. Consultants, too, are captives to the range of their skills and their special interests. Any organization hiring consultants should thoroughly explore the particular biases and procedures that they bring to the situation.

The "iceberg" phenomenon. Another problem that arises in the diagnosis process is the "iceberg" phenomenon. An adequate diagnosis may be done on an apparent problem that is only symptomatic of more serious ones. Very often the visible problem is no more than the tip of a deeper-seated problem. The overt symptom may be corrected, but the deep-seated problem may remain.

For this reason a comprehensive diagnosis of organizational problems is needed if any change is to be attempted. Experts from throughout the organization must participate in the diagnostic stage, for the definition of problems should not be limited to the world views of a few people. Symptomatic surface problems should be probed to determine whether there are more basic issues, and it is most important that the process take into account all the different organizational subsystems mentioned earlier—technology, structure, environment, and group processes. Difficulties in any of the subsystems may spin off so that the problem touches areas far from the original source.

Rule Two: Proposed Changes Must Be Relevant to the History of the Organization

Organizations have their roots deep in history; they have traditions and patterns of life that have evolved over a long period of time. It is important to realize that organizational change is always relative to a specific situation and to the unique circumstances of a given organization. Change simply cannot "take" if the history and tradition of the organization conflict with the proposed innovation. For example, in this period of tightened financial resources there is a demand for "efficiency" and "scientific management" in educational organizations. All too often, well-intended programs are undermined because there is little or no regard for the special conditions and historical procedures of educational organizations. Many changes that are potentially valuable must be severely modified if they are to mesh with the ongoing life of the organization. To be sure, assessing the fit between a new change and an organization's history and tradition up to that point is complex, but it is a task that must be done, and it must be done carefully.

Rule Three: Organizational Changes Must Take the Environment into Account

Organizational changes are almost never fully dictated by internal factors. The environment is a major impetus for change, for new environmental demands are a critical source of new ideas, new procedures, and new activities. Not only is change promoted by the environment, but changes made internally must also be supported by environmental connections. A change in student rules in a college, for example, may be popular with both students and teachers, but totally opposed by the surrounding community. New accounting procedures for business firms may generate enormous hostility among clients because of their complexity. In short, there are two basic questions: What does the environment *need*, and what will it *support*? The answers to these two questions are often the key to substantial organizational change.

Rule Four: Serious Changes Must Affect Both the Organizational Structure and Individual Attitudes

We noted earlier that a prime problem with much organizational change literature is that it often focuses narrowly on individual attitudes. Although individual attitudes are obviously important, it is also important to stress that organizational structure must be changed to support any changes in attitudes. For example, let us assume we want instructors to teach differently. One strategy would be persuasion—convincing the professors that the change was important. We could, however, reinforce that persuasion by changing organizational features such as the sanction and evaluation process. If professors got paid more for carrying out the new procedure, this would reinforce changes in their attitude. Attitudinal change is also encouraged by shifts in the authority structure, participation in decision making, and development of new technologies and procedures.

In short, any change that requires a shift in the attitude of key personnel can be reinforced by changing the organizational structures that support and undergird those attitudes.

Rule Five: Changes Must Be Directed at Manipulable Factors

It makes no sense to plan organizational change around factors that simply cannot be changed, a statement that sounds almost tautological. It is remarkable how many times strategies are proposed that simply will not work. For example, in trying to implement school integration it was obvious that changing the attitudes of millions of people was virtually impossible, while actually changing the racial composition of the schools was more feasible. Either strategy would have promoted integration. Of the two factors, however, only one was actually manipulable in any reasonable sense—changing the racial composition.

This is one reason why we continually argue that individual attitudes are a weak basis for organizational intervention. Individual beliefs and opinions are almost nonmanipulable. They are almost impossible to change, and they remain essentially stable in spite of persuasion and preaching. Consequently, they can do little to advance serious organizational change.

Factors that are *very difficult* to manipulate include: major environmental relations, such as the nature of the organization's clientele (clients, customers, students, patients, or others); basic missions and fundamental goals; and attitudes, opinions, and beliefs of workers.

Examples of organizational features that are *more readily manipulable* include organizational rewards, evaluations, and sanction systems; administrative and departmental structure; personnel practices such as hiring, firing, and promotion policies; and technology and operational processes. Fertile imagination and careful thought will help to distinguish between factors that lend themselves to change and those that do not. Although this seems like a simple point, it is remarkable how many grandiose schemes for organizational change have been planned around factors that proved virtually impossible to change.

Rule Six: Changes Must Be Both Politically and Economically Feasible

It might be desirable to have sex education classes in a politically conservative community. Only the most foolhardy administrators would propose such a drastic change where the environment was hostile, however. Not only is it important to make changes that will survive in the organization's environment, but it is also important to gauge political opposition from within. Powerful interest groups which fight proposed changes in an organization may have the clout to stop change. A vital part of any shrewd administrator's job is assessing what things will survive politically and what things will not. Often it is best simply not to try changes that are doomed to failure. If a change is so important that it must be done despite political opposition, however, it is critical that interest groups and coalitions be mobilized in support. Rational planning often completely disintegrates as a result of poor political strategy.

The political issue is frequently tied to the cost issue. Many plans fail because they simply are not viable in terms of what the organization can afford. All too often those who planned the changes simply do not take into account the financial cost to the organization. It is important to do some preliminary calculations long before time and money have been expended in order to avoid hard feelings and wasted energy. Usually this means expert advice and help, with a variety of opinions brought to bear on the issue.

It is important to remember that one of the most expensive costs is personnel time. Before the change is undertaken, there should be a careful assessment of available personnel, talent, and expertise. If necessary skills or appropriate personnel are not available and there is no prospect of obtaining them, the proposed innovation might as well be forgotten.

Rule Seven: The Changes Must Be Effective in Solving the Problems That Were Diagnosed

The most cost-effective plans involving the most manipulable factors in the finest of political environments will still fail if they do not solve the problem. The critical questions are: Will the proposed changes actually solve the diagnosed problems? Will they involve costs, in terms of money and personnel, that make sense to the organization? Will they provide a permanent solution? Can the changes be structured into the organization itself, or are they overly dependent on individual personalities?

Too often changes are proposed that meet all criteria except the effectiveness one. Changes may be based on real diagnosis, sensitive to both the environment and the organization's history, be arranged around manipulable variables, and be politically and economically feasible. Unless they actually solve the problem, however, they are a waste of time.

Effective Change Strategies: An Example of the Rules in Action

The rules for a good change strategy can be applied to a concrete case of major educational change: the drive for equality of educational opportunity in the public schools. Although this is not an example of a higher education reform, the basic principles are the same. Are the change rules outlined above useful for analyzing the solutions that were proposed to this important national problem?

Equality of educational opportunity was advanced as a national goal after the Supreme Court's *Brown* decision in 1954. In 1964 a huge research effort culminated in a government report, *Equality of Educational Opportunity*, often called the Coleman Report. This research conclusively verified that racial minorities were getting a much poorer education and were achieving at much lower levels than majority groups. The Coleman Report identified a number of factors as causes of this problem:

Fate control. Minority students did not feel that they were able to control their social destinies. As a consequence, they often reported that their motivation to learn in school was much lower than majority students who had been given so many more advantages in life. The minority students felt, realistically, that they had been cheated by their position in society and that no amount of hard work in school would reap them reasonable benefits.

Family background. A larger proportion of minority students came from broken homes than did majority children. In addition, minority students often came from families where achievement in school was neither highly valued nor effectively promoted.

Teacher quality. Schools with a predominance of minority students often had teachers who were less well prepared.

Segregation. Segregated schools were shown to have a number of harmful side effects, including lowered self-esteem and fewer middle-class role models.

Resource equalization. Because of discrimination by middle-class-dominated school boards, minority schools simply did not get the per capita expenditure for their pupils that middle-class schools got. It is a reasonable assumption that less money meant lower-quality education.

The Coleman Report, then, diagnosed the problem and found that low achievement, high dropout rates, and generally poor educational performance were characteristic of some minority groups. In addition, the research identified five factors as essential causes. How does each of these factors meet the test for a good change strategy? If we wanted to design a program of organizational change that would help solve the problems, which of the causes would we try to manipulate, and which changes would be likely to succeed in light of our change strategy rules?

Both fate control and family background share the same problems. They are effective variables. If we changed them it would certainly make a difference, but they cannot be readily manipulated. There is nothing we can really do, in the short run at least, about family background and pupil attitudes toward their general life environment. These two factors can probably be eliminated as effective strategies unless acceptable means of manipulation can be found.

The other three factors fare somewhat better under our rules. Teacher quality is a variable that meets most of the rules' requirements: it is a manipulable factor that we can do something about; it is probably an effective factor that would actually make a difference; it is politically feasible in light of the political muscle of teachers' groups; it is a change that would be supported by the environment. The major difficulty in manipulating teacher quality is the extremely high cost. Teachers' salaries account for the bulk of school system budgets, and to manipulate this factor in any serious manner might literally bankrupt half the school districts in the country. As a consequence, only marginal changes have been made in this area.

Integration meets many of the requirements of a good change strategy: integration is probably effective and would have impact on student learning; it is a variable that could be manipulated with the help of busing and redistricting; it is probably a cost-effective measure that is well within the financial resources of most districts; it does affect the structure of the school system itself while it is changing individual attitudes. In spite of the many advantages, however, there are some obvious liabilities. The political cost of integration activities has always been phenomenal, and it is doubtful that the environment around most school districts is supportive of such attempts. In many ways, then, integration is a strategy that meets most of our tests, but, at the same time, carries with it serious liabilities.

Finally, resource allocation is also a mixed blessing. The equalization of resources under court-mandated plans emerging from decisions such as California's *Serrano v. Priest* should be relatively effective in producing changes in school opportunities for minorities. To be sure, there has been considerable debate about whether merely adding dollar resources actually changes pupil performance. Nevertheless, there is still a very strong commonsense appeal to arguing that equalizing money might help equalize other opportunities. Resource changes are moderately effective, manipulable, and usually financially feasible. Again, the liabilities are political. There has been strong opposition to equalizing school expenditures because it means a redistribution of money from wealthier areas into poorer ones, a procedure that invariably stimulates political opposition.

This example teaches us something about our rules for efficient change strategies. Several of the proposed solutions were impossible because critical variables simply could not be manipulated—fate control and family background being prime examples. Another factor that was on other grounds reasonable but faced stiff opposition because of its enormous costs was upgrading teacher quality. Finally, political costs are often, as they were in this particular situation, a major barrier—especially where integration and resource equalization are concerned.

From the illustration above, what do we learn about evaluating change strategies? First, any strategy has to meet the minimal requirements of *effectiveness* and *manipulability*. Without these characteristics there is no sense in making the effort. Second, almost any strategy has some liabilities, perhaps *cost* or *political opposition*. It is important, however, not to be so concerned about liabilities that we are paralyzed into inaction. The basic lesson, then, is to evaluate any strategy in terms of all these factors and then to act on the most feasible possibilities. Often a complex mixture of *alternative strategies* can help balance liabilities and maximize opportunities for effective change.

References

Baldridge, J. Victor. "The Impact of Individuals, Organizational Structure, and Environment on Organizational Innovation," Research and Development Memorandum no. 124. Stanford, Calif.: Stanford Center for Research and Development in Teaching, 1973.

Bowers, David G. "O.D. Techniques and Their Results in Twenty-three Organizations." *Journal of Applied Behavioral Science* 9 (January 1973): 21-43.

Campbell, Donald. "Reforms as Experiments." *Evaluating Action Programs: Readings in Social Action and Education,* edited by Carol H. Weiss. Boston: Allyn & Bacon, 1972.

Coleman, James S. *Equality of Educational Opportunity.* Washington, D.C.: National Center for Educational Statistics, 1966.

Rogers, Everett. *Diffusion of Innovations.* New York: Free Press, 1962.

Rogers, Everett, and Shoemaker, F. Floyd. *Communication of Innovations.* New York: Free Press, 1971.

Udy, Stanley. "The Comparative Analysis of Complex Organizations." *Handbook of Organizations,* edited by James G. March. Chicago: Rand McNally, 1965.

6

The Organizational Saga in Higher Education

Burton R. Clark

Saga, originally referring to a medieval Icelandic or Norse account of achievements and events in the history of a person or group, has come to mean a narrative of heroic exploits, of a unique development that has deeply stirred the emotions of participants and descendants. Thus, a saga is not simply a story but a story that at some time has had a particular base of believers. The term often refers also to the actual history itself, thereby including a stream of events, the participants, and the written or spoken interpretation. The element of belief is crucial, for, without the credible story, the events and persons become history; with the development of belief, a particular bit of history becomes a definition full of pride and identity for the group.

Introduction

An organizational saga is a collective understanding of unique accomplishment in a formally established group. The group's definition

Reprinted from *Administrative Science Quarterly* 17, no. 2 (June 1972): 178-184. *Authors note:* Revised version of paper presented at the 65th Annual Meeting of the American Sociological Association, September 1970, Washington, D.C. I wish to thank Wendell Bell, Maren L. Carden, Kai Erikson, and Stanley Udy for discussion and comment. Parts of an early draft of this paper have been used to connect organizational belief to problems of governance in colleges and universities (Clark, 1971).

of the accomplishment, intrinsically historical but embellished through retelling and rewriting, links stages of organizational development. The participants have added affect, an emotional loading, which places their conception between the coolness of rational purpose and the warmth of sentiment found in religion and magic. An organizational saga presents some rational explanation of how certain means led to certain ends, but it also includes affect that turns a formal place into a beloved institution, to which participants may be passionately devoted. Encountering such devotion, the observer may become unsure of his own analytical detachment as he tests the overtones of the institutional spirit or spirit of place.

The study of organizational sagas highlights nonstructural and nonrational dimensions of organizational life and achievement. Macroorganizational theory has concentrated on the role of structure and technology in organizational effectiveness (Gross, 1964; Litterer, 1965; March, 1965; Thompson, 1967; Price, 1968; Perrow, 1970). A needed corrective is more research on the cultural and expressive aspects of organizations, particularly on the role of belief and sentiment at broad levels of organization. The human relations approach in organizational analysis, centered largely on group interaction, showed some awareness of the role of organization symbols (Whyte, 1948, chapter 23), but this conceptual lead has not been taken as a serious basis for research. Also, in the literature on organizations and purposive communities, "ideology" refers to unified and shared belief (Selznick, 1949; Bendix, 1956; Price, 1968, pages 104-110; Carden, 1969); but the concept of ideology has lost denotative power, having been stretched by varying uses. For the phenomenon discussed in this paper, "saga" seems to provide the appropriate denotation. With a general emphasis on normative bonds, organizational saga refers to a unified set of publicly expressed beliefs about the formal group that (a) is rooted in history, (b) claims unique accomplishment, and (c) is held with sentiment by the group.

To develop the concept in this paper, extreme cases and exaggerations of the ideal type are used, but the concept will be close to reality and widely applicable when the phenomenon is examined in weak as well as strong expression. In many organizations, even some highly utilitarian ones, some segment of their personnel probably develops in time at least a weak saga. Those who have persisted together for some years in one place will have had, at minimum, a thin stream of shared experience, which they elaborate into a plausible account of group uniqueness. Whether developed primarily by management or by employees, the story helps rationalize for the individual his commitment of time and energy for years, perhaps for a lifetime, to a particular enterprise. Even when weak, the belief can compensate in part for the loss of meaning in much modern work, giving some drama and some cultural identity to one's otherwise entirely instrumental efforts. At the other end of the continuum, a saga engages one so intensely as to make his immediate place overwhelmingly valuable. It can even produce a striking distortion, with the organization becoming the only reality, the outside world becoming illusion. Generally the almost complete capture of affect and perception is associated with only a few utopian communities, fanatical political factions, and religious sects. But some formal rationalized organizations, as, for example, [in] business and education, can also become utopian, fanatical, or sectarian.

Organizational sagas vary in durability. They can arise quickly in relatively unstructured social settings, as in professional sports organizations that operate in the volatile context of contact with large spectator audiences through the mass media. A professional baseball or football team may create a rags-to-riches legend in a few months' time that excites millions of people. But such a saga is also very fragile as an ongoing definition of the organization. The story can be removed quickly from the collective understanding of the present and future, for successful performance is often unstable, and the events that set the direction of belief can be readily reversed, with the great winners quickly becoming habitual losers. In such cases, there seems to be an unstable structural connection between the organization and the base of believers. The base of belief is not anchored within the organization nor in personal ties between insiders and outsiders, but is mediated by mass media, away from the control of the organization. Such sagas continue only as the organization keeps repeating its earlier success and also keeps the detached followers from straying to other sources of excitement and identification.

In contrast, organizational sagas show high durability when built slowly in structured social contexts, for example, the educational system—specifically, for the purposes of this paper, three liberal arts colleges in the United States. In the many small private colleges, the story of special performance emerges not in a few months but over a decade or two. When the saga is firmly developed, it is embodied in many components of the organization, affecting the definition and performance of the organization and finding protection in the webbing of the institutional parts. It is not volatile and can be relegated to the past only by years of attenuation or organizational decline.

Since the concept of organizational saga was developed from research on Reed, Antioch, and Swarthmore, three distinctive and
highly regarded colleges (Clark, 1970), material and categories from
their developmental histories are used to illustrate the development
of a saga, and its positive effects on organizational participation and
effectiveness are then considered.[1]

Development of Saga

Two stages can be distinguished in the development of an organizational saga, initiation and fulfillment. Initiation takes place under
varying conditions and occurs within a relatively short period of
time; fulfillment is related to features of the organization that are
enduring and more predictable.

Initiation

Strong sagas do not develop in passive organizations tuned to
adaptive servicing of demand or to the fulfilling of roles dictated by
higher authorities (Clark, 1956, 1960). The saga is initially a strong
purpose, conceived and enunciated by a single man or a small cadre
(Selznick, 1957) whose first task is to find a setting that is open, or
can be opened, to a special effort. The most obvious setting is the
autonomous new organization, where there is no established structure, no rigid custom, especially if a deliberate effort has been made
to establish initial autonomy and bordering outsiders are preoccupied. There a leader may also have the advantage of building from
the top down, appointing lieutenants and picking up recruits in ac-
cord with his ideas.

Reed College is strongly characterized by a saga, and its story of
hard-won excellence and nonconformity began as strong purpose in a
new organization. Its first president, William T. Foster, a thirty-year-
old, high-minded reformer, from the sophisticated East of Harvard
and Bowdoin went to the untutored Northwest, to an unbuilt campus in suburban Portland in 1910, precisely because he did not want
to be limited by established institutions, all of which were, to his
mind, corrupt in practice. The projected college in Oregon was clear
ground, intellectually as well as physically, and he could there assemble the people and devise the practices that would finally give

1. For some discussion of the risks and tensions associated with organizational sagas, particularly that of success in one period leading to later rigidity
and stagnation, see Clark (1970, pp. 258-261). Hale (1970) gives an illuminating
discussion of various effects of a persistent saga in a theological seminary.

the United States an academically pure college, a Balliol for America.

The second setting for initiation is the established organization in a crisis of decay. Those in charge, after years of attempting incremental adjustments (Lindblom, 1959), realize finally that they must either give up established ways or have the organization fail. Preferring that it survive, they may relinquish the leadership to one proposing a plan that promises revival and later strength, or they may even accept a man of utopian intent. Deep crisis in the established organization thus creates some of the conditions of a new organization. It suspends past practice, forces some bordering groups to stand back or even to turn their backs on failure of the organization, and it tends to catch the attention of the reformer looking for an opportunity.

Antioch College is a dramatic example of such a setting. Started in the 1860's, its first sixty years were characterized by little money, weak staff, few students, and obscurity. Conditions worsened in the 1910's under the inflation and other strains of World War I. In 1919 a charismatic utopian reformer, Arthur E. Morgan, decided it was more advantageous to take over an old college with buildings and a charter than to start a new one. First as trustee and then as president, he began in the early 1920's an institutional renovation that overturned everything. As president he found it easy to push aside old, weak organizational structures and usages. He elaborated a plan of general education involving an unusual combination of work, study, and community participation, and he set about to devise the implementing tool. Crisis and charisma made possible a radical transformation out of which came a second Antioch, a college soon characterized by a sense of exciting history, unique practice, and exceptional performance.

The third context for initiation is the established organization that is not in crisis, not collapsing from long decline, yet ready for evolutionary change. This is the most difficult situation to predict, having to do with degree of rigidity. In both ideology and structure, institutionalized colleges vary in openness to change. In those under church control, for example, the colleges of the more liberal Protestant denominations have been more hospitable than Catholic colleges, at least until recently, to educational experimentation. A college with a tradition of presidential power is more open to change than one where the trustees and the professors exert control over the president. Particularly promising is the college with a self-defined need for educational leadership. This is the opening for which some reformers watch, the sound place that has some ambition to increase its academic stature, as, for example, Swarthmore College.

Swarthmore began in the 1860's, and had become, by 1920, a secure and stable college, prudently managed by Quaker trustees and administrators and solidly based on traditional support from nearby Quaker families in Pennsylvania, New Jersey, and Maryland. Such an organization would not usually be thought promising for reform, but Frank Aydelotte, who became its president in 1920, judged it ready for change. Magnetic in personality, highly placed within the elite circle of former Rhodes scholars, personally liked by important foundation officials, and recommended as a scholarly leader, he was offered other college presidencies, but he chose Swarthmore as a place open to change through a combination of financial health, liberal Quaker ethos, and some institutional ambition. His judgment proved correct, although the tolerance for his changes in the 1920's and 1930's was narrow at times. He began the gradual introduction of a modified Oxford honors program and related changes, which resulted in noteworthy achievements that supporters were to identify later as "the Swarthmore saga" (Swarthmore College Faculty, 1941).

Fulfillment

Although the conditions of initiation of a saga vary, the means of fulfillment are more predictable. There are many ways in which a unified sense of a special history is expressed; for example, even a patch of sidewalk or a coffee room may evoke emotion among the believers, but one can delimit the components at the center of the development of a saga. These may center, in colleges, on the personnel, the program, the external social base, the student subculture, and the imagery of the saga.

Personnel. In a college, the key group of believers is the senior faculty. When they are hostile to a new idea, its attenuation is likely; when they are passive, its success is weak; and when they are devoted to it, a saga is probable. A single leader, a college president, can initiate the change, but the organizational idea will not be expanded over the years and expressed in performance unless ranking and powerful members of the faculty become committed to it and remain committed even after the initiator is gone. In committing themselves deeply, taking some credit for the change and seeking to ensure its perpetuation, they routinize the charisma of the leader in collegial authority. The faculty cadre of believers helps to effect the legend, then to protect it against later leaders and other new participants who, less pure in belief, might turn the organization in some other direction.

Such faculty cadres were well developed at Reed by 1925, after the time of its first two presidents; at Antioch, by the early 1930's, after Morgan, disappointed with his followers, left for the board of directors of the new TVA; and at Swarthmore, by the 1930's, and particularly by 1940, after Aydelotte's twenty years of persistent effort. In all three colleges, after the departure of the change agent(s), the senior faculty with the succeeding president, a man appropriate for consolidation, undertook the full working out of the experiment. The faculty believers also replaced themselves through socialization and selective recruitment and retention in the 1940's and 1950's. Meanwhile, new potential innovators had sometimes to be stopped. In such instances, the faculty was able to exert influence to shield the distinctive effort from erosion or deflection. At Reed, for example, major clashes between president and faculty in the late 1930's and the early 1950's were precipitated by a new change-oriented president, coming in from the outside, disagreeing with a faculty proud of what had been done, attached deeply to what the college had become, and determined to maintain what was for them the distinctive Reed style. From the standpoint of constructing a regional and national model of purity and severity in undergraduate education, the Reed faculty did on those occasions act to create while acting to conserve.

Program. For a college to transform purpose into a credible story of unique accomplishment, there must be visible practices with which claims of distinctiveness can be supported; that is, unusual courses, noteworthy requirements, or special methods of teaching. On the basis of seemingly unique practices, the program becomes a set of communal symbols and rituals, invested with meaning. Not reporting grades to the students becomes a symbol, as at Reed, that the college cares about learning for learning's sake; thus mere technique becomes part of a saga.

In all the three colleges, the program was seen as distinctive by both insiders and outsiders. At Swarthmore it was the special seminars and other practices of the honors program, capped by written and oral examination by teams of visiting outsiders in the last days of the senior year. At Antioch it was the work-study cycle, the special set of general education requirements, community government, and community involvement. At Reed it was the required freshman lecture-and-seminar courses, the junior qualifying examination, and the thesis in the senior year. Such practices became central to a belief that things had been done so differently, and so much against the mainstream, and often against imposing odds, that the group had generated a saga.

Social base. The saga also becomes fixed in the minds of outside believers devoted to the organization, usually the alumni. The alumni are the best located to hold beliefs enduringly pure, since they can be as strongly identified with a special organizational history as the older faculty and administrators and yet do not have to face directly the new problems generated by a changing environment or students. Their thoughts can remain centered on the past, rooted in the days when, as students, they participated intimately in the unique ways and accomplishments of the campus.

Liberal alumni, as those of Reed, Antioch, and Swarthmore here, seek to conserve what they believe to be a unique liberal institution and to protect it from the conservative forces of society that might change it—that is, to make it like other colleges. At Reed, for example, dropouts as well as graduates were struck by the intellectual excellence of their small college, convinced that college life there had been unlike college life anywhere else, and they were ready to conserve the practices that seemed to sustain that excellence. Here, too, conserving acts can be seen for a time as contributing to an innovation, protecting the full working out of a distinctive effort.

Student subculture. The student body is the third group of believers, not overwhelmingly important but still a necessary support for the saga. To become and remain a saga, a change must be supported by the student subculture over decades, and the ideology of the subculture must integrate with the central ideas of the believing administrators and faculty. When the students define themselves as personally responsible for upholding the image of the college, then a design or plan has become an organizational saga.

At Antioch, Reed, and Swarthmore, the student subcultures were powerful mechanisms for carrying a developing saga from one generation to another. Reed students, almost from the beginning and extending at least to the early 1960's, were great believers in the uniqueness of their college, constantly on the alert for any action that would alter it, ever fearful that administration or faculty might succumb to pressures that would make Reed just like other colleges. Students at Antioch and Swarthmore also offered unstinting support for the ideology of their institution. All three student bodies steadily and dependably transferred the ideology from one generation to another. Often socializing deeply, they helped to produce the graduate who never quite rid himself of the wish to go back to the campus.

Imagery of saga. Upheld by faculty, alumni, and students, expressed in teaching practices, the saga is even more widely expressed as a generalized tradition in statues and ceremonies, written histories and current catalogues, even in an "air about the place" felt by participants and some outsiders. The more unique the history and the more forceful the claim to a place in history, the more intensely cultivated the ways of sharing memory and symbolizing the institution. The saga is a strong self-fulfilling belief; working through institutional self-image and public image, it is indeed a switchman (Weber, 1946), helping to determine the tracks along which action is pushed by men's self-defined interests. The early belief of one stage brings about the actions that warrant a stronger version of the same belief in a later period. As the account develops, believers come to sense its many constituent symbols as inextricably bound together, and the part takes its meaning from the whole. For example, at Antioch a deep attachment developed in the 1930's and 1940's to Morgan's philosophy of the whole man and to its expression in a unique combination of work, study, community participation, and many practices thought to embody freedom and nonconformity. Some of the faculty of those years who remained in the 1940's and 1950's had many memories and impressions that seemed to form a symbolic whole: personnel counselors, folk dancing in Red Square, Morgan's towering physique, the battles of community government, the pacifism of the late 1930's, the frequent dash of students to off-campus jobs, the dedicated deans who personified central values. Public image also grew strong and sharp, directing liberals and radicals to the college and conservatives to other places. The symbolic expressions themselves were a strong perpetuating force.

Conclusion

An organizational saga is a powerful means of unity in the formal place. It makes links across internal divisions and organizational boundaries as internal and external groups share their common belief. With deep emotional commitment, believers define themselves by their organizational affiliation, and, in their bond to other believers, they share an intense sense of the unique. In an organization defined by a strong saga, there is a feeling that there is the small world of the lucky few and the large routine one of the rest of the world. Such an emotional bond turns the membership into a community, even a cult.

An organizational saga is thus a valuable resource, created over a number of years out of the social components of the formal enterprise. As participants become ideologues, their common definition becomes a foundation for trust and for extreme loyalty. Such bonds give the organization a competitive edge in recruiting and maintaining personnel and help it to avoid the vicious circle in which some actual or anticipated erosion of organizational strength leads to the loss of some personnel, which leads to further decline and loss. Loyalty causes individuals to stay with a system, to save and improve it rather than to leave to serve their self-interest elsewhere (Hirschman, 1970). The genesis and persistence of loyalty is a key organizational and analytical problem. Enduring loyalty follows from a collective belief of participants that their organization is distinctive. Such a belief comes from a credible story of uncommon effort, achievement, and form.

Pride in the organized group and pride in one's identity as taken from the group are personal returns that are uncommon in modern social involvement. The development of sagas is one way in which men in organizations increase such returns, reducing their sense of isolation and increasing their personal pride and pleasure in organizational life. Studying the evocative narratives and devotional ties of formal systems leads to a better understanding of the fundamental capacities of organizations to enhance or diminish the lives of participants. The organization possessing a saga is a place in which participants, for a time at least, happily accept their bond.

References

Bendix, R. *Work and Authority in Industry.* New York: John Wiley & Sons, 1956.

Carden, M. L. *Oneida: Utopian Community to Modern Corporation.* Baltimore, Md.: Johns Hopkins Press, 1969.

Clark, B. R. *Adult Education in Transition: A Study of Institutional Insecurity.* Berkeley: University of California Press, 1956.

Clark, B. R. *The Open Door College. A Case Study.* New York: McGraw-Hill, 1960.

Clark, B. R. *The Distinctive College: Antioch, Reed, and Swarthmore.* Chicago: Aldine, 1970.

Clark, B. R. "Belief and Loyalty in College Organization." *Journal of Higher Education* 42, no. 6 (1971): 499-515.

Gross, B. M. *The Managing of Organizations* (2 vols.). New York: Free Press, 1964.

Hale, J. R. "The Making and Testing of an Organizational Saga: A Case-Study of the Lutheran Theological Seminary at Gettysburg, Pennsylvania, with Special Reference to the Problem of Merger, 1959-1969." Ph.D. dissertation, Columbia University, 1970.

Hirschman, A. O. *Exit, Voice, and Loyalty.* Cambridge, Mass.: Harvard University Press, 1970.

Lindblom, C. E. "The Science of 'Muddling Through.'" *Public Administration Review* 19 (1959): 79-88.

Litterer, J. A. *The Analysis of Organizations.* New York: John Wiley & Sons, 1965.

March, J. G. (ed.). *Handbook of Organizations.* Chicago: Rand McNally, 1965.

Perrow, C. *Organizational Analysis.* Belmont, Calif.: Wadsworth, 1970.

Price, J. L. *Organizational Effectiveness: An Inventory of Propositions.* Homewood, Ill.: Richard D. Irwin, 1968.

Selznick, P. *TVA and the Grass Roots.* Berkeley: University of California Press, 1949.

Selznick, P. *Leadership in Administration.* New York: Harper & Row, 1957.

Swarthmore College Faculty. *An Adventure in Education: Swarthmore College under Frank Aydelotte.* New York: Macmillan, 1941.

Thompson, J. D. *Organizations in Action.* New York: McGraw-Hill, 1967.

Weber, M. *From Max Weber: Essays in Sociology,* translated and edited by H. H. Gerth and C. Wright Mills. New York: Oxford University Press, 1946.

Whyte, W. F. *Human Relations in the Restaurant Industry.* New York: McGraw-Hill, 1948.

7

Who Sank the Yellow Submarine?
Eleven Ways to Avoid Major Mistakes in Taking Over a University Campus and Making Great Changes

Warren G. Bennis

One cannot expect to know what is going to happen. One can only consider himself fortunate if he can discover what has happened. —Pierre du Pont

On December 19, 1966, I received a phone call from an assistant to President Martin Meyerson [now President of the University of Pennsylvania] at the State University of New York at Buffalo. The assistant began the conversation with almost sinful empathy: "I bet you don't know what's going on here at Buffalo, do you?" I allowed that I did not, and he proceeded to describe an academic New Jerusalem of unlimited money, a new $650-million campus, bold organizational ideas, a visionary president, a supportive chancellor and governor, the number of new faculty and administrators to be recruited, the romance of taking a mediocre upstate college and creating—well—the Berkeley of the East. Would I consider taking part in the effort? I was smitten by the verve, the *chutzpah*—and by the thought of having a hand in the transformation. S.U.N.Y. at Buffalo had been a relatively unnoticed local college founded by the thirteenth U.S. President, Millard Fillmore, "His Accidency." It had gained an uneven distinction between 1930 and 1962, the year it became part of the University of New York.

Reprinted from *Psychology Today* 6, no. 6 (November 1972): 112-120. Copyright Ziff-Davis Publishing Company.

New York wanted to create a multiversity and in 1966 had lured Meyerson from Berkeley (where he was the acting chancellor) to make the dream materialize.

Meyerson arrived with a monumental plan to redesign Buffalo's conventional academic structure. Within two months, the faculty senate had ratified the plan, which provided as follows:

1. The ninety existing departments would be restructured into seven new faculties, each with a provost as the chief academic and administrative officer. Each faculty would consist of the basic disciplines within the newly defined area, plus the relevant professional schools. (Meyerson wanted me to head the social science disciplines that included anthropology, psychology, and—to the chagrin of the Arts and Letters Provost—philosophy and history. My domain also would include the schools of management and social welfare.) The provosts would have ample resources and administrative leeway to create interdisciplinary programs and launch new education ventures.

2. The university would build thirty small colleges on a new campus. Each would house only four hundred students with up to six hundred day students as affiliates. Faculty and students would live and work together in the intimate atmosphere of these intellectual neighborhoods. Meyerson hoped the small college would offset the apathy and anomie that characterize enormous campuses. In addition, they would break the stranglehold that traditional departments traditionally leave on the university. Undergraduates would not get a watered-down version of what professors taught their graduate students; they would learn directly from their teachers in a communal setting.

3. Action-research centers and councils on international studies, urban studies, and higher educational studies would unite scholars and students from the entire university (and from the outside) for work on vital issues.

Esteem. Meyerson's overall concept impressed me. Several aspects of the plan were especially attractive: the decentralization of authority, the potential of the program (if you did not fit in with a department, you could always connect with a college, center, or council), and Meyerson's clear intent to raise the self-esteem of the university, the self-esteem of the faculty and students, and the self-esteem of the Buffalo community. Meyerson assured me that, with the new campus, there would be enough money to build quality on top of the university's inevitable deadwood.

I was sold on the man and his conceptual vision. The timing

seemed perfect, the new organizational design would go into effect on the same day my term of office was to begin. I arrived at Buffalo in the fall of 1967 and during 1967-68 I recruited nine new chairmen and two deans for the faculty, and changed about 90 percent of the leadership structure in the social sciences area. The faculty gained forty-five new full-time teachers. I spent almost three-fourths of my first year in recruiting.

Buffalo raided Harvard, Yale, and Princeton. Each new appointment increased enthusiasm, generated new ideas, and escalated the Meyerson optimism. The tiny, crowded campus barely contained the excitement. Intellectual communities formed and flourished.

Steam. The change was pervasive. Almost 75 percent of the present Buffalo faculty got their appointments under Meyerson.

The newcomers were eager recruits—committed to innovation and risk taking. The student body also was changing. By 1968, eight in ten of the entering freshmen were from the top 10 percent of their high school graduating classes, compared to only one in ten a decade before. Buffalo was regarded as one of the State University's radical campuses according to *Esquire* magazine (along with Stony Brook on Long Island). Meyerson's Berkeley-of-the-East approach may have had an appeal that he had not fully calculated. For one year, Buffalo was an academic Camelot. The provosts met around the president's conference table to work miracles. Occasionally I got signals that not everyone on campus took us quite as seriously as we took ourselves. One morning I found a Batman cape on my coatrack. The anonymous critic had a point: the atmosphere was a bit heavy with omnipotent fantasy.

Although construction had not started for the living quarters on the new campus, the six human-size colleges got underway at once. Almost immediately they provoked controversy. Rumors began to circulate that course cards for College A—the unit devoted to independent study and self-evaluation—were being sold, snatched up by students who did little or nothing and rewarded themselves with A's at the end of the semester. "Why do you think they call it 'College A'?" one cynical student asked. There were tales of credit for trips to Europe and the building of bird cages.

The master of College A regarded any impugning of its grading system as an antirevolutionary tactic. No one in the Meyerson administration, including myself, wanted to take a harsh public stand against this nonsense, particularly after College A and its master became the target of vicious community attack.

Status. There were other rumblings in paradise. The centers were not doing well. We learned that it was easier to break down barriers than to build bridges. For example, the Center for Higher Education did not generate new programs or attract faculty and students as planned. The Center for International Studies began to publish a newsletter—the only substantial sign of its new status. The Center for Urban Studies undertook a series of much-needed but thoroughly conventional projects in Buffalo's inner city.

In one form or another all the faculties had problems. Many departments raised questions about the new faculty structure. I felt that the many individual accomplishments, the promising new programs, [and] the appointment of a particularly good teacher or administrator did not add up to a significantly changed university. We were not consolidating our gains, and I feared that they might somehow slip away. These feelings were eventually confirmed. Camelot lasted barely a thousand days.

Setting. I took part in many of the crucial decisions that affected the progress of the Meyerson plan. And I now see, with all the unsettling clarity of hindsight, that we undermined many of our own best aspirations for the University. If I were asked today how to bring about change in a university setting, I would offer the following guidelines:

1. Recruit with scrupulous honesty. Most of the faculty who came to Buffalo shared the academic vision of its new president, Martin Meyerson.

Meyerson's gift as a recruiter was his ability to transmogrify all of the highly visible and terribly real drawbacks of Buffalo and make them reappear in the guise of exhilarating challenges. Those he attracted recruited others.

Sweetener. My personal recruiting at Buffalo depended on a falsely bright picture of the situation. It was not that I lied. But, consciously or not, I sweetened the package even when I was trying to be balanced and fair. Recruiting is a courtship ritual. The suitor displays his assets; the recruit, flattered by the attention and the promises, does not examine the assets closely. We were naive. The recruiting pitch at Buffalo depended on the future. We made little of the past and tended to deemphasize the present. Buffalo was the university of the future—of course, it would take time to catch up.

New arrivals had barely enrolled their kids in local schools before reality intruded. A labor union dispute delayed construction of the promised new facilities. Inflation nibbled away the buying power of the allocated construction funds at a rate of one and a half percent a month. It was easy to put up with the inconvenience of overcrowding when one was sure that the condition was temporary. But the dispute dragged on for months, and there was no room on the old campus. The situation might have been challenging if we had not led the new faculty to expect something magical. We had urged them to reveal their most creative, most imaginative educational thinking, then had assured them that their plans would receive generous support. In reality, money to staff new programs was difficult to come by. After one year, the state legislature began to pare the budget. Many new faculty members felt they had been conned. As recruiters, we had not pointed out our ultimate inability to control the legislatively determined budget. We had promised a new university when our funds could provide only an architect's model.

Shock. Inadvertently, we had cooked up the classic recipe for revolution as suggested by Aaron Wildavsky: "Promise a lot; deliver a little. Teach people to believe that they will be much better off, but let there be no dramatic improvement. Try a variety of small programs but marginal in impact and severely underfinanced. Avoid any attempted solution remotely comparable in size to the dimensions of the problem you are trying to solve. . . ."

The intensity of the disaffection felt by some of those I had brought to the university came to me as a shock. We had raised expectations as high as any in modern educational history. When our program met only a part of these expectations, the disillusionment that followed was predictable and widespread. The disparity between vision and reality became intolerable. No one had said a word during the seductive recruiting days about triplicate forms, resentful colleagues, and unheeded requests for help from administrative headquarters.

Support. Those who rose above the mundane annoyances provoked by university bureaucracy felt cheated in other ways. Recruits had joined our academic revolution because they shared our goal and wanted to participate. To keep such a cadre committed, an administration must keep them involved. But the warmth of our man-to-man recruiting interviews was not evident in later meetings with administrators. In fact, such meetings became fairly infrequent. The continuing evidence of personal support that might have overcome the unavoidable lack of concrete support was not forthcoming.

2. Guard against the crazies. Innovation is seductive. It attracts interesting people. It also attracts people who will take your ideas and distort them into something monstrous. *You* will then be identified with the monster and will have to devote precious energy to combating it. A change-oriented administrator should be damned sure about the persons he recruits, the persons who will be identified as his men or women.

A few of the persons who got administrative posts under the new administration were committed to change, but they were so irresponsible or antagonistic that they alienated more persons than they converted.

Sense. It is difficult to distinguish between agents of responsible change and those who rend all they touch. The most successful innovators often are marginal to the institution, almost in a geographical sense. They have contacts in other institutions, other areas. Their credentials are unorthodox. They are often terrible company men with little or no institutional loyalty. Change-oriented administrators must be able to distinguish the innovators, however eccentric they may be, from the crazies. An academic community can tolerate a high degree of eccentricity. But it will brutally reject an individual it suspects of masking mediocrity with a flashy commitment to innovation.

3. **Build support among like-minded people, whether or not you recruited them.** Change-oriented administrators are particularly prone to act as though the organization came into being the day they arrived. This is an illusion, an omnipotent fantasy. There are no clean slates in established organizations. A new president cannot play Noah and build the world anew with two hand-picked delegates from each academic discipline. Rhetoric about new starts is frightening to those who suspect that the new beginning is the end of their own careers. There can be no change without history, without continuity.

Stayers. What I think most of us in institutions really want—and what status, money, and power serve as currency for—is acceptance, affection, and esteem. Institutions are more amenable to change when they preserve the esteem of all members. Given economic sufficiency, persons stay in organizations and feel satisfied in them because they are respected and feel competent. They are much freer to identify with the adaptive process and much better equipped to tolerate the high level of ambiguity that accompanies change when these needs are heeded. Unfortunately, we did not attend to these needs at Buffalo. The academic code, not the administrative one, determines the appropriate behavior in the university. The president is a colleague, and he is expected to acknowledge his intellectual equals whatever their relative position on the administrative chart. Many old-guard professors took the administration's neglect as a personal snub. They were not asked for advice; they were not invited to social affairs. They suspected that we acted coolly toward them because we considered them to be second-rate academics who lacked intellectual chic and who could not cut it in Cambridge or New York. Ironically, some of the old-guard academic administrators who kept their positions were notoriously second rate. Meyerson extended the appointments of several such, perhaps hoping to avoid the appearance of a purge. Among the incumbents were a couple whose educational philosophy had rigidified sometime in the early 1950's. Instead of appeasing the old guard, these appointments added insult.

The old guard suspected that the new administration viewed them as an undifferentiated mass. They wondered why we kept these second-raters and overlooked a pool of potentially fine veteran candidates.

We succeeded in infusing new blood into Buffalo, but we failed to recirculate the old blood. We lost an opportunity to build loyalty among respected members of the veteran faculty. If veteran faculty members had been made to feel that they, too, had a future in the transformed university, they might have embraced the academic-reorganization plan with some enthusiasm. Instead the veteran faculty members were hurt, indignant, and—finally—angry.

4. **Plan for change from a solid conceptual base—have a clear-cut understanding of how to change as well as what to change.** Buffalo had a plan for change, but we lacked a clear concept of how change should proceed. A statement of goals is not a program.

The Buffalo reorganization lacked the coherence and forcefulness that would have guaranteed its success. The fault may have been that it was too abstract. Or perhaps it was too much a pastiche. A great many influences were evident: the late Paul Goodman and the community of colleges; the colleges and sense of academic tradition of Oxbridge; the unorthodoxy and informality of Black Mountain; the blurring of vocational-professional lives practiced at Antioch and Bennington; the collegiality of Santa Cruz; the college-master system of Yale. Each of these elements was both desirable and educationally fashionable, but the mix never jelled. No alchemy transformed the disparate parts into a living organism.

Students. We had no coherent mechanisms for change. Instead we relied on several partially realized administrative models. The burden of change fell upon the faculty senate, which emphasized the small-group model. Change depended on three things: 1) participation by the persons involved, 2) trust in the persons who advocate the change, and 3) clarity about the change itself. None of these conditions was fully present at Buffalo, and, as a result, the change was imperfectly realized.

Radical students utilized a revolutionary model. The students saw an opportunity for radical educational change in the Romantic tradition—the result was the College A controversy. The administration relied heavily on the model of successive limited comparisons, popularly known as muddling through. This is the model of most organizational decision making. It is a noncomprehensive, nontheoretical approach. Most administrators are forced to muddle through because the decisions they are called upon to make are simply too complex to treat comprehensively—even by committees. As a result, we neglected possible outcomes, overlooked alternative solutions, and could not predict the ultimate impact of the resulting policy on values.

Sensitivity. Ultimately the reorganization failed to concentrate its energies on the model that would have satisfied the ambitions of all parts of the university: an incremental reform model. Revolution inevitably produces reaction. All power to the French people one day, and to Thermidor the next. If change is to be permanent, it must be gradual. The incremental reform model depends on a rotating nucleus of persons who continuously read the data provided by the organization and the society around it for clues that it is time to adapt. These persons are not faddists, but they are hypersensitive to an idea whose hour has come. In a university such persons know when an idea is antithetical to the values of an academic institution and when it extends the definition of a university and makes it more viable. One cannot structure these critical nuclei, but an organization cannot guarantee continuous self-renewal without them. At Buffalo a few departments and programs developed these nuclei. Most did not.

5. Do not settle for rhetorical change. We accomplished the change at Buffalo by fiat. The faculty senate announced that the president's plan had been ratified. (This was a good beginning, but only that. Ratification occurred only two months after Meyerson arrived and almost one year before the plan was implemented. The senate was not exactly representative and the plans were barely understood. It was basically a paper plan with virtually no commitment except to a vague and poetic vision.) Significant change does not take place that way. An organization has two structures: one on paper and another one, deep, that is a complex set of intramural relationships. A good administrator creates a good fit between the two. We allowed ourselves to be swept along by our rhetoric and neglected the much more demanding business of building new constituencies and maintaining established ones.

6. Do not allow those who are opposed to change to appropriate

such basic issues as academic standards. I became Meyerson's academic vice-president in August of 1968. Members of the old guard soon began to accuse me of being soft on standards. I had refused to disavow some of the more flagrant abuses of self-evaluation in the new colleges, and I had failed publicly to chastise faculty who subverted traditional academic practices as part of the radical revolution (although I did so unofficially).

Silence. The problem of academic standards soon became a political issue. Privately we avowed our commitment to standards; publicly we were silent. The approach was notably unsuccessful. We did not want to undermine the fledgling colleges or violate the rights of radical faculty members. After "fascist," "McCarthyite" is the dirtiest word you can use on a liberal campus, and none of us was eager to hear it. We allowed the least change-oriented faculty members to make the issue of standards their own. They persuaded a great majority of moderate faculty members that administration was committed to change-for-change's sake, whatever the price in academic excellence. We made a mistake that no successful revolutionary ever makes: we did not make sure that respectable people were unafraid of what was about to happen.

7. Know the territory. A peculiar balance exists between the city of Buffalo and its one major university. Buffalo is not a university town like Princeton or Ann Arbor. The university is not powerful enough to impose its style and values on the city. Philadelphia and Los Angeles have several powerful universities that divide the city's attention and diffuse its rancor. Buffalo has a single target for its noisy anti-intellectuals. Two years ago some powerful forces in the town tried to close the university. I do not know of another campus in the country that has had to function with such constant unsympathetic pressure from the surrounding community. (The period I had in mind was the year of Kent State. From all I have heard about Meyerson's successor, he has worked hard at reviving a more sympathetic and supportive reaction to the campus.)

Meyerson barely had arrived in Buffalo when a group called "Mothers Against Meyerson" (MAM) began to petition for his removal. Their argument was that he was a Jew (a charge erroneously made against Meyerson's predecessor by an earlier group, "Mothers Against Furnas") and that the campus harbored such dangerous criminal types as critic Leslie Fiedler.

Buffalo blamed the disruptions of 1970 on the "permissiveness" of the new administration. I got mail recommending that Curtis LeMay succeed Meyerson as university president. The local exmarine who nominated LeMay believed that only the general's exotic blend of authoritarianism and right-wing values could undo the harm that we had perpetrated.

We never mastered the politics of local chauvinism. At the same time that the national press was romancing the university, one of the two local dailies was libeling her unmercifully. We devoted too little energy and imagination to public relations.

8. **Appreciate environmental factors.** Like any other human activity, change proceeds more smoothly in optimal environmental conditions. Buffalo's chief environmental problem was not its miserable weather. (Buffalo has two seasons—winter and the 4th of July. Residents recognize summer as three weeks of bad ice skating.) The problem at Buffalo was (and still is) overcrowding. The faculty we recruited expected to move their books into futuristic offices like those promised by the architect's model of the new campus. Instead, they moved in on top of the faculty already there. The university assembled some prefab annexes for the overflow. Barbara Solomon, writing on the paranoia at Buffalo, noted that we pursued the life of the mind in quarters so ugly as to seem calculated. (Her article, "Life in the Yellow Submarine," appeared in a 1968 issue of *Harper's*. It pictured S.U.N.Y.-Buffalo at the crest of the Meyerson dream, zany, careening, spectacularly lush, as played by the Marx Brothers in a World War II movie set of sallow, wooden barracks.)

The new university campus barely had begun to rise by the time we reached the originally proposed completion date of 1972. The university had to lease an interim campus near the new campus site. Eleven academic departments moved out to this temporary facility in the spring of 1971. The leased buildings had been designed for commercial and light industry use. The fifteen-minute bus trip is a drag for students and the isolation of the interim campus is contrary to the whole spirit of the Meyerson plan.

We neglected to protect new programs from external forces. College A began an experimental program in community action that was housed off-campus because of space priorities. College A is located directly across from a parochial grammar school and a diocesan center for retarded children. Every time a Scarsdale Maoist wrote "fuck" on the wall or a braless coed played her guitar in the storefront window, the residents of the neighborhood understandably reacted. Students of College A were determined to interact with their neighbors; mothers of the schoolchildren were equally determined not to interact. They picketed. The whole business snowballed, increasing the community's normally high level of outrage against the university.

9. Avoid future shock. Buffalo aspired to be the university of the year 2000. The future limited the campus just as the past limits the neurotic. The future insinuated itself into every attempt to deal with current issues and distorted our perception of the present. The unfinished new campus became an albatross, reminding everyone of the limited progress that was being made toward limitless goals. We put so much stock in the vision of future greatness that our disillusionment was inevitable. The problem with planning for the future is that there are no objective criteria against which to measure alternative solutions. There is not yet a contemporary reality against which to test. As a result the planner generates future shock along with valid ideas, and there is no surefire way to separate the two.

10. Allow time to consolidate gains. The average tenure of an American university president is now 4.4 years and decreasing. It is impossible to transform a university in so short a time. Only a year after Meyerson assumed the Buffalo presidency, rumors began to circulate that he was leaving. Supporters of the new administration feared abandonment. Social critic David Bazelon commented to me, "In every other university I've been to, the faculty hated the administration. Here they worry about desertion." The changes proposed by Meyerson depended on continued presidential support for their success. The campus had, in effect, undergone major surgery and did not have sufficient time to heal before a series of altogether different demands, including a semester of unrest, a new president, and a major recession, were made on it.

When Meyerson finally did resign in late January 1970, it was as though someone had prematurely pulled out the stitches.

The last guideline I offer to the would-be university reformer is so basic that it might well come first:

11. Remember that change is most successful when those who are affected are involved in the planning. This is a platitude of planning theory, and it is as true as it is trite. Nothing makes persons as resistant to new ideas or approaches as the feeling that change is being imposed upon them. The members of a university are unusually sensitive to individual prerogatives and to the administration's utter dependence on their support. Buffalo's academic plan was not generated popularly. Students and faculty did not contribute to its formulation. People resist change, even of a kind they basically agree with, if they are not significantly involved in the planning. A clumsier, slower, but more egalitarian approach to changing the university would have resulted in more permanent reform.

Surprise. The problems surrounding innovation and change in an entrenched bureaucracy are not peculiar to universities. Every modern bureaucracy—university, government or corporation—is essentially alike and responds similarly to challenge and to crisis, with much the same explicit or implicit codes, punctilios and mystiques.

Bureaucracy is the inevitable—and therefore necessary—form for governing large and complex organizations. Essentially we must find bureaucratic means to stimulate the pursuit of truth—that is, the true nature of the organization's problems—in a spirit of free inquiry, and under democratic methods. This calls for those virtues our universities and colleges have proved so capable of inspiring in others: an examined life, a spirit of inquiry and genuine experimentation, a life based on discovering new realities, of taking risks, suffering occasional defeats, and not fearing the surprise of the future.

The model for truly innovative and creative organizations in an era of enormous change becomes nothing less than the scientific spirit. The model for science becomes the model for all.

Assault. Now, four years after the dream was born, the campus mood is dismal. Many of the visionaries are gone—those left must live with the wreckage. The spirit of change has been stamped out.

Meyerson has officially disappeared. The state considers his administration to have been the reign of an educational antipope. There is rarely mention of him or his works.

Last year the American Council on Education released its current evaluation of the nation's graduate programs. Buffalo had improved dramatically in the ACE ratings. The university proudly held a news conference at which campus officials announced that the upgrading of graduate education at Buffalo took place under the late President Furnas.

What saddens me is a suspicion that this gross assault would have been successful if we had been more effective. Meyerson wanted to transform the university, but the current administration resembles that of Meyerson's predecessor, Clifford Furnas. By all appearances, our efforts changed nothing.

Epilogue

I wrote the above several months after I resigned from Buffalo—an outsider, though still living in Buffalo, supported by a grant from the Twentieth Century Fund. Outsiders and expatriates adopt a more critical perspective, I suppose, than those who remain.

Perhaps this article is not "objective" truth but "exiled" truth, not especially appropriate for those presently at Buffalo. Still and all, I would hope that some external validation of their former plight will help sustain their vitality.

At the same time, I hope that this critique of the Buffalo attempts at change will provide a template of action—for myself and my new Cincinnati administration, for faculty and students as well—that will conform more closely to a humane and democratic effort at university reform. We begin with more total community support and involvement than is enjoyed by any other urban university.

8

Organizational Change: Institutional Sagas, External Challenges, and Internal Politics

J. Victor Baldridge

For decades New York University's uptown Bronx campus, with its excellent liberal arts college, had been the pride of the university. In summer 1973 the university took a drastic step and sold the entire campus to the state of New York for the modest sum of $62,000,000. The storm clouds of financial crisis that had threatened the very existence of NYU had finally reached their darkest point. This event, the culmination of dramatic changes that had shaken NYU for fifteen years, provides a focal point for analyzing a major organizational change.

Organizational Change Themes

Although organizational theory has spawned a large amount of literature about organizational change, most of those studies are part of the organizational development group and its "human relations" approach to organizational changes. (See the excellent review of the literature in Katz and Kahn, 1966, chapter 13.) The development group's strategies typically focus on small-scale changes involving intergroup relations, communication patterns, and authority relationships between subordinates and superiors. Although this literature is

Reprinted from J. Victor Baldridge and Terrence Deal, *Managing Change in Educational Organizations* (Berkeley, Calif.: McCutchan, 1975).

rich in its implications for some kinds of organizational change, it is not always useful for those concerned with large-scale organizational dynamics, institutional survival, and the relationships between institutions and their environments.

This study concentrates on the major organizational change of a massive university during its fight for survival. It was a situation charged with major shifts in organizational mission and goals, with heavy threats from outside forces, and with conflict-filled plays for power. Three intellectual themes interweave as they form a framework to examine the problems of organizational change.

The Organizational Saga Theme

Burton R. Clark (1970, 1972) has argued that some organizations develop deeply rooted institutional missions and mythologies. The "organizational saga" encapsulates the *content* of an institution's missions and goals. What does the institution believe in; what are its major guidelines; in what direction is it moving? Knowing the direction of an institution's mission is especially necessary to understand large-scale organizational changes because missions that shift or are attacked by outside forces demand major adjustments within the organization.

The Environmental Theme

Many theorists have concluded that the prime impetus for large-scale change in organizations usually comes from external forces. (See Katz and Kahn, 1966.) This is an interesting shift in perspective since most change-oriented literature examines small-scale human relations problems within an organization and ignores the massive organizational changes that occur under powerful external pressures. This research analyzes the external environment, the *source* of the forces for change.

The Political Conflict Theme

While the saga theme focuses on content and the environmental theme focuses on the source of change, the political theme, in turn, examines the *processes* of change. (For a development of the political process in organizations, see Baldridge, 1971.) These processes include the responses of organizational interest groups to external pressures and their attempts to influence decisions during change. Rarely are organizational responses to external threats rationally planned. Instead, the conflict-filled process pits competing blocs within the institution against each other to gain the power to protect their threatened domains.

This study, then, is about a series of large-scale changes that affected New York University. The three themes blended together help to interpret the process. NYU had developed an institutional saga, a set of beliefs and mission statements that guided its actions. The viability of the institution and its missions were threatened by a series of massive external changes. In response to these changes, heavy organizational conflict and political activities emerged as the institution tried to revitalize its saga. This case study demonstrates the usefulness of the three themes for the study of large-scale organizational change.

Methodology

Two methodological thrusts are made. One has been widely used (case studies); the other has been largely neglected (historical analysis). The case study approach focuses on events within a single institution, a strategy common to organizational research. In 1968-69, eighteen months were devoted to an analysis of change processes at NYU. The principal research techniques were interviews with eighty-one faculty and administrators, a survey of all faculty, and participant observation in executive decision councils. In 1974 follow-up visits were made to update the materials.

There was a major attempt to assemble a historical study of the institution, primarily through the use of document analysis. This strategy is too often omitted in organizational analysis. Sociologists, in general, and organization theorists, in particular, tend to ignore the historical roots of a social system: tradition, culture, ethos, and deep-rooted values. It may be, in studying organizational change, that attention is on immediate interventions and findings that can be quickly translated into administrative policies. The neglect of history may also stem from the fact that most sociologists lack training in historical analysis. The case study technique, coupled with serious attention to organizational history, does, however, provide a depth and richness that highlights many problems of organizational change.

Organizational Saga

The study of organizational goals and values has often been the subject of theorizing and research, but one of the most penetrating studies was Philip Selznick's *TVA and the Grass Roots* (1948). Selznick recounts how the original institutional mission of TVA gradually eroded as powerful interest groups from the local community were co-opted into the decision councils. The mission became sharply redirected.

Following in Selznick's tradition, Burton R. Clark has always been fascinated by problems of institutional values, goals, and missions. His early work, *Adult Education in Transition: A Study of Institutional Insecurity* (1956), examined the "precarious values" of an organization that was lodged in a hostile environment. Later Clark looked at the consequences of the "open door" mission statements of community colleges and how that philosophy produced major changes in the San Jose Community College (1960). Clark develops the notion of "organizational saga," a belief system that provided purpose and direction for the three elite colleges he studied: Reed, Swarthmore, and Antioch. Clark defines an organizational saga in the following terms:

> An *organizational saga* is a collective understanding of unique accomplishment in a formally established group. The group's definition of the accomplishment, intrinsically historical but embellished through retelling and rewriting, links stages of organizational development. The participants have added affect, an emotional loading, which places their conception between the coolness of rational purpose and the warmth of sentiment found in religion and magic. An organizational saga presents some rational explanation of how certain means led to certain ends, but it also includes affect that turns a formal place into a beloved institution, to which participants may be passionately devoted . . . .
>
> The study of organizational sagas highlights nonstructural and nonrational dimensions of organizational life and achievement. Macroorganizational theory has concentrated on the role of structure and technology in organizational effectiveness . . . . A needed corrective is more research on the cultural and expressive aspects of organizations, particularly on the role of belief and sentiment at broad levels of organization . . . . With a general emphasis on normative bonds, organizational saga refers to a unified set of publicly expressed beliefs about the formal group that (a) is rooted in history, (b) claims unique accomplishment, and (c) is held with sentiment by the group [Clark, 1972, pages 178-179].

Clark seems to imply that an organization either has a saga or it does not, and he picks small, elite colleges that have clearly articulated, rich cultural belief systems—attitudes intensely held by the faculty, the students, and the community at large.

A Continuum Formulation of Saga

It probably would be an improvement on Clark's notion if we saw the structure of organizational beliefs as a continuum varying on the dimensions of clarity, degree of cohesion in accepting the beliefs by organizational participants, and environmental reinforcement. At one end of the continuum would be organizations with sharply defined sagas, widely shared among participants and reinforced by the environment. At the other end would be organizations with weak sagas or flabby fragmented beliefs, poorly articulated, that produce many subunit goals that have no unifying effect. Environmental support of the values in such cases is low.[1]

If we use the continuum concept, then we can propose some hypotheses about conditions that promote strong sagas:

—the smaller the size, the more likely the acceptance of the saga by most participants;

—the older the organization, the more likely a strong saga will develop;

—the more organizations screen entry, the more likely participants will share the saga;

—the fewer the tasks of the organization, the more likely it will articulate a clear, cohesive saga;

—the more homogeneous and stable the environment, the more likely a cohesive saga will develop and persist;

—the more insulation the organization can build (for example, reserve resources, physical isolation, rigid entry requirements) against environmental opposition, the more likely the saga will persist.

These are only suggestive hypotheses, but they illustrate the potential theoretical value of understanding organizational saga as a continuum and of proposing hypotheses that explain why a given organization may be located at some position on the continuum.

NYU's Traditional Role

What kind of saga could an organization as large and fragmented as NYU muster? Obviously, it might not be as clear or intensely held as that of small, elite institutions such as Reed or Swarthmore. Fragmentation and massive size certainly dilute intensity of feelings about any single institutional mission and probably lead to the development of miniature sagas around organizational subunits. On the other side of the balance, however, was a fairly clear set of institutional goals articulated by a broad spectrum of the institution and supported by a significant segment of its salient environment. Thus, even an institution as complex as NYU had all-encompassing mission statements and values that to some extent directed the organization's future. It probably had a medium-strong saga.

The role that a university plays in society is both planned and acci-

---

1. Clark would probably wish to reserve the term "saga" for only those belief systems at the clear, cohesive end of the continuum. However, this leaves the difficulty of identifying the other points on the continuum with other labels. Thus I suggest we simply use "strong-weak" sagas instead of restricting the term.

dental, both deliberate and a whim of fate. The role that NYU plays as an institution of higher education, for example, is shaped by a mixture of historical events, deliberate planning, and pressure from many sources. For many years NYU had a consistent interpretation of its role in higher education in New York. From its founding the university offered educational advantages to all types of people, including underprivileged minority groups. NYU accepted students with relatively low academic scores, allowing them entry into the world of higher education as part of the long-standing philosophy that it was a "School of Opportunity"—in the best tradition of the "Great American Dream." This philosophy became an organizational saga, a belief that faculty, students, and outsiders held firmly.

This orientation was more than idle rhetoric; it was an operating principle of the university that gave the campus a distinct institutional character. Generations of students testify to the importance of that philosophy in their lives, and many a Wall Street businessman and New York teacher gives credit to the chance afforded him by NYU. Large groups of the faculty, dedicated to this ideal, were willing to fight when that saga was threatened.

Times were changing, however, and this image of NYU was challenged. Not all members of the university community were happy with a philosophy that accepted large numbers of relatively poor students and then failed many of them. As one professor said during the case study field work:

Sure, we were the great teacher of the masses in New York City. In a sense this was a good thing, and we undoubtedly helped thousands of students who otherwise would never have had a chance. But we were also very cruel. We had almost no admissions standards and we were brutal about failing people. There were many years in which no more than 25-30% of an entering class would graduate. Sure, we were the great "School of Opportunity" for New York, but the truth of the matter is that we were also the "Great Slop Bucket" that took everybody and later massacred them.

From the inside, there was mounting opposition to the "School of Opportunity" philosophy, with its low admission standards and its high failure rates. At the same time, professors, particularly from liberal arts and graduate units, objected to lowering standards. Pressure was slowly building internally that would produce a different saga for NYU, even as events on the outside also indicated change.

The Environmental Threat

A number of major organizational theorists have suggested that the impetus for large-scale change almost always comes from outside an organization (for reviews, see Katz and Kahn, 1966; Thompson, 1967). Katz and Kahn state the environmentalist theme very clearly:

The basic hypothesis is that organizations and other social structures are open systems which attain stability through their authority structures, reward mechanisms, and value systems, and which are changed primarily from without by means of some significant change in input. Some organizations, less open than most, may resist new inputs indefinitely and may perish rather than change. We would predict, however, that, in the absence of external changes, organizations are likely to be reformed from within in limited ways. More drastic or revolutionary changes are initiated or made possible by external forces [Katz and Kahn, 1966, pages 448-449].

Certainly the events at NYU show the impact of heavy environmental influences, for external events were pressing the university toward a reevaluation of its mission, image, and saga. NYU exists in an environment in which other universities are competing for resources, students, and social influence. For many years NYU was the major "service university" in New York that took the masses of students. High admission standards at both the City University of New York and Columbia excluded most of the student population.

In the late 1950's, however, both the state and the city assumed more responsibility for educating the masses. A rapidly expanding network of junior and senior colleges caused public university enrollments to skyrocket. Public institutions charge little tuition. Even though privately supported NYU raised its fees until they were among the highest in the nation, it still lacked the resources to compete with public colleges and universities, and public institutions began usurping the role of educating the city's student population.

The effects of the shift in student population were rapid and dramatic. In 1956 NYU published *The Self-Study*, a major attempt at long-range planning that predicted many of the coming changes. The authors of that farsighted document were aware of the impending threat, but it is doubtful that they understood how immediate it was. In fact, they stated, with some confidence,

Even the enormous expansion of the tuition-free city college system with its excellent physical plan has not as yet substantially affected the character of NYU. . . . [New York University, 1956, page 11]

The Self-Study also predicted increasing enrollments for NYU from 1955 to 1966. By the early 1960's, however, it was obvious that the expected growth was not materializing. Thousands of students who previously would have attended NYU were going to public institutions. Figure 8-1 compares *Self-Study* projections with actual enrollments for the period 1955-73. By 1966 the actual figures

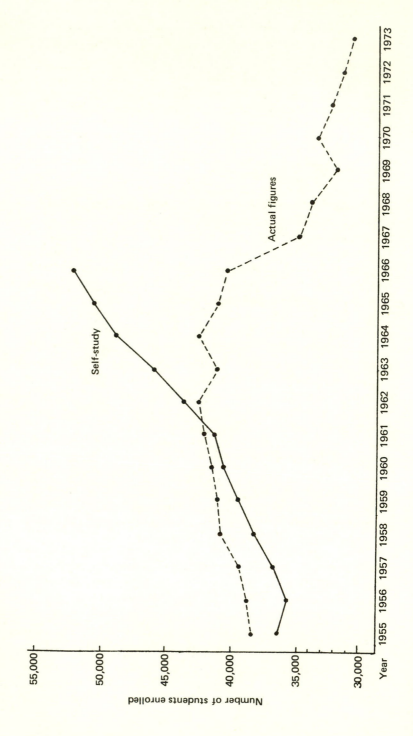

FIGURE 8-1

Comparison of Enrollment Figures: Self-Study Projections and Actual Figures, 1955-1966;
Actual Figures Extended to 1973 (New York University, 1956, page 9)

were running a full 20 percent, over 9,000 students, behind the predictions. As one administrator viewed it, "We certainly anticipated pressure from the City University, but frankly the pinch came ten years ahead of our expectations." Throughout the 1960's and into the 1970's, enrollments fell well behind the number needed to sustain the university's operation, and the situation grew progressively worse.

NYU was not alone in facing the threat from the public universities. Throughout New York State in the 1960's enrollment in the public institutions shot from a relatively small percentage to over 60 percent of all students by 1973. During that period private colleges and universities closed their doors as more and more students attended state institutions.

NYU did not die, but it was certainly sick. The financial impact was alarming. From 1964 to 1973 NYU accumulated deficits of over $32,000,000 that ate away a significant portion of its $62,000,000 endowment. In 1970, in a desperate attempt to gain more revenue, the university's undergraduate tuition went up to $2,700, a figure that exceeded even Harvard's. The financial picture was overwhelmingly bleak.

Burton Clark suggests that often during periods of crisis, when the established organization proves inadequate, organizational sagas are attacked, making way for change. Those in charge, after years of attempting incremental adjustments (Lindblom, 1959), realize finally that they must either give up established ways or the organization will fail. In order to survive, they may:

relinquish the leadership to one proposing a plan that promises revival and later strength, or they may even accept a man of utopian intent. Deep crisis in the established organization thus creates some of the conditions of a new organization. It suspends past practice, forces some bordering groups to stand back or even to turn their backs on failure of the organization, and it tends to catch the attention of the reformer looking for an opportunity [Clark, 1972, page 180].

NYU was an institution almost overripe for a new saga. Seriously weakened by competition from public universities, it was losing students, and its financial stability was being undermined by the loss of vitally needed tuition. It was a question of how to meet the challenge —how to frame a new saga that would serve the educational needs of the community and the survival needs of NYU. The changes that resulted were the source of intense political controversy.

Political Controversy and the Emergence of a New Saga

Once the saga of the institution had been challenged and external pressures had forced the university into a crisis condition, a series of essentially political processes began. Several organizational theorists have looked at decision processes as political activities (Cyert and March, 1963; Thompson, 1967). In an earlier work, I argued:

When we look at dynamic processes that explode on the modern campus today we see neither the rigid, formal aspects of bureaucracy nor the calm, consensus-directed elements of an academic collegium. On the contrary, student riots cripple the campus, professors form unions and strike, administrators defend their traditional positions, and external interest groups and irate governors invade the academic halls. All these activities can be understood as political acts. They emerge from the complex, fragmented social structure of the university, drawing on the divergent concerns and life styles of hundreds of miniature subcultures. These groups articulate their interests in many different ways, bringing pressure to bear on the decision-making process from any number of angles and using power and force whenever it is available and necessary. Once articulated, power and influence go through a complex process until policies are shaped, reshaped, and forged from the competing claims of multiple groups. All this is a dynamic process, a process clearly indicating that the university is best understood as a "politicized" institution [Baldridge, 1971, pages 8-9].

A political image brings with it a number of basic assumptions about decision-making processes, all of which definitely apply to the NYU situation.

Basic Assumptions of a Political Model

The political model assumes that complex organizations can be studied as miniature political systems, with interest group dynamics and conflicts similar to those of cities, states, or other political situations. All stages of the political model center around policy-forming processes. Policy formation becomes a focal point, for major policies commit the organization to definite goals, set the strategies for reaching those goals, and determine the long-range destiny of an organization. Policy decisions are critical, not merely routine; they are decisions that have major impact and mold the organization's future.

Since policy decisions bind the organization to important courses of action, people in the organization use their influence to see that their special values are implemented. Policy becomes a major point of conflict, a watershed of interest group activity that permeates a university's life. In light of its importance, policy becomes the center of the political analysis. Just as the political scientist may select legislative acts in Congress as the focus of his analysis of the state's political processes, organization theorists may select policy decisions as the key for studying organizational conflict and change. Some basic assumptions about political processes in organizations are:

Inactivity prevails. Policy making may be a political process, but not everyone becomes involved. On the contrary, policy activity generally follows a "law of apathy," that is, much of the time the process is an uninteresting, unrewarding activity avoided by most people. Both in the world of academia and in the larger society, administrators are allowed to run the show. Voters do not vote, people do not attend city council meetings, and, by and large, the decisions of society are made by small elites.

Fluid participation. Even when people are active, they move in and out of the decision-making process, not spending much time on any given issue. Decisions are usually made by those who persist, those small groups of political elites who govern most major decisions.

Fragmentation into interest groups. Like most social organizations, colleges and universities are split into interest groups with varying goals and values. These groups usually exist in a state of armed coexistence. High resources and benevolent times create minimal conflict; tight resources and attacks from pressure groups act to mobilize interest groups to defend themselves and their own causes.

Normalcy of conflict. In dynamic social systems such as colleges and universities, conflict is natural and expected. Instead of indicating breakdown in the academic community, conflict can be vital to promoting healthy organizational change.

Limitations of formal authority. Formal authority, as prescribed by the bureaucratic system, is severely limited by the political pressure and bargaining power of interest groups. Decisions are not simple, bureaucratic orders. Often they are negotiated compromises between competing groups. Officials are not free to issue a decision; instead, they must jockey between interest groups, building viable positions between powerful segments.

External interest groups. Academic decision making does not occur in a vacuum, for external interest groups exercise much influence over the policy-making process. External pressures and formal control by outside agencies, especially in public institutions, are powerful shapers of internal governance processes.

Challenges to the Old Saga

Political processes accompanied the struggle at NYU for institutional viability in the face of massive external threat. By the end of

1961 a debate about the university's future was raging behind closed doors, with disagreements going far deeper than the question of how to recruit more students. The essential issue concerned NYU's total educational mission. Could it continue with business as usual, or was this a critical turning point? Many top administrators felt that it was time for a sweeping evaluation of NYU's destiny, particularly in light of the financial crisis facing the institution.

The debate at this point involved the goals and long-range commitments of the university. The assessment was not only that the university should adopt new management techniques to solve its financial crisis, which it did, but that it would also have to develop new goals and new orientations toward the future to survive as a significant contributor to higher education. Confronted with multifaceted pressures, university leaders deliberately "tinkered with the future." NYU consciously sought to change its saga by creating and projecting a revised self-image, a new institutional character.

Several events accelerated the changes. In 1962 James Hester, former executive dean of the liberal arts units, was selected to be the new president. He was acutely aware of the problems facing the university and made it his first order of business to confront them. In addition, the Ford Foundation invited NYU to apply for a comprehensive development grant. This opportunity was seized as a means of providing financial support for the planned changes, and eventually the Ford Foundation granted $25 million to NYU.

In early 1962 several committees were appointed to formulate plans for the Ford request. It became progressively clearer that NYU's problems had to be faced if the grant was to be educationally meaningful. Although faculty bodies were asked to prepare plans to be included in the Ford proposal, many faculty members claim that the critical decisions were really made by a small group of administrators. Some administrators claimed that the faculty's contribution was limited because of their inability to look beyond individual departments to the needs of the entire university.

In any event, it is fascinating to observe the conscious efforts of the university community as it planned its future. The debates, fact-finding, and committee work for the Ford requests continued for more than a year, one of those rare periods when an organization really maps out its destiny and redesigns its saga. Rather than responding impulsively to the pressures of the moment, the university attempted to realistically plot a future based on a careful study of its needs, and then to engage in explicit decision making.

By fall 1963 the Ford report was completed, and the foundation responded generously, expressing strong confidence in the plans for the reshaping of NYU. The university was challenged to raise $75 million from other sources to match the $25 million grant. A complex, interconnected series of changes to promote NYU's new saga emerged from the Ford report. They included:

1. Undergraduate admissions standards would be raised substantially.
2. The fragmented undergraduate program (with Education, Commerce, Washington Square College, Engineering, and University College each having separate programs) would be unified.
3. An "urban university" orientation would be developed.
4. More full-time faculty and students would be recruited, and more on-campus residences would be provided.
5. More energy would be directed toward graduate and professional training, so that direct undergraduate competition with the state university would be avoided.

It is important to note several things about these decisions. First, they represented a basic, far-reaching transformation of the very nature of NYU. Second, the relation to the external social context was particularly critical, for, in large measure, these decisions represented a "posture of defense" for NYU. Third, the posture of defense allowed a confrontation with reality and the development of new future images that could turn NYU from potential disaster toward a revitalized educational role. A crisis situation had promoted the birth of a new saga.

From a sociological perspective it is important to realize that the resultant plans were framed by a context of conflict and that pressures were impinging on the decision makers from many sides. Although the forces for change were great, both inside and outside groups had strong vested interests in the status quo. At least two major units, the School of Education and the School of Commerce, as well as many influential alumni, were committed to the "School of Opportunity" image. It was, of course, exactly this philosophy that was being challenged as the university searched for its revised educational role. A confrontation was virtually inevitable.

The Role of Strong Leadership in Developing a New Saga

Burton Clark argues that major changes in organizational sagas, while often provoked by crisis circumstances, are usually fulfilled through strong institutional leadership. In fact, one could almost argue that the crisis produces a hero to make the decisions. The early presidents at Reed (William T. Foster), Antioch (Arthur E. Morgan), and Swarthmore (Frank Aydelotte) capitalized on critical situations to build new organizational sagas.

NYU had its aggressive leadership in James Hester and the chancellor, Allan M. Cartter, a noted economist specializing in higher education. The central administration team took strong action. In fact, most people at NYU felt that a small group of top administrators made critical decisions with little faculty consultation. To be sure, the University Senate was consulted about most of the plans, but at that time it was believed that the relatively weak Senate merely rubber-stamped decisions. As one member put it:

We were "informed" about these matters, and we were asked to vote our approval, but I wouldn't say we were actually "consulted" in any meaningful way. It was a one-way street—they told us what they were going to do and we said "OK."

In addition, faculty committees were working on the Ford report, but many people suggested that the critical decisions were not actually made by these committees. Instead, most of the faculty learned about the decisions when they were publicly announced. One rather bitter professor in the School of Commerce commented:

The School of Commerce was about to have its throat cut and we didn't even know about it until after the blood was flowing! Sure, Hester came over and gave us a little pep talk about how much this was going to improve things, but he didn't really ask our advice on the issue. He didn't exactly say it was going to be his way "or else," but we got the point.

From their perspective, the administration clearly saw the threats facing NYU from the public universities and knew that something radical had to be done—quickly. Administrators, disappointed in the faculty's conservative contribution to the Ford report, felt that their broader perspective gave them the duty to act as the key "change agents." It is also clear that they knew some moves would be vehemently opposed, and extensive consultation might arouse enough hostility to kill the whole matter. As President Hester explained it:

The University was confronted with critical conditions. We had to undertake action that was radical from the standpoint of many people in the University. Some of these changes had to be undertaken over strong opposition and were implemented by administrative directives. In two of the undergraduate schools a number of faculty members had accepted the "school of opportunity" philosophy as a primary purpose of their school. This had been justifiable at one time, but no longer. Many faculty members simply did not recognize that circumstances had changed and did not accept the fact that the service they were accustomed to performing was now being assumed by public institutions at far less cost to the students.

At this point the administration had to be the agent for change. It was incumbent upon us to exercise the initiative that is the key to administrative leadership. In the process, we did interfere with the traditional autonomy of the schools, but we believed this was necessary if they and the University were to continue to function [personal interview].

It might be helpful to examine some of the factors that enabled the administrators, as a critical leadership group, to execute this change so successfully. Strong opposition to the planned changes could be expected from those adversely affected. How did the policy succeed despite this opposition? What factors were working in favor of the central administration as it moved to implement these transformations?

First, the central administration's power had been greatly enhanced through centralization under the strong leadership of President Henry Heald. Before Heald's administration in the 1950's, NYU had been a loose collection of essentially autonomous schools. President Hester's success, then, was very dependent on Heald's earlier preparations.

Second, Hester, as a new popular president, could still rely on the "honeymoon effect" to win support from both the trustees and a substantial part of the faculty. As one professor of commerce noted, "He's as close to a popular president as any you'll find, and that makes him a hard man to beat on most issues." In 1969, for example, the general faculty indicated their "General confidence in the central administration of the university" on a questionnaire. Compared to the identical question on a Faculty Senate Survey for 1959, this represents a sharp increase in the level of confidence (see Table 8-1).

Third, large segments of the faculty supported the changes. Cross-pressures from various interest groups can allow decision makers

TABLE 8-1
Degree of Confidence in the Central Administration

Survey	Degree of confidence				Number of cases
	High	Medium	Low	Total	
		(percent)			
1959 (Faculty senate)	40	18	42	100	(596)
1968 (Baldridge)	47	32	21	100	(693)

more freedom than would be possible if most groups lined up in opposition. In the NYU case, many liberal arts professors favored raising admission standards, and they were joined by graduate-level professors who felt that higher undergraduate standards would indirectly improve the graduate programs.

Fourth, the decisions were successful because of the obvious bureaucratic weapons controlled by the central administration. The centralized admissions office, for example, could be instructed to raise standards, thus effectively bypassing the opposition. In addition, the twin powers of the budget and personnel appointments were brought to bear often in the struggles that followed the decisions.

Finally, one of the most important reasons that these dramatic changes could succeed was the external threat from the public institutions. A common finding of sociological research states that groups threatened by outside forces will tolerate internal changes that they otherwise would oppose. The administration recognized that NYU was truly under attack and fought to implement changes that would protect the university. The trustees, convinced that these changes were imperative, stood solidly behind the administration in the struggles that erupted—as they did all over the campus!

The Political Conflict: One Example

There is no question that NYU was in a crisis, demanding a strong leadership to make radical changes. The inevitability of conflict over the changes is especially clear in the issues provoked in the School of Commerce, a school dedicated to the "School of Opportunity" saga, and a large core of its professors fought to retain that concept.

The situation is complicated, however, because not all the business education faculty was opposed to the changes. The Graduate School of Business (GSB), a separate unit for graduate and advanced professional degrees in business, allied itself with the central administration. GSB wanted to become a major research center and a nationally reputable business education unit. Its professors were more interested in scholarly research on industry and business, and they feared that the undergraduate School of Commerce was damaging the reputation of business studies. Thus, the business education professors formed two distinct interest groups with two different emphases, each fighting for their image of NYU's future.

Most of the commerce professors believed their jobs would disappear if the changes were instituted. They feared reduced enrollments, a loss of the night school program, decreased faculty size, and a general weakening of their influence in the university. It is now clear that what they feared most was to happen in a short time!

Probably the majority of the commerce faculty opposed any major changes in their basic philosophy and admission policies. Moreover, the administration's chief representative, Dean John Prime, was not totally convinced that the changes were desirable. A power struggle developed, but the administration had most of the weapons. As one professor said in a personal interview:

> I guess now that it's all over these changes were good for us, but we fought it all the way; there was a fantastic battle. Actually, I'd say it was rammed down our throats. Several foundations made reports which suggested we were too "provincial," and we needed to upgrade standards and eliminate the duplication in our undergraduate programs. But remember, this was done by academic types, who really didn't understand a professional school and were prejudiced against us. This would not have happened a few years ago when the whole University lived off Commerce's surplus money. It is only our growing weakness which made this change possible. The various schools are always competing and at this moment we are in a bad relative position.

For many months the task of convincing the faculty to cooperate with the changes continued against strong opposition. Finally, two key appointments were announced. First, in April 1962 an "executive dean" was appointed to supervise both the School of Commerce and the Graduate School of Business. Second, in September 1963 Dean Prime resigned, and Dean Abraham Gitlow became local dean of the School of Commerce. To no one's surprise, both deans favored the administration's plans to upgrade quality in the School of Commerce, and a major breakthrough in faculty cooperation came at about the same time.

By almost any yardstick the School of Commerce is radically different from what it was a few years ago. By deliberate policy decision, S.A.T. scores went up, and enrollment figures went down. Of course, the cut in enrollments caused an equally drastic decrease in faculty positions. From a high of nearly three hundred members in the late 1950's, the number of faculty dropped to sixty-one in 1967-68. Many part-timers were dropped, many nontenured people were never tenured, a few senior men were "bought off" to retire early, few new people were hired, and many current faculty members left. Although NYU lived up to its contractual obligations, professors had to find positions elsewhere.

These changes hit the School of Commerce hard, yet the quality of the students, the faculty, and the program vastly improved. Those at NYU today, including members of the original faculty, now believe that the changes were necessary.

The Political Process: Summary Comments

The struggle over the School of Commerce only illustrates the larger political process occurring throughout NYU as it struggled over its new saga. Some characteristics of that general process can be summarized:

1. Many interest groups were threatened by the changes (in the Schools of Commerce and Education).
2. Influence was exercised by whatever weapons the interest groups could muster (threats of faculty resignations or withdrawal of alumni support).
3. Strong leadership was demonstrated from the top, and administrative authorities mustered political support from change-oriented groups (the liberal arts faculty).
4. Administrators were caught in a complex set of cross-pressures coming from different groups (the School of Commerce and the Graduate School of Business demanded different things).
5. Coalitions were formed to fight or press for the changes (the Schools of Commerce and Education united to fight changes; the School of Liberal Arts and the Graduate School united to promote them).
6. Bureaucratic mechanisms—budget, early retirement policies, reorganization of departments—were used as political weapons by administrators.
7. Outside pressure groups were often involved (alumni of the School of Commerce).

In short, the formulation of a new institutional saga for NYU was an eminently political process involving high conflict, influence tactics, and coalitional behavior. It reflected the general political dynamics outlined earlier.

The New Saga in Action

From the mid-1960's on, the decisions based on the new saga were carried out at NYU. The effects were dramatic and had repercussions throughout the university. First, undergraduate admissions dropped sharply—a stunning 20 percent from 1962 to 1965. This sharp dip was largely due to raised admission standards. At the very moment when a sum of approximately $10 million above normal costs was desperately needed for quality upgrading, the drop in enrollment cut off vitally needed tuition funds. From 1962 to 1973 the total number of students gradually decreased in the face of higher tuition, an expanded network of state institutions, and the same overall decline in enrollment that affected all of higher education.

A second indication that the planned changes had a strong impact was the tremendous rise in freshman S.A.T. scores, an increase of nearly one hundred points in the years 1961 to 1966; after that the scores once again leveled out at a higher plane.

A third indicator of the changes is related to student housing. The school's new role emphasized recruiting more students from outside New York City, and more full-time resident students. The university was forced to provide both housing for students on a large scale and residences for the full-time faculty. New housing units were constructed as part of a $75 million capital improvement program that spanned the 1960's. From 1960 to 1974 the number of on-campus students increased by over 500 percent.

A fourth change that accompanied the reconceptualized saga occurred in the composition of the graduate student enrollment. There was a shift toward more full-time graduate students, while the number of professional students remained relatively constant. In 1960 only 23 percent of the graduate enrollment was full-time, while by 1967 the percentage increased to 55. This meant that the absolute number of full-time graduate students had tripled in only seven years. This pattern continued into the early 1970's. In fact, the commitment to graduate and professional education is shown by the fact that, of the total number of degrees granted in any given year, nearly two-thirds are either graduate or professional.

The Crisis Continues: The Politics of Survival

To many observers it appeared that the drastic changes planned in the early sixties and implemented during the last half of the decade would solve most of the university's problems. Unfortunately, the rosy predictions were overly optimistic. City and state institutions in the area continued their phenomenal growth, and NYU still faced difficulties with student recruitment. In turn, deficits continued to mount so that, by the early 1970's, the institution seemed ready for bankruptcy. By this time the faculty opposing the administration's changes had realized that the university's survival was at stake, and more and more senior faculty rallied to the administration's support.

In 1972 a series of severe measures was taken. First, there was a university-wide freeze on salaries. Second, many nontenured faculty were fired. Third, a university task force was set up to make emergency recommendations toward controlling the financial crisis. The task force proposed a number of stringent changes:

1. Every School in the university would operate on a strictly balanced budget, or cut back their programs to fit their budgets. Except for the College of Arts and Sciences, which was allowed an annual $1,000,000 subsidy, no help would come from the central endowment for the schools that exceeded their income.
2. The university campus in the Bronx was to be sold. Subsequently, New York State bought the campus for $62 million, a sum desperately needed to shore up the shrinking endowment.
3. A sharp cut of $10.5 million in instructional costs was begun.
4. It was recommended that the School of Social Work be phased out. (It would be interesting here to expand on the political controversy around the School of Social Work as we did with the School of Commerce, but space does not permit it. The School of Social Work was not willing to give up; in fact, its faculty and students mobilized to raise $1,000,000 and the campaign successfully bought additional time for the school.)
5. The mandatory retirement age was reduced from 68 to 65, and people were encouraged to retire at 62. Over 100 faculty and staff were pushed out because of this move.

As these radical proposals were implemented, the faculty casualty toll was high. Many members supported the administration and its tough but necessary action; others were bitter and anxious to fight back with whatever political weapons they could muster. The controversies that raged around attempts at organizing unions would fill a book, but by 1974, when the issue was presented, the majority of the faculty still voted "no bargaining agent."

In spite of all the problems confronting NYU, a new spirit has begun to pervade the institution. Recently an enormous $300,000,000 fund-raising campaign was initiated, enrollments have taken a slight upturn, and the deficits plaguing the school have been reduced so that a break-even budget is anticipated for the 1974-75 school year.

Most important, in the face of disaster NYU has struggled to change its image and to develop a new organizational saga. It is unlikely, of course, that an institution as fragmented and as complex as NYU will ever exude a simple, cohesive saga. But this massive institution seems to have captured some direction in its drift, seized opportunities in the midst of crises, and created the self-image of a high-quality private institution.

Just as dynamic presidents led the moves toward new sagas at Reed, Swarthmore, and Antioch, much of the credit for NYU's rising hopes can be attributed to the capable leadership of President James Hester. A recent editorial in *Change* magazine paid tribute to Hester's leadership:

One is left with the impression that, even in this very large place, the influence and contribution of its president are unique and life-size. He is a capable, agile administrator and a consummate fund raiser finely attuned to the sensitivities of his faculty. In these days of tight finances he could carry a big stick, but he does not. Instead, he gives much of each day to the infinite process of consensus building among his 5,450 full- and part-time faculty, and in doing so he seems to be succeeding where many others have failed. It may be the new miracle on Washington Square, and an eloquent testimonial to the ability of complex universities to spring back to life [*Change*, 1974, page 13].

Summary

The story is obviously not complete. NYU's new institutional saga is only partly fulfilled, and devotion to the revised image is largely untested as yet. Although NYU often seems to be going in every direction at once, the notion of saga has some usefulness, even in the face of such diversity. A new belief, a renewed spirit, and a rekindled hope are placed in plans that emerged from fifteen years of crisis.

Impetus for change came largely from outside the institution. It is doubtful that NYU would have undertaken such severe transformations had it not been confronted with survival in a changing environment. The external threats were real; the internal responses were drastic.

Finally, the imagery of politics and interest group dynamics are particularly useful to an examination of major organizational changes. At NYU different groups had different goals. As external pressures buffeted the institution, powerful interest groups maneuvered to protect traditional activities and domains. Only the interference of strong, able leadership from the central administration was able to contain the conflict and move the institution toward survival.

This has been a study of massive organizational change. By using the case study method and a historical framework, we have tried to show how three themes in organizational literature can be enlightening for the study of institutional change. The notion of saga gives insight about the *content* of the changes; the environmentalist themes are powerful in showing the *sources* of change impetuses; the political theme is helpful in analyzing the *processes* necessary to institutionalize a new saga.

References

Baldridge, J. Victor. *Power and Conflict in the University.* New York: John Wiley & Sons, 1971.

Change (April 1974).

Clark, B. R. *Adult Education in Transition: A Study of Institutional Insecurity.* Berkeley: University of California Press, 1956.

Clark, B. R. *The Open Door College. A Case Study.* New York: McGraw-Hill, 1960.

Clark, B. R. *The Distinctive College: Antioch, Reed, and Swarthmore.* Chicago: Aldine, 1970.

Clark, B. R. "The Organizational Saga in Higher Education." *Administrative Science Quarterly* 17, no. 2 (1972): 178-184. Reprinted as chapter 6 in this volume.

Cyert, R., and March, James. *A Behavioral Theory of the Firm.* Englewood Cliffs, N.J.: Prentice-Hall, 1963.

Katz, E., and Kahn, R. *The Social Psychology of Organizations.* New York: John Wiley & Sons, 1966.

Lindblom, C. E. "The Science of 'Muddling Through.'" *Public Administration Review* 19 (1959): 79-88.

New York University. *The Self-Study.* New York: New York University Press, 1956.

Selznick, P. *TVA and the Grass Roots.* Berkeley: University of California Press, 1949.

Thompson, James. *Organizations in Action.* New York: McGraw-Hill, 1967.

9

The Evolution of an Urban University

Roger E. Dash and Gary L. Riley

"Off-Ramp University," "Freeway Tech," and "Concrete Jungle" are terms frequently used to identify California State University, Los Angeles. "Urban University," "Commuter College," and "Campus of Busy People" are more sophisticated descriptions of the same institution. At its birth, Cal State L.A. set out to be a model "urban university," determined to serve the needs of its environment, and to resist pressures to become just another traditional college. But the forces of traditional academic programming and faculty professionalism have seriously undermined that unique goal.

This chapter is a case study of this developing institution, its original goals, and the forces that helped transform its early distinctive mission into a less than unique role. The task of the chapter is three-fold: (1) to examine the original mission of the university as expressed in the urban university theme; (2) to analyze the forces of traditionalism that pushed it back toward the "mainstream" of higher education; and (3) to suggest some lessons that university management might learn from the Cal State L.A. story.

The Urban Mission

Located within the urban spread of the city of Los Angeles, the CSULA campus is only five miles from the downtown city center area. Over 25,000 students travel daily to and from the campus sometime between 8:00 a.m. and 10:00 p.m. Only one-half of the students are enrolled full-time. Almost 80 percent are in the upper division or graduate level of study. Over one-third are married; over one-half are totally self-supporting; 40 percent are racial minorities; the median age is twenty-eight. The students of CSULA live in the city, work in the city, and bring to the campus an array of social activities and attitudes that are clearly urban-oriented. Therefore, on the basis of its location, its ethnography, its proximity to urban-centered activities, and its social orientation, Cal State L.A. is properly labeled an urban university.

But the geographical location and physical characteristics of a university reflect only one aspect of its identity. A second aspect, and one which is far more critical to the concept of an urban university, is the mission of the school. An urban university is a school committed to experimentation and innovation in urban education. Its primary purpose is to train and educate for urban leadership. Its programs cross traditional lines of academic disciplines, utilizing multi-disciplinary approaches to learning and problem solving. An urban university uses to the fullest extent possible the resources of the city as its laboratory. Applied research, as opposed to basic research, is the proper focus of the urban university as it pursues its objectives (Dvonin, 1969).

We can summarize the mission of an urban university: it serves as an effective laboratory for higher education; the characteristics and career activities of the students are linked to the life of the city; the basic orientation of the campus is heterogeneous, reflecting the diverse populations and interests of the city. The problem, of course, is that colleges and universities often claim to have a particular set of purposes, but rarely have they translated their written and spoken commitments into structures, programs, policies, and practices that reflect their commitments operationally. Thus, the reconciliation of stated purposes and actual accomplishments has been a pervasive problem for higher education researchers, particularly those who study urban universities.

The task of the researcher is two-fold: (1) environmental factors, current and historical, having an impact upon the evolution of the institution must be identified; (2) organizational support—structural, administrative, and programmatic—must be examined to determine whether it helps or hinders the mission of the institution. Using Cal State L.A. as a case study, researchers at the University of California, Los Angeles, addressed this two-fold research task (Dash, 1975). Members of the research team represented several disciplines including history, organization theory, social psychology, administrative studies, and student personnel services. A variety of information sources were used including institutional and public documents, state legislative records, interviews, and specially developed questionnaires.

Data obtained from the documents and interviews were used to formulate a descriptive historical perspective of the development of the university into its present form. The emphasis was not on reconstructing a full and detailed historical account, but rather to focus on pivotal events in the history of Cal State L.A. that had an impact on four key components: organization, environment, program, and personnel.

An Historical Perspective

As are all California state colleges and universities, CSULA is a creation of the state legislature and, as such, is controlled by that body. Interests of the general public are often expressed through legislation. The founding of CSULA in 1947 is an example of public needs and interests being articulated through law. Los Angeles City College, a two-year, lower division community college, was saturated with World War II veterans, armed with the G.I. Bill and eagerly pursuing undergraduate degrees which would launch them into the postwar technological revolution. Then in its infant stages, the University of California at Los Angeles was unable to accommodate the large numbers of upper-division transfer students. Clearly, there was need for an additional upper-division institution in the Los Angeles metropolitan area. But what services was the new institution to perform in addition to simply accommodating vast numbers of students? After considerable debate, delays, and often open hostility among all parties with vested interests in the creation of the new institution, the state legislature set forth the following conditions and guidelines:

1. The primary instructional objectives of the new college would be to provide general liberal education and teacher education;
2. The new college would provide upper-division instruction exclusively; lower-division courses would be added later, but only in the event that the local two-year campus was unable to accommodate all eligible students;
3. The scheduling of classes would be similar to the scheduling practices followed in the local two-year college, with allowances made for part-time students, working students, evening students, and commuters.

Scarcely one year later, the impact of needs emanating from the Los

Angeles urban environment influenced the state legislature to add a fourth objective to be met by the new college:

   4. The "Los Angeles State College of Applied Arts and Sciences" would provide for the training of persons in gainful occupations related to business and urban industry.

In so ordering the college to meet this objective, the legislature revealed its expectation that the school would develop a cooperative arrangement with business and industry, providing programs which would coordinate practical work experience with classroom instruction (Earhardt, 1967).

   In response to the applied arts and sciences objective, the college's Executive Council initiated a study which involved members of the academic community and business leaders of the city of Los Angeles for nearly a year. From this study grew numerous occupational, vocational, and technical programs, among the most significant being the Cooperative Education (Work-Study) Program of 1950. This program was designed to create an alliance with urban business and industry, and a learning sequence which required participating students to be enrolled for at least six academic units at the college while being employed at least half-time in jobs related to their academic majors.

   Much of late 1950 and early 1951 was devoted to curricular development and program implementation. Today, many of those programs would sound routine, even trite. But, at the time, they represented major breakthroughs in making upper-division college training relevant to the career interests and human resource needs of an urban population. Areas which received the most intense review and planning were nursing, home economics, business education, journalism, radio-television, public service, merchandising, urban planning, and recreation.

   Moreover, in 1951 the college's Executive Council was notified by the State Board of Education that the campus had been granted tentative accreditation for an initial period of three years for granting the following credentials: kindergarten-primary, general elementary, junior high school, special secondary in art, business education, music, nursing, education, physical education, speech arts, correction of speech defects, teaching of the mentally retarded, child welfare and attendance, school psychometrist, elementary school administration, and elementary school supervision. In the context of the times, accreditation in these badly needed service areas in the growing Los Angeles metropolitan region enhanced markedly the "urbanization" of the new college.

Indeed, in the broad scheme of things it seemed that Los Angeles State College of Applied Arts and Sciences was well on its way to meeting the expressed interests of the state legislature and the city's population. In summary form, the following factors prevailed on the new campus in the 1950's:

1. Enrollments burgeoned quickly, ten-fold, twenty-fold, in the first half of the decade. As early as 1951, the college had over 50 percent of its students enrolled less than full-time; 40 percent were married; their average age was 25, four years above the state average for members of comparable college classes.

2. Part-time teaching faculty predominated, most having joint teaching appointments at the local two-year college campus and at the new college. Teaching staff, under this arrangement, maintained very flexible class and office schedules, thereby initiating the concept of the "extended day" campus.

3. Community, business, and industrial advisory committees proliferated. In the tradition of the Executive Council's development of the Cooperative Education (Work-Study) Program, the institution maintained liaison relationships with numerous public and private agencies with interests in the local higher learning enterprise.

4. Facilities of both the two-year college and the senior institution were open to use by students enrolled at either school, so that supplemental training activities or laboratory experiences could be obtained by persons working on two-year "technical" certificates or by those working on the four-year "applied" credential.

5. Certificate and degree programs were open to students of either campus, the two-year or the four-year, no matter which school a student attended. Moreover, classes at both campuses were open to students enrolled at either school. Communication between the two segments was largely unencumbered by regulatory or attitudinal constraints.

6. Administratively and structurally, the new college reflected certain desired qualities of urbanization. Intimately related to each other in terms of programs offered, joint faculty assignments, and student articulation practices, Los Angeles City College and Cal State L.A. proposed an administrative arrangement whereby the two campuses would be mutually governed and led by a single president. This pattern prevailed until 1958.

Reflecting upon the fifties, educational researchers today may cite the Los Angeles campus as one of a very few that went beyond rhetoric and actually tried to become an Urban University in programming and curriculum. In large part, its success was due to the interest and involvement of the public, often expressed through the California state legislature and local governmental agencies. However, public interest is only one of several environmental influences that help to shape the destiny of a college or university. And for CSULA, other external influences were soon to change the course of the institution's growth and development.

Environmental Counterforces

Although local influence over institutional purposes and missions may be prevalent, other agencies also impose guidelines, regulations, and limitations upon colleges and universities which counteract local influence. Examples include accreditation agencies, coordinating boards or councils, and system-level administrative officers. Granted, such agencies serve a vital function in American higher education. But often there exist conflicts between externally imposed sanctions and locally preferred options with regard to role, function, and purpose of a particular campus.

In the 1950's, three such agencies became involved in setting the direction for the development of CSULA: the Western College Association (an accreditation agency), the California State Credentialing Committee, and the California State College Advisory Board. Having achieved temporary accreditation in selected curricular and credential areas in early 1951, the college requested formal accreditation review by the Western College Association and credential review by the State Credentialing Committee. The results were negative; accreditation and credentialing were denied in numerous disciplines and areas of professional training. A study by the State College Advisory Board supported the findings and recommendations of the other two agencies. Their findings and recommendations were:

1. Housed on the City College campus, the college was judged to have inadequate facilities for the programs and credentials it proposed to offer.
2. The college had not developed an adequate graduate program in the subject matter areas in which it wished to offer professional credentials.
3. The college lacked organizational and administrative distinction from the City College, thus threatening the potential for independent growth and development.
4. The college lacked curricular and programmatic distinction from the City College, especially in the lower-division courses and programs of study; credits earned at the two-year college

were accepted without restriction by the senior institution when students decided to pursue a four-year or first-professional degree.

5. As indicated by the prevalence of part-time, joint-appointment faculty, the college lacked professional and academic distinction from the two-year college and, therefore, lacked the degree of specialization among the teaching faculty that was necessary to engage in professional and graduate training.

Thus, in spite of the dominant urban focus, extreme pressures were placed upon the new college throughout the fifties to move in a more traditional direction—a direction common to the other California State College campuses at the time. The fifties were years of turmoil for the Los Angeles campus: intense battles took place over the location of the campus; new administrative staff members were appointed to develop an elite faculty and a correspondingly elite undergraduate and graduate curriculum; and the campus was referred to in higher education circles as one of two "Siamese twins joined at the head"—in reference to its relationship to the City College.

Accreditation was finally granted in late 1953, but only on the basis of the college's potential. None of the reviewing agencies were satisfied that the college's organization, administration, facilities, programs, or faculty objectives had been met. But progress toward reaching objectives was being made, and there was great need for the college and its degree and certificate programs.

In a sense, torn between the mandates of the original legislation which gave the institution its "charter," and the prevailing pressures of various accreditation and credentialing agencies, Cal State L.A. was without any distinct direction and mission. Intense debates developed among state and local officials regarding the future of the college. Other institutions of higher education in the Los Angeles area, public and private, became involved in the debates, obviously attempting to protect their own future interests and academic "markets." Even the faculty association became politically involved in the development of the campus as its members confronted state officials and local administrators over such matters as faculty access to decision making and long-range planning. But, aside from the decision to locate the campus at its present site in central Los Angeles, virtually nothing had been resolved by the late 1950's. Indeed, it seemed that the campus was like a train moving down a track composed of two rails, each leading in a slightly different direction. Many in the state were concerned that the new campus would not survive the strain placed upon it by trying to keep both wheels on the track.

Finally, during the 1959 session, the California state legislature requested that a Master Plan for California higher education be developed. The Master Plan was to determine "the future role of junior colleges, state colleges, and the University of California in the state's tri-partite system, and how the three segments should be governed and coordinated so that unnecessary duplications will be avoided" (California State Department of Education, 1960).

In 1960, the legislature passed the Donahoe Higher Education Act which included the following provisions directly affecting the state colleges:

1. A new State College Board of Trustees was created, effective July 1, 1961, with jurisdiction over all fourteen campuses;
2. The state colleges were assigned the primary function of providing instruction through the master's degree in liberal arts and sciences, applied fields, and the professions;
3. The Trustees of the state college system were given more flexibility and discretionary powers in the use of funds available for state colleges;
4. The state colleges were directed to select first-time freshmen from the top one-third of all graduates of California public high schools, with graduates of private and out-of-state secondary schools selected from equivalent levels.

In establishing the State College Board of Trustees, the state legislature concurrently provided for a more centralized statewide administration of the fourteen campuses. The legislature believed that a central staff of business and academic officers would be required to set standards of performance and to verify campus compliance with these standards. Thus, the Chancellor's Office of the California State Colleges was established. Under this system of organization and administration, the Board would have jurisdiction over matters of policy; the chancellor would have control over matters of system standards and compliance; and the local campus presidents would have the responsibility for operating their campuses within these policies and guidelines. The Chancellor's Office brought tighter controls to the state college system, resulting in greater uniformity among the individual campuses.

For Cal State L.A., the effects of the Master Plan and the direction provided by the Chancellor's Office were mixed blessings. In one sense, these environmental factors forced the campus to settle many of its differences regarding mission, function, program, student admissions, faculty characteristics, and administrative organization. Externally imposed guidelines and regulations helped to ensure that the college would meet all of the requirements that had been established for accreditation and credentialing.

In another way, new internal conflicts were created among those with vastly different opinions and philosophies regarding the proper role of Cal State L.A. It was not clear what program options were available to the college. It was not clear what extended functions the college might serve in relationship to the urban environment. And it was not clear whether the faculty, which was required to meet the uniform standards of the state college system, would also meet the demands and requirements defined by *local* needs and interests. Even with external guidance, Cal State L.A. still faced the question of institutional identity.

Organization, Program, and Personnel: Conservative Forces

The 1960's were years of growth, turmoil, and change for all of American higher education. Events that took place on the campus of Cal State L.A. were not unique. Rapid growth dominated higher education in all segments. New programs were developed in response to specialized human resource needs and to the educational needs of disadvantaged student populations. Financial resources were pleasantly adequate, even abundant. Highly specialized, highly professionalized faculties organized themselves into strong academic senates and departments, and into powerful political enclaves.

Amidst this "academic revolution," Cal State L.A. discovered a number of political and economic incentives to reaffirm its commitment to urbanization. On many campuses during the sixties, students protested higher education's relationship to national and international policies and practices. But at Cal State L.A., students fought for issues closer to their own needs: a quarter system, a year-round academic schedule, and an institutional commitment to an "urban focus." In 1967, the Academic Senate resolved that seeking solutions to urban-related problems through applied research, instruction, and public service would become a major objective of the college. An Urban Affairs Committee was formed as a policy review body for all urban-related programs. A Center for Urban Affairs was established through the use of specially generated federal, state, and foundation monies totaling nearly $1,000,000. The Greater Los Angeles Consortium on Urban Higher Education was created, in part, to help local colleges and universities reconcile their provincial differences. The Consortium helped coordinate programs, services, and fundraising efforts through grants and contracts in urban education.

Throughout the late sixties, commitment ran high. But this commitment was supported almost exclusively by "soft money" sources.

The saga of soft money programs is well known to educators at all levels—from kindergarten through graduate schools. As with so many programs during the 1960's, financial support was totally external to the educational agency. At Cal State L.A., special urban programs proliferated, soon ran out of special funds, and consequently died. Naturally, when program funds were eliminated, so were most of the academic and support staff who were employed on "soft money." Dozens of satellite programs and ancillary services, lacking the necessary organizational momentum to remain in "orbit," were incinerated in the traditional academic atmosphere.

First to falter was the Urban Affairs Center. Soon to follow was the Urban Studies Program, which had not been accepted as a full-fledged academic degree program with an independent departmental status. College administrators, recognizing the need for departmental cooperation in urban education efforts, charged each academic department with the responsibility for working toward the objectives set forth by the Urban Affairs Committee. Through several minor grants, some departments were able to develop working relationships with community-based programs and agencies. But, in the tide of the 1970's, most of these funds were lost, too. Operationally, the urban focus at Cal State L.A. was doomed.

The implications are clear. The students, administration, Academic Senate, and community patrons of Cal State L.A. voiced a commitment to urban education. But the survival of innovative urban efforts was utterly dependent upon external incentives and resources. Institutionalization of these efforts failed due to a lack of local resources, a lack of appropriate organizational structures and practices. There was little solid support from power holders, support badly needed for converting abstract principles into operational academic practices. Three elements of the academic organization seem critical for starting and maintaining innovation: (1) organizational support, (2) programmatic congruity, and (3) positive support among academic personnel.

1. *Organizational support:* The organization of colleges and universities is predominantly departmental in character, and this has important consequences for the institution's ability to carry out an urban mission. Whatever the particular mission advocated by campus administrators and formal faculty bodies, academic structures tend to follow an order that is largely determined by departments. The personnel are organized within their academic disciplines and intellec-

tual specializations. The programmatic content and the learning resources for earning degrees are arranged by departments. Departmental structure has a logic of its own and all change agents in academic organizations must overcome powerful forces of "structural inertia" in their efforts to introduce new ideas.

One type of structural inertia originates with the faculty organization in colleges and universities. At Cal State L.A., academic personnel evolved from a loosely coordinated confederation of part-time teachers into a tightly organized body of academic specialists. "Areas" evolved into "divisions," and divisions became a multitude of academic departments, each with its own cadre of specialists, instructional objectives, and professional identities.

The traditional focus of the academic department is specialized and singular. But urban problems are typically without focus, and are multidimensional. Organization into academic departments serves the needs of the scientist, for example, who must have immediate and convenient access to the information pool necessary to the performance of his intellectual tasks. But such an organization actually serves to frustrate interdisciplinary arrangements which are vital to urban problem solving.

Academic departments are almost exclusively *content* oriented. But the search for satisfactory solutions to controversial urban issues and problems demands *process* orientations from many diverse specialties. Academic departments are often very rigid in their structures and practices. But within the context of the urban environment, which is a swirl of political, economic, and social conflicts, urban problems demand flexibility. Indeed, the problems of the city do not correspond well to the traditional structures of academic departments. However, Cal State L.A. moved quickly and with considerable determination into a traditional departmental organization.

Under such circumstances, change is difficult. Institutional changes of any kind require either new resources or the reallocation of existing resources. But departmental structures serve as the basic units of resource allocation in colleges and universities. Resources do not follow institutional goals. They do not follow instructional objectives. In reality, they do not even follow learners. Resources are generated and allocated on the basis of the departmental unit. Given the character of the academic department, it is understandable that Cal State L.A. is unable to allocate resources to facilitate an "urban focus." The departmental structures simply do not lend themselves to such decisions.

2. *Programmatic congruity:* Academic programs are organized so

that disciplinary specializations are the pathways to graduation. These disciplinary curricula are generally designed to provide students with narrow information, and with skills in "convergent thinking." Frequently these skills are learned as a result of highly focused, even narrow experiences. The arrangement of course sequences is based upon this principle of narrowing and specializing one's intellectual skills. Urban problem solving, on the other hand, requires training in modern applied fields as well as in specialized academic fields. Such training is based on the principle of "divergent thinking," thought that incorporates multidisciplinary approaches and broadening activities.

There is another aspect to the academic program that hinders innovation in response to urban needs. Student performance data, as measured by standardized achievement tests, are often used as measures of institutional success. Similarly, an institution's graduate program is often evaluated by the academic and scholarly achievement of its students, and by their eventual placement into advanced graduate degree programs or into prestigious professional positions. Academic programs which encourage various kinds of field experience in lieu of course experience fail to produce learner outcomes which are measurable in these traditional manners. "Applied programs" do not offer students, faculty members, or the institutions themselves many rewards. Indeed, if success is determined on the basis of student achievement scores, advanced placement, and prestigiously placed graduates, there are distinct liabilities associated with such applied programs.

Cal State L.A. has moved almost entirely away from lower-division, general education programs of study. As cited earlier, less than 20 percent of the college's enrollment are currently freshmen and sophomores. Furthermore, longitudinal studies of the degree programs at Cal State L.A. show clearly that applied studies are declining in number. On the one hand, the students reflect a strong urban orientation in their attitudes, values, and orientations. On the other hand, they reflect an increasing conformity to traditional college programs and degrees (Dash, 1975). The "urban" theme may be dying.

3. *Support by academic personnel:* Faculty typically prefer the organizational characteristics of traditional departments. Faculty members are highly specialized in their academic disciplines, and highly professionalized in their departmental associations. As specialists, they adhere to peer group norms, even beyond their commitment to the broader missions of the university. Faculty reward systems are typically based upon research, scholarly productivity, and

specialized teaching. In short, college and university faculty members reflect their training and their acquired professional values through their attitudes, professional practices, and departmental associations. This specialized focus, coupled with a strong professional orientation, shows considerable resistance to change and innovation.

Distinction must be made, however, between the full-time faculty member and the part-time instructor. At Cal State L.A., part-time faculty still account for over 45 percent of the instruction. In the fields of business, health services, and some of the sciences, 50 to 60 percent of the faculty are part-time. Because it is located in Los Angeles, the college is able to hire practicing professionals willing to teaching part-time. The net effect is economical in one sense, but costly in another.

The services to the institution and its students provided by part-time faculty members are not comparable to those provided by full-time faculty members. Generally, an increase in part-time faculty creates a proportionately increased service burden on full-time faculty. Students still require advisers. Committees still require members. And the more time that faculty members must stay on the campus, the less time they have to conduct research and provide services to the urban environment.

In 1975, the full-time faculty members at Cal State L.A. were not heavily involved in community-based activities, perhaps because of interest, perhaps because of time, perhaps because of the academic reward system. At the same time, the part-time faculty members were not heavily involved in scholarly activities. The high percentage of part-time faculty apparently does not increase flexibility, at least in terms of the diversity of academic activities.

In 1975, there was little evidence that the Cal State L.A. faculty was much different from the faculties at other campuses of the California State University system. In fact, uniformity in personnel policies, academic review policies, teaching standards, research practices, and curriculum ensures that faculties throughout the system are quite similar.

Academic Tradition versus Environmental Demand

Is it legitimate to say that in higher education uniformity prevails and diversity is disappearing? Some researchers think so. However, there is evidence that the student population at Cal State L.A. is very diverse, and becoming more pluralistic each year (Dash, 1975). Faculty members are still predominantly from western graduate schools, but slowly the numbers are increasing from the midwestern and eastern sections of the country. By these measures, diversity is still prevalent on the campus.

The debate does not seem to be between diversity and uniformity, but rather between academic tradition and environmental demands. In this sense, the story of Cal State L.A. is relevant not only to other urban colleges and universities, but to nearly all postsecondary institutions today. Perhaps as at no other time in the twentieth century, American higher education must develop methods to reconcile the conflict between public expectations and institutional capabilities.

Cal State L.A. is fully capable of becoming a model urban university. Although there are structural, procedural, and traditional barriers to urbanization reforms, the tools are available for such reform. These tools are the organization of the campus, its programs, and its faculties.

For higher education, the great lesson of the 1960's should be that satellite programs and ancillary services do not survive without institutionalization. The urban focus of Cal State L.A. must be institutionalized: in its programs, not simply its departments; in its faculty employment, promotion, and review practices, not simply its assignments to teaching courses; and in its student recruitment practices. Some have argued that increased centralization of the California State University and College system has cost campuses their individuality and their autonomy. But Cal State L.A. has not lived up to its charter. And without a serious effort to institutionalize the necessary supports for an urban university, that vision will probably be lost.

References

California State Department of Education. *A Master Plan for Higher Education in California 1960-75.* Sacramento: The Department, 1960.

Dash, Roger Evans. *A Developing State University: California State University, Los Angeles.* Ph.D. dissertation, University of California, Los Angeles, 1975.

Dvonin, E. *Urban University.* San Diego: Public Affairs Research Institute, San Diego State College, 1969.

Earhardt, A. *Twenty-one.* Los Angeles: California State University, Los Angeles, 1967.

PART III

The Environmental Context

10

The Public and Higher Education in California

John Vasconcellos and Patrick Callan

Our commentary will deal primarily with the conflict between egalitarianism and competitive excellence and the implications of those values for planning the future of California higher education. In our initial comments, we discuss our impressions of the general cultural and social context of higher education in the 1970's. We are in a period of remarkable and unprecedented differentiation of values which must be taken into account as we ponder the future. In the latter part of the commentary, we suggest some specific implications of this value differentiation for higher education.

Excellence and equality must be reincorporated or redefined to be operative values, with operative meanings, relevant to our place in time, in our culture. Almost everything about us is changing—our world, our society, our institutions, and our people. And each of us must wonder what *excellence* and *equality* mean for human beings sharing our culture today.

Institutional change and crisis are the hallmarks of our times. Many of our important social institutions—the family, church, school, government, and the university—are either besieged financially, rapidly losing the people's allegiance, or finding their very

Reprinted from *Public Higher Education in California*, edited by Neil J. Smelser and Gabriel Almond (Berkeley: University of California Press, 1974). Copyright 1974 by The Regents of the University of California.

legitimacy challenged. Throughout our society, we are in a time of radical change, accompanied by a remarkable loss of credibility among those persons and institutions which have traditionally been the sources of value, authority, and power. Higher education and the university are not immune to this change, and their future must be explored in the light of their intimate relationship with our entire cultural transformation.

We find our society existing at this point in history between conflicting cultures, each experientially grounded and each with its own value system and ethic. Although the diversity of persons and views is very great and simplification can be hazardous, we believe the contemporary cultural conflict can best be understood as the clash of two cultural models. Let us refer to them as the old culture and the new culture. The old culture was generated in a world of scarcity—most notably from our basic struggle for survival and from the insecurity of the depression. The new culture has been more recently generated—since World War II—in a time of affluence (the problems of distribution notwithstanding).

For persons whose gut experience is scarcity, the moral imperative is competition; but for persons whose gut experience is plenty, the moral imperative is sharing. The old culture emphasizes work, intellectuality, accumulation, elitism, and conformity. In more difficult times, these values were necessary for personal and collective survival. But the new culture rejects the work ethic, rejects conformity, is more sensuous in its orientation, more democratic, and more trusting of diversity, feelings, and the human body.

Such different cultures, with such different moral imperatives, result in contrary attitudes and values about almost everything—the value of human life, freedom, responsibility, war, peace, consciousness, drugs, marriage, sexuality, God, religion, pleasure, property, emotions, the human body—even human nature and human potential—and, likely, even about excellence and about quality. The most fundamental divergence has to do with the nature and value of human life. The implicit bias underlying the traditional culture and its institutions is that man is evil, depraved, sinful, or—at best—neutral, and that he must look to institutions, authority, religion, education, and the like to save him. The new culture assumes man's fundamental and spontaneous responsibility and trustworthiness and sees the old culture's institutions, with their negative assumptions, as the greatest threat to personal wholeness and integrity.

It is ironic that the achievements of our old culture and its traditional values, along with the sacrifices and generosity of its people,

have helped give birth to a new and different culture. Beyond this
irony is the painful realization that the experiences and perceptions
of many persons who have grown up in this new kind of world—in
the past twenty-five years—are radically different, in their expectations as human beings, in their attitudes, and in their most deeply
held values. It is not so much a matter of choice, nor a matter of
preference, nor a matter of right and wrong that underlies our split
cultures, but rather a matter of experiencing the evolved character of
our world. And along with affluence we have technology, automa-
tion, universal education, rapid transportation, and the mass media—
all leading to an evolving consciousness, an evolving character of
humanity. This takes shape as something very different in the way
human beings experience life, how they think, how they feel, how
they believe, how they hope, and even how they love.

No wonder we recognize a cultural crisis and an institutional crisis.
Our institutions, including the university, were conceived and constructed out of the old experience, the old culture, the traditional
ethic—and they served them well. In fact, though, our institutions
served traditional values so well that they evolved a new world, a new
experience, a new culture, a new consciousness, and a new ethic.

Along with the new experience, and probably as a result of universal education and the mass media, there exists a curious, and by now
obvious, demystification process. It is much like the way science in
the past served to demystify religion, and all the world was transformed as persons began to see through old myths of power, authority, and truth. Today, in similar fashion more and more persons are
unwilling to accept without argument, to swallow whole, what is told
them by persons in positions of power, command, and governance.
Questions are being asked, little is taken for granted, the burden of
proof is often on those in authority.

And along with the new experience comes a process of *horizontalization,* especially the horizontalization of institutions. Our traditional institutions depend on a model of someone up above, with
power, truth, and answers, making the decisions for all the rest of us
and handing these decisions on down, often in the form of rules for
us to follow. In our society today such vertical authority is under
attack within most of our traditional institutions—family, religion,
work, government, and education, including the university. The new-
culture persons are much less willing to accept from on high what
some authority says is true, or right, or what you ought to do, or
how you ought to be; instead, there is a thrust from the bottom that
is upending almost every institution in our society.

And along with the new experience of our radically changed external world comes a radically different experience of our internal world. Throughout history, we have lived in a world of scarcity; as a result, man chose—in order to survive—to limit himself, to suppress his body and his emotions in order to concentrate all his energy in his intellect and thereby encounter and conquer the threatening environment.

Now, in this new world which we have created and entered, man can relax some, let himself be and become more whole, functioning not only through his intellect but as a complete person of mind and body and emotions, functioning holistically. Franklin Murphy, former chancellor of UCLA, has characterized this evolution as man now choosing to become the being of "I feel, therefore I am."

Somewhere, somehow, in this movement out of an old world culture, we see emerging something new in the way human beings experience and envision themselves—a radically different way for human beings to see human nature, potential, values, relationships, and institutions.

What are the significant implications for the future of our institutions, for the future of the university?

First, we must recognize that the tensions between excellence and equality are endemic to our entire society. From our legislative-political perspective, the conflict between these values seems to be present in all our public institutions and public policy processes. It is not surprising, then, that we have institutionalized this tension in our system of higher education.

It is important to recognize that Americans have always defined both excellence and equality in terms of competition. Just as excellence has usually meant competitive excellence, equality has meant equality in competition. Richard Hofstadter made this point well when he stated that "American traditions . . . show a strong bias toward egalitarian democracy, but it has been a democracy in cupidity rather than a democracy in fraternity."

The problem with competition is that it tends to imply a single standard of excellence and a single standard of equality. This works reasonably well when there is consensus about values and standards. But it breaks down when there is disagreement and polarization about values. Today there is in our society and culture just such a breakdown of consensus. And the times demand a rethinking and restatement of the meaning of *excellence* and of *equality*.

The most basic assumptions and premises about human life are at issue here. It is from what persons experience of themselves and their lives that they derive their vision of man and human nature and human potential; thus it is from their vision of man that they derive conceptions of excellence and equality. And it is in a society divided over the nature of man and the meaning of life that we are now faced with the necessity to reexamine our values and their relationship to institutions of learning.

Second, it might be hoped that the university could be the place where both models—of culture and of man—could be tested, and where a valuable dialogue between new and old would occur. But the university is so much a part of the traditional culture that it shares most of its assumptions and, for the most part, resists the notion that there might be another legitimate model.

The university is the servant of the traditional culture in at least three important ways: for one, in its exclusive emphasis upon intellectuality, abstraction, and theory. There is little regard for experiential learning, little respect for the affective domain of human life. The university fragments man just as its disciplines fragment knowledge. The affective and cognitive are split, and as a result, it is forgotten that the whole man may be greater than the sum of his separated parts. (Yet recent research demonstrates the relationship of affective and cognitive development.)

In addition, the university assumes that most persons learn at the same rate in the same sequence—the *lockstep* so much discussed recently. This is basically an industrial assembly line model of learning, which relies on an external uniform standard rather than on the needs and wants of the individual person. It also implies that the institution, and not the persons served, knows best what its clients need.

Moreover, the university is elitist. In its educational processes, the university has perpetuated the socioeconomic dominance of the haves while doing little for the have-nots. California's Master Plan provides a good case study here. Despite our claims that higher education provides an avenue of social mobility, we persist in using culturally, economically, and socially biased admissions criteria that exclude most lower- and lower-middle-class persons from our "better" institutions. The same holds true in research, where universities and their faculties have served the powerful (agribusiness, the Department of Defense) and, in so doing, have helped perpetuate a socioeconomic order stacked heavily in favor of those with wealth and power. We are suggesting that the new culture challenges our universities to become genuinely person-centered and pluralistic—not only in its intellectual dialogue but also in its teaching, learning, and research.

Third, our difficulties are not simply the simpler ones of different thinking; rather, they are the more complex and painful ones of different feelings, and different visions, and different values. This is true throughout our society. The conflicts on our campuses, in our streets, cities, and ghettos are conflicts of differing experiences, perceptions, and values. So we cannot expect our path to be comfortable or easy.

Fourth, it is in our institutions of higher education that this cultural revolution has been experienced most painfully, because it is precisely within them that the persons and aspirations of the new culture collide with the traditional way things have been.

In *The Pursuit of Loneliness,* Philip Slater suggests that higher education may be hopelessly caught between the new and the old cultures. The persons who pay for colleges and universities are mostly persons of the old culture, who will not continue to pay if higher education caters to the perceived needs, wants, and goals of new-culture persons. But if higher education refuses to cater to the new culture, young persons may well destroy or abandon it (there is already much evidence of both). If Slater is correct, the universities are in danger of being destroyed in the collision of the two cultures.

However, there is another possibility. The universities could become the place where our society learns the value of tolerating and respecting and encouraging diversity. If we can envision and realize this possibility, the conflict between excellence and equality may be much less severe than we have imagined. And because these are indeed revolutionary times which (to paraphrase Lincoln) respect neither old lines nor old laws, we may ultimately come to the place where excellence and equality converge. Somehow, then, discovering how to bridge this gap between cultures is a life-or-death adventure for our public institutions of higher education.

Fifth, we must confront and accept the realization that there is no going back. There is no way to abolish television, or technology, or universal education—and these are precisely the forces and conditions that bring us into a new world, with its new culture and new persons. Because the old balance cannot be revived, we must discover and strike a new balance.

Sixth, in so doing, we must recognize that persons at the bottom of our society, who have not shared equally in opportunity (for whatever reason), have now seen, for the first time, what they are missing. The availability of television and other media in every home, in every city, in every part of our country, has let every person at the bottom see what others have. And they are constantly urged to want and to expect and to struggle for those very things. And besides the thrust toward material equality, we have the liberation movements—black or women or gay or Chicano or children or whatever.

The have-nots—materially or psychologically—aren't going to be put aside or ignored; they are here to stay, and they deserve to stay. What they are probably doing, most profoundly, is proposing and reaching for a new operative definition of *equality* (what does it mean to be equal as a person?)—a definition that recognizes the inherent and equal value and worth of each individual human being and the inherent right of each person to be himself.

Seventh, we must recognize that it is not only those persons at the bottom who are envisioning themselves and life and human existence in a new way. At the same time we find those students, our pride and joy, who have done the very best in school, who come to "the best" of our educational institutions, experiencing and envisioning life in a new way. The most sensitive of our better students are the persons who are most readily sharing in the attempted redefinition of *equality*.

They are asking our society and higher education to redefine *excellence* and adapt to pluralistic models of excellence. Certainly, the traditional model and traditional learning experiences should be available to those who wish to pursue them. But other models should be available, including noncompetitive models which recognize that: (a) learning and growth are valuable in themselves; (b) learning and growth are often best judged by the learner in relation to his own life, rather than by comparison with the achievements of others; (c) experiential learning is as valuable as purely intellectual learning; and (d) affective and cognitive learning are inextricably interrelated. And they may well be searching out another new and operative definition of *excellence*. What does it mean to be an excellent human being, what does it mean to be a person?

Thus we have, at this point in time, persons on the bottom and persons on the top reaching toward a new vision, a new search, a new ethic. Persons at the top and bottom are moving away from allegiance to institutions toward allegiance to persons. They are moving away from elitism and competition and moving toward a more democratic society. This ought to be recognized as a rejection neither of excellence nor of equality, but only of our traditional idea of these terms, in a search for new and more human meanings for both.

Eighth, we must recognize, and nourish, the movement of our society away from elitism (although not away from excellence) and toward equality. We have already experienced some movement away from a social, political, or religious elite. More powerfully now, we are experiencing a rejection of racial elitism and of sexual elitism—each so deeply ingrained in so many of us and in our public institutions.

But there is another elitism which is now being questioned—our bias about who we are as human beings, and about the respective values of the various parts of ourselves as human beings. For many years, Western man has assumed the elitism of intellect over body. We have so elevated the intellect as the measure of a person that we readily judge and categorize him by measuring his intelligence quotient. And the university is the very embodiment of this most basic elitism—no wonder it is experiencing so much challenge and conflict and pain. We must now examine the origins and the appropriateness and the ramifications of the mind-body split which underlies Western culture. This examination is not intended to separate out our intellects; rather, it ought to elevate our bodies to their existential place as coequal partners of the whole human being.

Ninth, Rosemary Park suggests that the problem of institutions is the lack of consensus about the definition of an *educated man*. Far deeper and more vital is the lack of consensus about the nature of man, and about the meaning and value of individual human life.

The answers are not clear, but each of us must begin by asking the right questions. Those questions and our responses must fully recognize and accept all the human reality of our times.

We must recognize ourselves, and all other human beings, and all that is happening within and between and to human beings today. In times of scarcity, persons need to curtail themselves, and conform and fit together artificially, in order to survive; in times of affluence, they can and will be more unique and whole and diverse.

In times of ignorance, persons could be kept down; in times of universal education and mass communication, persons must be encouraged up! Individual persons are bringing themselves, with their minds and bodies and feelings and needs and wants, to institutions of higher education. They will be differing persons, with differing experiences, needs, wants, goals, and expectations. The true criterion for higher education is whether it will respond to each of them, to their individuality.

The real challenge for higher education today is whether it is ready and able and willing to envision a new model of man, and to recognize and respond to the new man and woman knocking at its doors.

11

Law and Higher Education in California

Robert M. O'Neil

Late in the spring of 1965, after calm had returned to Sproul Plaza and Mario Savio had retired from campus politics, the University of California received claims for special police costs from the cities of Berkeley and Oakland and the county of Alameda. The amounts were substantial, reflecting many hours of arduous duty clearing Sproul Hall during the December sit-in. For several reasons, the legal posture of these claims was quite uncertain. An obscure provision of the California Government Code obligated the mayor or police chief to "direct a sufficient number of policemen to attend and keep order at any public meeting at which, in his opinion, a breach of the peace may occur"—a prescription which arguably covered the finale of the Free Speech Movement. Yet the university, unlike many institutions of higher learning that rely on the local police, had its own security force. Some fifty uniformed officers were assigned to the Berkeley campus alone, and they were on duty during the sit-in. Thus the university's liability for supplemental police services was problematical.

Scarcely had the claims been presented, however, than the vice-president and general counsel advised the regents that they need pay only the city of Oakland; Berkeley and Alameda County, he argued,

Reprinted from *Public Higher Education in California*, edited by Neil J. Smelser and Gabriel Almond (Berkeley: University of California Press, 1974). Copyright 1974 by The Regents of the University of California.

were legally required to police the campus and thus could claim no extra compensation for the unusual services rendered at Sproul Hall.

Several important lessons emerge from this episode. First, it suggests that more vital decisions concerning the legal status of the university are probably rendered by the judge in University Hall than by the judge in city hall. Like many university and college attorneys, the regents' general counsel has the power and authority to determine when the university's decisions and policies will be tested in court, and under what circumstances. On countless occasions, in negotiations, in the writing of briefs, and during argument in court, he and his associates must represent the legal views of the regents on questions about which there has been little or no time for actual consultation.

Second, this process of lawmaking and adjudication occurs almost exclusively in University Hall. Although many, perhaps most, large state systems of higher education have decentralized legal services along with other aspects of administration, the University of California (and the state colleges) have kept a very tight central rein. Moreover, the tendency has been to impose on the other eight campuses a set of legal principles responsive to the special problems of Berkeley, because the flagship campus generates the bulk of the difficult legal controversies. There is neither mechanism nor occasion to determine fully the appropriateness of such principles for the vastly different needs of Riverside, Santa Cruz, or Santa Barbara. Once the law has been made for Berkeley, it applies, however imperfectly, to the rest of the system.

Third, and perhaps most important, the general counsel's advice in 1965 reveals much about the University of California's legal status. The much vaunted autonomy of the university has in fact been invoked when convenient or necessary, but is often disregarded when unnecessary or inconvenient. If the issue in 1965 had been the right of city or county police officers to enter a campus building without invitation, the official response would likely have been quite different. But for the question of which governmental agency should bear the cost of several thousand hours of overtime police pay, the protective aspect of the constitutional autonomy was conveniently overlooked.

These observations suggest several pertinent themes in the relationship between law and higher education. At the heart of the matter is the concept of autonomy, to which I devote most of my attention here. Autonomy exists or occurs in California at two distinct levels. The role of autonomy within the public sector—deriving from the special constitutional status of the regents—tends to be considerably exaggerated. Yet another form of autonomy—that which differentiates the public institutions of higher learning from their tax-supported counterparts—is largely neglected in studies of California higher education. We shall consider both the intrasystem and the intersystem aspect of this elusive concept.

Autonomy: The Unimportance of Being Constitutional

It is widely believed, at least among educators, that the University of California derives some mystical independence from Article IX, Section 9 of the state constitution. In recent testimony before the Constitutional Revision Commission, President Hitch argued that this provision has given the university "a necessary measure of autonomy for one hundred years" and that "constitutional protection [is] vital to the University. . . ." This view is widely shared throughout the state, among faculty and students as well as citizens, parents, and taxpayers. Were the constitutional status of the university seriously jeopardized, a cry of opposition would doubtless arise. The vital question for consideration here is what justifies the faith in constitutional autonomy.

Whose autonomy? First, it must be understood that whatever autonomy the constitution does confer extends directly to the regents rather than to the university—much less to the individual campuses. In an ideal world, of course, the interests of university and governing board would be virtually identical, so that a guarantee enjoyed by one would be fully shared by the other. However, few persons would be naive enough to claim that such a harmonious relationship exists in California.

A few recent examples will suggest how grave is the threat to campus autonomy from the governing board. Having delegated to the chancellors all responsibility for reviewing and approving nontenure academic appointments, the regents nonetheless withdrew that authority in the summer of 1970 just long enough to terminate the employment of Angela Davis—well before any charges arose from the Marin Courthouse shoot-out. About the same time, the regents withdrew curricular responsibility delegated to the faculty. Some years ago the board had invested the Committee on Courses of the Berkeley Division of the Academic Senate with broad authority to review and approve new courses for academic credit. As against the campus chancellor, this power substantially limited administrative initiative in curricular innovation. Yet when the regents learned that Eldridge

Cleaver was scheduled to give several lectures in Social Analysis 139x during the fall of 1969, they withdrew that authority from the Committee on Courses and denied credit—not only for the originally scheduled course, but also for a hastily devised independent study option offered by a regular department. This action soon became the subject of a lawsuit, brought by a group of aggrieved students and faculty members.

Such incidents suggest that there may in fact be an inverse correlation between the governing board's legal independence and the effective autonomy of the university. Two explanations are plausible. The regents may feel that because of the constitution they are less likely to be held accountable by judges or legislators for violations of campus or individual freedom. Alternatively, the board may fear that a failure to keep their own house in order—even to the extent of anticipating the demands of hostile constituencies—would ultimately jeopardize their constitutional stature. Ironically, the regents' autonomy may have been diluted and cheapened by the very process of trying to preserve it. Whatever the explanation, the evidence does suggest that the University of California campuses may be less autonomous than their counterparts in other states precisely because the body that governs them enjoys a special constitutional status.

Autonomy *within* the systems—both California systems—is diminished in another important way. Unlike most large and complex state university networks, the vital function of legal counseling and representation remains wholly centralized. No provision is made for quick rendering of legal advice by a local attorney, or for the handling in local courts of small matters that may involve a campus several hundred miles from Berkeley or Los Angeles. The fact is that campus autonomy is only as substantial as the chief administrative officer's capacity to make his own decisions and defend his actions when challenged. Even if all other administrative functions were to be decentralized in both systems, the continued reliance upon a single legal office would measurably circumscribe campus autonomy.

Ultimately, whatever autonomy the regents or the university may enjoy is *gubernatorial,* because the governor retains the sole authority to appoint all but the ex officio members of the board. When the Michigan constitutional model was borrowed and adapted, the provision for popular election of regents was omitted. Subsequent attempts to require senate approval as a check have been resisted, although the state college trustees must now be confirmed and the proposed new California constitution would add this step to the selection process. The vesting of exclusive appointment power in the state's chief executive is a mixed blessing, to be sure. Popular election of regents works quite well in Michigan, giving the university a striking degree of real autonomy. Yet in Colorado, a popular election several years ago subjected the university to the ultraconservative hegemony of a Denver brewer and precipitated a crisis in academic freedom. Moreover, one need hardly point out that the sixth of the California board that *is* popularly elected—four of the ex officio Regents—has caused a disproportionate share of the university's problems in the last decade.

Senate confirmation or legislative assent is not a complete guarantor of integrity. The University of Minnesota discovered this several years ago, when the state senate declined to confirm several nominees for reappointment because of apparent pique with the board's tolerance for student and faculty activism. Had the governor had exclusive authority, these renominations would have gone through unchallenged.

Clearly the result in each state depends very much on the vagaries of partisan politics and other rapidly changing realities. But a special risk inheres in the California system. A governor can, in four years, effectively impose his political and educational philosophy on the university to a degree that other constituencies may not undo for eight to ten years. (In fact it may not even take that long. Governor Reagan had working control of the regents—sufficient at least to obtain the discharge of President Kerr—within weeks of taking office.)

Recent events provide dramatic confirmation of the extent of gubernatorial control over the university. Few issues have been more troublesome of late than the level of faculty salaries. First the legislature refused to act, although University of California compensation was falling behind that of competitive institutions in other states. Then, after the 1970 election, a new liberal majority twice passed salary increase appropriations, only to have them vetoed by the governor. This experience suggests how far the fox has been entrusted with custody of the chickens; what the governor cannot accomplish in his role as president of the Board of Regents, he may nonetheless be able to achieve as chief executive of the state.

Autonomy and the courts. Any review of court cases would suggest that the University of California has fared quite well before the bar of justice. Seldom has a lawsuit against the regents gone much beyond the threshold. Countless claims have been dismissed on demurrer or by summary judgment after review of relevant policies and documents. From the successful suit by Berkeley students challenging compulsory ROTC in the 1930's to the unsuccessful suit by former ASUC President Dan Siegel to regain the campus office from which disciplinary action had removed him in 1970, the pattern of litigation has been quite uniform. Thus the general counsel argues with some force that the judicial deference of the thirties survives into the seventies, even if the university is not absolutely immune from suit for its acts and omissions.

The real explanation for the university's relative invulnerability to suit lies somewhat deeper. A vital difference between California and other states may lie in the relative accessibility of legal remedies. In New York, by contrast, institutions of higher learning—both public and private—are often brought to bar. Courts have required that degrees be granted, that courses be rescheduled, that students be reinstated, and even (although ultimately reversed) that tuition be repaid for classes missed during the Kent-Cambodia aftermath. But there is a special explanation for the New York pattern: Article 78 of the Code of Civil Procedure makes the acts of a wide range of public agents, corporate officials, and others readily reviewable in the state's trial courts. Institutional accountability is thus built into the procedural laws of the state, although the draftsmen of the code had no thought of universities when they framed Article 78.

There is a rather substantial deterrent to lawsuits against the University of California. A new section added to the Education Code in 1967 provides that the regents, when sued, may demand that a plaintiff post security to cover the probable costs of the litigation. The amount of the security is to be set at $100 for each plaintiff, or more if the court deems appropriate. If judgment is rendered in favor of the regents, "allowable costs incurred by the regents in the action shall be awarded against the plaintiffs." Thus one now sues the university at his peril.

It is difficult to measure the impact of such differences in state procedural laws, for the *volume* of potential litigation varies widely among states according to the number of litigable issues arising on campuses, the availability of legal services, the applicable substantive law, and other factors. At least it can be said that getting into court is somewhat more difficult and probably costlier for the aggrieved faculty member or student in California than in many other states, and that once in court the scope of review is likely to be narrower.

There is a second factor that tells more about the *integrity* of California institutions of higher learning than about their *autonomy*. Throughout the 1960's, California deans (both student and academic) were generally ahead of the courts with regard to procedures employed for student discipline and faculty termination cases. Thus the warrant for judicial intervention was lessened by the impression of fairness and tidiness within the academy.

When Arthur Goldberg and three other students brought suit challenging their suspension for leading the Filthy Speech Movement in the spring of 1965, the courts may have had some doubts about the looseness of the substantive regulations, but they were so favorably impressed with the thoroughness and impartiality of the Committee on Student Conduct that the suit was dismissed. A year or two later, when a former teacher at San Jose State College (by then a state assemblyman) sued to regain his position, the courts abstained for similar reasons after reviewing the exhaustive procedures followed on campus prior to the termination. A student at the College of San Mateo brought suit in the federal district court after he had been suspended on an interim basis pending a disciplinary hearing; again probable fairness of the procedure awaiting him led the court to dismiss without critical analysis of the substantive issues. Examples of such judicial deference are legion, and suggest that abstention reflects a basic confidence in the fairness of California public colleges and universities far more than it reflects the phrasing of the constitution. Were that confidence to be shaken by summary or arbitrary dismissals—a most unlikely prospect in California higher education—the judicial response would doubtless change to accommodate different conditions.

One very recent case will suggest the limits of constitutional autonomy in the courts. A third-year medical student at the San Francisco campus brought suit claiming he had been denied entry to the fourth year on arbitrary and improper grounds. The general counsel for the regents simply filed a demurrer—a legal claim that even if all the facts alleged in the complaint could be proved, no cause of action would be made out entitling the plaintiff to relief. The matter was obviously a sensitive one, because the suit asked in effect for a judicial inquiry into the fairness of an academic judgment about a student. Nonetheless, the Court of Appeal reversed the summary dismissal of the complaint. For the first time, a court held that even the *academic* judgments of the University of California are potentially subject to judicial scrutiny upon a showing of arbitrary, capricious, or malicious criteria. However unlikely it may be that the plaintiff could ever bring his claim within these criteria, the precedent is nonetheless important.

Autonomy and the legislature. Whatever the constitution may say, the university's actual autonomy extends only as far as the legislature is willing to respect it or the courts are willing to protect it when it is threatened. The practical differences between the university and the state colleges in this regard tend to be exaggerated. (The comparison may be imperfect. The university has been a more frequent target of criticism in recent years and thus perhaps more vulnerable to external threats because of its greater visibility. But recent events have begun to shift the focus from one system to another.)

There are essentially two ways of measuring the independence of the university from the legislature. The first and most obvious is to examine the legislation, to appraise the areas in which the lawmakers have deferred and those in which they have regulated. The pattern is quite mixed. One example of apparent deference concerns academic tenure and faculty promotions. In 1970, the legislature apparently felt the university was too lax about hiring senior faculty from outside the system without a probationary period. Rather than abolish initial tenured appointments, however, the lawmakers passed a joint resolution "call[ing] upon the University of California to alter its academic tenure policy" in the suggested manner. Apparently the regents duly received this advice, considered it, but took no steps to act on it.

Perhaps the strongest manifestation of legislative respect was the failure of the threatened investigation of the Berkeley campus to materialize after the Free Speech Movement. Yet the explanation for inaction at that time appears to lie much more in political realities than in constitutional autonomy. As speaker of the assembly, Jesse Unruh was an ex officio regent, and was thus called upon to authorize an investigation of events and actions he had partially condoned. Moreover, the regents had taken the initiative in launching a major investigation of their own, headed by a Los Angeles attorney seemingly satisfactory to both conservatives and liberals. Third, and perhaps most important, Unruh had developed early rapport with and strong confidence in the acting chancellor of the Berkeley campus. To have sanctioned the investigation while a new administration was trying to restore calm and order might have seriously undermined that relationship. Thus the investigation never did in fact materialize —and to this extent an important aspect of the university's integrity was apparently preserved.

It is also true that the University of California has been somewhat freer from legislative intrusion than large public systems in other states. There have not been the kinds of full-scale investigations launched in 1970 by the legislatures of Ohio, Indiana, Illinois, and Virginia, among others. The University of California faculties have been spared the work load conditions and restrictions imposed in

Michigan, Florida, New York, and Washington—although the reprieve may be only temporary. The California legislature has never imposed on student financial aids the sort of attaint imposed by Pennsylvania's lawmakers in 1969. Nor have the officers of the relevant California legislative committees ever given gratuitous "advice" to the campus presidents and chancellors, as was done in Minnesota after the close of the 1971 regular session. In these respects, a measure of autonomy seems to have accompanied the special constitutional status of the regents.

However, the impression is partly deceptive. A substantial, and apparently increasing, number of potentially intrusive California laws apply indiscriminately to all three public systems. The definition of resident student status is supplied by the legislature for all systems. The Coordinating Council has the power to "require" all public higher institutions to "submit data on costs, selection and retention of students, enrollments, plan capacities, and other matters pertinent to effective planning and coordination," and this applies equally to regents and trustees. All governing boards are required by recent legislation to keep records of rejected applicants, to develop and utilize "an information system" to reflect redirection patterns, and the like. All systems are to report regularly to the legislature "on the progress made on the implementation of the enrollment plans and admissions priorities system." In these and other respects, the university receives no special immunity from state legislation that reaches into internal affairs and system management.

There is a risk in looking too closely at the trees, however, and forgetting the forest—some might say jungle—that is the Master Plan itself. By the very process of insulating the university from the other two systems, the legislature has restricted flexibility and closed options. If the Master Plan tells the university what it may do (and what others may not do), it also tells Berkeley and UCLA what they may not do. Moreover, as Smelser has shown so forcefully, "in the last analysis the authorization for growth must come in large part from the state legislature." Without the assent and support of the lawmakers, there is very little the regents can do on their own to shape or change the character of the system.

To look simply at statutes, as we have done up to this point, is to neglect a major artery of legislative intrusion, the budget and appropriation process. Soon after the Kent-Cambodia crisis and the "reconstitution" of classes, key committees of both houses in Sacramento took clearly punitive measures against the university. First, the Finance Committee of the state senate struck from the budget a proposed 5 percent cost of living increase in University of California faculty salaries. A few days later the Ways and Means Committee of the assembly deleted an item earmarked for the support of the Academic Senate. This latter action, explained the committee chairman, was designed "to shake them up." "What does the Academic Senate do," he queried, "but make themselves obnoxious? Why don't they fund themselves out of their own dues?" With a stroke of the legislative pen, the mightiest organ of faculty self-government in the United States was badly crippled; a body that could terrify chancellors and worry regents was no match for the state legislature. (Some of the cuts were later restored, and the senate limped through the year on a meager austerity budget.)

What may be the sharpest blow of all has been reserved until last, because it is a glancing blow—the legislation to invest the state colleges with the nomenclature of universities. Superficially, this has no bearing on the university's status. Yet the relationship is too clear to require elaborate demonstration. Despite the insistence of supporters that the name change portends no abandonment of the Master Plan's structural distinction between systems, the prospects are ominous. Chancellor Bowker properly fears that a "state university" may soon be authorized to develop new doctoral programs, when "even within the University of California, Berkeley faces strong competition for scarce funds from new and growing campuses with their own plans for doctoral programs." Yet the governor, on signing the name change bill, claimed to be mystified by the university's anxiety, adding—as though to assuage the fears—"I love the university; I show no favorites."

The lesson is fairly simple: The autonomy of one entity can be impaired as much by strengthening a competitor as by weakening the original beneficiary. Whether or not the state college trustees ever attain constitutional status (as proposed by the constitutional revision), the major battle may already have been won simply by altering a single word in the title. The actual decision as to which campuses may become universities has been left to the trustees and the Coordinating Council—the very Coordinating Council that recently suggested dismantling the smaller foreign language programs at Berkeley, UCLA, and Davis.

How has the university's autonomy fared in the courts? Although this is not the place to examine the cases at length, a brief summary of the law may be useful. A group of early cases have been cited as establishing nearly absolute university autonomy in the face of conflicting or threatening legislation. But careful review suggests that the early decisions were rather narrow in sustaining the university's claims and that their holdings have been inflated by several later cases, and especially by a series of attorney general's opinions in the 1940's and 1950's. In 1913, for example, the California Supreme Court recognized that the regents possessed "a larger degree of independence and discretion with respect to [matters covered by general state law] than is usually held to exist in such inferior boards and commissions as are solely the subjects of legislative creation and control."

When the critical showdown came, forty years later, the limits of the regents' autonomy were clearly marked. The conflict was between the loyalty oath required of all state employees and the special supplemental oath the regents had imposed on the university faculty. The California Supreme Court held that a supervening statewide concern (loyalty of all public employees) gave the general law primacy over supplemental regents' orders. (It is possible, of course, that the court was simply making bad law in a good cause, lacking the votes to declare the oath unconstitutional, as the state's high court did fifteen years later. Bad law or not, the decision in the oath case is nonetheless important law on the issue of autonomy.)

The two issues that will really test the extent of university autonomy have yet to reach the courts. One of these is the validity of the Master Plan itself, which may someday be challenged because of the distinctions it draws between institutions and systems. Precisely such a challenge has already been mounted in the federal courts of New York against the CUNY-SUNY stratification. In a brief opinion several months ago, a district judge sustained the corresponding New York legislation. The judgment is rather superficial, however, and the last word remains to be spoken on this issue.

The other issue lurking around the corner is the applicability to the university of general public employee collective bargaining legislation which is almost certain to be enacted within the next five years. Perhaps for the first time in the autonomy struggle, challenges to such a law would pit the regents against the legislature, with the university faculties sharply divided. The dilemma for the professors would be acute: Those who most clearly favored collective bargaining would probably also be most reluctant to see the university's autonomy waived for other purposes, and those who opposed collective bargaining might be more willing to forfeit autonomy on other issues. Yet ultimately sides would have to be chosen, depending essentially on the relative importance of the immediate conflict versus the future value of the university's special status.

Autonomy and the regents. I began this section by suggesting that whatever autonomy does exist is more the regents' than the university's. If the original autonomy has been squandered, therefore, the governing board is primarily accountable, at least in its lack of vigilance.

There is, first, the matter of the charges for supplemental police services. Seemingly to avoid payment of a rather substantial bill, the general counsel declared that Berkeley and Alameda police were supposed to be on the campus anyway and could not claim overtime. Later, when an Oakland housewife demanded to see the confidential lists of officers and bylaws of student political organizations on the Berkeley campus, the files were opened on orders from University Hall—apparently in the belief that these were "public documents" made accessible to any applicant by a general state law. (Later, when a Berkeley law student brought suit to enjoin the university from disclosing such information, the university formally—and successfully—defended its open-file policy, thus in a sense making a virtue of its waiver of autonomy.) Then, on two occasions, demands for information from the Internal Security Committee of the United States House of Representatives and its predecessor have gone unchallenged by the university; in fairness it should be noted that very few institutions of higher learning have responded to these requests with much vigor or protection.

Finally, the regents have not consistently protested even serious incursions by the legislature, the governor, the Division of Finance, the Coordinating Council, and other external bodies. The experience of Michigan stands in stark contrast. This comparison is appropriate, not only because the California constitutional provisions were patterned largely after those of Michigan, but also because the universities of California and Michigan are generally regarded as the two great constitutional state universities. From time to time, the University of Michigan has been beset by an angry or a parsimonious legislature. Most recently, the 1970 higher education appropriations bill contained a variety of intrusive and restrictive conditions, on such matters as faculty work load, class size, level of student tuition and fees, accounting and reporting requirements, student conduct and discipline, and related matters. The regents of the university, joined by the governing boards of Wayne State and Michigan State, immediately filed a lawsuit in the state court challenging these conditions as invasions of the universities' constitutional autonomy. The governing boards won at least the first round of their current suit. Early in December 1971, the circuit court held the conditions imposed in the

1970 budget to lie beyond the constitutional powers of the legislature because they invaded the constitutional province of the respective governing boards.

The analogy between California and Michigan is not quite perfect.
It is true that the California legislature has not used budget conditions of the Michigan type to control the conduct of the university
and its disbursement of funds. Yet the selective budget cuts that have
become increasingly fashionable of late serve essentially the same
purpose, and just as effectively remove discretion and flexibility
from the governing board. If the legislature can take away teaching
assistants one year, the Academic Senate another, and faculty salary
increases a third year, the result is the same.

The differences between the statuses of these two constitutional
governing boards reflects a fundamental contrast in philosophy and
outlook. The Michigan regents apparently regard themselves as a
fourth branch of government and behave accordingly, while the California regents do not. Although a university governing board lacks
the checks and balances of the other branches—the veto, the power
of the purse, the injunction—Michigan's regents have protected and
bolstered their autonomy by seeking the aid of one agency against
another. The California Board of Regents has simply not acted as a
fourth branch of government, even though it may believe it enjoys
that status under the constitution. The power that has not been exercised may some day be found to have atrophied.

Coordination: The Importance of Being Private

It is impossible to talk of higher learning in California without taking note of the private colleges and universities. The state's system of
postsecondary education includes two nationally eminent private
universities, one of the most comprehensive private consortia, a number of smaller universities, and a large group of private two- and four-
year colleges. Although the vast majority of California college students attend publicly supported campuses, the role of the private
sector far exceeds its numerical proportion. Thus it is pertinent to
consider ways in which the law affects relations between the two sectors.

Less coordination or control exists between the two sectors in
California than in many, perhaps most, other states. Clearly the private colleges and universities are freer than in New York, where the
regents possess the constitutional power to charter and accredit every
private institution, to approve every new degree program, to make

visitations and require written reports as often as they wish, to set specific standards for the qualification and compensation of faculty members, and to grant or withhold permission for a private institution to close its doors. The independent higher institutions of California are also freer of state control than their counterparts in Massachusetts, where not only general health and safety requirements but even a loyalty oath (recently invalidated) have been imposed on employees of private colleges and universities. Nor do public officials hold ex officio seats on the governing boards of private universities, as in Connecticut, Louisiana, and Pennsylvania.

Where many other states have undertaken extensive studies of the private sector and the relations between tax-supported campuses and those that are not tax-supported, California has been relatively unconcerned. Late in the 1971 session, the legislature enacted a bill to create a Council on Private Postsecondary Educational Institutions, which would have made a modest start toward evaluation and coordination. But the governor vetoed the bill on two grounds: first, that the state already had enough commissions and agencies; and second, that the proposal "creates another board without changing the substance of the laws to be administered." Thus even this first and rather tentative step will not be taken, at least for a while.

The difference between California and other states might appear to be essentially a fiscal one. It is true that the state constitution precludes direct support of private colleges and universities—a ban which the proposed new constitution would dissolve. Yet this explanation is inadequate for two reasons. On the one hand, the *indirect* support of the private sector is quite substantial. Roughly half the state scholarships, accounting for an estimated 85 to 90 percent of the funds, go to students attending private institutions which enroll only 10 to 12 percent of the total California student body. Moreover, the governor recently signed into law a bill to create a medical contract program for the support of students in the private medical schools. This arrangement comes about as close to direct subvention of the private sector as would be possible under the present constitutional constraint. One additional factor is potentially relevant: The California constitution raises an unusually high wall between church and state, thus effectively precluding any direct support of church-affiliated colleges and universities. The California courts would not, for example, tolerate anything like New York's system of per capita payments to institutions of higher learning—a system initially extended to some Catholic colleges and denied to others but recently held available to most.

The relatively primitive relationship between public and private sectors in California must find an indigenous explanation. Surely the framers of the California constitution were not oblivious to the private institutions; the section immediately following the provision creating the University of California regents deals extensively with the Leland Stanford Junior University, conferring special status and tax exemptions on the property of the trustees. Doubtless the clear constitutional constraint against direct support of the private sector partially explains the current separation. Perhaps, too, the relative financial health of the private institutions and the steadily rising demand for higher education in California have deferred the issues of coordination and support. Moreover, the political strength of the two great private universities would probably have averted legislative conditions and exactions to which private universities in other states have been more vulnerable.

It seems unlikely that the present state of affairs can continue indefinitely. The situation may not yet have reached the critical pass of New York, Pennsylvania, and Ohio, but the private sector is clearly in trouble everywhere. Thus, the final comments of the Constitutional Revision Commission on a proposal permitting direct public support of private colleges and universities clearly point up the changing realities of the times:

The proposal reflects the view that these existing prohibitions are unduly rigid and may actually increase the cost of higher education to the public. In the decades ahead, the financial needs of private institutions are likely to exceed existing or forseeable resources. If private institutions begin to close, or become unable to expand, the number of students that must be absorbed by the public institutions will increase. In these circumstances it may prove less costly for the state to assist existing private institutions than to build new state facilities at public expense.

The end of an era is in sight. Some form of assistance to the private sector will almost certainly be sanctioned. Once that is done, the political pressures to appropriate the funds will be intense and cannot long be resisted. With this new infusion of state aid to the private colleges and universities, a measure of coordination and perhaps greater control seems inevitable. Thus, within a matter of years the one real form of autonomy that now exists, and which sharply differentiates the two sectors, may well come to an end. For a university, being private may someday be as relatively unimportant as being constitutional.

12

Coordination and Planning Despite Competition and Confusion

Lyman A. Glenny

State government is still the chief source of funding for higher education, and there is nothing new on the horizon to change this observation. Public senior institutions rely most heavily on the state, community colleges do less so, and private institutions, although not heavily subsidized in the past except for state tax exemptions, will seek more state aid in the future. At the same time, the state is confronted with serious policy issues relating to support of research, public services, and adult education, to falling enrollments in some public institutions, to the probable closure of some private and perhaps some public liberal arts colleges, to the continuing oversupply of doctoral graduates, to the competition between new educational forms and institutions and the established collegiate sector, and to financial problems in an inflationary and recessionary period.

In this article, I discuss ways to resolve some of the major issues at the state level, comparing the social and political climate that influenced such action in the 1960's with the different climate that exists today. (Observations on current conditions are drawn from five hundred field interviews of staff members of statewide higher education, executive budget, and legislative appropriations agencies, and from documents obtained from seventeen states being studied in depth for

Reprinted from *Assuring Academic Progress Without Growth*, edited by Allan M. Cartter (San Francisco: Jossey-Bass, 1975).

the Study of State Budgeting Practices of the Center for Research and Development in Higher Education, Berkeley.) In the last decade or more, vast changes have taken place in structure and in power relationships among higher education agencies. Further changes and some reform seem imperative if rational approaches to planning and coordination are to be used. I conclude with suggestions on how the state can make its planning and coordinating functions more effective and how institutions can help by taking the initiative.

Growth of State Planning

Planning and coordination came late to higher education, as they did to most social services in the United States. Until World War II, planning was somehow considered a venture alien to higher education. In the 1960's, the mood for establishing planning and coordinating agencies for higher education was one of expansion and optimism. Enrollments, funds, and buildings all grew greatly, and each senior institution, new or old, seemed to aspire to the status of a great graduate research institution.

Expansion and complexity. The states responded to growing problems of complexity and expansion by creating a variety of coordinating and planning boards or councils. Some had only advisory powers, others had authority to implement plans and control institutions. These new agencies operated without much involvement with or interference from politicians. Most governors' offices had small staffs of politicians rather than professionals and rarely included a specialist for higher education. In state legislatures a political assistant might be found on joint finance and budget committees, but professional staffs were virtually nonexistent. Under these conditions, coordinating boards or councils entered a near vacuum with their new staffs of specialists in planning, budgeting, and program development. They were in an ideal position to leave a favorable record of accomplishment and, as far as the governor and the legislature were concerned, did so. By the late 1960's, most coordinating agencies and statewide governing boards had completed one or more planning cycles. Both governors and legislatures relied increasingly on coordinating boards for planning and initiating policy. Geared to expansion, the plans—almost without exception—anticipated unending increases in the number of young people and in the proportion of high school graduates who would attend college.

Proliferation of state agencies. Today coordinating agencies and statewide governing boards (as well as institutions) face a different political climate and new operational problems (Glenny et al., 1971). In the late 1960's the staffs of many governors' budget offices were expanded to include professional specialists for higher education. These analysts reviewed the budget and programming work of both institutions and statewide boards. Later, as funding constrictions and unexpected enrollment drops occurred, coordinating staffs tended to move under the control of the governor and hence away from the legislature. By 1970 many legislatures began to actively combat the continuing accretion of gubernatorial power. They hired their own professional staff for research units and legislative councils, and many of them hired professionals for the appropriations and finance committees. In the past four years the growth of these legislative staffs has been the most distinguishing characteristic of state government. (Drawn from ongoing research, Study of State Budgeting Practices for Higher Education.) Economists, political scientists, accountants, and managers now aid legislators in dealing with government agencies. Moreover, many legislatures have either established new program review and performance audit agencies or added that function to an existing office performing fiscal audits. It is not uncommon for college and university budget requests to be reviewed seriatim by the state coordinating board, the executive budget staff, and from one to four different legislative committee staffs. Committee staffs may even be divided along partisan lines as in Illinois and Pennsylvania, thus further fragmenting the review process. Top administrators of colleges and universities increasingly exhaust their planning and management resources in responding to a plethora of executive and legislative staff requests. Little time remains for the educational and program planning and development that must be done if institutions are to survive in the next twenty years.

The political situation for coordinating boards was further complicated by the ineptness of many states in administering federal programs for buildings, continuing education, and instructional equipment. Rather than assign the administration of such programs to existing coordinating or statewide governing boards, new agencies were often established. So while planning responsibilities generally lay with the coordinators, other agencies whose functions had marked effect on the course of higher education could plan independently of the coordinating boards. Planning became more difficult and coordination among the agencies became unlikely, even when mandated by law.

The 1202 commissions and state power. Primarily because of this proliferation of state agencies, the federal government sought to create a single comprehensive planning agency in each state by means of the Education Amendments Act of 1972. The membership of these so-called 1202 commissions (named after the section number of the law) was to include representatives from all areas of post-secondary education. The federal statute also encouraged states to consolidate their higher education facilities commissions and continuing education councils with the new 1202 agencies. (In early drafts of the bill this consolidation was a requirement.) A few states took advantage of this opportunity for greater unification, while many others assigned the functions of 1202 commissions to their existing coordinating and planning boards. However, some states created still other new agencies without changing, abolishing, or consolidating any existing ones. The unfortunate result was to increase the ambiguities of state planning and operation, particularly for the coordinating board.

Representatives of the federal government are not especially pleased with the confusing results of their attempts to achieve comprehensive planning. Not only are more agencies planning and operating higher education, but the 1202 commissions themselves often have been authorized to obtain only meager federal funds for planning; few state dollars are committed. Furthermore, the composition of these agencies sometimes creates doubt about their planning capabilities.

As a solution, one might say that the states should look out for their own interests and let the federal government do the same. Yet the problem is not so simple. Federal funding policy during the past five years has been to award less money directly to institutions and more to students through grant and work-study programs. Federal administrative funds for higher education facilities commissions have been drastically cut and are likely to be eliminated in the coming years. The federal policy of aiding students through the institution they attend has led the government into an extremely complicated set of administrative arrangements with colleges and universities. As a result, it is not clear whether federal objectives or the more parochial objectives of the institutions are being achieved. Congressional leaders and staffs are seriously considering giving the states the authority to administer these aid programs. The 1202 commissions were initially authorized to include this possibility. Yet the continuation of fragmented responsibility in some states and its increase in others necessarily causes skepticism among federal officials about delegating these important programs.

State planners have seldom considered the administrative problems associated with federal student aid programs, much less recognized that projecting consequences should be integral to planning the total financing of higher education institutions. Moreover, some new 1202 commissions are authorized only to plan, not to coordinate or administer. Yet if the thrust of federal funding is toward student aid, the operation of these programs should be integrated with comparable state aid programs and financing and guided by comprehensive planning.

More Programs, Fewer Students

Political and organizational complexities for state coordinating and planning agencies continue to baffle policy makers. But probably more important for social welfare is resolving the discrepancy between the growth of new educational forms, modes, and institutions on the one hand, and drastically changing enrollments among new and old institutions on the other. The best use of resources for higher education is already hindered by a lack of consensus on long-range planning strategies. These new instructional forms and modes are not minor adjustments in education. They have revolutionary import and should be at the heart of the planning process. Yet they are largely ignored or taken for passing fads, soon to be outmoded. Nisbet (1974) has called for reassessment of institutional missions and goals in the face of change. He predicts that most colleges and universities will become more parochial, meeting local and regional needs rather than national ones. Although some state leaders may be satisfied by this turn of events, it nevertheless calls for a complete review and reassignment of roles, missions, and objectives of every state-supported institution.

Not only do new types of institutions offer education to students who do not attend traditional colleges, but so do the colleges and universities themselves. As enrollments drop or level off, institutions search for new constituencies to serve, such as low-income students and adults. Private colleges contract with industry for adult education programs, and they provide extension programs that were formerly the sole province of large metropolitan private universities. State colleges, badly affected by the enrollment slippage, offered few extension services in the past but now do so through off-campus centers, late evening and weekend classes, and correspondence courses.

If adults are successfully recruited to make up for enrollment declines among young people in public institutions, the state will face an important policy issue. In the past, most direct costs of extension and off-campus courses were paid by the student; now many state institutions not only give resident credit for such work but by doing so bring these enrollments within state funding formulas for regular daytime students. A few states face this issue directly, but others seem unaware of it even though it is fundamental to funding commitments. As a nation we are turning more and more toward becoming a "learning society," as some scholars dub it. Most of us look with favor on this development, but the question of responsibility for financing it has yet to be explicitly resolved by most states.

Resolving Planning Problems

Many state and federal policy makers seem to believe that special management techniques, particularly those related to costing, will help solve most budget and resource allocation problems if applied to institutions of higher education. However valuable management techniques may be for increasing the efficiency of internal operations, they will not help much to solve state and federal policy issues. These issues transcend any impact management can have on production effectiveness. They concern controversial problems with political overtones and the resistance of strong special interests to any major reductions or cutbacks. Reducing the mission of an emerging university by eliminating doctoral work, closing some institutions unable to shift away from a primary focus on teacher education, eliminating obsolete programs backed by powerful lobbies, or supporting new types of education in settings other than colleges are issues of the present and future. They involve social, economic, and political considerations to which management efficiency or unit costing can contribute little.

Given current problems of programming, delivering education, reallocating resources, and eliminating programs and institutions, how are coordinating agencies and statewide boards resolving them? How *should* they be resolving them? To find out, the Center for Research and Development in Higher Education is conducting an in-depth analysis of budgeting for higher education in seventeen states. Among other concerns, we find policy makers disturbed and frustrated by the unfocused and disorganized way colleges and universities confront present exigencies and by their failure to plan for the long run. Coordinating agencies are supposed to supply needed planning, yet we find only a few instances of long-range planning in educational programming, setting goals, redefining missions, or establishing parameters for institutional development. The reason coordinators give for their failure to plan is that they exhaust themselves in negotiation and information gathering and dispensing between institutions and myriad state staffs. Particularly time-consuming are the many different legislative staff members they must deal with. Further, they assert that the concerns of legislative staffs often reflect only the interests of individual legislators but require hours or even days of work. Coordinating officers say that with these pressures and the limitations of their own staff and resources, long-range plannning and fundamental studies get short shrift.

As coordinators and planners fail to respond to long-range policy needs, legislative and governors' staffs are forced to make judgments on current issues that may have unanticipated long-term consequences. Political staffs are not employed to plan, nor are they trained in the complexities of higher education. Their jobs often require quick answers to urgent questions, and they often give little thought to the eventual consequences of their decisions or to valid alternatives.

Unquestionably, the complaints expressed by policy makers and coordinators have a good deal of validity. The proliferation of state staffs is almost matched by the proliferation of separate state agencies dealing with different aspects of higher education, and both put the board or council responsible for planning in a weak and ambiguous position.

The most tangible evidence of a viable coordinated system is ongoing planning that involves the priority goals and objectives of the system and keeps them before the public. As organizational and procedural means for implementing plans are conceived and made public, better understanding and more commitment results. In this way planners can guide coordinators' day-to-day decisions as well as the larger ones related to state budgeting and finance. The state wants and expects such advice from coordinating and planning boards.

Single-agency responsibility. From previous research on planning and coordination, I have concluded that state coordinating agencies have done the most and best planning for higher education (Glenny et al., 1971). A recently completed survey by the Center for Research and Development in Higher Education of 2500 college and university presidents supports this conclusion: of thirteen states in which presidents of institutions reported the most planning and what type of planning was most helpful to them, eleven states have coordinating agencies and two have statewide governing boards. In spite of this testimony to the effectiveness of coordinating agencies, we observe governors and legislatures attempting to solve the problems of higher education by consolidating all their public institutions under a single governing board and abolishing the coordinative structure in the process. Now, because of federal intervention and insistence, most states have 1202 commissions, often in addition to existing organizations.

It is more imperative than ever that as educational forms and methods change, as new types of institutions emerge, and as the federal government increasingly aids students rather than institutions, both coordinative and statewide planning activities be lodged in the same agency rather than in competing ones. Legislators and governors, responsible for the creation of state agencies, should know from long experience that plans and policy laid down by one agency are often altered beyond recognition when they are implemented by another. The placement of both planning and coordinating functions within the same agency strengthens the state's ability to respond rationally to current exigencies and to those that will inevitably follow in the next twenty years.

Placing full responsibility for planning and coordination with one agency does not require that the same professional staff perform both functions. To avoid dissipating all the agency's resources in grappling with current issues, the long-range planning staff can—perhaps must—be separately organized. Keeping such planning staff in close touch with institutional and agency operations is a challenge to management, but one which can be met. The lack of a combination of coordinating and planning with vigorous, imaginative professional staff decreases the likelihood of long-range statewide planning and ensures that legislators will make only politically expedient decisions.

Contributions by institutions. Despite current confusion over state planning responsibilities, individual institutions can still strengthen their own planning and operation. However, this task requires new perspectives on the institutional role across the wide spectrum of postsecondary education. It also requires new data bases for providing more meaningful assessments of internal operations and faculty and student trends bearing on policy issues. Accurate current data with a ten-year historical base are necessary to assess an institution's position. Data bases need to be laid for determining what types of students are attending now compared with in the recent past; how these types are distributed among courses and programs; whether new and adult students fit successfully into existing curricula; which types of students drop out now compared with in the past; why they drop out and where they go; how faculty age, training, and tenure affect program change and student attendance; how well students perform after graduation or certification; how program is related to student self-development, social adaptation, and career success; what internal procedures exist for admission, transfer, and graduation; what rates of student entry, admission, and graduation are; and how responsive, durable, and successful curricular innovations are with different types of students.

An institutional research staff and policy analysis group, if adequately informed, can contribute substantially to the well-being of the institution by aggressively pursuing with state agencies objectives and goals backed by data-supported realism and imaginative analysis. State plans can then support strong institutional plans rather than impose state-conceived models and procedures. An institutional planning vacuum invites state intervention and domination, either through an imposed state plan or ad hoc legislative decisions. A well thought out plan based on realistic assessment of an institution's strengths invites state support and cooperation rather than control. At a minimum, institutions ought to know more about their students, faculty, programs, operations, and plans than state agencies do—knowledge that current research indicates is sadly lacking.

References

Glenny, L. A., et al. *Coordinating Higher Education for the '70s.* Berkeley: Center for Research and Development in Higher Education, University of California, 1971.

Nisbet, R. "The Decline of Academic Nationalism." *Change* 6, no. 6: 26.

PART IV

The "Estates" and Their Role

13

The Constituencies and Their Claims

Morris Keeton

There is no simple formula as to who should govern an American college or university. Four grounds for claiming the right to share in governing are put forward:

Students 1. Those whose concerns and lives are most affected by campus activities should surely have a part in their control.

Faculty 2. Those who are most competent to do the work of the campus should have a voice that ensures the effective use of their competence.

Admin. 3. Those whose cooperation is essential to the effectiveness of the campus in its work should have a place in governing that facilitates their continuing cooperation.

Trustees 4. Those whose sponsorship and resources created and sustain the institution, and thus make possible the opportunity of higher education, are entitled to protect and further their purposes and interests.

Difficulties in Satisfying the Claims

These four grounds for a voice in governance can be presented both as ethical claims to rights and as practical requirements of effective campus operations. In this study, emphasis is put upon the prac-

Reprinted in an abridged version from *Shared Authority on Campus* (Washington, D.C.: American Association for Higher Education, 1971).

tical requirements of effectiveness. If a "constituency" is defined as a group whose sponsorship, cooperation, competencies, or concerns are important to the work of a campus, then each campus has numerous constituencies. Once the merits of any claims to a share of authority are granted, we still do not know how these claims can be effectively implemented. The very existence of diverse grounds for authority with different applicability to different groups presents a difficulty in deciding who should govern.

A further complication in the inquiry as to who should govern is the fact that legal control and effective day-to-day control in the crucial campus choices need not be the same. To enfranchise a group who can help the institution succeed better, it is not necessary that the group sit in the board of trustees or in the university senate. How the group can thus obtain the optimum influence and power and how it can ensure continuance of an optimum relationship is a question involving both formal and informal authority and permitting the use of a great variety of means.

A third difficulty lies in the effect of changed circumstances. Changes of circumstance in turn change who is most affected, who is most competent, whose cooperation is essential, and even at times whose sponsorship and resources sustain the campus. A substantial change of circumstances can thus have a major effect in determining how an abstract right to influence can best be implemented.

In the past decade there has been unusual attention on American campuses to these complexities and to the need for realignment of authority to reflect a deliberate judgment by the parties in conflict about the issues. Where the issues have been debated and resolved, the outcome has generally been an increased provision for formal voice and vote for faculty, students, or both. The question here as to who should govern is not primarily a question about participation in boards, councils, and committees. It is a question of the influence and effect appropriate to the rights and responsibilities of those who constitute the campus and its constituencies. Assuming the four bases for influence just stated, what application do they have to the claims for governing authority by faculty, students, and other constituencies of today's campuses?

Grounds for Faculty Authority

The primary justification for faculty voice in campus governance is the fact that faculty alone have the kinds and degree of qualification essential to the task of the college or university. They are selected and appointed on the basis of those qualifications. Most faculty are teachers; some are researchers; others are specialists in other forms of public service provided by their institutions; and many combine these competencies. In the subject matter in which they teach, serve, or do research, the great majority of faculty are further specialized as philosophers, physicists, historians, economists, sociologists, biologists, or the like.

Normally the faculty as a professional body represent a further type of competence—that of experience and commitment. Though faculty mobility has in the past quarter-century reduced the average span of faculty service, the turnover of presidents has changed even more dramatically; trustees rotate more commonly than was once the case; and even those students who pursue uninterrupted studies have a short tenure. The largest element of continuity and experience with the tasks and problems of the campus is increasingly that of the faculty. . . .

The overwhelming consideration in fixing the role of faculty in governance should be the desire to improve the performance of the institution. If this is so, the necessity of faculty cooperation should be seen as a problem of how to maximize the use of faculty competencies in meeting campus objectives. Involvements in governing can ensure and energize both cooperation and the devotion of faculty expertise to improvement. The full participation of their own representatives in crucial decisions can win a faculty's belief in the rightness of a policy or decision when otherwise it would not seem credible to them. Bringing their knowledge and perspective to a problem as decision about it is shaped can win their cooperation and improve the solution. . . .

There are difficulties and disadvantages to faculty participation in campus governance. A party at interest in a decision affecting others may press his interest improperly at their expense. In a complex matter, an expert is prone to overestimate the weight of that part of it in which he is expert. Moreover, in rendering a service an expert may not rightly arrogate to himself the client's rights in choosing the type and priorities of service he intends to obtain. Those who have most experience with a task fall too easily into the assumption that new circumstances do not alter the way it can best be done. Those with greatest continuity in an organization become too readily preoccupied with institutional maintenance at the cost of changes of purpose or work which might better serve the trust for which the institution exists. The use of faculty time to govern withdraws that time and talent from the tasks for which the faculty were employed and in which they are most expert.

How do the bases for faculty sharing in campus authority and the disadvantages of their doing so permit a resolution of the question as to their proper role in governance? That resolution can take form through specific attention to the relevance of faculty competencies, cooperation, and interests in the specific types of policy and decisions being shared. . . . If influence is to follow the contribution which each constituency of an institution can best make, the mechanisms and channels for influence will have to reflect this complexity and interweaving of essential contributions and essential precautions against constituency biases and limitations. . . .

Current practice leaves a great deal to be desired if faculty are to be accorded influence fitting to the principle just stated. In 1966-67 the Campus Governance Program's Task Force on Faculty Representation and Academic Negotiation studied thirty-five campuses where the issues of faculty voice were in ferment. The Task Force judged that the sample underrepresented campuses where faculty had acquiesced to administrator dominance and possibly also underrepresented those with faculty dominance, faculty primacy, or shared authority. The Task Force estimated that about 50 percent of the campuses studied were marked by administrative primacy, another 25 percent by shared authority between faculty and administration, only a few campuses by faculty primacy, and most of the last 25 percent by administrative dominance. . . .

The Task Force also found a defect of representation in systems which place crucial authority over higher education in coordinating boards, superboards, or state administrative offices and legislatures. In these situations faculty often were provided no vehicle or poor vehicles for their own representation at the levels of governance where decisions were actually made. Again the decision as to the level of taxation to support public higher education is appropriately reserved to publicly chosen representatives or their delegates. It is not prudent or right, however, to screen these public representatives from knowledge or interaction with those who can best present the interests, relevant knowledge, and experience of faculty to them.

A similar problem of representation in denominational colleges may call for a different resolution. In one such college an impasse between trustees and faculty, with administration in the middle seeking to mediate, was resolved by establishing regular participation of faculty and students in trustee committees and occasional, more inclusive, informal meetings of trustees with faculty and students. In Catholic institutions where faculty have often been dominant numerically in the controlling board, they have often failed to exercise an independent perspective because they were members of the controlling church order and were appointed by the college president or the presiding bishop.

A final example of types of inadequate faculty role in governance emerged in the course of data taking in the Nineteen Campus Study. The data do not dictate, but suggest, that faculty in different disciplinary groupings (e.g., humanities or social sciences as contrasted with applied sciences or administrative studies) bring different perspectives and priorities to campus concerns. On a few issues the age of faculty correlated significantly with their reporting of problems and their reflection of priorities in interviews. Interviews showed that in recent campus unrest about ethnic studies and ideological issues it was helpful to problem solving if faculty representatives of the contending factions could be formally involved in efforts to work out resolution of the issues. Some of the groupings significant for governance were persistent and could appropriately be reflected in the formal structure of governance; others were transitory and might best be treated through ad hoc legislative or administrative mechanisms.

What Voice for Students—and Why?

Teaching is primarily for students. They are the principal learners. They are the original clients for the campus services. On private college campuses they or their families are also consumers in a second sense: they pay most of the cost. On public campuses they pay an increasing share. It is their daily lives that are most affected by policies on campus life and the conditions of learning. How should the interests of client, buyer, and resident be protected and represented in campus governance?

In higher education, some say, the buyer must beware. He has many choices of campuses. Once he has chosen, he should not complain; or, to be more precise, he is entitled to only such relief as complaint will gain. He is a petitioner, without further rights. Moreover, he is a petitioner whose preferences may not serve his own best interests. Others know best, or at least better than he.

But, without his help, do they know best? And is his choice of campus altogether free? Granted that his interests as learner and resident may be his paramount basis for a say in campus affairs, is learning an enterprise in which his cooperation and his competencies play a crucial part if the campus is to achieve its greatest effectiveness? . . .

Although the interest of a student as client may seem to be his paramount basis for a right to vote and a voice in campus governance, it is probably a poorer basis for discerning his optimal role than is the contribution he can make to the effectiveness of the campus. In higher education the cooperation of the learner is absolutely essential to good results. He can give or withhold that cooperation in multitudinous ways and in many different dimensions of his work as learner. The damage he can do to campus effectiveness is a far less helpful basis for designing his participation in governance than is the promise he alone can make real, but both the potential damage and the realizable promise are substantial. . . .

Aside from petition and persuasion, the main resort of students for influence on campus in the past has been noncooperation and selective cooperation. The elective system was a mode of enfranchisement of students. Their choices of majors and elective and "service" courses play a heavy role in the allocation of faculty positions, departmental support, and eventually facilities and degree programs. As options on housing and dining services have been opened in recent years, students' selections have slowed down dormitory building programs and have bankrupted some options in dining services. In some colleges today there is more than one way for a student to meet each or some of the degree requirements, with the result that courses which become unfavorably known on the campus grapevine may have to be dropped or altered. "Voting with the feet" is a crude instrument for deliberation and reform in an enterprise as sophisticated as a college or a university. Nevertheless, it has sometimes been more effective than committees in eliciting change. . . .

For the practical demands of campus governance, one of the most useful ways to view potential student contributions to governance is to examine the requirements which campus purposes place upon campus life and instruction under contemporary conditions. For example, students arrive on campus today more mature than did those of a century or a half-century ago, and the college is expected to contribute further to their maturity. In contemporary society, matters which once were considered appropriate for institutional regulation are now defined as properly matters of personal choice as long as there is not interference with other people. While the definition of what is private and personal varies among American and collegiate subcultures, there has been change throughout American higher education on the proper scope and nature of parietal regulations. Even the sharpest critics of some forms of student role in governance normally grant the importance of their taking part in the creation and application of these regulations. Given a society in which change and mobility make even the ordinary citizen's life less protected and stable than before, the task of developing maturity in students cannot be well done if they themselves do not take major responsibility for the quality of student life. To insist otherwise is demeaning of their maturity and futile in practice. Moreover, it builds resentment and resistance against legitimate exercise of authority in other quarters.

Still more critical is the relation between learning and self-determination. A scholar is a person who wants to learn, chooses his own objectives in learning, and knows how to enlist competent assistance in choosing the ends and means of further inquiries. An inquirer who is not a mature scholar should be on the way toward the capacity for scholarship. Some college instruction is still a matter of acquiring information on how to do a job or how to pass a certification test, and some students are present primarily to escape adult responsibilities or to get a degree. But these practices, where they exist, are deficiencies to be overcome, a caricature of what higher education should be. If the capacity for self-determination in learning and in life is to mature as it should in students, the conduct of life and instruction on campus must elicit growing autonomy among them. No particular structures of governance are implied by that requirement, but a climate acceptant of students' sharing in critical decisions and mechanisms suited to the particular campus will be increasingly essential to effectiveness.

The difficulties and disadvantages of student participation in governance are substantial, and in practice these must be heeded if both student and institutional interests are to be well served. Students are charged with transiency, inexperience, immaturity, ignorance of crucial aspects of campus governance, special interests that conflict with institutional goals (e.g., keeping charges at a minimum), and lack of sufficient time and interest to do well with the responsibilities of governance. The principle proposed for designing a faculty role in governance should apply to students as well: Design the role to obtain the contributions available from student competencies and cooperation and to protect the other constituencies and the institution against undue effects of the special interests and limitations that apply on the particular campus. . . . When established institutions are studied in the light of this principle, there has been a remarkable change in practice since the early 1960's; but participation in campus governance is still much less effectively provided for students than for faculty. . . .

In designing the structures and processes by which students exert power in campus governance, some further considerations should also be kept in mind. Among these are the relative effectiveness of informal processes where the intention to share authority is genuine and pervasive, the need for different patterns of participation in different types of policy and program decisions, and the possibility that an adversary proceeding may be the only effective means available or the best of the feasible options when an impasse develops. . . .

It is also important to keep in mind that students differ among themselves even more than do faculty or campus administrators. Extensive research is already available about the variety of American student cultures. A single university campus sometimes harbors several distinctive subcultures. Neither students nor faculty may be thought of as a single constituency, a monolith of opinions, values, and interests. For example, on some issues third-year students identify more clearly with disciplinary groups (such as humanities and social sciences faculty) than with other students. On some ideological issues, the groupings are less appropriately identified as student groups than as radical or conservative constituencies which cut across faculty, student, and other lines. Similarly, certain ethnic minorities which see themselves as having a particular cultural mission enlist and organize across faculty, student, and noncampus groupings. To cope with this pluralism of identities of individuals and groups and with their changing character, campus governing structures and processes will need a flexibility and complexity uncommon in our presently complex society.

The Proper Powers of Administrators

In most colleges and universities, the administrators are dominant. The Task Force on Faculty Representation considered the administrators too powerful in the great majority of campuses, and almost never underrepresented. The sharing of authority with other constituencies clearly involves curtailment of that power.

To curtail administrative power at a time when there is a public outcry against campus disorders may seem the reverse of what is needed. Three distinctions may be helpful in seeing why the sharing of some powers may actually strengthen the hand of administrators in their proper roles. First, the sharing of legislative authority is not to be confused with a sharing of managerial powers, though legislative policy does set the purposes and policies within which management operates. Second, the management tasks in a college or university are partially carried out by faculty and students, as in the faculty's management of instruction and the students' assumption of some tasks of dormitory management or control of social life. A division of labor on these tasks may facilitate the performance of administrative functions rather than hinder it. Third, the surrender or sharing of particular powers in policy making or management can strengthen the administrative leaders in other functions and in their capacity to achieve the overall goals of the institution. For example, under certain circumstances the use of honor systems has been more effective in limiting cheating than instructor proctoring; administrative efforts to exert direct control over academic standards is generally less effective than insistence that faculty carry responsibility for those standards; and the delegation of budgetary control over lines within departmental budgets is often more effective in both fiscal and educational outcomes than detailed preauditing of all expenditures by the central administration.

Prior to World War II college presidents typically achieved outstanding results by their powers of charisma, competence, and prerogative. As campuses became large and complex, these resources ceased to suffice, particularly for institutions striving to become excellent in their field. Under contemporary circumstances, administrators must find ways to exercise their leadership which draw upon the capabilities and the willing cooperation of the leaders of the other campus constituencies.

The dominant claim of administrators to voice and vote in the policy making of a campus is that of their essential competencies. At the levels of leadership, they are chosen for these competencies. They may be removed from office if they fail in either competence, support of constituencies, or cooperation with the board and the other administrative leaders. The tasks of administrators put them in a unique position to have or to obtain the information crucial to understanding and solving the institution's problems and to achieving its purposes. As professionals, they have an interest in working conditions which maximize their capacity to do their tasks well. Crucial among these conditions is that of being free to carry out their work in a manner of their own choosing and to know at the outset the limits within which this choice is theirs.

Because of the intimate relationship between policy and implementation and the importance of good information to wise policy making, direct participation of major administrators in policy-making bodies is a normal part of currently recognized good practice. Thus presidents sit ex officio on boards of trustees, and deans take part ex officio in the councils shaping policy for the deans' jurisdictions. The presence of the administrators is more critical than whether they have vote as well as voice. Often campus committees are served regularly by administrative staff who do not vote but who supply essential data and judgments on the effects of alternative policies. A formal vote for administrators is a way of making sure that everyone on a board or in a council is aware of the administrators' judgment. Since the administrators' convictions bear heavily upon their ability and willingness to make the councils' and committees' actions work, the formal vote also helps to ensure a workable agreement. . . .

Trustees: Their Makeup and Changing Roles

A college or university is a public trust. In the American polity, even a private college bears this character. The legal basis for trustee authority is a charter issued by a state or, in rare cases, by the federal government. All of the seventeenth century American colleges were private, though in the small and close-knit communities of that time the private-public distinction hardly had the meaning which it has today. The rise of public colleges and universities, particularly since the Civil War, and the sharply increasing proportion of public campus enrollments since World War I have introduced a division of labor between private and public institutions which is still undergoing change. A growing self-consciousness about institutional purposes has resulted from these trends and from efforts to divide labor efficiently and apply limited resources effectively to the improvement of performance.

In his work on trusteeship, Morton Rauh identifies the principal tasks of trustees as three: choosing the mission or purposes of the institution, choosing and replacing the chief executive at appropriate times, and making sure that the management of the institution is good. In state systems of higher education, the trustees or regents may be subject to, or dependent upon, statewide coordinating boards, the legislature, or other agents of public control in the exercise of these functions. Once named, private boards with rare exceptions enjoy full formal authority, though some have in practice been subordinate to other authorities, as in the case of some denominational colleges.

The makeup of the previously discussed constituencies represented in campus governance is determined by their roles; e.g., student, faculty, or administrator. With trustees, it is appropriate to ask: Are trustees to be viewed as constituencies in the sense that applies to these other groups? Who should be considered for the position of trustee? To answer that question, it is helpful to review the functions of trustees, the present makeup of trustee bodies, and the recent changes of circumstance which have a bearing upon the appropriate makeup of campus governing boards.

In 1968-69 Morton Rauh did the first comprehensive survey of the makeup of campus boards of trustees in the United States and inquired as to their work and their attitudes as trustees. As disclosed in the survey, the actual work of trustees is less concentrated in the functions just listed (choice of mission and of president and monitoring of overall effectiveness) than in matters of finance, plant, and fund raising. In a college with an unquestioned mission and a strikingly successful president, it may well be that the most critical functions of the trustees call for relatively little of their time. In these respects their task is to stand by for the time of need. Moreover, a small college often cannot afford all of the staff it needs, much less the quality of staff it can obtain as a contributed service through its board. However, the minimal board time given to purpose and effectiveness may be less a function of need than of the interests and capabilities of the preponderant membership.

Fault can be found with typical practice. One fault is the inadequate attention given to the distinction between the role of trustees as a board and the managerial services which particular members or groups may render. If the trustees' activity in finance, plant development and management, and fund raising goes beyond evaluation of performance and counsel to the actual conduct of the managerial functions, this is likely to cause their preoccupations with that activity to carry undue weight in their deliberations. . . .

The demand for higher education has never been greater than today. Yet the financing of both public and private colleges has much of the air of a mendicant operation. Why must those who render such a crucial service beg for resources to meet its costs? What alternatives are feasible in our society? These are questions for trustee resolution and action. . . .

Higher education needs the collaboration of others, who must finance it. Unless they believe in it, they will not use it, and colleges will wither or weaken from disuse. Also, the life and institutions of society are playing an increasing role as realities in which students and professors engage as the subject matter of their studies. This change is not merely a matter of pedagogical changes involving an increased use of travel, television, work, and other means of firsthand engagement with the world of today. It is also a product of growing relative emphasis upon the arts, the humanities, and the social sciences, and an apparent tendency in all of these areas to put increasing emphasis upon the present and future as against the past. As the social sciences become increasingly sophisticated and powerful in their research methods, they depend upon increasingly extensive access to the day-to-day activities of the people and institutions they study. The pace of growth of knowledge and the rate of change in society also make for the investment of greater energy in direct interactions with the contemporary world as a condition of both effective research and effective teaching.

Our changing wants interact with our changing ways of getting them to produce a growing interdependence between higher education and other activities and institutions of society. That interdependence is a key to the lost consensus on campus and to a crisis in public confidence in higher education. It provides a context in which trustee attention is urgently needed for the overall issues of purpose, priority, design of campus-community relations, and rationalization of the choices on those relations with the mode of financing of the institution.

The actual makeup of boards of trustees is not related well to this recommended task at all. For example, trustees are occupationally atypical of the types of expertise that are relevant to the problems just outlined. They are heavily concentrated in manufacturing, money management, and law, and enjoy high incomes (median between $30,000 and $49,000 per year), which are a mark of success of a kind. While not all high earners share one another's biases, and good income need be no disqualification in itself, the proportion of wealthy trustees is likely to deprive a board of the mix of perspective and of urgency appropriate to some of the issues just outlined. In a society facing urgent problems of racial justice, in which higher education should be an example of good practice, the proportion of Negro trustees is only 1.3 percent in the aggregate and is not evenly distributed among types of institutions. Age brings experience and often marks continuity of service and high competence in a calling, but 88 percent of trustees in 1968 were over fifty years old. A larger infusion of younger members could again diversify trustee perspectives, help in their communications with youth, and preserve a better balance of new life and developing leadership. Trustees are also typically male (86 percent) in a society still struggling to enfranchise the female majority. Even in religious affiliation (75 percent Protestant), after allowance is made for the special distributions of trustees by religion on denominationally sponsored campuses, the trustees are not typical of the public they serve. In race, religion, occupation, and income, the trustees of selective institutions are even less typical than those of others.

Still different problems of makeup emerge when particular boards or types of boards of trustees are studied. A quiet revolution has developed within the last decade in the change of Catholic college boards from clerical to lay control. A number of community colleges formerly governed by boards for lower schools now have separate and differently constituted boards. As mentioned already, some states have recently subordinated the formerly independent boards of individual campuses to a statewide authority or required certain forms of statewide coordination which have the effect of changing the composition as well as the prerogatives of controlling boards. Negro college boards which were formerly dominated by white trustees in a position to help have adjusted their membership to changed perceptions of who can help and who can best define the proper functions and interests of those institutions.

It is, of course, not important that trustees be typical in some of these respects. Those who protect the public interest in governing need not be altogether typical of the public they protect. The constituencies should have effective advocacy before, and response from, the board; they need not be, and cannot always be, equally well represented on the board. Moreover, the complexity and novelty of contemporary problems of campus governance might well be best met by new divisions of labor and new methods of empowering the constituencies. Three examples, related to the faculty, students, and the community respectively, will illustrate the possibilities.

A typical board of trustees is minimally involved in academic and student affairs. A recent exception, the reversal of a faculty appointment by the University of California regents, "earned some sort of prize for the most inappropriate action of the year," according to Morton Rauh. Yet while a board should not intrude upon management and professional functions, either academic or financial, how can it monitor the work of a campus without major attention to, and competence in, academic affairs if the preponderant public interest in that campus is in the performance of intellectual services?

The faculty are a natural resource for the trustee function of evaluating institutional performance of this public interest. As professionals, the faculty hold the intellectual life as their peculiar concern and trust. In the British and Canadian systems of campus governance, this fact is recognized in the dominant role of faculty in governing boards. In these systems the purse strings are watched by government

as well as by the governing boards. In the United States where finance and other resources are more fully controlled at board level,
the pecuniary and personnel interests of faculty have acted as barriers to their direct participation on boards.

In addition, the tradition in the United States has recognized that
values other than the intellectual enter into the choice of institutional purposes and task. Lay control has existed in part to see that
these other values—whether religion, national purpose, pedagogy, or
ideology—were chosen according to the sponsors' lights. Perhaps,
then, other means must be found in the United States for bringing
educational expertise into, or to the disposal of, trustee bodies. One
such device is the provision for the faculty or a campus senate to
select a portion of the members of the board or, in public systems,
for a qualified panel of educators to nominate candidates for the
choice of the public appointing authority.

When Princeton University announced that a graduated senior
would now regularly be named to its board of trustees, Rauh objected on multiple grounds: The presence of students as board members may tempt the board to inject itself into actions it is not competent to take and should keep delegated to management. In any case
one or two or three students cannot represent the range of views held
by students, especially with the rapid shifts of concern typical today.
Worst of all, the appointment of students as trustees may "fool some
people into thinking that student aspirations are being met by a
move that at best is but a token of good intentions." Rauh suggests
more powerful and practical modes of enfranchisement: requiring
boards to meet publicly where students and other constituents may
attend, empowering students as well as faculty to select some of the
trustees, focusing agenda upon issues vital to student concerns (e.g.,
the roles of students and faculty in determining curricular policies),
and allowing students to participate as working members in task
groups or committees which shape the resolutions coming to the
board for action. "It is sheer fantasy," says Rauh, "to think that a
change as superficial as giving the student a token seat on the board
of trustees will satisfy his aspirations for influence, participation,
and, above all, some measure of control over his own education."

The case of representation of the immediate and more remote
communities concerned with a campus is even more difficult in
theory, if not in practice. In the past community relations have been
largely left to trustees and administrators except when the outside
world threatened intervention on campus. The attitude underlying
this assignment of functions is changing. On some campuses it is

already a matter of policy to confer and collaborate actively with representatives of the community about the educational services the campus should render. This applies particularly to community and state colleges. On city campuses today it is becoming increasingly essential to confer with neighbors before expanding facilities or undertaking programs with a direct impact upon the neighborhood. But the change to which we refer is more fundamental. It is one toward active interest in collaborative planning and continuous communication with a view to finding the most appropriate response to the emerging interdependence of campus and community.

This change of attitude or philosophy will generally involve the consideration of new mechanisms. These may include changes in membership of the campus trustees and will surely include new arrangements for communication and joint problem definition and problem solving. They should in many cases include an attempt to understand with greater precision who are the constituencies on and off campus whose interests and concerns are most vitally affected by the choice among options as to how campus and community interact. It will no longer do to assume that an appointed public board ensures effective representation or advocacy for community constituencies.

For the system of higher education as a whole, diversity and decentralization of control will be of increasingly critical importance at the very time when they are increasingly difficult to achieve. The financing of private and public colleges and universities is becoming less and less distinct as public universities mount large fund-raising efforts among private sources, and private colleges turn increasingly to federal and state subsidies to avoid pricing students out of their market. There is an inevitable pressure from funding sources to impose at least minimal definition and monitoring upon the use of their funds. In times of political crisis and controversy, that pressure often touches upon the very freedom of inquiry and teaching. If added to these financial pressures is a more intimate pattern of communication to cope with the increasing interdependency of campus and community, the result could be a further subtle and pervasive blanket of constraint upon intellectual freedom. A pressure for homogenization not unlike that besetting secondary and elementary education could plague higher education.

Interdependence need not produce such unwanted change. Given the variety of subcultures in our society, the diversity of interests and concerns, and the degree of commitment to political and constitutional freedoms, a closer interaction of campus and communities could produce a new variety in the functions and styles of American campuses. The possibility of creating within higher education a new relevance to social need and a renewal of intellectual potency should preoccupy the boards of trustees as they address the changes now in store.

Realignment of Authority on Campus

The tasks and trends confronting those who govern campuses dictate the need for a new sophistication in the design of governing structures and processes, but they do not dictate any one solution that will serve for all campuses. What can be proposed is criteria to be heeded by particular campuses and types of campuses in the design of their own authority structures. The following statements summarize criteria implicit as assumptions or proposals in the preceding discussion.

1. The authority structure should reflect a genuine commitment to enfranchise constituencies previously unrepresented or underrepresented. This principle does not imply direct participation of particular constituents in the board of trustees, but it does require arrangements which provide for effective advocacy for, and response to, their concerns.

2. The processes and prerogatives in governing should be designed to foster the cooperation of each constituency and to further the contributions for which it has special competence. At the same time the pattern of sharing authority should avoid any undue effects of the special interests and disadvantages which the different constituencies bring with their roles.

3. The system of governance of a campus should provide for a division of labor between policy making and managing, and between the board of trustees and other councils and committees. The system should provide effective means for constituencies to be heard and heeded at the level and locus where their particular concerns receive final disposition. In state systems and private institutions with multiple campuses this principle calls for mechanisms for these campuses and their constituencies to be heard at the statewide or systemwide level.

4. The existence of diverse constituencies with often conflicting interests and perspectives need not imply that all fundamental policy making become a process of group negotiation—of collective bargaining, compromise, and accommodation. At the same time, not every issue can be settled on rationally persuasive grounds in the eyes of

every constituency. To reduce the frequency of impasse and to minimize damage from it, the system of governance should provide mechanisms of accommodation short of coercion and violence. The enfranchisement recommended in criterion 1 should result in purposes and priorities which will reflect constituency concerns and minimize the likelihood of coercive confrontations.

5. The rapidity of external and internal changes affecting campuses requires processes of governance which are more flexible in everyday operation, capable of more rapid and effective response to crisis, and less cumbersome to change in response to new working agreements than have been typical in the past.

The implementation of these principles will affect substantially the concepts and practices with regard to consent, accountability, and leadership. . . .

14

Administration: The Impact of Management Information Systems on Governance

Michael L. Tierney

Colleges and universities have been developing management information systems for the last fifteen years. The basic purpose of these systems is to support the decision-making process, particularly those decisions concerning the internal allocation of resources. However, unanticipated consequences of these systems may substantially affect the decision-making process. This chapter will (1) present a taxonomy of management information systems, (2) illustrate how one type of system may be used in a typical resource allocation problem, and (3) discuss some unanticipated consequences for the behavior of academic departments and the distribution of power within the institution.

A Taxonomy of Management Information Systems

The growth in the number of institutions having computer-based management information systems has been phenomenal. A 1970 survey of 1,873 colleges and universities indicated that 13 percent had some type of information system (Bogard, 1972). Stratifying the institutions by control (public versus private) and enrollment size indicated that such information systems were more likely in larger, public institutions. A more recent survey of forty-eight institutions indicates that administrative computing expenditures increased at an average annual rate of 33.4 percent between 1963 and 1968, and averaged 2.3 percent of an institution's total operating budget (Mann et al., 1975).

Computer-based management information systems do not, however, form a homogeneous group. The category includes the collection of data according to standardized definitions, the development of integrated data files for information retrieval, and the use of sophisticated software to relate elements of various data files. Because the phrase "management information system" can refer to so many different types of systems, it is necessary to develop a taxonomy of these systems.

The taxonomy employed in this chapter is borrowed directly from the work of R. O. Mason (1970). According to Mason, there are basically four types of computer-based information systems to support organizational decision making: databank information systems, predictive information systems, decision-making information systems, and decision-taking information systems. Because these information systems support organizational decision making, they are classified as "management information systems." And because most of the actual data processing is performed by computer rather than by hand, these information systems are labeled "computer-based." (For the present purpose, no distinction will be made between batch and on-line modes of computer data processing. The interested reader is referred to Davis, 1974 and Cushing, 1974.)

Databank Information Systems

This type of information system involves the collection of data according to standard definitions. The data collected might include a student's grade point average, year in school, and sex, or it might include the number of full-time equivalent faculty, by rank, in a given department. The important point is that everyone concerned, both inside and outside the institution, employ the same data definitions. A great deal of confusion can arise within an institution when different offices employ different data definitions, as when the registrar's office defines the total enrollment as full-time equivalent students and the academic dean defines the total enrollment as the total number of students enrolled.

Once the data have been collected, similar data elements are grouped to form "records." For instance, all of the data collected on one student constitutes that student's record. All similar records are combined into one data file which is stored on either cards or magnetic tape. An institution may have any number of data files: a student master file consisting of student records, an accounts payable file, a course file, etc. These various data files constitute the database or databank.

The impact of databank information systems on the institution's decision-making process is relatively small. Campus decision makers are only able to retrieve descriptive information concerning various aspects of the campus operation. Such information systems are able to answer such questions as "how many students enrolled in History 102 last semester?" or "how many student accounts receivable are overdue six weeks?" Such information systems are generally necessary for the development of more sophisticated information systems.

Predictive Information Systems

This type of information system involves the development of software to simulate the behavior of the institution. The system is usually used to model instructional and capital costs. (There are several surveys of the currently available simulation models. See Johnson and Katzenmeyer, 1969; Minter and Lawrence, 1969; Schroeder, 1972; and Hussain and Freytag, 1973.) Such simulations predict the long-range cost implications of changes in various institutional policies.

This predictive capability allows campus decision makers to ask "what if" questions. For instance, it is possible to determine the instructional cost implications of increases in the student-faculty ratio prior to actually altering that ratio. Or campus decision makers may want to compare the cost implications of two different methods of increasing the student-faculty ratio. Consequently, predictive information systems are an important asset to the decision-making process.

Decision-Making Information Systems

This type of information system is rare in colleges and universities. Basically, these systems involve computer programs which determine optimal solutions to certain types of problems. An example in a business organization is the application of linear programming techniques to the shipment of goods from a firm's factories to its various warehouses. Once the solution to the problem has been determined, the manager simply implements it; hence the characterization of these information systems as "decision-making."

The usefulness of such programmed decisions in colleges and universities is limited. Such techniques may be useful in some routine tasks such as purchasing supplies for departments, the scheduling of classes, or ordering food for dormitories. Most academic decisions, however, are ambiguous, politically contested, and do not have clear goals against which to measure success.

(The final type of system, the decision-taking information system, is applicable only to highly automated business organizations. The reader is referred to Mason, 1970 for a discussion of this system.)

The remainder of this chapter will focus on the impact of predictive information systems on the decision-making process of academic organizations. The discussion will include the *intended* impact of the information system on one type of institutional decision (i.e., the internal allocation of resources), and two possible *unintended* consequences resulting from the implementation of the information system.

Predictive Information Systems and Resource Allocation Decisions

One of the basic decisions made by colleges and universities is the allocation of resources to academic departments. Traditionally, the budgeting process has relied upon across-the-board increases or decreases in departmental allocations, based on the assumption that the historical pattern of expenditures is correct. However, this traditional budgeting process has been criticized as an ineffective use of the institution's scarce resources (Carnegie Commission, 1972).

Academic organizations have tried a number of alternative budgeting procedures in order to overcome this problem. The initial alternative involved the implementation of Planning Programming Budgeting Systems (PPBS) on various campuses. These budgeting systems attempted to relate the allocation of resources to *objectives* of the organization rather than to the historical pattern of expenditures by departments within the organization. However, the inability of academic organizations to operationalize an overall measure of organizational performance has led to the abandonment of PPBS at most institutions (Carnegie Commission, 1972; Balderston, 1974).

A second alternative has been the adoption of "zero-based" budgeting procedures. These procedures require that each academic department justify its program each year. However, the criteria for justification become a basic problem with this approach to the allocation decision. One possible criterion might be the goals of the organization, which would lead to the same problems faced by PPB systems. Another problem with this budgeting procedure is that part of an academic department's costs are fixed. It is not possible to start from zero when 60 percent of the faculty are tenured.

Whatever budgeting procedure is used by the institution, predictive information systems can support the resource allocation decision in two ways. First, these systems determine the *total workload* which is placed upon the various departments. Second, these systems estimate the *cost* of meeting this expected workload demand. How these two tasks are accomplished is discussed below.

The Generation of Departmental Workload

The first problem involved in the determination of departmental workload requires the estimation of the level of enrollment for the next budget period. Such enrollment forecasts must take into consideration such factors as the number of students who continue at the college, the number of students who will transfer to the college from other institutions, and the number of first-time, full-time students. Further, these forecasts are sensitive to changes in the rate of unemployment and the rate of student attrition. In order to deal with these complexities, institutions have increasingly turned to "student flow models" to supplement the informed guesses of campus administrators.

The second problem is to relate the average student enrollments to the workload placed on the various departments. The principal method for establishing this relationship is the calculation of an Induced Course Load Matrix or ICLM.[1] (This discussion follows the ICLM as formulated by Clark and Huff, 1972. Alternative ICLMs are discussed in Hussain and Freytag, 1973.) *The ICLM displays the average distribution of student enrollments by major and level (e.g., freshmen, sophomores) in the lower and upper division courses of each academic department.* For instance, the ICLM might indicate that the typical freshman history major enrolls in twelve semester credit hours of lower division history courses, twelve credit hours in a foreign language department, and six credit hours in a biological science department. Assuming that these average course enrollments are constant over time (which is equivalent to the assumption that the technical coefficients of an input/output analysis are stable over time), the institution is in a position to estimate the total workload for each academic department for the next budget period.

The total workload for the various departments within the institution is simply the product of the estimated student enrollments (by major and level) and the average distribution of student course enrollments in the upper and lower division courses of each academic department. For instance, if the college estimated that there would

---

1. In technical terms, the Induced Course Load Matrix is essentially the technical coefficient matrix of an input/output analysis in which the inputs are student enrollments and the outputs are student credit hours.

be fifty freshmen history majors during the next budget period, and
these fifty students were multiplied by the average of twelve semester credit hours in lower division history courses, then a workload of
600 credit hours could be expected in the history department's lower
division program from these students. Repeating this process for
other student major and level categories and summing the results
would estimate the total anticipated departmental workload.

The Estimation of Instructional Costs

Once the total anticipated workload has been calculcated for the
various departments, it is possible to estimate the total costs of operating each department. These costs are divided between direct and
indirect. Direct costs are a function of faculty salaries, the salaries of
departmental administrative personnel, and departmental supplies
and expenses. Indirect costs are a function of the services provided to
the department by other units within the organization. These services
may include the use of the campus computer or the library, as well as
general administrative support. Each of these costs will be discussed
in turn.

Direct Costs

The single largest component of the direct costs for a particular
department is the total number of faculty positions required to meet
the anticipated workload. The actual number of faculty positions for
any given workload is based upon institutional policies such as the
average class size and the number of courses each faculty member is
expected to teach. However, the fundamental implication is that the
allocation of faculty positions is dependent upon the anticipated
level of demand for courses in the department.

Some institutions may decide to include more (or less) faculty
positions in a department than would be determined by strict application of organizational rules. Such decisions are based upon the
expectation that the additional supply will increase demand for
courses within the department. Further, some institutions may have
to be willing to allocate additional faculty positions during the initial
phase of new programs due to the lag in student demand for new
courses (Balderston, 1974). Eventually, however, there will come a
time when it must be determined whether or not the level of enrollment in a particular program is sufficient to support the number of
faculty positions allocated to it. In times of financial exigency,
reducing a department's academic program in order to reduce costs,
and the concern that this will result in decreased enrollment, is a
source of constant tension.

In addition to estimating the absolute number of faculty positions required to meet anticipated course demand, predictive information systems are able to answer "what if" questions. While the number of variables which can be manipulated varies with the type of simulation model available, the two variables given the most attention are faculty salaries and the student-faculty ratio. For instance, Wesleyan University has estimated that each 1 percent increase in the average faculty salary costs the institution approximately $100,000. Further, each 1 percent increase has a cumulative effect over time due to the addition of the previous year's salary increase to the salary base for the current year's increase. Thus, changes in faculty salary can have a substantial effect upon the direct costs of operating the academic departments.

The second planning variable involves changes in the ratio of students to faculty in the various departments. This ratio may be increased by either maintaining the current level of enrollment and decreasing the number of faculty in a department (by not filling faculty vacancies), or by increasing the level of enrollment while holding the number of faculty constant, or by some combination of these two strategies. The cost implications may be considerable. In the case of Wesleyan University, the first alternative would save the institution $920,000 in the third year of a three-year phase-in, while the second strategy would reduce expenditures by $2,209,000 in the same period.

Full Costs

The state of the art of "full costing" in colleges and universities is still rudimentary. In order to estimate the full costs of operating an academic department, it is necessary to allocate indirect costs (such as the computer center or the library) to each department in such a manner as to reflect the institutional cost structure as accurately as possible.

Because academic institutions are nonprofit, there has been no motivation to depreciate their physical plant and equipment. Further, when costs are attached to these facilities, they are generally historical and not replacement costs. As a consequence, colleges and universities may not only seriously underestimate the actual costs of operating an academic department, but also "the condition of their capital resources" (Jenny and Wynn, 1972, page 46).

The allocation of costs for services and physical plant has essentially two aspects: the basis upon which costs will be allocated and the method of allocation used. The preferred method for allocating indirect costs is to determine the actual amount of service consumed by the various academic departments. For instance, the actual use of the computer center by the department of physics during the current budget period could serve as a basis for estimating the cost of this service for the physics department during the next budget period.

Lacking direct usage data (as is usually the case for such services as the library and administrative support), it is necessary to develop reasonable parameters for allocating indirect costs. These parameters may involve the direct labor costs of a department (i.e., the total costs for faculty salaries) or the number of student credit hours generated by a department. In order to accurately reflect the institution's cost structure, it may be necessary to use different parameters for different types of indirect costs.

In order to allocate these costs to the various academic departments, one may directly apply the indirect costs in question or use a single- (or multi-) step allocation procedure (Topping, 1972). The latter alternative takes into account the possibility that some support services render services to other support services (e.g., the services provided by the institution's accounting department to the computer center).

By allocating indirect costs, it has been argued that it is possible to anticipate the full cost implication of changes in a department's academic program. One wonders whether public and private universities would have leaped at the opportunity of implementing the variety of graduate programs that they did in the 1960's, had they been able to anticipate the full costs (for such items as computer services or sophisticated equipment) of these programs.

Having described the basic capabilities of predictive information systems generally, mention of several specific cost simulation models should be made. The most common direct cost simulation model is the National Center for Higher Education Management Systems' (or NCHEMS) Resource Requirements Prediction Model 1.6. Models which simulate both the direct and indirect costs of a college are System Research Group's Comprehensive Analytical Methods of Planning in University Systems or CAMPUS, and NCHEMS's Resource Requirements Prediction Model 1.3.

Unanticipated Consequences

Predictive information systems are intended to assist the campus in the more effective use of its resources. However, these systems may also establish a new set of rules within the organization which will affect the behavior of academic departments generally and departmental chairpersons in particular. Specifically, the rules for calculating workload and for estimating costs may produce incentives to maximize enrollments while limiting the indirect costs assigned to the department.

Proposition No. 1

The adoption of predictive information systems will increase departmental motivation to maximize departmental enrollments. The use of the Induced Course Load Matrix or ICLM to allocate resources ties faculty positions directly to the number of student credit hours generated by the department. Thus, if the department is to increase its academic program, it must increase the number of students who enroll in the department. Academic departments may increase their level of student enrollments in at least four different ways.

First, academic departments may *add new courses* in order to attract more students, or at least maintain their current level of enrollment. An apparent desire on the part of academic departments to be "relevant" may in fact be an attempt to play upon the current curricular tastes of students. Getting academic departments to admit that new course offerings result primarily from a desire to increase enrollments is, however, difficult.

In some cases, the development of new courses results from a calculated study of the market. For example, at Adelphi University, the School of Business Administration developed its Educa-train in which commuters between Long Island and New York City would be able to work toward an MBA degree while commuting. On the west coast, a number of public and private institutions (e.g., Pasadena City College and Mount St. Mary's College) have been expanding nursing programs in order to acquire a share of the large student demand. (Such an approach to potential student markets indicates, in part, an increasing management orientation on the part of college and university administrations, as well as the desire on the part of academic departments to generate new enrollments.)

A second way in which academic departments may increase their level of enrollments is to *eliminate courses which generate few student credit hours*. If the rule for allocating faculty positions to a department involves an average class size of fifteen students, it is clear that courses enrolling more than fifteen students are subsidizing courses enrolling less than fifteen students. Most departments have been willing to accept lower division subsidization of upper division courses. However, certain lower division courses may not generate enough student credit hours and thus a department may cancel one course in the hope that a more attractive course will be substituted.

The traditional manner in which academic departments bolster their level of student enrollments is to *require students to take certain courses*. There is probably no faster way to increase student credit-hour demand upon foreign language departments than to impose a five-course foreign language requirement (and no faster way to decrease student credit-hour demand than to drop such course requirements). Within the Graduate School of Education at UCLA, for example, there has been a substantial shift in student course demand to certain specializations due to a change in the courses which satisfy the research methods requirement. One could go on and on with examples of this sort.

Finally, the ICLM provides a clue to yet another way in which academic departments may increase student credit hours. The fact that students enroll in courses outside their major points to *interdependencies between academic departments*.[2] For instance, increases in the number of students enrolling in a college's nursing program have the effect of increasing the number of students enrolling in biology courses. A clever biology department chairperson would thus welcome efforts on the part of the nursing program to expand, knowing that his department would be the beneficiary of some student "fallout." Generally, however, department chairpersons view the allocation of faculty positions as a type of zero-sum game in which there are a fixed number of faculty positions available, and any allocation of an additional faculty position to one department will come at the expense of another department.

Proposition No. 2

The adoption of predictive information systems will increase departmental motivation to minimize the amount of indirect costs assigned to it. The implementation of full costing procedures is intended to assist campus decision makers in anticipating the total costs of operating each academic department. However, these procedures may lead to organizationally dysfunctional behaviors on the part of the departments. Such behaviors may minimize the total indirect costs assigned to a department, but also defeat the purpose of full costing procedures.

One type of dysfunctional behavior is a *drop in the use of support services*. For instance, if an academic department is charged for the use of counseling services, on a direct usage basis by the students majoring in its department, there is a possibility that the department

---

2. These interdepartmental dependencies are revealed by the number of non-zero technical coefficients in the matrix.

may attempt to discourage its students from using the service. Although the indirect costs assigned to the department have decreased, the number of students who might need the service has remained the same; costs are lower, but so are services delivered to the students.

A second type of dysfunctional behavior is the increase in *departmental distrust* and lack of cooperation as a result of full costing. Because departments are charged for services over which they have little, if any, control, the situation is ripe for contentions that unfair charges are being made against a department's accounts. The resulting bickering between departments and administration may detract from the effectiveness of full costing procedures.

There are instances in which departments are motivated to maximize total indirect costs. This occurs when the services provided to the department, such as computer support, are highly valued. However, full costing procedures may still lead to dysfunctional consequences. At UCLA, for example, the allocation of computer funds for intramural users is based on the total expenditures for computer services during the previous year. Such a procedure motivates potential users to request more computer funds than they actually anticipate using, and to spend all of the funds which are available prior to the end of the fiscal year, even if funds are spent unwisely. This kind of behavior indicates the need for empirical investigation into the unanticipated consequences of predictive information systems.

Behavioral consequences are not necessarily negative. On the contrary, strong management information systems can have some very positive impacts on departmental management. Many of the pitfalls outlined above can be avoided if wise use is made of these information systems. For example, Furman University has developed an integrated management system composed of an institutional research office, an information system, and organizational development strategies. Using information distributed to departments on a need-to-know basis, the University has been able to develop a participative management system.

Proposition No. 3

The adoption of predictive information systems will increase the degree of centralization in academic organizations. Two supplementary arguments support this proposition. One involves factors which promote centralization; the second attacks assumptions which support a decentralized management system. These arguments are discussed below.

Predictive information systems seek to provide better information for decision makers. Information itself does not produce change, but may motivate college personnel to select courses of action which will produce the desired changes (Katz and Kahn, 1975). However, in an "information poor" organization, such as a college or university, information can have a substantial effect on the distribution of power (Cohen and March, 1974).

First, the bulk of the information provided by predictive information systems is in the hands of campus administrators. This information is required if administrators are to allocate resources, such as faculty positions, effectively. The increasing use of data-based decisions constitutes a fundamental change in college management practices.

Second, administrators can devote a considerable amount of time to studying this information. Academic organizations have been characterized as institutions in which time is a scarce resource (Cohen and March, 1974). For the most part, faculty members have little time for the study of the operation of various academic departments. Consequently, administrators are able to develop substantial and unopposed expertise in important areas of the operation of academic departments.

Third, the new information produced by predictive information systems may bring changes of "high leverage" but "low salience" for the campus community. These changes have high impact but are not directly in the arena of political concern. For example, the provost of one prestigious university indicated that the most important thing he had done in ten years was to change the "indirect cost" charge on federal and foundation grants, a measure which caused little controversy but which produced substantially greater income for the university.

The argument for decentralizing authority usually assumes that decentralization will motivate departmental supervisors to manage their departments more effectively and efficiently (Benston, 1970). This assumption underlies various management strategies, such as management-by-objectives, in which the participation of department heads in setting goals and assessing accomplishment is supposed to increase their commitment to the organization. Such strategies seem especially appropriate in nonprofit organizations which lack clearly defined measures of organizational outcomes (Anthony et al., 1972). However, it is important to delineate some false assumptions which underlie the idea of decentralization.

The first false assumption is that the college actually evaluates the effectiveness of departmental chairpersons. Under a model of organization decentralization, the departmental chairpersons are assigned certain responsibilities by the administration (e.g., ensuring that departmental appropriations are not exceeded), and then evaluated in terms of the effectiveness with which these responsibilities are carried out. However, this evaluation is rarely carried out.

A second false assumption concerns the ability to distribute rewards that are important to chairpersons. For the most part, departmental chairpersons are elected by the members of their department (it is often said that the person elected is the one not present at the time of the election). Chairpersons are usually teachers and scholars first, and departmental administrators second. Further, other than some released time, most departmental chairpersons do not receive additional compensation for their additional responsibilities. Thus, the organizational rewards for department chairpersons are generally nonexistent and certainly unrelated to the values which motivate academic personnel.

The third false assumption is that chairpersons are management-oriented. Under this assumption, departmental chairpersons hold the campus administrators as their referent group. In seeking to be like administrators, department chairpersons make judgments that are consistent with the concerns of the administration. For the most part, however, departmental chairpersons are not concerned with becoming members of the administration. They perform their duties until such time as they are able to get back to their primary concerns of teaching and research.

We have seen that most decentralization arguments are founded on a set of false assumptions. In addition, a number of forces are pressing for centralization. First is the impact of management information systems. Further, most management theorists know that scarce resources cause centralization of power, and the financial crunch in higher education is definitely having such an effect. When a resource scarcity is coupled with powerful information systems, which are in the hands of the central administration, there is double pressure for centralization. Under these conditions, the principle that decisions in academic organizations should be based on a joint effort between academic departments and college administration becomes little more than a formality.

Some Implications for Restructuring Governance

The central issue involved in the governance of academic organizations is: who is to control the organization? Since the turn of the century, the governance of the campus has been defined in terms of a joint effort between the administration and the faculty (AAUP, 1973). This joint effort is constituted by the "structures and the processes of decision making. We thus distinguish it from administration or management" (Carnegie Commission, 1973, page vii). With the development of computer-based information systems and similar techniques, this separation of decision making and management is no longer tenable.

A definition of academic governance which more closely corresponds to the realities of the current situation has been offered by Garbarino (1975). By governance, he refers to "the total system of institutional administration," a system which consists of a mix of three basic components: (1) management in the traditional sense (i.e., planning and control), (2) participation by colleagues in academic policy decisions, and (3) bargaining as decision making between interest groups. In light of the changes occurring in campus management, one might include in this definition the access of various campus constituencies to organizational information, and the role of these constituencies in decision making based on information.

There are a number of ways to increase participation in information utilization and campus management. Most campuses have a (formal or informal) budget committee consisting of the president and the vice presidents for academic and business affairs. These committees have a great deal of influence in determining the actual budget for the various departments. More importantly, they usually control and use the management information system. How can the strong centralizing tendency inherent in this situation be mitigated? A few suggestions are offered.

First, membership in the central budget committee might be expanded to include faculty and student representatives. There would be at least three basic functions of this expanded budget committee. First, it would collectively develop the assumptions upon which the academic budget for the following year would be based. These assumptions would pertain to such issues as the projected level of enrollment by department, the rate of inflation, the amount of gift revenue to be expected, etc. Second, the committee would jointly review the long-range impact of alternative budget allocations and

changes in institutional policies. Based upon such a review, and discussions with departmental chairpersons, the committee would allocate institutional resources to academic and nonacademic departments. Third, the committee would be responsible for monitoring
the various departments in order to ensure that the established policies (e.g., average class size) were being followed.

Such a committee could have a number of beneficial effects for
the campus. First, it would provide for greater representation by various campus constituencies in an increasingly centralized organization. Centralization in academic organizations is not necessarily to be
avoided, as long as power is centralized in the hands of a representative committee and not a few individuals. In addition, such participation would lead to the realization by members of the campus community of how little flexibility exists in the budget of the institution;
the committee would have a major educational function. The campus
which is able to consider 10 percent of its operating budget discretionary is extremely fortunate. This "cooptation" may lead to increased understanding on the part of the campus community of
problems faced by the campus administration.

An opposite strategy is to adopt a budgeting procedure in which
"every tub has its own bottom" (Carnegie Commission, 1972). Each
department would develop its own budget in terms of anticipated
revenues and expenditures. Revenue estimates would include tuition
generated by students enrolling in the department, gifts made explicitly to the department, and research grants awarded to departmental faculty. Based on these revenue estimates, departments would
decide how many faculty positions would be needed, the amount to
be spent on supplies and equipment, and, under full costing, the
amount of space to be rented from the institution.

The benefits of this approach to campus management is the institutionalization of a highly decentralized budget process. Departments would exercise complete control over the distribution of
resources within their boundaries. However, such a budget system
may result in the erosion of an institution's overall mission. Further,
such a budgeting system emphasizes the department's dependence
upon student curricular tastes. There may be situations in which certain academic programs have sufficiently high value to the academic
community to warrant institutional subsidies.

What is most important, perhaps, about these and other budgeting
strategies, is that a definition of academic governance is operation-
alized which is meaningful in the context of American higher educa-

tion. There are indeed strong pressures toward centralizing management, but administrative domination of academic organizations can be avoided.

References

American Association of University Professors. "Statement on Government of Colleges and Universities." *AAUP Policy Documents and Reports.* Washington, D.C.: AAUP, 1973.

Anthony, R. N.; Deardon, J.; and Vancil, R. F. *Management Control Systems.* Homewood, Ill.: Richard D. Irwin, 1972.

Balderston, F. E. *Managing Today's University.* San Francisco: Jossey-Bass, 1974.

Benston, G. J. "The Role of the Firm's Accounting Systems for Motivation." *Information for Decision Making,* edited by A. Rappaport. Englewood Cliffs, N.J.: Prentice-Hall, 1970.

Bogard, L. "Management in Institutions of Higher Education." *Papers on Efficiency in the Management of Higher Education* (Technical Report). Berkeley, Calif.: Carnegie Commission on Higher Education, 1972.

Carnegie Commission. *The More Effective Use of Resources.* New York: McGraw-Hill, 1972.

Carnegie Commission. *Governance of Higher Education.* New York: McGraw-Hill, 1973.

Clark, D. G., and Huff, R. A. *Instructional Program Budgeting in Higher Education.* Boulder, Colo.: National Center for Higher Education Management Systems at the Western Interstate Commission for Higher Education, 1972.

Cohen, M. D., and March, J. G. *Leadership and Ambiguity.* New York: McGraw-Hill, 1974.

Cushing, B. E. *Accounting Information Systems and Business Organizations.* Reading, Mass.: Addison-Wesley, 1974.

Davis, G. B. *Management Information Systems: Conceptual Foundations, Structure, and Development.* New York: McGraw-Hill, 1974.

Garbarino, J. W. *Faculty Bargaining.* New York: McGraw-Hill, 1975.

Hussain, K. M., and Freytag, H. L. *Resource, Costing, and Planning Models in Higher Education.* Munich: Verlag Dokumentation, 1973.

Jenny, H. H., and Wynn, G. R. *The Turning Point: A Study of Income and Expenditure Growth and Distribution of 48 Private Four-Year Liberal Arts Colleges, 1969-1970.* Wooster, Ohio: The College of Wooster, 1972.

Johnson, C. B., and Katzenmeyer, W. G. (eds.). *Management Information Systems in Higher Education: The State of the Art.* Durham, N.C.: Duke University Press, 1969.

Katz, D., and Kahn, R. "Organizational Change." *Managing Change in Educational Organizations,* edited by J. V. Baldridge and T. E. Deal. Berkeley, Calif.: McCutchan, 1975.

Mann, R. L.; Thomas, C. R.; Williams, R. C.; and Wallhaus, R. A. *An Overview of Two Recent Surveys of Administrative Computer Operations in Higher Education.* Boulder, Colo.: National Center for Higher Education Management Systems at the Western Interstate Commission for Higher Education, 1975.

Mason, R. O. "Basic Concepts for Designing Management Information Systems." *Information for Decision Making,* edited by A. Rappaport. Englewood Cliffs, N.J.: Prentice-Hall, 1970.

Minter, W. J., and Lawrence, B. (eds.). *Management Information Systems: Their Development and Use in the Administration of Higher Education.* Boulder, Colo.: Western Interstate Commission for Higher Education, 1969.

Schroeder, R. G. *A Survey of Operations Analysis in Higher Education.* Paper prepared for the 41st national meeting of the Operations Research Society of America (April 26-28, 1972).

Topping, J. R. *Cost Analysis Manual.* Boulder, Colo.: National Center for Higher Education Management Systems at the Western Interstate Commission for Higher Education, 1972.

15

The Changing Role of Trustees in Academic Governance

Gary L. Riley

Despite the increased attention that has been given recently to the study of the American college and university trusteeship, 1977 is not a particularly good year to offer a definitive statement concerning the existing role and function of governing boards. Many traditions in academic governance—based upon conditions of high public trust, high client demand for educational services, high degrees of professionalism and autonomy among academic faculties, and high public resource commitments to postsecondary education—are eroding as the nation and its institutions face major changes in social policies, economic conditions, and public expectations. In the wake of these changes have come modifications in traditional governance patterns, especially as evidenced by increased faculty unionization, increased centralization of decision-making power and authority, and increased pressures for institutional accountability.

At the apex of the academic governance structure, college and university trustees serve as the primary links between the institutions that they hold in trust and the public which has endowed them with that trust. Caught between pressures from within and from without, today's trustee is thrust into the role of negotiator, mediator, statesman, and accountant. Under these conditions, the relationship between the trustee and the college is strikingly less avuncular and more managerial. The relationship between the trustee and the public is decidedly more political. Ultimately, these changes will have a marked effect upon the characteristics of academic governance structures and processes in American postsecondary education.

An Overview of the American Trusteeship

Boards of governance have a variety of official names. They are most commonly known as Boards of Trustees, Directors, Governors, Boards of Regents, or State Boards of Higher Education. Of less importance than the particular name given to a governing board is the distinguishing relationship that exists between the board and its institution or other governing agencies. Three types of governing boards in the United States can be distinguished on the basis of these relationships. They are: (1) the governing board of a single college or university; (2) the governing board of a multicampus system; and (3) the board of governance that coordinates all of higher education in a particular state.

The governing board of a single college or university is the predominant type in the United States today. Such a board is legally responsible for the affairs of a single institution, public or private. Until well into the present century, when the number of institutions greatly increased, this was almost the only type of board in existence. In structure and purpose it was the prototype for the more recent multicampus and coordinating boards of governance.

The term *Board of Trustees* directly states the purpose of the governing board. It is a corporate organization which accepts a responsibility or trust. The trust is the college or university itself. Decisions of the board are, by definition, corporate decisions. Legally, there is no aspect of the institution's affairs for which the trustees are not ultimately responsible. Until early in this century, boards of trustees took this mandate quite literally. They not only defined and interpreted the goals and standards to be met—they also actively administered the institutions.

There are many ways in which boards of governance can ensure the fulfillment of their extensive responsibilities. For this reason educators can and do vigorously debate the role of trustees. But, despite this disagreement, the principal functions of boards of trustees can be clearly stated:

1. Boards ensure that the institution is financially solvent.
2. They provide for the good administration of the campus through the appointment and dismissal of executive officers.
3. They monitor the quality of instruction, research, and student performance.

4. They serve as the "court of last resort" by resolving internal disputes among administrators, faculty, and students.
5. They act as a buffer between the institution and society, ideally protecting the best interests of both.

The governing board of the multicampus system is patterned after the single campus board, but has a markedly different relationship to the institutions governed. A multicampus system can be defined in many ways; Lee and Bowen (1971) offer one of the more widely accepted definitions. A multicampus system is: (1) one with responsibility for only a portion or segment of higher education in a given state; (2) one with more than one campus; (3) one with a systemwide executive who does not have specific responsibility for any single campus.

The trust of a governing board of a multicampus system is composed of an identifiable segment or subsystem of the total higher education enterprise of the state. The principles of trustee governance do not differ from those cited with respect to single institutions. The unique aspect of trusteeship at the multicampus level is the nature of the trust. By definition, members of the board ensure fulfillment of only some of the goals which the state has set for higher education—or for the segment of higher education that is governed by the board. Moreover, the board not only governs the various member institutions but also assigns responsibilities to the campuses within the system—in effect, it coordinates the work of individual institutions.

As Lee and Bowen (1971) note, the fundamental rationale for multicampus systems of governance and administration is based on two assumptions:

In contrast to a single statewide system of higher education, multiple goals, evidenced by alternative approaches in academic plans and programs, can be better achieved if the state divides responsibilities among separate institutions.

However, in contrast to a system of completely autonomous campuses, these differences can be coordinated and sustained more effectively if campuses are grouped under common governing structures.

Multicampus boards must not only be concerned with the policies and issues of their particular segment, but with interinstitutional cooperation and the distribution of resources and responsibilities throughout the system.

The coordinating board of all postsecondary education is the most recently originated form. Most states now have a board whose function is to coordinate all public (and sometimes private) institutions of higher education. Coordinating boards, sometimes called coordinating councils, do not govern individual educational institutions or segments. Rather, they are responsible for ensuring that the post-secondary mission of the entire state is coordinated and delegated to the appropriate segments and individual institutions. These boards vary markedly from state to state, however, in their specific responsibilities, structures, and governance procedures.

To some extent, these differences depend upon the existence of multicampus boards. In some cases coordinating boards merely review the budgets and make policy recommendations. In other instances, the coordinating boards consolidate the budgets of all institutions and have effective control over the development of higher education—institutions and degree programs—throughout the state.

The current trend toward statewide coordination is most pronounced at the two-year, community college level. Day and May (1973) observe that, in most states, coordinating boards regulate most strongly institutions in the two-year public sector, while statutory provisions affecting the governance of other segments emphasize the scope of responsibility of local institutional boards. However, Wattenbarger (1972) argues that, as the national trend toward centralization continues, it is likely that four-year colleges and universities in the public sector will also be subsumed under coordinating boards granted authority by legislative amendments.

The Composition of American Boards of Governance

In American higher education, the size of governing boards varies greatly from institution to institution in both the public and private sectors. The Carnegie Commission on Higher Education (1973) has indicated that the size of governing boards ranges from approximately five to over one hundred members. Since there are more than 2,000 governing boards in the nation, the total number of trustees is estimated to be over 30,000.

One of the most important distinguishing characteristics of American (and Canadian) governance boards is that control is vested in individuals who are not professional educators. This is commonly described as "lay" control. Clark (1961) describes trustees as instruments of external control, as persons who are part-time and amateur rather than full-time and expert. Trustees should possess the following qualifications: (1) a college education; (2) an active interest in the institution; (3) a genuine interest in higher education; (4) the ability to attend meetings regularly and to work in behalf of the institution; (5) reasonable economic stability; (6) a good reputation in business or professional life; and (7) a good reputation in the community for sound character and moral judgment (Burns, 1966).

While these qualifications are not necessarily limited to a small stratum of society, the membership of governing boards is quite limited in actual practice. Men who controlled businesses, finances, and industries constituted an inordinately high percentage of trustees in 1947 (Beck, 1947). Twenty years later, the Educational Testing Service found that this had not changed much. "In general, trustees are males, in their fifties, white, well-educated, and financially well-off. . . . As a group, they personify success in the usual American sense of that word" (Hartnett, 1969).

In 1976, the Association of Community College Trustees conducted a survey of public two-year college trustees. The ACCT hypothesized that if the two-year community college represents the innovation, opportunity, and freedom espoused in the literature of the "community college movement," then the characteristics of community college trustees should be different from trustees governing four-year elite institutions. However, when the ACCT compared the results of their 1976 study to the ETS results of 1967, no significant differences were found between the two samples. ACCT concluded that 92 percent of community college trustees are white; 85 percent are male; 59 percent earn more than $20,000 a year; 74 percent reside in the suburbs; and 39 percent hold postsecondary degrees.

Board membership is, of course, partially determined by the method of selection employed. Public and private institutions differ in the way in which they select their trustees. In the public sector, the governor of the state normally chooses the members of the state-financed public boards. In some cases, however, members are elected by the general public. This is particularly true in the case of the public community college where the local district elects the board of governors.

State governing boards often include at least one ex-officio member. These are usually governors, superintendents of public instruction, and presidents of the institutions. In some cases, legislative representatives serve in an ex-officio role as well—especially where the governor wishes to have direct linkages between the board and the state's budget committee.

Private institutions follow a pattern of self-perpetuating boards of trustees. That is, the boards select their own membership. Occasionally, the president of the institution is entitled to make recommendations to the board. Similarly, alumni associations may have the right to elect one or two trustees. However, with a median number of twenty-four members on private college and university boards, administrative and alumni candidates are clearly in the minority.

The Power and Authority of the Trusteeship

Governing boards in the United States generally have final legal corporate authority over their institutions; this is assured by law and by the principles of public trust. However, in order to function effectively, boards customarily delegate major elements of their power and authority to other groups and individuals within their institutions. Boards depend upon others to share the trust, and this most often means presidents and faculties.

Both administrative and academic positions often require highly specialized skills. In a complex environment like the modern university, trustees must rely upon the judgment of others and upon information provided by others with specialized skills and analytical methods. In other words, trustees are in need of groups and individuals to administer the trust. The faculty must be included in this category; in recent years, faculties have assumed more responsibility for the academic aspects of governance through such organizations as the academic senate.

Thus, although instruments of incorporation entrust the board of trustees with the total welfare of the educational institution, in practice there is substantial collegial governance as well as conflict of interest among trustees, administrators, faculty members, and students. Under the jurisdiction of board authority, administrative appointees have assumed nearly all of the managerial responsibilities of the academic organization. Academic faculties have assumed nearly all of the control over academic programs and the appointment and promotion of their own membership. Some observers have concluded that college and university boards of trustees have relinquished their power and authority so extensively that they have become nearly impotent. The net result is that institutions of higher education have become inner- rather than outer-directed (Newman, 1973).

Since the early 1970's, criticism of lay governing boards has increased markedly, both within and outside the academy. Lack of role clarity, lack of assertiveness, lack of concern for the maintenance of intellectual standards in student performance, and lack of managerial accountability are among the more commonly voiced criticisms leveled at today's trustees (Budd, 1974; Paltridge, 1973; Zwingle and

Mayville, 1974). Lee and Bowen (1971) voice a strong position on the contemporary responsibility of trustees. They argue: "Both internal and external pressures suggest the necessity—contrary to the criticism of many students and faculty—for a strong governing board: to prod and support the administration, to make difficult decisions of educational policy, to hear appeals from the faculty and students, to interpret the university to a questioning and demanding community and the community to the university—in short, to represent the public interest in the governance of the multicampus university."

The strength of a governing board is, of course, relative to that of others who are delegated power and authority to make academic policy and to implement decisions. Indeed, it is probably the case that both internal and external groups are in favor of boards of trustees retaining their legally constituted authority over academic policy. The differences of opinion arise, however, when the board exercises its power, thereby favoring one interest group over another. The question is, should a strong board of trustees exercise its power to buffer the academic organization from external influence? Or should its power be used to translate external demands into institutional reforms? Perhaps the critical issue is not simply whether boards of trustees have great power and authority, but whether institutional policies reflect the prevalent attitudes of the external environment or those of the professionals within the university.

A Changing Environment and a Changing Professional Climate

In 1971 and again in 1974 a survey of colleges and universities was conducted by Baldridge and associates at Stanford University in order to determine the relationship between patterns of academic governance and a variety of environmental and professional influences (Baldridge et al., 1973; Kemerer and Baldridge, 1975). These researchers wished to know what effects external environmental conditions have upon decision making and policy formulation in colleges and universities, and whether environmental conditions affect the distribution of power and authority within certain decision structures. Specifically, they wished to know whether a tightened economy, increased legislation, student needs, market demands, and special interests expressed by the public permeated the academic organization in ways that would visibly affect power, authority, and certain kinds of institutional autonomy.

Simultaneously, the researchers wished to study the impact of academic collective bargaining upon decision-making power and authority. Does academic unionization contribute to major shifts in power? What procedural reforms in academic governance are necessitated by the negotiated union contract? What is happening to the professional climate on campuses that have elected to unionize?

Although the results of the studies varied somewhat according to the type of institution examined (i.e., public or private, two-year, four-year, or university), several findings apply to all postsecondary institutions:

1. *Increased environmental pressure leads to increased centralization of decision making.* This centralization occurs at the individual campus level, at the level of the chief executive officer in a multi-campus system, and at the level of the state board or coordinating council. Under conditions of high external pressure, those with the formal power to make policy decisions tend to take back much of the authority that, previously, was delegated to others in the educational system. Trustees reclaim authority delegated to administrators; administrators reclaim responsibility delegated to faculty senates or other associations. Powerful coalitions of trustees and chief executive officers rally around issues and problems raised by external influence groups.

2. *Increased environmental pressure leads to an increased demand for accountability.* Higher education has become one of the largest businesses in America, with the total enterprise representing slightly over 3 percent of the Gross National Product. Taxpayers, students as consumers, employers, and others have begun to articulate their economic concerns to higher education through legislators and trustee organizations. The net effect had led scholars such as Ralph M. Besse to state that: "If we are to maintain the vitality of institutions of higher education, someone must be accountable in the basic areas of academic substance and methods. The trustees themselves must either exact this accountability or see to it that somebody else does and reports to them" (Scully, 1974). The demand for accountability is equally present in the private college, although it is not expressed quite as formally as in the public sector where state boards and legislatures provide a ready means of articulation.

3. *Increased environmental pressure leads to increased trustee involvement in day-to-day decision making and matters of institutional management.* Under conditions of high external pressure, the traditional distinction between the trustee as policy maker and the administrator as manager weakens markedly. To ensure that the public's interest is represented, trustees seem more inclined to become directly involved in routine administrative functions. Many scholars

have cautioned against unchecked trustee involvement in these routine practices—fearing that fundamental questions of institutional growth, direction, educational policy, and public accountability might be crowded out of the board's agenda to make room for the details of educational administration (Cheit, 1971). However, in practice it is difficult to satisfy the demand for accountability without getting involved in administrative procedures. So long as the trustee believes that the public interest is best served in such a manner, it will be difficult to distinguish between fundamental policy questions and routine administrative issues.

4. *The climate for academic governance is becoming increasingly legalistic in all aspects of decision making and policy formulation.* Trustees are affected in at least two ways by increased legalism in colleges and universities. First, one of the principal functions of the board—that of serving as a court of last resort in cases of internal disputes—is seriously undermined by an encroaching legal appeal system that takes disputes off the campus and into the courts. Second, the function of the board as a buffer between the institution and society is seriously threatened as the board is placed in the legal position of plaintiff or defendant. Of course, the settlement of disputes according to points of law can reduce conflict growing out of ambiguous definitions of role, authority, and responsibility. But the shift in the role of the trustee from "caretaker" to "adversary" has significant consequences for all concerned. Under these circumstances, power shifts *outward,* threatening to overwhelm the delicate balance of authority.

Academic collective bargaining and faculty unionization reinforce the effects of environmental pressure on college and university governance. In fact, academic collective bargaining depends upon a legalistic, adversarial, and centralized system of governance.

Collective bargaining amounts to a turning away from collegiality and self-governance and a moving toward an adversary system which recognizes that the central fact of life in the academy is that there are those who manage and those who are managed, that there are employers and employees, that conflicts arise from these relationships, and that in a collective bargaining system they are resolved by a process predicated upon the proposition that people whose interests conflict are, at least in respect of those conflicts, adversaries [Wollett, 1973].

Although the movement toward coordination of public higher education occurred before academic unions appeared, collective bargaining and the centralization of decision making are ready-made stimulants for each other. In order to be effective, unions must deal directly with centers of power. Contracts affecting an entire multi-campus or state system are managed by the authorities at the peak of the system's pyramid. Similarly, there has to be a union power center which is equivalent to the administrative central offices. Moreover, centralized power usually means financial power—the legislature, its budget committees, and the office of the state governor.

Interestingly, the movement toward collective bargaining reflects in part faculty anxiety over the erosion of local campus autonomy by statewide boards and coordinating agencies. Many faculty members embraced collective bargaining as a weapon to use against accountability and economy-minded legislators and trustees who insist upon cost reductions and improved efficiency. Yet, ironically, collective bargaining promotes centralization through large bargaining units and by focusing on economic issues that must be settled off campus and personnel issues that must be settled in the courts. Thus the circle is complete: anxiety about system control stimulates unionism, and unionism accelerates system control (Kemerer and Baldridge, 1975).

To summarize, under the conditions of environmental pressure and academic collective bargaining, power shifts upward and outward: upward into multicampus boards and statewide coordinating agencies; outward to the courts, the unions, and the legislature. To the extent that the local campus trustee and the chief executive officer participate in the resulting centralized decision making, their powers are maintained or even enhanced in relationship to the faculty and other mid-level administrative officers (Kemerer and Baldridge, 1975). But, to the extent that campus presidents and local boards are subordinate to central administrative offices and system-wide coordinating boards, their power to formulate policy is reduced.

The implications should be clear: as power is shifted upward, with local trustees held responsible for implementing systemwide policies and local campus administrators held responsible for managing negotiated contracts or legislated regulations, trustees and administrators will function as joint participants in administrative management teams (Riley, 1976). Trustees, now bombarded with demands that they be involved on a continuous basis with the administration and the monitoring of academic operations, must work with administrators to develop procedures whereby the public interest can be served while institutional autonomy is preserved. Collective bargaining and collective management are the two newest and most important elements of academic governance to be faced over the next decade.

References

Association of Community College Trustees. *Trustee Profile 1976.* Washington, D.C.: The Association, 1976.

Baldridge, J. Victor; Curtis, David; Ecker, George; and Riley, Gary L. *Academic Politics, Morale and Involvement: Preliminary Findings of the Stanford Project on Academic Governance* (Research and Development Memorandum no. 100, Stanford Center for Research and Development in Teaching). Stanford, Calif.: Stanford University, 1973.

Beck, Hubert P. *Men Who Control Our Universities.* New York: Kings Crown Press, 1947.

Budd, John F. "Are College Trustees Obsolete?" *Saturday Review* (March 9, 1974).

Burns, Gerald P. *Trustees in Higher Education: Their Functions and Coordination.* New York: Independent College Funds of America, 1966.

Carnegie Commission on Higher Education. *Governance of Higher Education: Six Priority Problems.* New York: McGraw-Hill, 1973.

Cheit, Earl. *The New Depression in Higher Education.* New York: McGraw-Hill, 1971.

Clark, Burton R. "The Role of Faculty in Administration." *Studies of College Faculty.* Boulder, Colo.: Western Interstate Commission for Higher Education, 1961.

Day, C. W., and May, R. *Effects of State Coordination upon Two-Year College Boards of Trustees.* Los Angeles: ERIC Clearinghouse on Junior Colleges, 1973. ERIC, no. ED097924.

Hartnett, Rodney T. *College and University Trustees: Their Backgrounds, Roles and Educational Attitudes.* Princeton, N.J.: Educational Testing Service, 1969.

Kemerer, Frank, and Baldridge, J. Victor. *Unions on Campus.* San Francisco: Jossey-Bass, 1975.

Lee, Eugene C., and Bowen, Frank M. *The Multicampus University: A Study of Academic Governance.* New York: McGraw-Hill, 1971.

Newman, Frank. "Trustee Accountability and National Policy." Association of Governing Boards, *Reports* no. 16 (October 1973).

Paltridge, James G. *Boards of Trustees: Their Decision Patterns.* Berkeley: Center for Research and Development in Higher Education, 1973.

Riley, Gary L. "Collective Bargaining and Collective Management: Two New Partners in Community College Governance." *Preparing Trustees with Better Tools of Boardsmanship.* Washington, D.C.: Association of Community College Trustees, 1976.

Scully, Malcolm G. "Many Trustees Seek to Assert More Control." *Chronicle of Higher Education* 8, no. 31 (May 6, 1974): 1.

Wattenbarger, James L. *The Two-Year College Trustee: National Issues and Perspectives.* Washington, D.C.: Association of Governing Boards, 1972.

Wollett, D. "Historical Development of Faculty Collective Bargaining and Current Extent." *Proceedings, First Annual Conference, April, 1973,* edited by M. C. Benewitz. New York: National Center for the Study of Collective Bargaining in Higher Education, Baruch College, 1973.

Zwingle, J. L., and Mayville, William V. *College Trustees: A Question of Legitimacy* (Higher Education Research Report no. 10). Washington, D.C.: American Association for Higher Education, 1974.

16

Student Participation in Governance:
A Review of the Literature

Gary L. Riley

Student participation in the governance of American higher education is a fairly recent development. Before the Civil War, student
behavior in all types of postsecondary institutions was tightly controlled by regulations set forth by the trustees, enforced by the administration, and welcomed by the teaching faculty. With the establishment of the land grant college, authority loosened somewhat—
largely because of the student transience and anonymity that resulted from the urban location and greater size of the campuses
(Hodgkinson, 1971). During the twenties, student governments
began to appear in many institutions, public and private. And by the
early thirties, associated student organizations had become widespread.

Student participation in these early forms of government was
limited to matters relating to the "quality of student life" (Kapp,
1975). Undergraduates seemed content to select homecoming
queens, elect prom committees, and write school songs. It was this
condition that returning veterans of World War II faced when, armed
with the G.I. Bill, they turned to higher education as a means of preparing themselves for careers in the postwar technological American
society. Veterans, insisting upon sharing in academic decisions which
would, ultimately, affect their careers and their lifestyles, quickly

This chapter was prepared with the assistance of Gloria J. Kapp, student activities administrator at California State University, Los Angeles.

realized that existing forms of student government were ineffective as decision-influencing tools. Having little in common with eighteen-year-old cheerleaders and football players, the vets organized separate associations through which their needs and interests could be expressed to trustees and academic administrators.

When the 1960's began, very few colleges and universities involved students in decision-making processes. But, by the end of the period of student activism, student participation in campuswide decision bodies had become generally accepted throughout the nation. For the first time, student government was not merely a form of developmental activity, but became a political activity—stimulated by motives and behaviors that are typical of other kinds of political interest groups working to achieve access, recognition, and efficacy in matters of policy formulation and governance. That is, as one consequence of the student activism of the 1960's, students have *formalized* their access to and their participation in academic governance.

The Formalization of Authority and Influence

The principle of formalization is central to our understanding of students' contemporary role in academic governance. At the time that Stam and Baldridge (1971) completed their study of student activism, student influence over matters of policy was expressed through ad hoc associations of interest groups variously labeled "alienated," "radical," and extralegal. Reflecting all dimensions of the political spectrum, associations such as Students for a Democratic Society and Young Americans for Freedom had a marked "awakening" effect upon faculty, administrators, trustees, legislators, and college student populations (previously moderate in their politics and inactive in their day-to-day lives as members of student government).

Today, in contrast to the late 1960's and early 1970's, student influence over academic decisions is predominantly exercised through formal participation in committees and other academic decision bodies. Indeed, such participation is generally considered to be common to the routine governance procedure of many colleges and universities. While the exact pattern of student membership and participation on administrative and faculty committees varies significantly from campus to campus, by incorporating many of the principles of student activism into contemporary student government, the extralegal activities of the sixties have become routinized, formalized, and, to some degree, bureaucratized.

Political evolution of the type described above is not uncommon in other social and organizational settings. Labor unions, professional associations, taxpayer groups, and other special interest organizations throughout the American social-political network have historically sought out and found means by which their particular interests might be officially represented in decision processes affecting them and their welfare. Such political evolution is not without its problems, however—particularly as applied to the development of student participation in governance. As Hodgkinson observed at the White House Youth Conference in 1971, "At the same time that more power is going to the [student], more authority is being concentrated in the hands of centralized boards at the state and federal levels." To become a part of the decision-making system does not necessarily ensure that students become influential over the outcomes of decision processes. Apathy may prevail; in addition, the cooptation of under-represented student interest groups threatens to reduce the diversity, autonomy, and creative polarity of thinking that so typified the student movement of the 1960's.

Gamson's treatise on power, authority, and partisan influence in decision making offers us one explanation of the changes that occur when interest groups gain formalized access and recognition in traditional decision structures (1967). During the 1960's, students (as partisans) had virtually no formalized power and authority over academic policies and decision outcomes. Traditionally, power and authority were vested in boards of trustees, delegated in specific instances to the administration, and shared by the faculty through their affiliations with academic departments and the academic senate. In Gamson's language, student interest groups gained *access* to formal decision-making bodies by means of independent political behaviors—persuasion, negotiation, coercion, and even violent confrontation. Student status in decision-making processes was demanded and negotiated through external affiliations, and not through formalized structures such as student government, membership on the academic senate, or employee organizations.

However, subsequent to the activities of the sixties, national councils, trustee organizations, professional associations, and numerous other authority groups that had responsibility for the development and preservation of higher education stimulated campuses to formalize student participation, frequently via existing student government organizations. Under these conditions, students no longer demand *access* to power, but instead are forced to deal with the problems of *sharing* formal power and authority. Moreover, in the

former situation, students rallied around interest-specific causes. Resources were assembled around these political causes, and influence
was channeled in rather narrow—at least, focused—directions. Under
the present circumstances, with students having gained routine access
to decision making, interests and energies are disseminated over a
multitude of issues causing energies to be drained and influence to be
severely watered down.

To summarize, contemporary forms of student government involve a sharing of decision-making powers among students and traditional authorities—namely, trustees, administrators, and faculty.
Routinized participation in decision making has a constraining effect
rather than a liberating effect. That is, students have learned that formalized participation often means that others control the decision
agenda; that the principles of democracy and majority rule can work
to their disadvantage; that committee work is, essentially, a bureaucratic process requiring much time and perseverance; and that professionalism and academic expertise outweigh the appeal of academic
reforms—no matter how well they are presented.

Current Problems and Issues

A study of the current literature on student government reveals
that the major issues, problems, and concerns stem directly from the
formalized and legalistic patterns of student participation that have
evolved since the 1960's. Three issues stand out as being particularly
troublesome: (1) student participation and voting rights on governing
boards and other key committees; (2) state and federal student lobbies which, paradoxically, seem to be more effective than student
participation at the local campus level; and (3) the impact of academic collective bargaining and unionization on student participation
in governance. It seems that the sharing of power and decision-
making authority has, for students, as many drawbacks as advantages. The three issues cited above are the result of attempts by students to engage in governance within the confines of traditional
academic structures and procedures.

Student Participation on Governing Boards

In June 1972, the United States Congress enacted the higher education bill (Public Law 93210), which included the following statement: "It is the sense of the Congress that the governing boards of
institutions of higher education give consideration to student participation on such boards." Reactions to the congressional statement by

college and university officials were mixed. Some institutions which had already begun to initiate actions leading to student participation in governance welcomed the statement as an endorsement of a "controversial" policy. Others declared that the action of Congress was inappropriate—centering their argument on "the principle of institutional autonomy and freedom from governmental interference" (Blandford, 1972).

In response to numerous inquiries from colleges and universities across the nation, the Association of Governing Boards of Colleges and Universities asked the Higher Education Panel of the American Council on Education to conduct a survey to assess the extent of student participation on institutional governing boards and to learn more about such questions as: How many institutions have students on their governing boards at the present time? How many are planning such a move? What means are used to include students on the boards? What authority do students hold on boards? What is the attitude of board members toward student participation? (Blandford, 1972).

Results of the American Council survey revealed that only about 14 percent of all postsecondary institutions in the United States had, in 1972, students as members of their governing boards—voting or nonvoting members. Public four-year colleges, with approximately 25 percent having students represented on boards, were at the high end of the scale. Public two-year colleges, at 8 percent, and private two-year colleges, at 6 percent, represented the other end of the scale. Although more institutions included student members in 1972 than in years past, these institutions were clearly in the minority. Moreover, the Council declared, "very few intend to involve students in decision making at the board level" (Blandford, 1972).

By 1974, a study of student participation on governing boards of public colleges and universities revealed that little change had taken place since 1972 (Joint Committee on Post-Secondary Education of the California State Legislature, 1974). Although twenty states had made provision for students to sit on the boards of one or more public institutions, the actual number of colleges and universities involved was not significantly different from the number reported by the American Council on Education two years before.

Analyses of information gathered by the American Council in 1972 and the Center for the Study of Higher Education at Berkeley in 1974 indicate that by the mid-1970's most of the colleges and universities that supported the idea of student participation on boards had made provision for student representation. Conversely, institutions opposed to the idea of student participation indicated that they had absolutely no intention of initiating the question again in the near future (Kapp, 1975).

Widespread student membership on college and university boards will probably not occur in the immediate future. Arguments in support of student membership are balanced by arguments against it. Common arguments in support of student membership are: as consumers of education, students ought to have an appropriate share of the decision-making authority in academic and curricular matters; boards of trustees with student members are more responsive to student-oriented issues and concerns; student membership on boards of trustees opens new lines of communication among students, trustees, administrators, and members of the faculty.

Arguments on the negative side are: students are largely unaware of existing power-integration mechanisms; few issue-oriented student groups are ever formed; students primarily play a protest role, using board membership to act out authority problems; complex problems are dealt with superficially by joint groups of students, trustees, and administrators—with the real problem solving done later by smaller groups of trustees and members of the administrative and faculty decision structure.

Trustees and administrators also complain that students feel inadequate to deal with the issues involved, that they become frustrated, lose their motivation, and withdraw either physically or psychologically (Hawes and Truax, 1974). One solution to this problem, of course, is to provide them with orientation and training. But this is a costly and time-consuming proposition—particularly when the average period of student tenure on boards and board committees is slightly less than one calendar year (Hawes and Truax, 1974).

Perhaps because of the problems involved, the vast majority of colleges and universities that currently include students in decision making at the level of the trustees do so by various alternative means. For example, board committees allow students to serve in an advisory rather than a policy-making role. Committees such as those related to curriculum, financing of educational programs, special study programs, and student services offer students the advantage of selective participation in matters most directly related to their interests and welfare. Selective committee membership, as opposed to general board membership, also helps to reduce the problem of limited student time and expertise.

Although such strategies seem to solve most of the institution's problems with student membership at the policy level, the students themselves are far from satisfied. With heavy restrictions on their voting rights, limited representation on boards of trustees, and almost no authority over academic issues, students have begun to take their problems off the campuses and into the state and federal capitals.

State and National Student Lobbies

Increased student influence on state and federal legislative bodies and on other agencies external to the college and university campus is an issue which has received much attention of late. This is particularly true with regard to the formation of state and national student lobbies. In a 1973 report, *Governance of Higher Education,* the Carnegie Commission suggested that increased student influence with the legislature might lead to a situation where students feel it is more desirable to maintain this external influence than to work toward influence and autonomy on campus (Carnegie Commission on Higher Education, 1973). Others such as Kapp (1975) and Kemerer and Baldridge (1975) suggest that centralized student lobbies might be the only means available to students in the late 1970's to exercise concerted influence over an increasingly centralized system of American higher education.

Governance is, essentially, a legal term. It suggests that financial responsibility and authority over the maintenance and operation of the institution are entrusted to a corporate board. Further, the board may delegate specific responsibilities and decision-making authority to those who may be held accountable in the eyes of the law. In recent years, the administration and coordination of colleges and universities in the public sector has become increasingly centralized as a result of the formation of state coordinating councils, the strengthening of multicampus system offices, and the passage of federal legislation affecting higher education. Consequently, authority and accountability have been delegated to persons and agencies at higher and higher levels of the educational pyramid (Kemerer and Baldridge, 1975).

In a centralized system, influence over campus decisions might affect certain procedures—while influence over legislative decisions will affect guidelines, rules, regulations, and policies. It is this principle that has caused campus administrators to attack movements favoring increased centralization, for one result is a lessening of local campus autonomy and administrative authority. It is also this principle that has led student associations to concentrate attention and resources on pieces of legislation that, ultimately, set the tone for local campus practices.

The National Student Lobby, drawing its membership from the various state student lobbies, is currently attempting to influence federal legislation on student financial aid, higher education financial appropriations, national collective bargaining, and numerous issues related to the controversial Equal Rights Amendment. Student interns from the nation's large public universities regularly participate in special state and federal committees on finances, equal educational opportunity, institutional governance, and systemwide educational planning.

At the 1975 meeting of the Association for the Study of Higher Education in Chicago, professors of higher education met to discuss recent trends and developments in the teaching of college and university administration. Among the developments cited was the proliferation of specially designed courses offered to undergraduates who are involved in local, state, and national student lobbies. California, Illinois, Michigan, New York, New Jersey, Ohio, Florida, and many other large state universities currently provide for undergraduate student instruction in academic governance—on a special seminar or regularly scheduled course basis. The purposes of such courses is to help compensate for a lack of student expertise in matters of academic governance, planning, financing, and management.

In many states, student governments maintain full-time student lobbyists in state capitals. Some employ legal and educational specialists to assist in the preparation of legislative reviews and proposals. Although the overall effectiveness of student lobbies is yet to be officially determined, state legislative committees have reported that student input is not only desired, but clearly needed in situations where student needs may conflict with the vested interests of faculty and administration (Smith, 1975).

One of the problems with student lobbies is that they are not particularly compatible with existing forms of student government. Hodgkinson points out that, while no one pattern of student government prevails today, there is a clearly visible trend away from the traditional separation of powers to unicameral models (Hodgkinson, 1971). With local campus trends leading toward a *sharing* of certain powers and responsibilities, and state and national trends leading toward a *separation* of policy and decision influence among administrators, faculties, and students, the relationship between student lobbies and local campus student government is uncoordinated and frequently dysfunctional.

The "representative assembly" model of student government, currently dominating the two-year and four-year campuses in both public and private sectors, requires substantial numbers of students on individual campuses to involve themselves on a continuing basis in committees, senate assemblies, special councils, and subunits of the administration and the board of trustees (Creamer, 1975). The "bicameral" model involves a negotiating group of students, faculty members, and administrators, who bargain toward compromises in recommendations to the trustees or appropriate administrative groups. Negotiation for compromise is fundamental to the idea of traditional academic governance—governance among peers. But it is inconsistent with independent political activities via student lobbies aimed at direct influence over decision-making authorities.

Among others, Creamer (1975) proposes that the "student syndicalist" model of government might be more appropriate to the wave of student lobbyists—whereby students form a national or regional power base for the purpose of bringing pressure to bear upon decision makers at the local, state, regional, and national levels. Local campus agencies would, under such a model, stand by the regional or national "platform," while attempting to influence locally relevant decisions and practice. The student syndicalist model has yet another appeal: it might be the only option available to students in relationship to academic collective bargaining.

The Impact of Collective Bargaining on Student Government

Research on the impact of academic collective bargaining on student participation in governance is almost nonexistent—having taken a back seat to the study of faculty roles and attitudes toward unionization (Kemerer and Baldridge, 1975). However, one must recognize that collective bargaining is associated with an increased incidence of conflicting and adversarial relationships between academic managers (administrators) and employees (faculty members). Students, having no employee status, are generally excluded from the bargaining process.

Shark (1973) notes that the traditional industrial model of collective bargaining assumes a clear employer-employee relationship, and fails to recognize any contractual rights and privileges outside that relationship. In campus bargaining situations, students are generally among those denied these rights and privileges (Ort, 1975). Olsen (1974) suggests that the influence of the industrial model over academic collective bargaining leads to a confusion between "the institution as a 'corporation' (management of enterprise) and the 'college' (curriculum, instruction, standards, admissions, etc.)." He further argues that "the clashes yet to occur on the campuses are those between the student leaders who have successfully gained student power and the faculty collective bargaining units because, almost invariably, collective bargaining agreements ignore the student interest of the trichotomy and abrogate the student voice and role gained in recent years."

Bond (1974), having studied several examples of academic collective bargaining contracts, concludes that students have few formal rights to governance participation as expressed or implied in contracts. She suggests that students will attempt to correct this situation by working directly with their state legislatures to influence "enabling legislation," thereby making provision for some kind of student involvement. Bond believes that students may seek observer status at collective bargaining negotiations, participatory status in bargaining between faculty and administration, or the establishment of tripartite bargaining in the law. Indeed, state and national student lobbies appear to be moving in these directions—but with little success, to date.

One of the most significant barriers to student participation in collective bargaining is the law. Bucklew (1973) observes that "there is little evidence to indicate that students will be interpreted as covered by most state labor relations acts." Nevertheless, he reminds us that "if students are not granted the legal right to bargain by state labor statutes, an institution may choose to grant that right to its students." However, to assume that many colleges or universities will do so contradicts the observed tendency on the part of higher educational institutions to exclude students from collective bargaining (Kemerer and Baldridge, 1975; Ort, 1975).

What About the Future?

The future of student participation in academic governance is uncertain. One must be particularly scrupulous in reading contemporary literature, for some of the most appealing theories are based on untested assumptions about the law, about the formal status of students, and about public and professional attitudes toward governance and accountability.

For example, some authors argue that students relate to academic governance in three contexts—as employees, as affected third parties, and as consumers. Most current legislation, however, does not include students in any of these categories. Of course, some college and university systems may adopt one of these status definitions. And state and national student lobbies may eventually influence legislation that will specify students' rights and their relationship to the academic governance process. But it is unlikely that uniform policies will be adopted from state to state or from one institution to another. American higher education is simply too diverse and too jealous of institutional autonomy to agree to uniformity in student participation.

Those involved with student government must carefully assess the legal, constitutional, and political conditions in their particular states and individual institutions. Colleges and universities should decide what issues, decisions, and policies might be appropriately addressed by their unique student populations. Each institution should be encouraged to adopt a judicious definition of student status in academic governance. The time is past when colleges and universities can simply declare what students *are not*. If higher education will not determine a clear definition of student status, recent experience tells us that other interested agencies most certainly will.

References

Blandford, Barbara A. "Student Participation on Institutional Governing Boards." *Higher Education Panel Report* (Survey no. 11). Washington, D.C.: American Council on Education, 1972.

Bond, Linda. "Collective Bargaining and Its Impact on the Learning Environment: The Need for a Closer Look." Los Angeles: University of California, 1974. ERIC, no. ED 090814.

Bucklew, Neil S. "Unionized Students on Campus." *Educational Record* 54, no. 4 (Fall 1973).

Carnegie Commission on Higher Education. *Governance of Higher Education.* New York: McGraw-Hill, 1973.

Creamer, Don. "Alternatives to Traditional Student Government." *Peabody Journal of Education* 52, no. 2 (January 1975).

Gamson, William A. *Power and Discontent.* New York: Dorsey Press, 1967.

Hawes, Leonard C., and Truax, Hugo R. "Student Participation in the University Decision Making Process." *Journal of Higher Education* XLV, no. 2 (February 1974).

Hodgkinson, Harold. "Student Participation in Governance." *The Research Reporter* VI, no. 2 (1971).

Joint Committee on Post-Secondary Education of the California State Legislature. *Governing Boards of Public Universities and Colleges: Composition, Selection, Length of Terms.* Sacramento: The Committee, 1974.

Kapp, Gloria J. "Faculty and Student Participation in Governance." Los Angeles: University of California, 1975.

Kemerer, Frank, and Baldridge, J. Victor. *Unions on Campus.* San Francisco: Jossey-Bass, 1975.

Olsen, James K. "Governance by Confrontation: Adversarialism at the University." *Intellect* 102, no. 2356 (March 1974).

Ort, Larry V. "The Student and Collective Bargaining in Higher Education." *The MSU Orient* 10, no. 1 (1975).

Shark, A. "The Student's Right to Collective Bargaining." *Change* (April 1973).

Smith, Glen. "A Survey of Student Lobbies." Los Angeles: University of California, 1975.

Stam, James, and Baldridge, J. Victor. "The Cycle of Student Conflict: A Study of the April Third Movement at Stanford University" (Stanford Research and Development Memorandum no. 96). Stanford: Stanford Research and Development Center on Teaching, 1971.

PART V

Collective Bargaining

17

Images of Governance: Collective Bargaining versus Traditional Models

J. Victor Baldridge and Frank R. Kemerer

Over the past few years, faculty collective bargaining has achieved significant visibility in the complex governance processes of higher education. There has been continued debate about the suitability of collective bargaining strategies in higher education, about the destruction of the "shared governance" principle, and about the imposition of "industrial model unionism" on the delicate processes of professional decision making. Much of the debate has been at a symbolic level, with assumptions and fears about collective bargaining meeting assumptions and beliefs about the proper strategies of academic decision making. In fact, it is fair to say that much of the debate has focused on images, beliefs, and abstract models rather than on concrete events.

We believe it would clear the air of many misconceptions—but reinforce some legitimate concerns—if the basic assumptions behind collective bargaining could be contrasted to the basic images that have dominated academic governance. We propose to do three things in this chapter: (1) outline some patterns of action and systems of belief that characterize collective bargaining; (2) discuss three images that have shaped thinking about academic governance—collegial, bureaucratic, and political; and (3) compare and contrast the new collective bargaining strategies with the more traditional governance models, indicating some of the developing tensions.

Defining Collective Bargaining

Although the traditional patterns of academic governance have not included union action, the collective bargaining movement in higher education has its roots deep in other sectors of the society. By first examining patterns of unionization that have developed over fifty years of experience in industry, we can then contrast union patterns with the traditional academic governance images. There are at least four basic assumptions which characterize the philosophy of unions:

1. There is conflict between those who are employed and those who administer.
2. The employee group accepts an organization as its exclusive representative vis-à-vis management.
3. Individuals and small groups are protected; for example, there is the concept of "fair representation" of all individuals, even if they don't belong to the union.
4. The employee group must win representative status as a collective bargaining agent within a legal framework that has authority beyond the employer. The organization must not depend on the employer's good graces for its continued existence.

Industrial employees spent long years struggling for the right to choose unions independent from the employer and able to negotiate a binding contract with management. The first major piece of collective bargaining legislation was the Railway Labor Act in 1926. It was followed by the more encompassing National Labor Relations Act (NLRA) in 1935. Both made the clear refusal of an employer to bargain with the employee representative an unfair labor practice subject to fine and imprisonment. (There continues to be no effective remedy to what has been labeled "surface bargaining" by an employer—continued discussion that does not result in agreement. The Supreme Court has denied the National Labor Relations Board the power to compel a concession from an intransigent employer.)

The National Labor Relations Act conveys to the private sector employee, including most employees at private colleges and universities, a full complement of collective bargaining rights. The NLRA defines collective bargaining as

... the performance of the mutual obligation of the employer and the representative of the employees to meet at reasonable times and confer in good faith with respect to wages, hours, and other terms and conditions of employment, or the negotiation of an agreement, or any question arising thereunder, and the execution of a written contract incorporating any agreement reached if requested by either party ... [Section 8d].

In addition, the NLRA supports the employee's right to organize collectively. The obligation to bargain on the employer's side and the right to organize on the employee's side are the foundation for a full bargaining relation that also includes (1) the right of employees to be represented by an exclusive agent; (2) bilateral (management-labor) determination of wages, hours, and other terms and conditions of employment; (3) the right to a binding contract between the employer and the representative of his employees, a contract that does not depend on the employer's good graces but can be enforced by the courts; and (4) the right to strike or to negotiate binding arbitration of both grievance disputes (those arising under the contract) and interests disputes (those arising from the negotiation of a new contract).

Although the NLRA extends these bargaining rights to the private sector, state or federal government employees are not included—and many faculty are employed by public institutions. For them, special state laws have been necessary for unionization, though most states have been reluctant to pass legislation offering the broad rights available under the NLRA.

Through collective bargaining, the parties arrive at an agreement that has much in common with a government charter or treaty. The agreement regulates the diverse activities and conflicting interests of groups within the organization. In many instances, collective bargaining does not replace past governance structures and procedures but is superimposed on them, particularly in the first few contracts negotiated by a new union.

In the private industrial sector, the collective bargaining agreement has been a charter through which workers have gained influence over organizational policies. Collective bargaining, one authority writes, "is . . . the means of establishing industrial democracy as the essential condition of political democracy, the means of providing for the workers' lives in industry, the sense of worth, of freedom, and of participation that democratic government promises them as citizens" (Shulman, 1954-55, page 1002).

Not only does collective bargaining affect the *formulation* of organizational rules, it also affects their *interpretation* and *adjudication* through grievance and arbitration procedures. A majority of collective bargaining contracts in the industrial sector contain a grievance system.[1]

1. A recent study of contracts in the United States covering 1,000 or more workers showed that 1,314 of the 1,339 agreements (98.1 percent) contained

Images of Academic Governance

We have dealt with our first objective—outlining some observations about collective bargaining as a system of governance and negotiated management. Now let us turn to our second task, the analysis of more traditional images of academic governance. How do they compare to the collective bargaining model we have just outlined?

Academic governance is a complex and tangled web of decision making that translates scholarly goals and values into college and university policies and action. How we see that process largely depends on which pair of analytical glasses we wear. In many ways, academic governance also looks like a bureaucratic process, a system that translates complex organizational procedures into plans, actions, and policies. Using another set of ideas, academic governance appears to be a political process, a network of competing interest groups that pressure to influence the outcomes. Academic governance may also be viewed as a collegial process, a system by which the values of scholarly professionals are used to make the decisions that run institutions. These intersecting forces—collegial, bureaucratic, and political —make academic governance a complicated and often hectic process. These images often stand in stark contradiction to collective bargaining strategies.

Bureaucratic Images

Higher educational institutions have many characteristics associated with a bureaucratic interpretation of organizational decision making. To summarize several prominent features: (1) Higher educational organizations have a formal hierarchy with bylaws and organizational charts which specify organizational levels and role relationships between members. (2) There are formal lines of communication to be observed. (3) Authority relationships, while sometimes unclear, nevertheless are present. (4) Specific policies and rules govern much of the work of the institution. There are deadlines to be met, records to be kept, periodic reports to be made, and so on. (5) Decision making often occurs in a relatively routine, formalized manner using decision councils and procedures established by institutional bylaws.

The bureaucratic characterization holds truest for routine decision processes such as admissions, registration, course scheduling, and

---

both grievance and arbitration provisions. Twelve had grievance provisions alone; only thirteen contracts made no reference to either grievance or arbitration (U.S. Bureau of Labor Statistics, 1974, page 64).

graduation procedures. The application of management techniques to financial problems facing colleges and universities helps to systematize decision making in a bureaucratic manner.

In many ways, however, the bureaucratic paradigm falls short of explaining university governance, especially as it concerns decision-making processes. First, the bureaucratic model says much about "authority," that is, legitimate, formalized power. But it neglects the informal power based on threats, mass movements, expertise, and appeals to emotion and sentiment. Second, the bureaucratic image explains much about the formal structure but little about the dynamic processes of the institution in action. Third, the bureaucratic model deals with the formal structure at one particular time but does not explain changes over time. Finally, the bureaucratic image does not thoroughly explore the crucial tasks of policy formulation. The image explains how policies may be carried out after they are set, but it says little about the process by which policy is established. It slights the political issues, such as the struggles of groups within the university who want to force policy decisions in favor of their special interests.

Political Images

Another governance image, the political model of decision making, assumes that complex organizations can be studied as miniature political systems, with interest group dynamics and conflicts similar to those in cities, states, or other political environments. Baldridge (1971) used the political approach to examine the policy formulation process. Major policies commit the organization to definite goals, set the strategies for reaching those goals, and determine the long-range destiny of the organization. Policy decisions are critical; they have a major impact on the organization's future because they bind the organization to important courses of action.

Because policies affect their vital interests, people throughout an institution try to influence them. Policy making becomes the focus of interest group activity in a process that is basically political. To say that policy making is a political process is not to say that everybody is involved. Quite the contrary, because usually the "law of apathy" prevails. For most people, the policy making process is uninteresting and unrewarding, and administrators run the show. This is not only true in colleges; it is also characteristic of political processes in the larger society. Voters do not vote, people do not attend city council meetings, school boards usually do what they please, and the decisions of the society are made by small and elite groups. Even when people are active, they move in and out of the decision-making process. Rarely do people sustain their interest; they become active when they are directly affected. Decisions, therefore, are usually made by those who persist, the small groups of political elites who invest time in the governance process.

Colleges and universities, like most other social organizations, are fragmented into interest groups with different goals and values. These groups normally live in coexistence. When resources are plentiful, interest groups engage in minimal conflict. However, when resources are tight, interest groups mobilize; outside pressure groups attack, or internal groups try to take over the decision processes. In a fragmented, dynamic social system conflict is natural, and it is not necessarily a symptom of breakdown in the academic community. In fact, conflict is a significant factor in promoting healthy organizational change.

A political analysis of governance assumes that formal authority, as prescribed by the bureaucratic system, is severely limited by the political pressure exerted by groups. Decisions are not simple bureaucratic orders but negotiated compromises between competing groups. Officials are not free to issue a decision, but must jockey between interest groups, building lines of communication between powerful blocs.

In addition, academic decision making does not occur in a vacuum. The external environment generates pressures that affect internal governance procedures. External interest groups influence the policy making process, and formal control by outside agencies—especially in the public sector—are powerful shapers of internal governance.

These assumptions can be summarized in a "political process" model of academic decision making. First, powerful political forces—interest groups, bureaucratic officials, influential individuals, organizational subunits—push a particular problem to the front and force the political community to consider the problem. Second, there is a struggle over *where* the decision is to be made, because this can determine the outcome. Third, decisions are often "pre-formed" by the time one person or group is awarded the decision-making right, causing options and choices to be limited. Fourth, political struggles are more likely to occur over "critical" decisions than "routine" decisions. Fifth, a complex decision network is developed to gather the necessary information and supply the critical expertise. Sixth, during the decision-making process, political controversy is likely to continue—compromises, deals, and plain head-cracking are often necessary to get any decision made. Finally, the controversy often continues so that it is difficult to know when a decision *is* made, for the political processes appear to unmake and confuse agreements. The political model, therefore, may be especially descriptive of decision processes within a loosely coordinated, fragmented academic institution.

How does the political image relate to the collective bargaining process? To some people, unionization seems to signal a breakdown in the traditional approach to managing academic organizations. We believe, however, that the process is less alien than it seems and is a logical outgrowth of long-existing trends. We believe that much of academic governance is a dynamic political process, with competing interest groups trying to influence the decision process. In this light, formal faculty collective bargaining is a natural progression from the informal conflict processes.

Specialized interest groups, conflict, bargaining, and negotiation have always been part of decision making in large academic institutions. At the same time, the patterns of negotiation and conflict that characterize these *informal* processes are vital to the dynamics of *formalized* collective bargaining. In short, the argument is that unionization is a formal and crystallized form of the interest group dynamics that have continually occurred in higher education.

The early days of education in the United States were a period of informality; collegiality dominated in at least a few of the small, prestigious liberal arts colleges. Later, complex institutional governance forms grew to include academic senates, rigid departmentalization, the national AAUP, and special interest groups within the various academic disciplines. Now, in the latest phase of governance development, conflict over wages and working conditions has become a critical issue. Faculties feel threatened by economic conditions and the growth of large bureaucracies. Therefore, it is not surprising that interest groups have become more formalized and more structured around economic issues. In fact, it would be most unusual if this did not occur; future changes and environmental pressures will find new interest groups forming around new issues.

The political interpretation of decision making helps explain why collective bargaining has grown so rapidly in higher education. Political activity invariably encourages the formation of interest groups, and unions have traditionally been interest groups focusing on economic issues. In higher education, the political activity that previously centered on interest groups such as the AAUP has now generated unions concerned with economic issues. Of course, if we view the college or university only as a collegial system or a complex bureaucracy, then the growth of faculty unions may appear to be an anomaly and an aberration. If academic governance is seen as a political process, then unionization can be seen as a normal, legitimate, and reasonable outcome.

We believe that unionization is a logical progression of an ongoing political process, but we must qualify our argument in two important ways. First, although unionization in higher education has evolved from similar conditions and has similar characteristics of industrial-sector collective bargaining, this does not necessarily mean that higher education should adopt industrial union practices. On the contrary, there are some aspects of industrial unionization that could be hostile to higher education. Faculty unionization must be sensitive to the peculiar values and cherished traditions of the academic community.

Second, although unionization may be a natural outcome of the political process, we should not enthusiastically embrace all the possible consequences. Some of the results of unionization will undoubtedly be positive and will bring major benefits to higher education; it is also possible that a high cost will be paid.

Political and Bureaucratic Stages in Collective Bargaining

We have examined the political and bureaucratic images of governance. In understanding faculty unionism, the two images are not necessarily contradictory; each is helpful in approaching different phases of the collective bargaining process. Collective bargaining has three distinct stages. Stage one is unionization, stage two is negotiation. These two stages are primarily political. Stage three is the administration of a contract, a largely bureaucratic process.

Unionization is the drive to form unions in nonunion organizations. Competing unions campaign to represent the employees, and elections are held to determine the employees' choice of a bargaining agent. It is also possible to have "decertification" elections to terminate a union or replace it with another union. All this activity proceeds under strict rules set down by the law, and is highly political.

Once a union has been formed, the *negotiation* phase involves bargaining over the terms of a contract. There are demands, threats, offers and counteroffers, and perhaps even strikes, lockouts, or arbitration. The negotiation stage is best characterized as a power struggle between employers and employees conducted within the confines of a legal framework.

The negotiation phase of collective bargaining in the industrial sector usually has four characteristics: (1) It is bilateral (between employer and employee representatives). (2) It is essentially a power play between these two organized interest groups. (3) The least common denominator is the starting point. (4) It is adversary in tone (a "we/they" viewpoint). Experience with collective bargaining in higher education indicates that the negotiation phase is similar.

Once a contract is signed the activity shifts to a more routine, bureaucratic *contract administration* phase. Wages and working conditions are administered as the contract provides, and grievances are filed when employees feel dissatisfied. Arbitration is often used to decide these grievances. Contract administration highlights weaknesses in the contract and sets the stage for another round of negotiation in the next collective bargaining cycle.

Both in industry and in higher education a major factor influencing contract administration is the language of the agreement. A legal contract requires precise and operational definitions of terms. Loose wording provides arbitrators, particularly those who look beyond the intent of the parties, with an opportunity to modify the contract. Because arbitration is essentially interpretation, both parties must be careful in constructing the agreement to prevent arbitration from creating new contract language. The pressure to reach agreement will inevitably leave poorly worded and vague phrases that invite "creative" arbitrators to rewrite language outside of the bargaining process. The result can be disastrous for either or both parties.

In short, the administration of the contract is as important as the initial contract negotiation in forming the employer/employee relationship. Contract administration first specifies role relationships and establishes channels for conflict resolution. The contract implements organizational functioning, taking conflict out of the political arena and routinizing it in the grievance machinery. Second, the contract may also establish formal lines of communication and clearer and fairer policies and rules governing personnel decision making. Finally, the administration of the contract highlights misunderstandings, ambiguous contract wording, and clumsy processes that need streamlining. Thus, the bureaucratic contract administration helps set the stage for a new round of political negotiations to clarify and eliminate such problems.

Collegial Images

There is a third commonly used image of academic governance. Many writers have deliberately rejected the bureaucratic and political images and instead have declared that the academic institution is a "collegium," or a "community of scholars." The collegial model views decision making as a process of deliberation by academic professionals. It presumes that: (1) There is a consensus within the professional academic community as to the purposes and goals of higher education and the role of the faculty. (2) Academic professionals should be the key participants in governance because they alone have the expert knowledge required. (3) Administrators and faculty have a commonality of interests that transcends their role differences.

The supporters of this approach argue that academic decision making should not be hierarchical. The "community of scholars" should administer its own affairs, and outsiders and bureaucrats should have little influence. According to the collegial model, educational decision making, particularly regarding curriculum and personnel issues, requires the deliberative abilities for which professors are especially equipped. This is so because "it is they who possess the special training, competence, experience, special understanding, and professional commitment necessary for sound and reliable decisions" (Kadish, 1972, page 121). Since administrators are members of the profession, they supposedly share the same goals as the faculty.

But there are obvious cracks in the collegial armor. The experience of the late sixties demonstrated that all members of the academic profession do not hold similar views about the purposes and goals of higher education. As one observer has commented ". . . the modern university is most emphatically *not* a cloistered retreat for like-minded scholars" (Leslie, 1972, page 709). In 1972, the president of the AAUP called attention to three growing threats to the collegial view of the academy (Kadish, 1972, page 122):

1. Claims of the professor as an employee, which led to an adversary relationship with the institution.
2. Claims on behalf of direct social involvement by the university and its faculty, which split and embittered many faculties.
3. Claims for the application of democratic political precepts in decision making within the university, which undercut the professor's elitist claim to authority based on expertise.

Economic pressures and a trend toward egalitarianism in organizational membership have continued to fuel these threats. The growth of faculty collective bargaining across the spectrum of American higher education is testimony to a lack of faith by many faculty members in the ability of existing collegial governance mechanisms to satisfy their needs, especially their economic needs in an increasingly economy-minded environment.

Perhaps of equal significance in contributing to the breakdown of the collegial model is the growing apathy of academicians toward participation in governance, an apathy reinforced by the increasing complexity of campus management. Many would probably agree with a well-respected English professor at Central Michigan University who admits, "My interests are to teach; I don't want to get involved in governance."

Admittedly, the collegial model is a value-laden conception of organizational functioning in higher education. It seems less descriptive of what *actually* happens than of what many people believe *should* happen.

Is collective bargaining compatible with notions about shared governance, professional expertise, and collegial decision making? This is a difficult question, for collective bargaining can be supportive of collegiality in some situations, but clearly undermines it in others. In many institutions, the idea of faculty participation in governance and shared decision making has always been fictional. The institutions were actually managed by strong administrators and trustees, a pattern characteristic of some community colleges, state colleges, and undistinguished liberal arts colleges. In institutions where academic collegiality was a myth, collective bargaining may *promote* faculty rights and collegial decision making. Most observers have argued that collective bargaining will undercut collegiality, but we feel that in many situations strong union contracts will be instrumental in producing greater faculty participation in governance. (For one such example, see Orze, 1975.) In one sense, then, collective bargaining may bring some semblance of collegial management to institutions that never had such a tradition. The helpful role that unionization can play in extending faculty rights is noted by no less a collegial organization than the AAUP:

The longstanding programs of the Association are means to achieve a number of basic ends at colleges and universities; the enhancement of academic freedom and tenure; of due process; of sound academic government. Collective bargaining, properly used, is essentially another means to achieve these ends, and at the same time to strengthen the influence of the faculty in the distribution of an institution's economic resources. The implementation of Association-supported principles, reliant upon professional traditions and upon moral suasion, can be effectively supplemented by a collective bargaining agreement and given the force of law [*AAUP Policy Documents and Reports*, 1973, page 52].

Despite the benefits that unionization may bring to some institutions, it is nevertheless true that collective bargaining may threaten some collegial practices. In institutions with long histories of faculty rights, shared governance, and peer judgment, unionization may weaken faculty professionalism, because some collective bargaining practices are frankly in opposition to academic collegiality. In particular, it is critical to understand that collective bargaining does not accept the presumption of shared governance which is central to academic collegiality. Instead, collective bargaining divides the world into a "we/they" dichotomy, recognizing that people's perceptions and interests depend largely on their positions within organizations. The best way to guarantee shared decision making, according to the union viewpoint, is to mandate it in a legally binding contract.

Frequently, proponents of this view will stress that administration and faculty have essentially an adversary relationship. Donald Wollett, Director of Employee Relations for New York State, comments (1973, page 32):

Collective bargaining amounts to a turning away from collegiality and self-governance and a moving toward an adversary system which recognizes that the central fact of life in the academy is that there are those who manage and those who are managed, that there are employers and employees, that conflicts arise from these relationships, and that in a collective bargaining system they are resolved by a process predicated upon the proposition that people whose interests conflict are, at least in respect of those conflicts, adversaries.

Others acknowledge that occasionally administrators and faculty have different viewpoints, but believe bargaining can be a catalyst toward accommodation and thus reduce, not increase, polarity. At its best, collegial governance has enhanced faculty participation in decision making, but at the same time the differences between administrators and faculty have been glossed over. In contrast, collective bargaining brings those differences out into the open. While bargaining may be a means of increasing joint decision making in some situations, it may also lead to polarization, with the administration controlling certain decisions and the union contracts governing others.

There is another way in which collective bargaining threatens collegiality—the evaluation process. Professional evaluation of work is based on the skills and merit of the individual. It is difficult to judge merit in terms of subjective observation of professional behavior, but professional organizations have managed by using peer evaluation processes. Professionalism is, in many ways, an elitist concept built upon professional performance and knowledge. The tradition of unionism differs because it stresses the equality of all workers and emphasizes democratic control of the union. Unions sometimes negotiate contracts that level the differences among individuals— although this is not always true, as experience in some craft unions indicates. Under a one-man, one-vote system the elite may not control the union, and their concerns will not be uppermost on the union's bargaining list. This position is at odds with the notion of merit based on professional performance. In addition, unions have often used seniority, not merit, as a basis for promotion, a procedure that violates cherished principles of professionalism.

In short, there are many areas of tension between the assumptions behind collective bargaining and those behind collegiality: the rejection of shared governance concepts, the creation of a "we/they" mentality, the expression of open conflict between faculty and administrators, the rejection of status differences based on merit, and the use of seniority as a criterion for advancement.

Collective Bargaining Strategies and Traditional Academic Processes

In this section we will highlight a number of tensions between the patterns of activity inherent in collective bargaining and those that have traditionally characterized academic personnel practices and decision-making processes.

The Shift from Individual to Group Rights

Under both federal and state legislation, employees are provided with basic rights that assure an opportunity to organize and to bargain collectively with their employers. But collective bargaining does not confer these rights on the *individual* employee; rather, the *union* as the representative of all the employees is the party to the collective agreement. Individual employees cannot deal directly with the employer to pursue individual advantage, but must work through the union representative. This departs radically from traditional individualistic practices in most academic and professional organizations. A union agreement allowing individual contracts would, of course, modify this generalization, and some college and university contracts allow individual bargaining and salary increments based on merit.

When a faculty shifts from traditional informal practices to the formality of collective bargaining, many changes occur. First, the individual is no longer the negotiating agent and individual concerns are sublimated to group needs. Second, personnel practices are no longer informally arranged between the institution and the individual, but are highly specified under a contractual relationship. What is permissible or necessary in terms of faculty behavior and institutional performance is often spelled out in minute detail. The individual's employment relationship to the institution is no longer direct. In a sense, the relationship is no longer bilateral, but trilateral—professor, union, and institution.

The Union as Exclusive Representative

Under a comprehensive collective bargaining law such as the NLRA, the union has "exclusivity," it becomes the sole representative of all employees in the bargaining unit whether they are union members or not. The concept of exclusivity, long advocated by unions, stems from a conviction that members of groups rarely contribute time and money to group activities since they will receive collective benefits in any case (Olson, 1971). Thus, to prevent "free riders," unions have sought and usually won the right to be the exclusive representative of all employees in the unit, and to have all employees pay union dues. This often means that the individual's choice about union membership is severely limited.

As a by-product of exclusivity, the union usually has a legally enforceable obligation to represent all employees fairly—whether or not they are union members. This does not mean the union must always press an individual's claim. On the contrary, the union as a representative of *group* interest may well decide to settle an *individual* grievance early or simply refuse to process it at all.

The discretionary power to back grievants creates a dilemma for unions in higher education. For example, in a disputed tenure case, the union may incur the wrath of its membership by refusing to back a grievant. By backing the grievant, however, the union may be challenging the decision of a tenure committee who may also be members of the bargaining unit. Under these circumstances, the ironic result may be that the administration is placed in the role of defending the faculty, while the union is criticized for violating academic processes.

The Conflict Between Union Democracy and Professional Meritocracy

Both potential bargaining topics and disputes arising within the bargaining unit are resolved by majority vote of union members. Although majority rule is an efficient way to resolve policy disagreements, it does not allow for differentiation in status among various people in the union. That is, under a one-man, one-vote approach, such traditional status indicators as seniority, rank, or special skills are not considered—a difficult situation for professional organizations that historically have been status-oriented.

Some special professional statuses are preserved, however, because the federal NLRA and many comprehensive state laws allow professional employees to form their own unit separate from nonprofessionals. In practice, however, the separation of professional employees is diluted because regulatory agencies normally create large units incorporating different or "unequal" professional positions. Thus, tenured faculty may be lumped together with nontenured faculty, part-time staff, and nonteaching professionals such as librarians and counselors. Large units, combined with the industrial union principle of majority rule, clearly threaten academic elites who have held power in universities and colleges. "Majority rule" and "professional status" become strange bedfellows in academic unions.

Unionism and Uniformity

Many commentators fear that faculty collective bargaining will reduce institutional autonomy and diversity if imposed on higher education. Pressures toward uniform collective bargaining practices come from laws that vary little from state to state and that lump higher education in with other types of civil service employment. In addition, public employment relations boards often introduce practices based on their experience in the industrial sector when they resolve higher education bargaining issues, such as the geographic extent of units and the scope of bargaining.

Despite these pressures toward uniformity, collective bargaining can encourage diversity. Even where laws do not treat higher education differently from other institutions, administrative agencies often approve separate procedures for community colleges, senior colleges, and universities. Substantial differences remain between the private sector operating under the federal NLRA, and the public sector, as well as between various states. Most significantly, the contractual nature of bargaining enables the parties themselves to tailor the process to their needs, since they must decide what is to be included or excluded in the contract, as long as their decisions are in harmony with statutory provisions. It should not be forgotten that collective bargaining has long served the interests of such diverse groups as airline pilots, steelworkers, actors, truck drivers, football players, and symphony musicians. Obviously, different procedures are possible under the general umbrella of collective bargaining. Thus, although there are tendencies toward uniformity, strong currents exist for diversity as well. Whether or not the outcomes of bargaining in higher education will be uniform is open to question. Despite pressures toward uniformity, collective bargaining may not be as threatening to institutional diversity as some critics fear.

The Conflict Between Unionism and the Concept of Shared Authority

Because collective bargaining practices stress the differing interests of employers and employees, they could pose a threat to the concept of "shared governance" in higher education. Professional employees such as doctors, lawyers, and professors function in part as managers and in part as employees. They often have considerable control over personnel and institutional decision making, matters usually considered management prerogative. Because of this dual role, professional unions have sometimes tried to divide the representation effort, to maintain a dual bargaining stance. The coalition of AAUP and NEA chapters at the University of Hawaii, for example, supports a "dual-track" system of bargaining—one track preserving traditional faculty governance with the other using collective bargaining to deal with salary issues:

The University of Hawaii Professional Assembly (UHPA) proposes the "Dual-Track" approach to collective bargaining for University of Hawaii faculty. Under the "dual-track" approach faculty members are viewed to have two roles—as academic professionals, and as State employees. These dual roles are peculiar to a university system. The contract must be formulated, therefore, to maintain them; otherwise, faculty self-government and participation in the University policy-making process will disappear. . . . UHPA believes that the dual-track approach to bargaining will preserve faculty rights as academic professionals by using collective bargaining to assure these rights and will improve the economic status of the faculty.

UHPA will insist upon *continuance of the present policies and procedures* including existing Faculty Handbooks, except as specifically modified by contract provisions. The Faculty Handbooks and procedures could be altered only by mutual consent between the Regents and representative faculty bodies, such as senates, in dealing with academic freedom, due process and tenure, personnel evaluation by peer review, faculty control over academic policies and goals, including curriculum. These academic matters would continue as rights of faculty in their role as academic professionals. UHPA will support development and acceptance of Faculty Handbooks covering these matters where they do not now exist or require improvement [UHPA flier, March 5, 1974].

The AAUP is walking a fine line, upholding the faculty's union control over economic issues and the faculty's management prerogative over curriculum issues. This delicate balancing act may be jeopardized both by legal decisions based on traditional concepts of management prerogative and by the expansionist tendencies of unions.

The Conflict Between Unionism and Traditional Spheres of Influence

After three years of analyzing contracts negotiated in higher education, a team of researchers at West Virginia University reported a steady expansion of bargained issues (Andes, 1974, page 10). This creeping expansion appears to move out in successive waves of bargaining. The first wave is confined to economic issues such as wages and fringe benefits. The second adds issues of personnel decision making such as reappointment, promotion, tenure, and grievance procedures. The third adds bargaining over governance structures and processes. As unions move into these wider spheres, the traditional prerogatives of academic senates and departments are sharply challenged.

Progressively longer and more encompassing contracts result in part from external economic and social pressures, stronger unions, and the deepening relationship between the parties. Equally potent are the forces exerted by the contractual process itself. First, contracts expand because both parties may find unexpected results from contract wording that later needs renegotiating. A prime example occurred at Chicago City College where the administration discovered, to its horror, that it had agreed to negotiate *any* policy change on working conditions. Later, the contract was renegotiated at a cost to read any *uniform, systemwide* policy, thus allowing discretion for local campus changes to meet unique needs. In general, contracts expand to meet the need for language clarification and specificity, as well as the need to plan for unexpected consequences.

Second, contracts can expand without a single provision being altered, through constant grievance appeals that subtly change the administration of the contract. Traditionally, unions use grievance and arbitration provisions to gain what they could not win at the bargaining table. Third, contracts expand because activities previously handled by the traditional senates, departments, or other governance agencies are shifted to the union for better results. This process occurs particularly in those institutions where campus governance has been notoriously weak in the first place.

Fourth, contracts expand to account for interpretations by administrative agencies and the courts that have occurred between contracts. These interpretive decisions can substantially alter the contracts and extend bargaining far beyond what the parties originally intended. Fifth, contracts expand because of enlarged demands at each new bargaining session. Because a union is responsible to its membership and must confer benefits to justify membership dues, it can never afford to rest on its laurels. This is particularly true where the membership is under no compulsion to join the union or pay dues in lieu of membership. A long-term contract may diminish the union's importance in the eyes of its constituency. To counteract this attitude, the union may develop a comprehensive list of demands for the next negotiating session, or it may be particularly active in pressing grievances under the current contract. In addition, weak or new unions—like those in higher education—must be aggressive in order to grow. For these reasons, the collective bargaining process has often been characterized as a never-ending quest for more.

If the pattern of expanding contracts continues, then "dual-track" bargaining may be an unrealistic approach unless other countervailing forces stop the expansion. The power and influence of the union may grow at the expense of both traditional academic senates and administrative groups. In any case, it is particularly important not to conclude too much about collective bargaining from the first few contracts—change is inevitable as bargaining progresses.

Summary

The task of this chapter was threefold: to outline one of the basic strategies and assumptions behind collective bargaining, to compare and contrast it with traditional images of academic governance, and to describe some of the critical tensions that are likely to develop with the advent of faculty unionism.

There are many more assumptions behind collective bargaining, of course, and several stand as critical: (1) conflict between employer and employee is the basic stance; (2) the union demands and usually obtains the exclusive right to represent the employees; (3) legal authorities beyond the campus back up the contracts—third parties enforce the agreements; (4) sanctions (strikes, lockouts) are used to support negotiating positions in interest disputes arising out of the bargaining process; (5) individual grievances are handled by pre-arranged machinery, often including arbitration procedures; (6) the union contract itself becomes a major element in the governance of the institution.

When traditional patterns of academic governance are compared with collective bargaining strategies, some areas complement each other and some areas create tensions. Collective bargaining may be considered a logical outgrowth of interest group dynamics that have been occurring in higher education, the extension of informal processes that have now become formal. The *unionization phase* and the *negotiation phase* are highly political. After the contract is signed, the political dynamics die down and a more routine bureaucratic process accompanies the *contract administration phase*. Through the grievance process the contract administration phase provides a mechanism for channeling and resolving conflict. In essence, the bureaucratic phase of contract administration helps regularize the political dynamics that occur in the unionization and negotiation phases.

It is more difficult to reconcile unionization with the collegial image of governance. On the one hand, unionization may protect and enhance faculty rights and shared governance at those institutions where they have been weak. The force of a legal contract can ensure rights that informal collegiality failed to obtain. On the other hand, unionization will undoubtedly undermine some central ideas of academic professionalism. Shared governance will become more polarized, individual negotiations will be subsumed under group bargaining, the subjective procedures of peer evaluation will be replaced by a more mechanical process, and seniority may substitute for merit as the prime criterion for promotion and tenure.

There are a number of other tensions that must be noted. As the shift from individual to group bargaining occurs, a trilateral relationship is formed between professor, institution, and the union that has gained exclusive representation. This effectively changes the relation of the individual to the institution, cuts out other groups that may wish to represent the faculty, and seriously undermines some professional criteria for advancement. Unionization also has some critical institutional impacts: it may press for homogeneity between institutions (thus threatening institutional diversity), may undermine the concept of shared authority between faculty and administration, and may jeopardize the traditional spheres of influence of academic senates and departments.

We are at a point of uncertain and tenuous beginnings. Decades of traditional academic governance patterns now stand face to face with the relatively new phenomenon of faculty collective bargaining. In some respects those patterns of action are in sharp contradiction, but in other ways collective bargaining is a natural consequence of trends that already existed in higher education.

References

Andes, J. O. "Developing Trends in Content of Collective Bargaining Contracts in Higher Education." Washington, D.C.: Academic Collective Bargaining Information Service, 1974.

Baldridge, J. Victor. *Power and Conflict in the University.* New York: John Wiley & Sons, 1971.

Kadish, Sanford H. "The Theory of the Profession and Its Predicament." *AAUP Bulletin* (June 1972).

Leslie, David. "Conflict Management in the Academy: An Exploration of the Issues." *The Journal of Higher Education* (December 1972).

Olson, Mancur, Jr. *The Logic of Collective Action: Public Goods and the Theory of Groups.* Cambridge, Mass.: Harvard University Press, 1971.

Orze, Joseph J. "Faculty Collective Bargaining and Academic Decision Making." Washington, D.C.: Academic Collective Bargaining Information Service, 1975.

Shulman, Harry. "Reason, Contract, and Law in Labor Relations." 68 *Harvard Law Review* (1954-55): 999-1002.

U.S. Bureau of Labor Statistics. "Characteristics of Agreements Covering 1000 Workers or More, July 1, 1973" (Bulletin no. 1882). Washington, D.C.: The Bureau, 1974.

Wollett, Donald H. "Historical Development of Faculty Collective Bargaining and Current Extent." *Proceedings, First Annual Conference,* edited by Maurice C. Benewitz. New York: National Center for the Study of Collective Bargaining in Higher Education, Bernard Baruch College, 1973.

18

Collective Bargaining: Evaluating the Issues

Joseph W. Garbarino and Bill Aussieker

It appears that the predictions of increased tensions and a higher level of conflict under unionized conditions are accurate. Even Rutgers' President Blaustein, whose generally favorable assessment of that relationship has attracted considerable attention, agrees that collective bargaining has "thrust administrators into a management role," but he argues that this change is desirable and long overdue. The most serious new problem he identifies is "creeping legalism," but he believes this is an independent development and not introduced by trade unionism (1973, page 6).

The principal merit of Blaustein's analysis is that he identifies the changes taking place in the internal relations of colleges and universities[1] and emphasizes that many of them exist independently of unionism and that unionism is as much an effect as a cause.

The AAUP officers at Rutgers may not agree with all the details of Blaustein's portrayal; in general it appears to be a reasonably accurate one. But Rutgers's situation is highly atypical. The impetus for

---

Reprinted from *Faculty Bargaining: Change and Conflict* (New York: McGraw-Hill, 1975).

1. Blaustein's "chamber of horrors," often attributed to unionism, is (1) a more explicit system of governance, (2) the deterioration of faculty quality, (3) the deterioration of department and school autonomy, (4) the polarization of the campus, (5) the decline of the senate, and (6) the replacement of consensus by bargaining in decision making.

organization was at least partly a shared concern by the administration and a large, active AAUP chapter that the new public employee bargaining law and a reorganized, and presumably more centralized, system of higher education might combine to threaten Rutgers' preferred position in that system. The AAUP was able to demonstrate support from 80 percent of the faculty, to agree with the administration on a definition of the bargaining unit, and to be recognized as the exclusive bargaining agent without going through the trauma of a representation election. Rutgers had previously experimented with a mixed academic senate with quite modest success from the faculty's point of view, and the AAUP supported the development of a faculty senate to participate in governance. (One unfortunate aspect of unionism that Blaustein detects is the effort by the AAUP to dominate the senate.)

Creeping legalism is a disease that affects unionized and nonunion universities alike (and virtually all other American institutions), but the union is a carrier that introduces legalism in a virulent form to the campus as a whole in a remarkably effective way. It is one of the great accomplishments of American unions that the grievance procedure has introduced due process and the academic version of what Sumner Slichter called "industrial jurisprudence" to employer-employee relationships. In the absence of unions legalism might have made due process available to prominent and controversial figures, but unions help to make it available to obscure assistant professors in departments of library science. Colleges and universities have long been vulnerable to charges of casual and erratic protection of the employment rights of nontenured faculty. With the loss of protection provided by a buoyant academic labor market and a serious oversupply of qualified new entrants to the profession, faculty members need and would in some way have secured more formal methods of job protection.

Nevertheless, the necessity for meeting the standards of what the typical union regards as due process may be incompatible with the subjective process of evaluating faculty performance in the institutions where such evaluations are taken seriously in retention and promotion decisions. Effective peer evaluation may not survive open personnel files, the right to reply, and, possibly, appeals to other forums. Administrators understandably appear to find amusement in the not infrequent instances in which a union pursues a grievance against a personnel decision made by their faculty colleagues (and sometimes fellow union members) sitting in peer judgment. Perhaps they should be wondering how the system will work if the faculty participants come to agree with Wollett's observation that "self-governance that thrusts the faculty into the performance of managerial functions serves primarily the interests of the administration" (1973, page 36). Many faculty members have accommodated to the pressures for less rigorous standards of performance for students; they may be amenable to doing the same for their colleagues.

No other organized institution has had as high a level of conflict for as long a period as CUNY. Virtually all social relations in New York City seem to be more problem-prone than anywhere else, and faculty unionism is no exception. CUNY is a gargantuan complex of institutions of great heterogeneity exposed to the problems of higher education in their most extreme form—for example, open admissions. Nevertheless, the level of sustained hostility in the union-administration relationship is unusual, particularly in view of the changes in the leadership on both sides that have occurred since the bargaining relationship was established, a factor that sometimes lessens the tensions created by the shock of adjusting to the introduction of collective bargaining.[2] During 1974 a new board of higher education was appointed, and this may lead to a change in the character of the relationships.

During the first three years of the CUNY agreement, 1969-72, 629 formal written grievances went through the first step (the campus president) of the grievance procedure. Another thirty class grievances were initiated at the second step (the chancellor) (Benewitz and Mannix, 1974). This record means that each year about fifteen grievances per 1,000 unit members got to this stage. Unfortunately comparable data do not exist for other institutions, but our own guess is that the 659 total may be two or three times the total grievances in all other organized institutions.[3]

Compared to the private industrial sector, an unusually high proportion of these grievances was taken to one of the nation's more expensive labor arbitration forums. Newton (1973) reports that

2. Since the bargaining election three of the four principals have changed: Albert Bowker and Bernard Mintz have been replaced by Robert Kibbee and David Newton as, respectively, chancellor and vice-chancellor with responsibility for administration-union relations. Belle Zeller, long-time head of the Legislative Conference, remains as head of the merged union, but Israel Kugler, former head of the AFT-controlled lecturers' unit and an officer in the merged organization, no longer plays a major role in the union. There appears to have been less turnover in the legal representatives.

3. According to the Benewitz and Mannix study, the grievant won one-sixth of the cases at step 1; about 55 percent of the denials were taken to step 2, where the grievant won in one-eighth of the cases.

during approximately the same three-year period more than 200 cases were filed for arbitration (some of them undoubtedly later withdrawn), but only sixty-one cases were actually decided by August 1972.

If Newton's figures are combined with those from Benewitz and Mannix, we can conclude that about one-third of the 623 individual grievances filed at step 1 eventually were filed for arbitration and that at least 10 percent and perhaps as high as 15 percent actually were carried through to final decision. Looked at another way, of the approximately 250 grievances denied at step 2, about 80 percent were filed for arbitration, and somewhere between one-fourth and one-third actually were arbitrated.

There is no question that the situation at CUNY is a difficult one, but in our opinion the best explanation of the conflict is the heterogeneity of the bargaining unit.[4] The administration seems to believe that the union (the Legislative Conference before the merger) does not represent the true interests of the full-time career faculty and that many of its demands are in response to the pressures from a diverse set of militant membership caucuses. During the difficult and prolonged negotiations for a second three-year contract, the administration declined to put the annual salary increments into effect on the defensible ground that it would be making a major concession in advance of an agreement. In the context of a deadlocked negotiation this move probably did more to nearly double membership in the Professional Staff Congress (PSC) than any other single factor. The membership proportion was at an all-time high of about 40 percent in 1974. If membership continues to rise, the union will gain in credibility as the representative of the group and the administration's position may change. The new New York Board of Higher Education also may bring some change to the situation.

CUNY Vice-Chancellor David Newton has provided a sketch of the escalated bureaucratization that has occurred at CUNY (Newton, 1973). It involves additional internal staff, more outside professional help, a great deal of staff time diverted to contract administration, and greatly increased expenditures on promulgating and administering procedures. His "conservative" estimate of the cost of financing the administrative side of the CUNY system is $2 million in 1973 for

4. The New York Public Employment Relations Board has faced the most difficult bargaining unit determination problems in the country in the several SUNY and CUNY cases. In no other instances have the bargaining unit decisions been so important in determining the character of the relationships, and, in our opinion, they have consistently been unfortunate in their consequences.

a bargaining unit of some 17,000 members. In addition to these costs
Kibbee (1973) stresses the effect of the rhetoric of the "negotiating
struggle" in shaping the "generalized view of the administration by
the faculty" and the consequences of this for day-to-day educational
relationships. One of the happier aspects of the CUNY situation is
that the relationships on many of the local campuses seem to be less
conflict-ridden than at the higher levels.

In most organized institutions the administration-union relationship is more like that at Rutgers than at CUNY. The escalation of
bureaucracy is widespread in the form of more staff, more explicit
and more detailed procedures, and more records, meetings, and reviews. Blaustein is right in emphasizing that all these trends were set
in motion independently of unionism, but the unions are a remarkably effective device for hastening and elaborating the process. The
recognition that the new procedures may increase the probability
that justice is done in individual cases does not change the fact that
there are substantial costs involved.

One man's loss of flexibility and discrimination in decision making
is another man's limitation of arbitrary authority. In the short run
the impact of bargaining may change the atmosphere of informal administration that many faculty and administrators feel existed previously to one of restricted authority through formalization and
rationalization. In the long run, however, administrations may gain
more freedom on more important issues by adopting a more aggressive adversary stance than appeared appropriate to a consensus system of decision making.

Collegiality guaranteed by contract may be given less scope to
operate than delegated collegiality had. The contribution of lawyers
to drafting contracts is a facility with the language of the law and a
training to anticipate and provide for dealing with the worst possible
occurrence in his client's interest. A governing board that feels that
in a crisis it can withdraw delegated authority without challenge will
be willing to delegate authority over a wider range of decisions than
it will grant irrevocably in a legally binding contract. The union's
answer to this argument is that its specialty is forcing the board to
grant contractually more authority than it would ever grant voluntarily. The net result depends on relative bargaining power, and in
higher education, at least in the four-year sector, this has not been
seriously tested.

Finally, collective bargaining legitimates adversarial behavior on
both sides of the table, and this may give management an advantage.
Bargaining strategy accepts the advancement of extreme demands as

a normal tactic, and this encourages not only thinking about the unthinkable but actually publicly proposing "unthinkable" changes. Bargaining means "packaging" gains and concessions so that an explicit tradeoff becomes possible. The resulting decisions need be acceptable to only a majority of those voting on the ratification of the contract. Forms of productivity bargaining are more likely to be achievable since a faculty concession on work load, for example, can be linked to higher pay or other benefits. Faculties enjoy the protections of many well-established "work rules" that might be difficult to challenge directly through traditional procedures but that might be changed as part of a bargaining package. Sophisticated administrations may in the next decade be able to take advantage of these characteristics of bargaining to make more changes more easily than they could through traditional structures.

Unions and Status Equalization

Status equalization is the reduction of differentials in pay and privilege that have existed between groups of academic staff and between different types of academic institutions.[5] A century ago the British socialists Sidney and Beatrice Webb identified the establishment of "the common rule" as a major goal of trade unionism. Much public discussion of faculty unions presumes a devotion to uniformity and equality that is exaggerated, but there is no question that employee organizations typically require a justification of differences in treatment in more explicit and objective terms than managements are likely to introduce on their own. The two areas of potential equalization that will be discussed in this section are tenure and pay.

Unions and Tenure

A credible threat to the traditional practices of academic tenure may be the most important single cause of unionization in a college or university.

Tenure is the academic version of job security, and its classic defense is its function in protecting faculty members in their intellectual independence in teaching and research from popular or political reprisal.[6] In addition to providing a bulwark of academic freedom in

---

5. The awkward but neutral term *status equalization* is used to avoid the depreciatory overtones of *leveling* or *homogenization* on the one hand and the laudable connotations of *correcting inequities* on the other.

6. Walter P. Metzger (1973) has contributed a historical review of the development of tenure for the Commission on Academic Tenure in Higher Education.

this sense, tenure should be considered as part of a system of personnel and salary administration. In this connection some of its important aspects are:

1. As a desirable condition of employment, it is one of the benefits that attract quality recruits to the profession.

2. The expensive and virtually permanent commitment it implies exerts great pressure to ensure quality of performance before tenure is awarded. The up-or-out decision after the expiration of the probationary period embodied in most tenure systems discourages taking the easy way out by making repeated short-term appointments of persons judged not to merit a long-term commitment.

3. Tenure plays a central role in the whole apparatus of collegiality and peer evaluation if this apparatus is to function effectively. Innumerable academic decisions made by faculty members are more objective than they would be if tenure did not protect those involved in the decisions and those affected by them from reprisals from their colleagues, from students, and from administrators.

4. In spite of administrators' impatience with the limits tenure places on their authority, they nevertheless are prime beneficiaries of faculty tenure. It protects them from constant pressures from students, other faculty, alumni, political factions on and off the campus, legislators, and a host of other groups to get rid of one or another faculty member for one or another reason.

5. It is an integral part of the system of salary administration. The operation of tenure means that a system of progressive advances in pay starting from a remarkably low level can be used to motivate performance. Surely the prospect of achieving a tenured career is one of the reasons that institutions of higher education are able routinely to recruit highly trained men and women in their late twenties with a lifetime record of top academic achievement for annual salaries of about $13,000 in 1973.

Tenure has its seamy side as well. The argument against it today is discussed in terms of "tenuring in," the situation that arises as the proportion of an institution's staff with tenure increases. Percentages of tenured staff of 70 or 80 percent are common in mature institutions, although the proportion overall is about 50 percent (Metzger, 1973, page 233).

Introducing new faculty members into a system that has reached a "steady state" depends on the rate of retirement, death, or resignation at one end and the level of recruitment and the rate of promotion to tenure at the other. It is not generally recognized that the "tenuring in" problem not only affects the rate of new recruitment and the proportion of probationary faculty awarded tenure but also leads to attempts to minimize the number of entry "ladder" appointments that might lead to tenure, to reducing the rate of promotion of faculty already tenured, and to drastically reducing the chances of lateral movement from one institution to another for all faculty with salaries much above entry levels. Unions thus are concerned not only with attempts to limit or abolish tenure but with the pressure that "tenuring in" produces for hiring part-time faculty, adjuncts, or lecturers, for holding down the proportion of eligibles given tenure, and for quotas in rank distributions.

The lengthy progression in salary and rank found in most public institutions does not denote changes in job content—professors and assistant professors do similar work—but is part of an incentive system to motivate behavior. As a faculty ages, it is likely to get increasingly expensive in salary terms. It is not surprising that some faculty members, both inside and outside of unions, suspect that much of the expressed concern with flexibility and obsolescence is really a concern with salary costs and the intriguing prospect of replacing expensive senior staff with inexpensive junior staff.

The other major argument against tenure is that it permits faculty to be unresponsive and irresponsible in meeting the needs of the institution and of their students. Discharge of a tenured faculty member is rare, and a system of discipline short of discharge is only now being developed. This again is a highly principled stance that has more pragmatic personnel overtones. A great deal of what is called governance by consensus or collegiality is really forced by the difficulty in getting faculty protected by academic freedom and tenure to do anything they really do not want to do or at least to get them to do it well. It is very difficult to elicit quality performance of an intangible professional service by discipline or compulsion. The client's replacement of one professional by another is one remedy, but at present, tenure stands as a barrier to this solution in higher education.

Again it is not surprising that faculty members and union officers suspect that the weakening of tenure is designed not only to enhance flexibility, intellectual dynamism, and responsiveness to societal needs but also to lower costs, to raise work loads, and to make faculty more subject to administrative direction and control in a wide range of day-to-day operating conditions.

In fact, administrators down through department chairmen have much more control over their faculties than is implied in tenure discussions. Promotions or pay increases can be manipulated to reward or punish individuals. Access to support services, research support opportunities for additional income, the assignment of offices, reduced teaching schedules, scheduling of classes, committee assignments, and travel opportunities—all can be used to influence behavior. The inclusion of rules governing many of these items in the collective bargaining agreements of faculty unions attests to their use and importance. Discharges of tenured faculty may be rare, but a substantial number are undoubtedly encouraged or harassed into leaving their jobs, and managerial control over a larger number is enhanced by the use of other aspects of the "reward system," of which tenure is one part.

Tenure and security of employment. Most collective bargaining contracts leave tenure arrangements unchanged, either by explicit language that maintains existing policies or by omitting any reference to the subject. Others, like the St. John's agreement, may have strengthened tenure arrangements by including language that expands previous rights.

The most significant fact about collective bargaining on tenure is that, in spite of all the discussion of weakening tenure, on balance the group enjoying some form of security of employment has been expanded and "nonreappointing" probationary faculty members has been made more difficult. In general, where some members of the bargaining units have not had tenure or security of employment prior to unionization, there has been movement toward an expansion of coverage. . . . The SUNY agreements and associated board policies are noteworthy for including a remarkably elaborate set of personnel policies for nonteaching professionals (NTPs) that dramatically improved their position. . . .

Unions and instant tenure. "Instant tenure" is one of the colorful phrases that appeared early in faculty bargaining. It is a misleading phrase in that no union has demanded, much less achieved, instant tenure for its faculty clientele. But as unions have pressed for "due process" for probationary faculty, the wide gap between the different procedures applied to the termination of tenured and nontenured faculty has been narrowed a good deal as more stringent procedures are required for nonreappointment. Instant tenure is an exaggerated description of the result, but the phenomena it represents are real.

Once again, the unions are reacting to a change in the institutional environment, not initiating one. Demands for due process are ubiquitous in American society, and the traditional processes of nonreappointment in higher education are unusual in the degree of secrecy and lack of review that have been maintained. In the not-too-distant past new recruits to the profession entered the pyramid of institutions of higher education at the highest prestige level available to them and, if unsuccessful at that level, found it easy to move laterally or to a lower stratum, possibly even at an increase in pay. With a reduced demand and an increased supply of job candidates, institutions at all levels find themselves able to raise their standards of recruitment and their standards of performance. It is both easier than it was to fail at a position at one level and harder to make a successful transition to another position. Institutions that ten years ago were glad to hire a holder of a Ph.D. degree and that granted tenure to virtually all eligibles are reviewing sheaves of applications, lengthening probationary periods, requiring records of research and publications, and reducing the proportion of probationary faculty awarded tenure.

Litigation has been used to press for due process, but most of the pressure for new procedures has come from the unions. The demands have taken several forms:

1. *Specification of procedures of evaluation.* Bargaining agreements commonly specify the character of reviews, a calendar of notifications, and reports of results. When department chairmen are required to observe these procedural niceties, the results are often less than ideal. Flaws of procedure can be challenged in a grievance hearing, and a large fraction of CUNY's hectic grievance record has resulted from complaints that procedure was not followed. CUNY has tried to reduce procedural complaints by negotiating a requirement that a faculty take positive steps to initiate the required action before a claim of omission can be made.

Complex procedures that create unpleasant duties for collegial supervisors or evaluators obviously reduce the likelihood that adverse actions will be taken. If an adverse evaluation must be based on frequent formal observation, if conferences are required at which evaluation reports must be defended against the faculty member and, perhaps, the union representative, and if decisions must be defended before an appeals panel, the administrative stamina needed for effective action may be lacking. Identifying specific contracts would mean imputing motives without information, but on a reading of some procedures it is hard to avoid the suspicion that they have been devised with strategic intent to discourage administrative authorities as well as to provide substantive protections.

2. *Open files.* Peer evaluation has often been done anonymously in committee on the basis of confidential reports secured from persons inside and outside the campus who are familiar with a candidate's

work and area of interest. In other cases the membership of evaluation committees is known, but their deliberations are secret. A large
number of negotiators have struggled with the obvious problems of
equity created by these arrangements. The candidate would like to
be sure that all information was considered, that the information was
accurate, that extenuating circumstances were recorded, that the persons expressing opinions were qualified to do so, and, finally, that
the decision reached was consonant with the evidence. On the other
hand, candid expressions of opinion may be difficult to collect if the
evaluators are asked to render sensitive judgments solely out of a
sense of professional obligation at the risk of personal unpleasantness
and possible reprisal.

The trend in contracts is to try to deal with this problem by keeping two sets of files. At a minimum, evaluations made at the time of
appointment are kept confidential. Most contracts also try to protect
the anonymity of outside evaluators at all times. Official correspondence and all formal evaluations by chairmen, deans, or committees of observers are usually available to the faculty members, and
responses can be entered in the record.

Because all the documents are not available and the deliberations
of the review committee itself are closed, the question arises as to
how full an explanation of the action taken will be provided—that is,
will reasons for adverse actions be given?

3. *Reasons for denial.* The key argument against giving reasons for
an adverse action is that it implies that the reasons must meet some
standard of adequacy if the action is to be regarded as justified. In
some instances giving reasons would compromise confidentiality, but
the real danger is that the published reasons may then have to be
defended and that over a succession of cases a kind of public common law would develop with the citing of precedents and a need to
prove distinctions among apparently similar cases.

These same considerations are cited as grounds for requiring that
the justification of decisions be made available to the faculty member. Unless the bases for the decisions are revealed, how can arbitrary
or discriminatory actions be challenged? . . .

4. *Appeals in academic cases.* In unionized four-year colleges appeals from academic decisions to outside bodies have been strongly
resisted. The collective bargaining contracts tend to distinguish carefully between a grievance procedure to appeal from disciplinary
actions and a procedure for grieving the interpretations of the provisions of the contract, including the procedures for academic review.

Where they exist, as at SUNY and CUNY, the disciplinary grievance procedures could eventually turn out to be an underrated inno-

vation. Discipline against faculty members has been rare in the past, and spelling out procedures for discipline could be interpreted as implying that they might be less rare in the future. (So far these procedures seem to have been little used.)

The CUNY provision (Article 21, CUNY Agreement, 1973) states that discipline can be imposed for "(a) incompetent or inefficient service; (b) neglect of duty; (c) physical or mental incapacity; (d) conduct unbecoming a member of the staff. This provision shall not be interpreted as to constitute interference with academic freedom." . . .

The introduction of these four elements into the tenure review process by faculty unions represents a major change in the way the system has operated, particularly in the colleges and universities that have taken tenure most seriously. In community and state colleges covered by tenure laws some elements of due process have been available in the past, but even here it appears likely that the new systems are more procedurally elaborate. In spite of the development of these procedures, the tenure review process is an example of a bargaining issue on which administrations have resisted any really significant inroads on the academic content of internal decisions.

Nontenured faculty, as the least favored of the professoriate, have been formally guaranteed procedural justice in unionized institutions, whereas previously they had to take the provision of justice on faith. Undoubtedly more justice is probably now being done, and certainly more justice is being *seen* to be done, which is important in itself. This does not mean that nontenured faculty are more likely to be promoted as a result. At CUNY, for example, it is probably true that, in spite of the new procedures and the vigorous and expensive prosecution of nonreappointment cases by the union, the proportion of eligible faculty being awarded tenure each year is smaller than was the case before unionization.

Junior faculty may be in the same position as senior faculty who have made relatively few positive gains from unionism but who may have benefited from a mitigation of possible negative developments in an unfriendly environment. Because the position of all nontenured faculty is much more unfavorable than it was formerly, it is important that negative decisions be seen to be procedurally fair. On balance, the procedural complexities and greater openness that bargaining has introduced do not seem to have been serious barriers to the continued exercise of academic judgment. The price in administrative expense and complexity has bought benefits by protecting a system that can still be meritocratic if the administration and the tenured faculty really want it that way.

There is a danger that over a period of time union pressure will eliminate the distinction between outside review on procedure and the review of academic judgment. If this happens in those institutions where a system of peer evaluation has operated effectively in selecting and providing persons of scholarly promise, the adversary nature of the arbitration process and the emphasis on the formal record could pose a threat to the maintenance of academic "quality." This could be particularly true if arbitrators were drawn from outside the institution. This possibility is mitigated by a number of factors. Institutions that take tenure seriously appear to be in the minority,[7] although they are a large and an inordinately important minority, and few of them have unionized to date. Even where the screening is taken seriously, it is not necessarily true that outside review by carefully selected academic persons would be less effective than internal selection; in fact, it might be more effective in protecting faculty quality.

In summary, unionization has had a substantial effect in extending security of employment similar to faculty tenure to other members of the academic staff. This may have significant financial and administrative costs but is unlikely to affect academic affairs directly. Unions have introduced lengthy and tedious procedures of selection, evaluation, and review of appointments, nonreappointments, and promotions. These are expensive and bureaucratic in operation, but until there is more evidence than exists to date that the academic content of decisions has changed for the worse, no final judgment can be made.

Is tenure negotiable? So far, the discussion of status equalization has assumed that the faculty unions are the aggressors in trying to expand the areas of academic privilege. In the long run, in some institutions it may be the administration that takes the offensive—at least as far as tenure is concerned.

The abortive contract negotiated by the AFT at the University of Hawaii but overwhelmingly rejected by the faculty attracted a great deal of attention because it contained a provision that weakened the tenure system. Part of the proposal was the modification of the up-or-out system by the concept of an "extended" appointment. Persons completing the probationary period and not going "up" to tenure need not have gone "out" but could have been awarded five-

7. The Commission on Tenure found that in all institutions combined, 42 percent awarded tenure to all candidates considered in Spring 1971. Only 25 percent denied tenure to as many as 30 percent of the candidates (Commission on Academic Tenure, 1973).

year term appointments and retained on the staff. Faculty with tenure would presumably have retained it, and new tenure appointments could have been made, but under the new system a new category of possibly long-term nontenured faculty would have been established. The possibility of an indefinite succession of term appointments was regarded as the thin edge of the wedge of an attack on tenure overall.

The administration initiated the proposal in bargaining, and the union could have rejected it outright and struck, negotiated its withdrawal by granting other concessions, or accepted it with or without securing compensating administration concessions. The AFT took the last alternative. If the AAUP wins bargaining rights and the same demand is pressed, they will face the same set of choices. Whatever their decision, tenure will be established as a negotiable item.[8]

If a frontal assault on the academic version of tenure is launched and succeeds, it will probably be replaced with its civil service equivalent in public institutions. A wave of organization would be stimulated. Under these conditions it is possible that management might gain more initiative and control than the present system permits, but experience with the operation of unionized civil service systems indicates that it is not obvious that the difference in practice actually realized would be significant.

Salaries and Salary Administration

Measuring the impact of unions on the level of salaries will attract increasing attention as collective bargaining spreads and more experience is accumulated. At this moment the data are too sparse to permit econometric analysis of any sophistication to be undertaken for the four-year institutions. The heterogeneity of institutions by size and type requires their separation into categories (the AAUP salary survey uses five categories), and there are only sixty to seventy separate four-year contracts to analyze. The data source most often used for the simpler analyses of salaries in higher education is the AAUP survey, published annually in the summer issue of the *AAUP Bulletin.*

Salary practices in institutions of higher education make it difficult to collect and analyze data to test the effect of unionization.

8. William Van Alstyne, the AAUP president, advances the suggestion that tenure might be considered a nonnegotiable subject that would be the faculty equivalent of an inherent management right. In Hawaii the law contains a strong management-rights clause that alone might rule out this interpretation, and, in general, tenure seems almost a classic "condition of employment" and therefore bargainable under virtually all laws and court decisions.

Changes in salary by rank of individual faculty reflect general salary increases, the granting of pay increases to individuals within a rank, and promotions to a higher rank. Averages computed for a single institution are affected by all these, plus changes in the number employed at the different pay levels. Changes in averages for groups of institutions are the result of all the foregoing, plus changes in the set of institutions reporting over the years and changes in the distribution of employment among the institutions. Isolating the effect of unionization is a difficult task.

One method of coping with these problems is to use pairs of union-nonunion comparison institutions chosen to resemble one another in all other pay-determining variables. Robert Birnbaum (1974) did such a study for eighty-eight pairs of institutions. He concluded that the average unionized institution had increased a pay advantage of $47 in 1968-69 to $824 in 1972-73. Birnbaum divided the institutional pairs into four categories[9] and found that in all categories unionized institutions increased their advantage over their unorganized counterparts, although the results for two groups were not statistically significant.

Not only is it hard to isolate the differential effect of unionism on salaries, but it is even difficult in many cases to calculate the correct percentage rate of increase from the collective bargaining agreements. Both the Rutgers and CUNY agreements, for example, do not contain a percentage increase figure; instead they reproduce salary scales and describe movements on the scale. Without other information an average percentage increase cannot be calculated, which may not be an accidental result. In other contracts—for example, Wayne State University—an across-the-board increase is specified, but then other adjustments are described in a way that presumably is clear to the administration and the union but is hardly clear to the outside analyst.

Under the circumstances we will fall back on advancing two propositions as to the behavior of average salaries under collective bargaining, based on an unsystematic mix of interviews, case studies, contract analysis, and intuition.

1. In the general case faculty salaries in public institutions of higher education have moved upward more or less in line with the salaries of the state civil service as a whole. This means a range within

9. Public universities, public four-year colleges, public two-year colleges, and independent colleges and universities. The differentials in public two-year colleges and independent colleges and universities did not meet statistical tests of significance.

one percentage point plus or minus of the state employees' increase
for the year. Examples of this pattern appear to be SUNY, Wayne
State, and the New Jersey institutions, including Rutgers.

2. In a number of special situations unions won increases substantially greater than civil service increases or the "going rate" in academia generally in the early years of negotiations, but the rate then
declined to the equivalent of the civil service rate. St. John's, for
example, started at 12 percent in the first year, dropped to 9 percent
in the second, and then to 5.8 percent for each of the next two
years. The Pennsylvania state colleges are unlikely to maintain the
rate of 5 percent every six months in their first three-year contract
plus annual increments and fringe improvements. Central Michigan
University and Oakland started off with increases of between 7 and 8
percent, and Oakland at least has tapered off to a 5.9 percent rate in
its 1973 settlement. The first St. John's contract followed several
years of institutional upheaval and reflects the resolution of a difficult internal situation. The other examples seem to represent "emerging institutions" whose faculties, possibly with tacit administration
support, were trying to move up a notch or two in what the British
would call the academic league standings in faculty salaries and perhaps also in institutional quality. Unionism has been the method
used by faculty and administrations to gain ground on the "elite"
universities in their states.

In the current climate the limits to this kind of academic boot-
strapping are narrow, and the civil service pattern, modified somewhat by differences in pay practices, is most likely to prevail in the
long run.

Salary Structure

The status equalization theme raises more questions of salary administration and salary structure than of general salary changes. Are
there any discernible tendencies for unions to negotiate systematic
changes in internal salary relationships?

There are several different dimensions of this question that can be
studied, and there is enough evidence available for three of them to
report in some detail:

1. *Changes in differentials among ranks.* The AAUP surveys show
that over five years, 1968-69 through 1972-73, the three major ranks
—assistant, associate, and full professor—each reached annual increases in pay totaling 30, 30, and 29 percent, respectively, although
the pattern of change was slightly different from year to year. These
data show a stability of rank differentials for the system as a whole.

Some of the unions have been negotiating across-the-board percentage wage increases that would have the same effect. Others provide for a wide variety of adjustments that tend to favor lower-paid faculty members to some extent.

Examples of the latter are the first St. John's University contract, which called for generous percentage increases or an absolute dollar-minimum increase, whichever was greater. Central Michigan University has used the device of across-the-board percentage increases plus a uniform dollar amount. Both of these approaches result in somewhat larger percentage increases for lower-paid faculty.

Perhaps the most egalitarian four-year contracts in existence are the two CUNY agreements. In the first contract the major move in that direction was the equalization of salary scales by rank for the senior and the community colleges. At the same time Table 18-1

TABLE 18-1
Salary Ratios by Rank, CUNY

	Professor/assistant	Associate/assistant	Assistant professor
1968-69	152.9	123.5	100
1971-72	150.1	122.4	100
1974-75	145.4	120.3	100

Source: Calculated from the CUNY agreements. Salaries are for the top step of each rank in each year.

shows a reduction in percentage differentials by rank from the differential existing in the year prior to the first contract and those prevailing in the final year of each of the two agreements. The trend toward a reduction of differentials is uniform through the table, with the rate of reduction increasing during the second three-year contract period. Because CUNY publishes salary schedules in their contracts instead of announcing an average percentage salary increase, little attention has been paid to the low rates of general pay increases built into the scales in the second contract. Salary schedules were raised a flat $600 for the first year, $750 for the second, and $850 for the third. These amounts for the first year produce percentage increases for those persons already at the top of the scale for professor, associate professor, and assistant professor of 1.9, 2.4, and 2.9 percent, respectively. The total increases over the entire three-year contract at the top of each rank will be 7.0, 8.6, and 10.6 percent. This compares with the three-year totals of over 20 percent for the same ranks in the first contract.

Those professors not at the top of the salary range for their rank receive annual increments in pay of $1,250 each year; assistant and associate professors each receive increments of $1,000 each year. If we choose a member of the faculty who receives an increment in each year plus the three general increases in the schedule, the combined increases in salary would be much more substantial: 21.6, 23.1, and 29.2 percent[10] over three years for professors, associate professors, and assistant professors, respectively.

The degree of emphasis on flat, relatively uniform dollar amounts of pay increases in the CUNY contracts is unusual. It operates to reduce percentage differences between salaries by rank as portrayed in Table 18-1. The emphasis on annual automatic increments in pay rather than general increases in the salary schedule explains why the promotion problem and the limits in the proportions in the several ranks are so important to the CUNY union. A person at the top of the salary range for his rank receives only the relatively low general wage increase unless he can move to the next higher rank. An associate professor at the top of his salary range at the end of the first contract received an annual salary of $25,500. If he were promoted to professor at that point, he would be paid $30,975 by the end of the next three-year contract; if he remained an associate, he would be getting $27,700. The promotion means the difference between a pay increase of 22 percent and 9 percent over three years.

It would be a mistake to assume that the union has initiated the policy of reducing differentials. CUNY salaries were tied to lower-school salaries prior to unionization, and schedules were rising as unions in the lower schools won increases. It is reported that there was some administrative concern with the political effect of the rising levels of the top of the professors' scale, and holding this ceiling down has resulted in the compression of differentials. Even so, two CUNY units had the highest-paid faculties in the nation, according to the 1974 AAUP survey report.

Although the AAUP data suggest that rank differentials have been maintained over the whole system, increases in pay that are "tapered" to favor lower-paid faculty have occurred in nonunion situations. The unions have reinforced this tendency and made it more general, but the overall trend seems to be little influenced by these efforts.

10. The corresponding figures for the first three-year contract were 40.5, 41.7, and 48.8 percent. Note that since the increments are in absolute dollar amounts the percentage increases would be even larger if we measured the gains at the low end of the salary range rather than at the top end.

2. *Compensation differentials in two- and four-year institutions.*
Baseball pitcher Satchel Paige's famous saying, "Don't look back,
something may be gaining on you," might well have been directed at
the faculty of four-year colleges. In terms of average compensation
community college faculty have been closing in on their four-year
college brethren for many years, with and without unionism.

The AAUP surveys for the academic years 1966-67 and 1972-73
illustrate the position of the faculty in two-year public institutions
relative to four-year public institutions. Although the institutional
categories used to report the data are different in the two years, the
main outlines of the relationship are clear from Table 18-2. In

TABLE 18-2

Compensation Ratios by Rank and Type of Public Institution

	Two-year colleges	Teachers colleges	Liberal arts	Universities
1966-67				
Professor	100	105	106	122
Associate	100	92	100	106
Assistant	100	94	101	105
1972-73	Category III	Category IIB	Category IIA	Category I
Professor	100	89	97	106
Associate	100	90	96	98
Assistant	100	88	94	95

Key: Category I—universities granting fifteen or more earned doctorates in the past three
years in at least three unrelated disciplines. Category IIA—institutions awarding degrees
above the baccalaureate not in I. Category IIB—institutions awarding only the baccalaureate
or equivalent. Category III—two-year institutions with academic ranks.

Source: *AAUP Bulletin,* Summer 1967, p. 150, and June 1973, p. 194.

1966-67 the compensation for every rank in all four-year public institutions (except for associate and assistant professors in teachers colleges) equaled or exceeded that of the corresponding ranks in the
two-year colleges. In the different classification of 1972-73, of all the
nine rank categories in four-year institutions, only the compensation
of the full professors in public doctoral universities exceeded that of
their counterparts in two-year institutions and then only by 6 percent.

Another indication of the changing relationship between two- and
four-year colleges that reflects the effect of unionism is the fact that
none of the seventy institutions with the highest average compensa-

tion in 1966-67 was a two-year college, but by 1973-74 eleven of the top seventy institutions were two-year colleges and all eleven were unionized.[11] Seven of the eleven were CUNY community colleges, three others were located in metropolitan New York, and the other entry was the Chicago city colleges.

This record emphasizes the role of the comprehensive union at CUNY in raising the compensation of the CUNY community college faculty by negotiating salary parity in 1970. It may be that a separate community college bargaining unit would have raised the salaries of their group relative to those of the four-year faculty, but we doubt if the differential could have been eliminated in three years with separate bargaining. Achieving parity in salary scales in the first three-year contract at CUNY required that the two-year faculty by rank receive annual percentage increases more than double those of the four-year faculty.

In the SUNY system there are pressures for parity between the four-year colleges and the university centers and between NTPs and teaching faculty, but there is relatively little public evidence of pressure for parity for the two-year campuses. This may be because of their relatively small size and because they are not community colleges but agricultural and vocational schools. One suspects that the pressure is only delayed.

Once again we have a situation in which the changing environment of one sector of higher education is leading to a change in traditional relationships. The community colleges are expanding in size and function, they are the legislators' favorite sector of higher education, and their close links to the lower schools have helped them benefit from the militant union campaigns in this sector. All of these factors are basic to an explanation of their relative gains.

Unionization also has been an independent factor in the community colleges' improved position. More than a third of all community college faculty are unionized. In California nearly all of the nation's largest system (ninety-six institutions, 24,000 teaching faculty) engage in collective negotiations under a "meet and confer" bargaining law, but these situations do not meet the test of unionization used in this study. If they are regarded as bargaining, almost half of all community college faculty is engaged in bargaining. Some part of the

11. As were nineteen of the four-year institutions. Note that some institutions on the 1973-74 list may not have existed in 1966-67 or may not have participated in the survey. The 1973-74 data are from the *Chronicle of Higher Education*, May 6, 1974, p. 6.

advances of this group results directly from this bargaining activity. The community colleges of CUNY are the most visible example of gains from unionization in the context of a comprehensive bargaining unit. Organization has given independent community colleges less obvious but nonetheless real benefits and has improved their relative position.

3. *Retrenchment and merit pay policies.* As more institutions find themselves forced to reduce staff, the importance of policies on "retrenchment" rises and provisions dealing with these procedures are appearing in agreements. Some agreements are silent on the problem; examples are Central Michigan, Oakland, and CUNY. St. John's and Rutgers provide for joint consideration of the problem by the union and the administration, with the St. John's agreement explicitly giving weight to the faculty's "worth" to the institution. But most agreements that mention retrenchment provide for reductions in staff to be made in inverse order of seniority, with some qualifications about the scope of the seniority districts and the ability of those remaining to carry out the educational program. Examples of agreements of this type are those at SUNY, Wayne State, Rhode Island, Southeastern Massachusetts, and the Pennsylvania state colleges. With the best intentions one wonders whether significant departures from seniority will occur when institutions such as Rutgers and St. John's actually face a retrenchment problem.

Discussions of faculty unionism sometimes are carried on under the assumption that unions are invariably hostile to differential pay for "merit." In rebuttal union sympathizers often point out that unions of entertainers, musicians, professional athletes, newspaper and television reporters, and columnists operate by negotiating basic pay scales while leaving individuals limitless scope for individual bargaining. Union officials have, on occasion, spoken out against the "star system" in academia, but there appears to be no evidence that any union in a four-year college institution has tried to limit the payment of special salaries or accelerated movement up a salary scale.

Where contracts contain salary scales, there is typically no mention of whether an over-scale salary may be paid. CUNY's agreement calls for $250,000 to be provided to create fifty distinguished-professor chairs that are not necessarily permanently assigned to individuals or equal in value. In the first year of its agreement the SUNY union negotiated money for a general increase and for payment of annual increments but did not include funds for merit increases. In the second year's pay negotiations merit increases were provided, but increments were eliminated.[12] The current CUNY contract makes no provision for increments but provides funds for "discretionary" increases, which can be used to reward "merit" or "correct inequities" as the local group decides.

It is probable that a substantial part of the total salary budget of a symphony orchestra is devoted to payments above salary scales to individual performers. If a unionized institution were to use a substantial part of its salary budget to pay above-scale salaries to a significant number of faculty, one wonders if the method of distribution would be a matter of indifference to their colleagues and the faculty union. Agreements often provide funds specifically for merit pay and sometimes specify a method of deciding on their distribution. It may be that the ability of administrations or peer committees to make differential pay adjustments will be eroded by the democratization of pay systems, but experience to date has not produced any evidence that this has happened.

In summary, the individual institutions of higher education have been stratified internally into occupational groups with substantial differences in job security, working conditions, and pay. The various types and levels of institutions have also been part of a stratified system of higher education, with significant differences among the sectors in the same characteristics. As higher education evolves toward a system of mass higher education, many of these relationships are changing. Faculty unions appeal to some of the affected groups as a way to take advantage of the new situation to improve their position. Among these groups the most prominent are the nontenured regular-rank faculty; the irregular teaching ranks, and the nonteaching professionals at university-level institutions; and the staffs of the lower-level institutions as a whole. The faculty unions also gain support from some of the more privileged groups as a method of protecting their existing position from erosion in a new environment. The less privileged groups and institutions have so far been more active in their concerns, and their aspirations are more in tune with the temper of society as a whole. As a result faculty unionism has been part of a holding action for the established faculty and the university sector, with most of the gains accruing to the other sectors of the academic and professional staff and to the "emerging" four-year institutions and the community colleges.

12. The agreement required that merit increases be limited to no more than 30 percent of faculty and 25 percent of NTPs to try to preserve the merit principle. This limitation is not included in the new contract.

References

Benewitz, Maurice C., and Mannix, T. "Grievance Procedures in Higher Education Contracts." *Community and Junior College Journal* 44, no. 44 (December 1974): 22-24.

Birnbaum, Robert. "Unionization and Faculty Compensation." *Educational Record* 55, no. 1 (Winter 1974): 29-33.

Blaustein, Edward J. "Collective Bargaining and University Governance." Speech to the American Association of Colleges (San Francisco, January 14, 1973).

Commission on Academic Tenure in Higher Education. *Faculty Tenure.* San Francisco: Jossey-Bass, 1973.

Kibbee, Robert J. "A Chancellor Views Bargaining in Retrospect and Prospect." *Proceedings, First Annual Conference, National Center for the Study of Collective Bargaining in Higher Education,* edited by Maurice C. Benewitz. New York: CUNY, 1973.

Metzger, Walter P. "Academic Tenure in America: A Historical Essay." *Faculty Tenure,* prepared by the Commission on Academic Tenure in Higher Education. San Francisco: Jossey-Bass, 1973.

Newton, David. "Management Structure and the Financing of Bargains in Public Universities." *Proceedings, First Annual Conference, National Center for the Study of Collective Bargaining in Higher Education,* edited by Maurice C. Benewitz. New York: CUNY, 1973.

Wollett, Donald H. "Historical Development of Faculty Collective Bargaining and Current Extent." *Proceedings, First Annual Conference, National Center for the Study of Collective Bargaining in Higher Education,* edited by Maurice C. Benewitz. New York: CUNY, 1973.

19

Effects of Unionism on Higher Education

Everett Carll Ladd, Jr. and Seymour Martin Lipset

It is too early to tell what degree of difference unionization will make in university life.[1] Like all unions, the faculty organizations have pressed hard for an improvement in economic benefits and working conditions. There is some dispute among observers as to how well they have succeeded and whether the increases secured under union contracts would have occurred in any case—since legislatures and governments have generally voted percentage increases in response to a variety of pressures, particularly the lobbying of more numerous associations of public employees and schoolteachers. In New York City, CUNY faculty have generally received a percentage increase comparable to that given to high school teachers. On the other hand, it is clear that the two CUNY unions secured one of the highest salary scales in the country in their first negotiation in 1969.

Salary Parity

More significant for the nature of the academic institution than changes in the size of the salary package, however, is the fact that

Reprinted from *Professors, Unions, and American Higher Education* (Berkeley, Calif.: Carnegie Commission on Higher Education, 1973).

1. For a valuable overview of some of the principal likely effects of faculty unionism, see Boyd (1971, pp. 306-318).

unionization inevitably fosters policies that seek to eliminate salary differentials among those in a given job category, other than those linked to seniority. Justice Jackson emphasized this aspect almost three decades ago:

The practice and philosophy of collective bargaining looks with suspicion on . . . individual bargaining. . . . The workman is free, if he values his own bargaining position more than that of the group, to vote against representation; but the majority rules, and if it collectivizes the employment bargain, individual advantages or favors will generally in practice go in as a contribution to the collective result [Wollett, 1971, pages 18-19].

More recently, two students of the collective bargaining experience across the country conclude that higher education

. . . bargaining agreements tend to substitute the "objective" standards of seniority and time in rank for the principle of merit. . . . The argument is that faculty members of equal rank and longevity are entitled to equal pay. While a few clauses are found which allow for merit raises above and beyond the minimum salaries provided for by the contract, pressure upon the administration to abide by the scale may inhibit the free distribution of merit increments [Mortimer and Lozier, 1972, page 27].

Faculty unions, the AAUP apart, have generally followed these principles. Richard Hixson, writing as AFT Director of Colleges and Universities, described merit-pay plans as "unionbusting disguised" (Hixson, 1972, page 23). Also speaking for the union, Israel Kugler proposed as a general policy to be applied everywhere "a professional salary schedule ranging from $10,000 to $30,000 to be attained in a reasonable number of steps by all faculty members in annual increments with a change in title upon reaching the maximum rank" (Kugler, 1969, page 184).

Both NEA and AFT affiliates in schools from New York to California have pursued salary equalization. In the CUNY system, collective bargaining resulted in parity between faculty at the two-year community colleges and the rest of the system. "Parity is achieved by the CUNY community-college full professors, who vault from their previous high of $21,950 to the new high of $31,275" (Margolin, 1969; Garbarino, 1972). The maxima at the junior colleges increased by more than twice that at the senior institutions. Two of the CUNY two-year schools are now reported by the AAUP as the fifteenth and eighteenth ranking colleges in the United States, as judged by the average compensation received by their faculty.

At SUNY, the question of parity in salary has been raised prominently.

The "parity" issue is very much alive in SUNY and surfaced in a mild form in the 1972 negotiations for salary changes. The university center's salaries by rank furnished the goals for the other segments and for the professional staffs. . . .

The most controversial element of the package of adjustments has been the problem of distributing the merit increases. . . . At SUNY, the failure of the union to secure funds for merit increases in 1971 was the subject of criticism in the university centers. . . . In 1972, in a reopening of salary negotiations, the teaching faculty received a 3.5 percent general increase with another 1.5 percent made available for differential adjustments . . . [Garbarino, 1973a] .

The NTP's secured a higher general increase of 4 percent, with another 1.5 percent available for merit or equity raises. More important, perhaps, than the limitations on merit increases is the fact that the union contract has shifted the decision power for such individual raises from the administrative structure to "peer judgments." This eliminates the power of administrators to implement the so-called "star" system, the emphasizing of "quality" or prestige distinctions among the faculty. The union also prefers to describe the sums available for personal raises as a "merit" and "equity" package. The latter term implies increases are designed to bring individuals up to parity, not ahead of others.

The situation was, of course, considerably different before unionization. Thus, in a more affluent year, 1966, the SUNY faculty was voted an 8 percent salary increase. At that time, however, the state provided "that 3 percent of that would be across-the-board and the other 5 percent would be left to the local campus president to play with. . . . [This] meant that some of the people got little, if anything, above the mandated 3 percent across-the-board . . . [while one] person got as much as 32 percent" (Garbarino, 1973a).

AFT and NEA have been able to press their opposition to individual merit increases, as compared to across-the-board lines, in the California University and State Colleges System. An attempt by the board of trustees to use limited uncommitted salary funds for merit adjustments in December 1972 was successfully lobbied against by the faculty unions. They persuaded the State Department of Finance to require a general percentage increase for all. In presenting its position, the United Professors of California (UPC) argued that once a man has been given tenure, there should be no further evaluation of his work as a condition for advancement. They presented their case in the following terms:

UPC's plan . . . rejects merit evaluation as a condition of advancement from one step within a rank to the next higher step. If a faculty member is adjudged good enough to be retained, he is good enough to merit a 5 percent salary increase. . . . We see no reason why some step 5 Assistant Professors are denied a step increase. . . .

Similarly, UPC rejects merit in moving Associate Professors 5's to step 6. If they are good enough to keep, they are good enough to be rewarded for their additional experience with more pay. Since there is not enough money for all step 5 Associate Professors to receive a step increase, *the choice should be on some non-invidious basis, either seniority or by lot. Of the two possibilities, seniority seems preferable.*[2]

At Rutgers, where the AAUP is the bargaining agent, the president of the Rutgers council of AAUP chapters challenged the University president's proposal "that an amount equal to a normal increment for each faculty member below the maximum of his salary range be '. . . awarded selectively to those members of the faculty who had demonstrated exceptionally meritorious performance. . . .'" Another AAUP leader issued a statement calling for "Price rise for everyone, not just the meritorious. . . . If all raises become merit increases, and if deans make the decisions about who is meritorious, we are putting a weapon into the hands of the administration that will humble the faculty and set back collegiality and faculty participation in university governance. . . ." ("Bloustein Asks State . . . ," 1972, p. 12).

Reappointment and Tenure

The tendency of unions to try to reduce or eliminate the power of "management" to differentially reward employees appears also with respect to the issue of job security, or tenure. Unions seek to have new appointments defined as "probationary" ones, which implies a claim to permanency for anyone who demonstrates that he can handle the job. Once appointed, a person should have a superior claim to a permanent position, even if a more able candidate should subsequently appear. Thus, the New Jersey NEA asserted during the 1972 bargaining election in the state colleges system that "if recruitment and selection procedures are sound, almost all new faculty members should qualify for tenure" (*Accomplishments in Higher Education,* 1972, page 4). Its AFT rival also contended that "tenure is the right of all qualified and competent faculty and professional staff" ("A Position Paper on Tenure," 1972).

Since it is untenable to argue that *all* faculty should be granted tenure after putting in so many years, academic unions have been

2. "On Implementation . . ." (1972, p. 1). For a comparable position by the NEA affiliate, see "CCUFA to Act . . ." (1972, pp. 1, 4). For UPC's report on the way they claim to have killed the proposal with the help of the California labor movement, see "UPC-Labor-Demo Coalition . . ." (1973, pp. 2-3).

concerned with spelling out the conditions under which professors may receive tenure, and their rights to appeal decisions either through arbitration or in the courts. These have become matters of widespread controversy (Smith, 1973; McHugh, 1973, pages 129-178; O'Neil, 1973, pages 178-199).

At the first major university to be unionized, CUNY, the unions won extensive guarantees of due process procedure to be followed with respect to reappointment and tenure decisions, as well as the right of faculty to outside arbitration. This achievement has been of central importance; for as Maurice Benewitz, Director of the National Center for the Study of Collective Bargaining in Higher Education, located at CUNY's Baruch College, reported, "the vast majority of all grievances filed concerned reappointment with or without tenure." The contract, however, limits the scope of arbitration to procedural matters in such cases. No consideration of academic judgment is allowed in the current contract. In fact, however, arbitrators have occasionally sought to go beyond their jurisdiction over procedural matters. In one case, where a man was turned down for renewal of appointment because he had not completed his Ph.D., the arbitrator ruled that because he held a teaching position that did not imply a research commitment the school had no right to refuse reappointment on those grounds: "The arbitrator recognizes that scholarly research could be helpful to teaching effectiveness. He also recognizes that many academicians equate the possession of a Ph.D. with scholarly research. However, the contract bars the university from using the criteria of scholarly research and the lack of a Ph.D. as the *sole* grounds for denying reappointment" (Finkin, 1973, pages 79-80).

The union is trying to broaden the rights of aggrieved nontenure faculty in its 1973 contract proposals by demanding that judgment also be subject to review by a committee of three—one designated by the union, one by the administration, and a third to be chosen by the two initially selected. As Benewitz notes: "Such review would tend to impose the 'just cause' rule for dismissal found in industrial situations to academic separations" (Benewitz, 1973). The university administration is vigorously opposing this demand "insisting that academic quality will become impossible to maintain if arbitrators trained in the standards of factory grievance procedure substitute their judgment for evaluation by academic juries of a teacher's peers" (Raskin, 1973). Efforts to involve nonacademic "judges" in tenure decisions have become a major goal of faculty unions. Opinion on the matter not only divides administrators from unions, but separates the concerns of the tenured faculty from the concerns of others at institutions that are, or hope to become, distinguished in terms of the scholarly quality of their professoriate. The *New York Times,* a paper with strong ties to the upper tier of academe, neatly delineated the concerns dominant there in an editorial discussing union demands in the City University of New York. The *Times* argued that the issues under negotiation raised the question

whether decisions concerning faculty tenure will continue to remain in the hands of the academic departments or increasingly be turned over to union grievance committees and outside arbitrators. These decisions have traditionally been left to academic juries of the teachers' peers. Failure to renew the individual contract of a nontenured faculty member normally does not constitute a verdict of incompetence; it merely suggests that the department believes it ought to look for a person of even higher promise or of different qualifications before committing itself to a permanent offer of tenure. . . . To abandon this approach in favor of what would in effect be automatic promotion and instant tenure, with appeals ultimately left to outside arbitrators, would seriously undercut the role of academic self-government. In plain language, it would mean adoption of the public school staffing model under which all certified teachers are essentially interchangeable parts. It is a model ill suited to the maintenance of high scholarly standards in universities.[3]

The positions that the editors of the *Times* oppose as unscholarly may, however, correspond both to the perceived interests of the nontenured staff and to the idea of justice espoused by most unions around the country in dealing with the rights of new "probationary workers." William McHugh has noted that the view of the initial-term appointment as one whose claim to renewal for a permanency should be dependent on the institution's or senior faculty's desire to be open to recruit "higher quality faculty" who may subsequently become available, runs counter to union norms.

[It] has been attacked by many faculty and certain employee organizations as subjective, elitist, institutionally oriented, and with no provision challenging nonrenewals founded upon unlawful, capricious, subjective, or punitive reasons. To some extent, there lies behind this position an underlying view that emphasizes the probationary aspect of the term appointment, the job security aspect. Assuming a term appointment is in effect a probationary appointment, it is reasoned that the individual is on a tenure track leading to a continuing appointment at the institution the moment he is appointed. The argument is that where the university has policies relating to notice appointment and requires a tenure decision after a prescribed period of service, it follows that an initial term

3. "Organized University" (1972, p. 42). For a union rebuttal of the *Times* editorial, see Shanker (1972, p. 7).

appointment may create an institutional obligation to grant tenure if certain conditions are met. This view says there is an implied obligation on the part of the institution to grant tenure, provided the individual does not do something wrong or does not fail to measure up to expressly articulated institutional standards. It is further argued that in cases of nonrenewal denying tenure, the burden should logically shift to the institution to show the reason for nonrenewal . . . [McHugh, 1973, pages 157-158].

This argument not only has been applied to schools that are primarily teaching institutions, but has even been advanced implicitly by unions at major research-oriented universities, such as the University of California. There, the AFT has successfully litigated the case of an assistant professor of speech at the Santa Barbara campus. After eight years in that rank, he was turned down for tenure when the chancellor reversed a favorable recommendation by the department on the basis of negative evaluations of the man's published work from authorities in speech outside the university.

In arguing the case, AFT's attorney contended that "the chancellor does not have unlimited discretion to determine plaintiff's right to continued employment, if the reasonableness of his decision is called into question." The union brief denounced as capricious "the *reason* given by the defendants—namely, the two comments by two negatively critical reviewers of his unpublished manuscript" and cited the "plaintiff's extraordinary record in every other area upon which he was judged [teaching, service, etc.], including the *quantity* of his publications . . ." ("UC-AFT Brief . . . ," 1972, page 5). The university agreed to an out-of-court settlement, which provided for an extraordinary nontenure reappointment for a ninth year, so that a new review of the case might be made.

This insistence by the union that administrative officers should not have the power to review faculty peer evaluations by seeking outside judgments of a candidate's scholarly qualifications runs directly contrary to an assumption shared at many leading schools: that it may be necessary, in upgrading "weak" departments, for administrators to seek confidential extramural advice to prevent faculties from becoming staffed with people like themselves. James Conant, when he was made president of Harvard in the 1930's, argued that the Harvard faculty had declined in calibre severely during the preceding decade or so and insisted that recommendations for tenure appointments from appropriate faculty and ad hoc review bodies were only that—recommendations. Unless a president concerned with scholarly calibre had the power to overrule, faculty quality would inevitably decline (Conant, 1970). Historically, the president and chancellors at the University of California had insisted on the right to overturn faculty recommendations, and had so acted in a number of important instances. Conversely, there can be little doubt that this power may be abused by administrations. Again, the significant variable may be the relative intellectual status of different institutions. The more concerned a school is with maintaining or securing a scholarly achieving faculty, the greater the necessity to build in procedures that negate the inherent tendency for academic "nepotism" appointing those who do not challenge their seniors. In high-calibre institutions, the problem of maintaining faculty prominence is complicated by the fact that "competence," even at a high level, may not be sufficient to keep a department among the leaders in its discipline. During periods in which new approaches and subfields develop, those trained in increasingly outmoded styles of work may be undesirable as permanent faculty, even though they are highly productive and intelligent. Standards such as these obviously are not relevant to the great bulk of academe, but do apply to those with the responsibility for frontier creative scholarship. Such considerations are deemed inappropriate by unions.

Many academics, even among distinguished scholars, find themselves supporting the union case on grounds that the profession has no right to "murder" large numbers of its juniors by firing them for lack of significant publications. They see the value of "humane treatment" as outweighing that of encouraging professional scholarship. Thus, the organ of the AFT at the University of California published a series of eloquent "Letters to My Colleagues" by the distinguished historian, Page Smith—author of five well-recognized books— opposing the University of California's emphasis on scholarly productivity as a condition for tenure.

Behind the publish-or-perish syndrome lies a simple if usually unspoken assumption: academic scholarship will insure the orderly and continuous advancement of mankind. Committed to pushing forward the famous "frontiers of knowledge" so beloved of commencement orators, the academic world, in order to insure the progress of the race, must insist that every professor privileged to labor within its walls play his part in this great work of "progress" by producing one or more monographs intended expressly to push forward the particular frontier of knowledge chosen as his "field."

Higher education thus [has come to believe that] . . . we could be saved by scholarship.

If in your heart of hearts you could believe that, you could commit the most cruel and wicked acts with a spirit of transcendent self-righteousness. You could kill the spirits and ruin the careers of thousands of young teachers and bully and intimidate the rest. You could do this, safe in the knowledge that you were maintaining "standards," defending your own academic balliwick against mediocrity, even doing what was "truly in the best interests" of the victim, meanwhile, of course, preserving the special privileges that you have euchred for yourself out of a compliant university. . . .

Each year we engage in the ritual murder of some of our colleagues in order to preserve our own privileges. . . . In order to do something cruel and inhumane, we must, of course, believe that it is for the good of mankind. . . .

I believe this is the proper time to unmask this tragic farce. The fact is we are no longer capable of believing that mankind will be saved by monographs . . . [Smith, 1973, page 2].

A similar argument has been presented by another University of California professor, Donald Wollett, who is a strong advocate of faculty collective bargaining. He states categorically that

from the standpoint of simple humanity and decency, the situation which exists at such places as the University of California where a faculty member can work his tail off for five years, receive no adverse evaluations and no indication of dissatisfaction with his work, and then be placed on one-year terminal appointment at the beginning of his sixth year of service has nothing to commend it other than the fact that, given the present labor market, money can be saved and a superior replacement obtained (perhaps) [Wollett, 1973].

Such highly controversial questions involving tenure have sprouted throughout the academic world. During the collective bargaining representation campaign at the University of Hawaii in the fall of 1972, the issues were discussed openly. The official AFT publication, *The Faculty Advocate,* described as unfounded the fear among some "faculty members that collective bargaining will somehow threaten professional standards. They are prone to use the word 'levellers' in voicing their apprehension over those trying to organize the faculty." Yet repeatedly, the AFT defined an initial nontenure appointment as "a probationary period for new faculty members." And in appealing to those without tenure, it argued that the decision should not be competitive: A candidate who does an adequate job should be given tenure even when a better-qualified outsider, particularly as judged by research creativity, is available. The traditional AFT trade union emphasis may be clearly seen in its policy statement: "There should be one standard definition of probation. If an individual meets the objective qualifications for a job, he is entitled to that job."

The union explicitly sought to deny senior faculty the right to differentiate among candidates for tenure through making qualitative, necessarily subjective, judgments about the scholarly worth of their work. "If some faculty members are given tenure and others meeting the identical qualifications are dismissed this can only mean that favoritism and discrimination are involved. . . . If the candidate meets the [objective tenure] standards he should have the position" ("Editorial . . . ," 1971, page 2).

Unions inherently seek to secure "more" in negotiating over the years. And clearly, reducing the power of the employer to discharge has been a continuing objective. Thus, the current contract proposals of the CUNY Professional Staff Congress include the following:

No classroom teaching member of the instructional staff, full-time or part-time, shall be denied reappointment for reasons of professional incompetence unless he has been evaluated according to the provisions of this Agreement, and either the last two semester teaching evaluations and the last yearly evaluations are all rated "Unsatisfactory"; or the last three semester teaching evaluations are rated "Unsatisfactory"; or the last two yearly evaluations are rated "Unsatisfactory" ["PSC Contract Proposals," 1972, page 5].

This demand, basically directed against the tenured faculty rather than the administration, since it is the more senior professors who must make these evaluations, is accompanied by arguments that insist that those faculty making the decisions do so publicly. Thus the co-chairman of the PSC Grievance Committee states that if the reasons for negative judgment are given,

and if they are valid academic reasons, then the charges of corruption prevailing in departments will become less and less. . . . It seems all of us know at least one case in which the "true" reason a person was not reappointed or promoted was not academic. . . . Just as we oppose the absolute right of the president to act without reasons on these crucial career decisions, we must oppose our absolute right to do it to each other [DeMelas, 1973, page 11].

Academe has traditionally relied on securing confidential evaluations about the quality of men's work from authorities in their field, as well as from former teachers. Current or prospective department colleagues have deliberated the significance of the scholarship of those they may hire or promote. Given the fact that those making the judgments are often acquaintances, friends, or competitors of those they are evaluating, it has been assumed that a guarantee of anonymity is a necessary condition for securing frank evaluations and votes. This situation, of course, differs from the typical one in industry, where personnel decisions are made by employers or their representatives rather than by peers who will often continue to live with those whom they must judge. The AFT and NEA, however, have insisted that secrecy must go:

Every faculty member . . . must have the right to examine his personnel file. . . . There should only be one such file kept and . . . it should be made easily available to the faculty members upon request. . . . One of the dangers in a closed file policy lies in the fact that malicious gossip and irrelevant but damaging unsubstantiated information could plague the faculty member the remainder of his working days.[4]

Although the national AAUP, in line with its emphasis on being primarily a professional association, has opposed submitting professional matters to outside arbitration, and has never endorsed the principle of "open" personnel files, it should be noted that chapters which have become bargaining agents have conformed to union principles. Thus at St. John's, where the faculty is represented by the AAUP, "faculty members gained access to their personnel files and were to be promptly notified of any material placed therein" (Hueppe, 1973, page 190). And both at St. John's and Oakland, AAUP-negotiated contracts provide that an unresolved grievance may be submitted to outside arbitration under the auspices of the American Arbitration Association (Finkin, 1973, pages 70, 72).

In a larger sense, as we have seen, the procedures established at schools seeking to maintain high scholarly standards for those awarded lifetime tenure are justified by reference to the needs of the profession. Harold Perkin, historian and former president of the British Association of University Teachers, offered the meritocratic argument, stating that members of the profession have their highest "responsibility in academic matters . . . to the subject they study, to the academic standards they profess, to their colleagues in the profession now and in the future, and to society which pays them to study and teach the truth as they see it and to guarantee the qualifications of those whom they educate" (Perkin, 1969, page 245). And to assure fulfillment of these responsibilities, some leading universities seek to establish the cruel principle, from the point of view of aspiring candidates for tenure, that they should resolve doubts about creative potential in favor of the university. Where there is doubt, the nontenured faculty member must be let go. A report prepared for the American Association for Higher Education pointed to the way in which "the positive features" of increased competition for jobs will "far outnumber and outweigh the negative. The oversupply of Ph.D.'s is going to raise the faculty talent level. Weaker institutions can become stronger in much less time, and higher education as a whole will be lifted appreciably" (Blackburn, 1971, page 38).

4. "Executive Board . . ." (1971, p. 4). For NEA position, see "Bargaining Brings Benefits" (1972).

These assumptions have become an overt issue in campaigns for unionization. At the University of Hawaii, the administration, faced, like many schools, with the prospect of relatively few new openings as the era of rapid growth comes to an end, announced that whenever a department is unable to reach agreement or consensus about a tenure recommendation that this would be regarded "as evidence of doubt and a strong *prima facie* reason for unfavorable action. . . ." The AFT reported that in such a situation "under an AFT contract the case would be a legitimate grievance which, if it went that far, would be won at the arbitration level . . ." ("Any Doubt . . . ," 1971, page 2).

To justify such policies—that is, to insist that when a junior faculty member has performed adequately any doubts be resolved in his favor—the AFT has pointed to the same structural change used by some as an argument for tightening standards. But it draws the opposite conclusion. It notes that in the past the

nonrenewal of a contract for untenured faculty members was not the greatest tragedy in the world, for the extraordinary expansion of colleges trying to meet the educational need created by the population explosion meant there were plenty of jobs available. Times have radically changed . . . professors are becoming a glut on the market. . . . There is literally no place to go anymore . . . ["The Intellectuals' Buyer's Market," 1971, page 2].

Although some see the new economic situation as one that will permit universities to upgrade the quality of those to whom they give tenure, others, as represented by the AFT, see it as reducing the job prospects for the younger faculty, and hence requiring formal rules enhancing the chances that "probationary teachers" will be kept on.

During the election campaign at SUNY, the AFT demanded that "tenure shall be conferred after an initial probationary period of not less than one year and not more than four years" (Scully and Sievert, 1971, page 6). The NEA has publicized, as an achievement to be pressed at other schools, the "landmark" rights that it secured in 1972 for the faculty at the fourteen-campus Pennsylvania State College system. These include: "No dismissal of nontenured faculty without just cause. . . . Full tenure following three years of satisfactory service" ("Pennsylvania . . . ," 1972, page 1). Some informed observers who have studied the situation at various unionized schools and universities have even concluded that the grievance procedures and union support will prevent the dismissal of any nontenured faculty member who really presses to stay on. David Riesman reports "the impression that procedures for assessment of faculty, for

tenure, and for the handling of grievances make it extremely difficult, at times, nearly impossible, to raise the level of faculty quality. . . ."[5] Perhaps the most difficult aspect in the situation is the
fact that collective bargaining agents assume, almost as a matter of
course, that they should take up the case of any faculty member
denied reappointment or tenure through all available channels, up to
and including arbitration and the courts. Such efforts place a considerable time burden on members of personnel committees, department chairmen, deans, and higher echelons of administration, who
are forced to defend the action. One consequence is that persons in
these positions will consciously lower their standards, and decide in
favor of a weak candidate—to avoid devoting the necessary time to
defend a negative judgment as well as to prevent the development of
a public controversy in which they are placed in the position of being
the "bad guys." These pressures to yield on a tenure issue in individual cases also encourage administrators and boards to look for more
formal rules limiting arbitrarily the number who can gain tenure.
Increasingly under the pressure of finances, as the publicly expressed
reason, but also of unions and court decisions, as a private one, colleges have been initiating policies requiring the dismissal of a fixed
proportion of those who might be considered for retention. Unions,
of course, strongly resist such proposals, but ironically, their very
policies and activities are one of the forces bringing them about.

Jack Cherniak of Rutgers has also emphasized the related pressures
on administrators to reduce the free scope senior faculty have traditionally had in making tenure decisions.

The problem then arises as to who is responsible for adverse decisions on appointment or reappointment. In the private sector the supervisor is a managerial
representative appointed by and responsible to the next higher level in the hierarchy. This is clearly not the case in colleges and universities where initial decisions are made at the department level. Although faculty bargaining groups may
have no intention of altering the traditional path to faculty membership and promotion, events may logically and inevitably move them in that direction. For the
processing of a grievance which claims an unfair or erroneous decision at the
departmental level places a higher administrative authority in the position of
automatically defending a departmental decision on grounds of faculty responsibility, or of upsetting it and thus nibbling away at the principle of faculty control. To avoid this problem of adjudication administrators will at least seek to
enforce more uniform adherence to rules governing the timing of decisions on
faculty status at the department level and insist on clarity in understanding of
the conditions of appointment and reappointment. But it seems possible that

5. Riesman (1973). For a discussion of the situation at CUNY, see Glazer
(1973).

because grievances will at least to some extent claim error in evaluation judgment, pressure towards bureaucratization will occur. Department chairmen and senior faculty will be obliged to follow more formal guidelines in reaching their decisions and the scope for independent judgment is likely to be constricted [Cherniak, 1972, pages 4-5].

Although the story of collective bargaining in higher education has hardly begun, the record is sufficient to indicate that the principles that evolved over many generations in "blue-collar unionism" have been successfully transferred to academe in spite of the enormous differences in structure and role. Our examination of its effects on salaries and tenure-granting practices reinforces the findings of Joseph Garbarino's earlier intensive study of collective bargaining at five institutions. As he notes, "a leveling process has occurred as most of the benefits have gone to the faculty of the lower level institutions and to the support of professionals. Among regular rank faculty the most significant benefits have accrued to a relatively small fraction of the junior faculty who have improved their chances of continuing employment in a weak labor market" (Garbarino, 1972).

Governance

There is, of course, a range of consequences of collective bargaining in academe beyond the impact on salaries and job contracts. Berkeley professor T. R. McConnell has particularly stressed the potential effects on university governance:

The consequences of unionism and collective bargaining to faculties will be complex; they will both lose and gain power. Individuals will lose freedom of action if they are represented by an exclusive bargaining agent, and faculties will lose power corporately when an external organization serves as the collective bargaining agent, or when matters under contention between the union and the employer are submitted to external arbitration. Power may be gained, however, through negotiations over conditions of tenure, duration, and service.

In addition to the reordering of relative power, unionism and collective bargaining will have other profound effects on governance; the roles, posture, and authority of academic senates may well be affected. If the bargaining agency and the senate are separate bodies, it may be difficult to divide jurisdiction between them. Conditions involving appointment, promotion, and tenure, traditionally established and applied by senates or senate committees, will become subjects for negotiation with the union. The collective bargaining agreements will define grievance procedures and the parties to adjudication. The issues will be between union and "management," and the faculty senate may become relatively impotent. It is difficult, too, to separate all of the conditions covered by a collective bargaining agreement from fundamental questions of educational policy. Again, the senate may be the loser . . . [McConnell, 1971, pages 43-45].

The ultimate effect of unionization on the authority of faculty senates and other self-governing institutions is clearly of enormous importance. Although it is obvious that such bodies have been generally dominated by small minorities of faculty oligarchs, who are often quasi-administrators primarily concerned with academic politics, these elective groups are *pro forma* representatives of the entire faculty who may overturn the decisions of the oligarchy (Clark, 1961, pages 293-302; McConnell and Mortimer, 1971, pages 24-39). Organizations that are designated as exclusive bargaining representatives of the faculty present the standard problem that they are prone to be controlled by an operative minority or oligarchy; but they also present a new one, arising from the fact that the voting membership is not coterminous with the faculty as a whole. As noted earlier with reference to the SUNY situation, many faculty may choose not to join the union. The same situation prevails at most four-year colleges or universities which have designated an exclusive bargaining agent, the majority of the faculty are not members of the organization that represents them (Garbarino, 1973b). Although some bargaining agents have allowed everyone covered in a unit, whether union members or not, to vote on a proposed contract, most do not allow this. Even AAUP chapters that hold bargaining rights limit the vote on a proposed contract to dues-paying members of the organization (Kerr, 1972, page 53). At Rutgers, the bylaws of the AAUP Council "provide that the agreement between the Rutgers administration and faculty shall be voted upon only by members of the AAUP at Rutgers." In the discussion of this bylaw, " 'Anyone can join, and everyone should support faculty bargaining,' was the argument that won" ("Dues Increase . . . ," 1972, page 6).

The right of faculty members who refuse to join an organization designated as a collective bargaining agent to vote on contracts has been taken up by rival groups that lost the initial election. Thus, in the New Jersey college system, where faculty were represented by the NEA from 1969 to 1972, the AFT denounced the NEA as controlled by a small clique of officers who largely ignored their members and refused to submit contracts to "the faculty at large for ratification." They promised to change this practice. Conversely, at Hawaii, it was the NEA's turn to denounce the AFT for undemocratic practices. Following the run-off victory of the AFT, backed by the NEA, a rift developed between the two groups over elections to the collective bargaining committee. "Nominations were open to the faculty but only HFCT (AFT) members could vote, which insured the HFCT would dominate the Committee." The NEA group canceled merger negotiations with the AFT on this issue, charging that in choosing the bargaining committee the faculty turnout was exceptionally low and hence unrepresentative, that, for example, only "25 people voted in the College of Arts and Sciences" ("Memorandum to the Faculty," 1973, pages 1-2). Thus, the senate oligarchy, responsible to the entire faculty, is replaced for certain purposes by the union oligarchy responsible to a more limited membership (Lipset, 1963, pages 387-436).

The shift from the academic senate or "campus politicians" oligarchy means a major change in the type of individuals "representing" the professoriate. There is evidence that those who serve on faculty committees or who have been department chairmen are more conservative and more friendly to the administration than the faculty as a whole. Lazarsfeld and Thielens (1958, pages 151-152, 443) reported this pattern among a national sample of social scientists interviewed in 1955. And in our 1969 Carnegie survey of the total professoriate, the relationships were somewhat similar. These findings reflect the fact that campus committeemen and chairmen, even when formally elected, are likely to be chosen from older faculty who are willing and even anxious to hold such "local" posts. In large measure, therefore, they come from the ranks of the less prestigious in scholarly terms, and as noted earlier, are therefore also more conservative politically. Heavily concerned with local status, they tend to seek ways of getting along with the higher ranks of administration, a group that itself is often recruited from the "committeemen." Unionization is likely to open a new avenue of prestige and power to another group of "locals" whose status will depend on their retaining the favor of the union members drawn heavily from the less privileged strata of the university. Presumably they will be more liberal politically, more inclined to take an adversary posture with administration, and more favorable to "a program of immediate across-the-board benefits for the existing majority" (Oberer, 1969, page 143).

The assignment of collective bargaining rights to a given organization that has won an election does not, of course, eliminate the existing faculty self-government institutions. Union spokesmen publicly contend that there is no conflict between faculty self-government and exclusive bargaining rights. Israel Kugler of the AFT insists "The union is not opposed to faculty senates." But the area of the jurisdiction would be clearly limited. "We wish them to be invested with *complete* authority in the areas of curriculum, scholastic standards, student activities with proper student involvement. Since there cannot be a unitary union line in these matters, we conceive of powerful senates as compliments of unions" (Kugler, 1968, page 416). On the other hand, a comprehensive survey of trends in faculty collective bargaining concludes unequivocally that "with the exception of the AAUP, comments about senates by the leaders of the dues-funded faculty organizations are uniformly critical, if not derisive" (Wollett, 1971, page 25). David Riesman, who has investigated the situation at a number of colleges, reports that "commonly, presidents find that a union tends eventually to weaken the power of the Faculty Senate, even though during a transition period they may have to deal simultaneously with both the union and the Senate" (Riesman, 1973, page 425).

In a discussion of the essential modifications in faculty governance made necessary by collective bargaining, Belle Zeller, President of the CUNY Professional Staff Congress, also described the continuation of a bilateral model, senate and union, as a "transitional step . . . necessary to assure faculty that they are not giving up their decision making powers, particularly on academic issues." She went on, however, in commenting on the continuation of previous governance procedures at CUNY, to state that "frankly I do not know how long they will last . . . [given the] question of overlapping [jurisdictions]" (Zeller, 1972, pages 107-111).

Some indication of the breadth of university issues that faculty unions see as within their scope may be gathered from the list of subjects that Israel Kugler (then President of the New York State AFT College and University Council) presented to the New York Public Employment Relations Board during the SUNY hearings:

Merit increases, number of students, promotions, compensation for extracurricular activity, TV and radio tape residuals, research staff, office space, secretarial services, travel funds, academic calendar, evening and extension assignments, sabbatic leave, leaves of absence, maternity and sick leave, tenure policies, grievance procedures, general regulations pertaining to campus affairs, consultation on educational matters, curriculum, admissions, student activities, choice of administrators (including deans, chairmen, presidents), pensions, health benefits, life and disability insurance, salary policy, moving expenses, tuition waiver for dependents, central faculty authority, master plan formulation, educational policy governing entire university, establishment of new campuses, intercollege agreements, and finally, but not least, selection of the chancellor and other central administrators [McHugh, 1973, page 42].

Various contracts have given unions the right to represent the faculty on a range of noneconomic matters. Thus, at Central Michigan University where an NEA affiliate is the bargaining agent, the agreement specifies that NEA representatives shall serve on a committee to establish a "distinguished professorship." At Southeastern Massachusetts University, the committee that controls sabbatical leaves is composed of two representatives of the local AFT and three other professors designed by the president. Nominations for dean-ships are to be made by three faculty members representing the union, three persons appointed by the president, and one representa-tive of the student senate. At Boston State College, the union is also involved with the curriculum. The NEA, while it was negotiating agent of the New Jersey state college faculty, won the right to desig-nate a representative "to each college-wide standing committee at each of the six state colleges, and to any presidential search commit-tee." The bargaining agent represents the faculty in preparing the col-lege calendar. The St. John's contract (AAUP and an unaffiliated local group as agents) provides that "presently constituted organiza-tions within the faculty (e.g., the University Senate, Faculty Council, departmental personnel and budget committees, etc.) or any other body composed in whole, or in part, of the faculty, shall continue to function provided that the actions of such bodies do not modify the agreement itself." A similar proviso is included in the CUNY contract (Finkin, 1971, pages 156-157). As the Ad Hoc Committee of the Michigan State Faculty concluded, "collective bargaining would in-creasingly come to cover subjects both economic and academic."[6]

Beyond the specific economic or academic powers taken up by collective bargaining agents, the very existence of union representa-tion must serve to reduce interest and participation in faculty sen-ates, councils, or other bodies. The adversary model of university governance contained in collective bargaining, with its consequent emphasis on formal, detailed spelling out of both rights and obliga-tions—e.g., student contact hours, research time, faculty-student ratios—is likely to weaken the "producers' cooperative," self-govern-ment aspects.

From a pro-union viewpoint, CUNY professor Myron Lieberman looks forward to these developments. He suggests that collective bar-gaining establishes a variety of criteria for running the university, and that once agreeing to them through their union, the faculty must give up

the operational responsibility for making and carrying out the decisions made according to these criteria. But their loss will be higher education's gain. The role of a faculty should not be to administer an institution but to ensure that admin-

6. *Report of the Ad Hoc University Committee* ... (1972, p. 21). This is a comprehensive report dealing with almost every aspect of the situation.

istration is fair and equitable. Unfortunately, pathetic confusions about professionalism have misled faculty members into believing that professors at each institution are entitled to make management decisions. . . . Collective bargaining will force professors out of administration, but administrators will be monitored by faculty unions in the performance of their administrative duties.[7]

The issue of self-government versus adversary managerial relationships is still in a confused and controversial state. On one hand, the AFT and NEA strongly reject the image of a collegial faculty-controlled university, arguing that the "professor is a professional employee for whom others make the key decisions. . . . Decision makers are not the practicing professionals, but that corporate hierarchy which includes trustees, presidents, deans. . . . The faculty member [is] powerless without a collective bargaining contract. . . ."[8] But paradoxically, the AFT has insisted that at various schools "the hiring, retention, and separation of division heads, associate deans, deans, vice-presidents, and presidents shall be done with the advice and consent of the faculty . . ." (Lieberman, 1969, page 62). In a statement distributed for national use, the NEA argues that the union, itself, shall play a major role in the process of selecting management. Thus, it insists on "screening of all candidates for administrative positions by a three-man faculty selection committee appointed by the association, and association representation on the committee to select the college president" ("Bargaining Brings Benefits," 1972). At Boston State College, where the faculty is repre-

7. Lieberman (1971). Significantly, this article was reprinted in its entirety in the University of California AFT organ, *University Guardian* (1971, pp. 1-3). A similar argument has been posed recently by a University of California law professor who is a strong supporter of faculty collective bargaining. Speaking of his experience with the reputedly powerful University of California Academic Senate system, Donald Wollett observes "that self-governance which thrusts the faculty into the performance of managerial functions serves primarily the interests of administration. . . . They can utilize the instrumentalities of self-governance as lightning rods for making unpopular decisions for which administrators do not want to take responsibility. . . . [But] if the faculty makes a managerial decision which is unacceptable to the administration, it can be vetoed if the administration has the guts to do so." Wollett is critical of the faculty's "romantic attachment to self-governance." Like Lieberman, he looks forward to a situation in which unionization forces university administrators to become stronger, more responsible, and more efficient, as a response to strong unions. "I believe in strong managements, and I believe that one of the pluses of the collective bargaining is that it will force educational institutions to improve their managerial structure and most importantly their management personnel" (Wollett, 1973).

8. See Kugler (n.d., p. 5). For a similar analysis by an NEA official see Keck (1972, pp. 4-5).

sented by the AFT, the union is directly involved in choosing department chairmen. The contract provides that department members
shall propose three nominees for the chairmanship in elections supervised by the union. The list of nominees is then submitted to the
college president by the union president. If the college president
refuses to designate any of the candidates, the procedure is repeated.
The New Jersey state colleges contract negotiated by the NEA, while
it was still the agent, stated that chairmen should be elected by department members, but that under exceptional circumstances, a college president could appoint a chairman with the consent of the local
union (Mortimer and Lozier, 1973, page 125). At Wayne State University, where the AAUP won bargaining rights, the first contract
negotiated provides "for the presence of members of the bargaining
unit on Selection Committees appointed for the purpose of giving
advice about selecting candidates for department heads, deans, directors, etc., of academic units" (Letter to Wayne AAUP members from
the Chapter Office, March 8, 1973, page 4).

The conflict inherent in the two models of academic governance
has come to a head at CUNY, where the administration and the
Board of Higher Education have begun to insist that collective bargaining means that the administration must be able to select all of its
members down to the level of department chairman. They seek to
reverse the traditional practice of election of chairmen by full-time
members of the faculty. The chancellor's office argues that the
CUNY contract gives the chairmen managerial functions in administering the contract, that the university is held legally responsible for
any violations of a contract by a chairman, such as in dealing with
nontenured faculty. The latter may file and win grievance complaints
about a tenure decision because of a chairman's actions. The union
takes the position that these "management" positions should be
filled through election by the "workers."

Union spokesmen repeatedly deny that formal collective bargaining will result in the replacement of "collegial" relations with administrators by "adversary" ones. Yet four years of negotiations at
CUNY have clearly exacerbated the relationships. A leading spokesman for the more "professionally" oriented of the two unions that
represented the faculty there preceding their merger in 1972, Arnold
Cantor, then Executive Director of the Legislative Conference
(NEA), and currently in the same post in the merged PSC, described
the university administration as "The Real Enemy." He wrote:

In my view we must not lose sight of the fact that our continuing battle must be
against the University Management—the BHE, the Chancellor, the Vice-Chancel-

lor and the College Presidents. These are the people to be held responsible for daily efforts at denigrating our contract . . . .

While the "real enemy" attempts to convince PERB that nonclassroom members of the instructional staff should be in a separate unit; while the "real enemy" is constantly trying to increase our workloads, deny us sabbaticals, our research funds, and generally making our lives miserable; I urge that we do not dissipate our energies and resources fighting with other groups of teachers [Cantor, 1972, page 2].

It is clear that the adversary relationship inherent in the very conception of collective bargaining does change the role and image of university administrators. Ideally, they have been viewed as the colleagues and representatives of the faculty in coping with off-campus power—the alumni, public opinion, the press, the legislature, the trustees. They are expected to be a buffer. In intramural matters, good administrators often operate informally; a good dean rarely inquires as to what given individuals are doing with respect to teaching load, sick leave, and the like.

Under collective bargaining, administrators, often down to the level of department chairmen, become responsible for a legally binding contract. The institution will be held legally responsible for their actions. They become, as the unions insist, representatives of management who seek to protect management's prerogatives and rights under the contract. Thus a self-confirming prophecy comes into play (Merton, 1968, pages 475-490). The union representatives deal with management in a constant battle over interpretation of the contract. And the tendencies toward rigidity and bureaucratization, inherent in any case in the sheer size and complexity of many academic institutions, are magnified.

Student-Faculty Tensions

The role of students in university governance may also be affected by the introduction of collective bargaining. Writing in *Harper's* in October 1971, Myron Lieberman, an analyst and strong supporter of faculty unionism, projected a future event occurring "sometime in the seventies" at a large state university in which the student union would announce that it has "voted in favor of a mass refusal to pay any tuition at all if it goes up as a result of the faculty union's intolerable pressure on the administration," and it would demand "real faculty accountability." He went on to predict that "student unions will seek to participate in bargaining between the faculty and the administration, and they will often be the decisive factor in resolving disputes between these groups. In these disputes, students will usually line up with the administration against the faculty."[9]

T. R. McConnell also suggests that the sight of faculty unions bargaining hard for their membership will stimulate student demands for a larger share. He predicts:

. . . that students will demand and get a review of the total work load of faculty members and of the distribution of faculty time. Collective bargaining will rapidly become a tripartite rather than just a bilateral negotiation. . . . It is easy to see why administrators and students may find it advantageous to combine against the faculty, not only in the distribution of the fundament, but also in moving toward evaluation of faculty services and in establishing standards for appointment, promotion, and tenure. It is not inconceivable that on many of these questions students may ultimately acquire the balance of power.[10]

Concern over negative consequences of faculty unionism for student interests is in no sense limited to conservative or pro-administration undergraduates. The National Student Association, controlled in recent years by fairly left-wing students, has also seen unionism as a threat. "Collective bargaining will co-opt the present system of university senates and faculty and faculty-student committees. In order to assure that students don't lose the little power they have, they need real voting power on boards of collective bargaining" (National Student Association, 1971).

The assumption that unionization may stimulate student conflict with faculty is not simply a hypothetical prognostication (Semas, 1973, page 4). "Already, some student organizations are questioning the merits of faculty tenure, while others are looking askance at

9. Lieberman (1971, pp. 61-62, 70). As noted, this article was reprinted by the University of California AFT. See also McHugh (1971, pp. 175-185). Much of the prospective sources of tension between students and faculty were anticipated by Clark Kerr in his Godkin Lectures in 1963. "The undergraduate students are restless. Recent changes in the American university have done them little good—lower teaching loads for faculty, the use of substitute teachers for the regular faculty, the choice of faculty members based on research accomplishments rather than instructional capacity, the fragmentation of knowledge into endless subdivision. There is an incipient revolt of undergraduate students against the faculty; the revolt that used to be against the faculty *in loco parentis* is now against the faculty *in absentia*. . . . Lack of faculty concern for teaching, endless rules and requirements, and impersonality are the inciting causes" (Kerr, 1963, pp. 103-104).

10. McConnell (1971, pp. 43-45). For a related discussion of the sources of tension between activist students and leftist faculty, see Lipset (1972, pp. 197-235).

teaching efficiency, both in terms of classroom effectiveness and in terms of hours worked and classes taught" (Bonham, 1971-72, pages 13-14). Student leaders at the first major unionized university, CUNY, have openly expressed their opposition at times to the high-pay package given to a "mediocre" faculty, arousing the natural ire of union leaders. In the spring of 1971, the student senate passed a resolution calling on the Board of Higher Education to rescind faculty pay increases and to use the monies to offset proposed tuition increases ("On Faculty Unionism," 1971, page 1). The University Student Press Service of CUNY released to the student press nationally, in January 1971, an article written by a student, George McCough, making a strong student-oriented case against faculty tenure.

A high ratio of tenured faculty will, in the long run, mean higher tuition and fees and a stagnant curriculum. Since neither of these can be regarded as being convergent with student interests, unconditional student support of faculty in tenure disputes is at least counterproductive and clearly contradictory . . . .

It must be concluded, that not only is student support or sympathy in faculty tenure disputes unwarranted, but students must actively seek to participate in those areas wherein tenure affects the character of the college and university community. . . . Students must become involved in collective bargaining as parties to the contract . . . .

A predominant factor in the reappointment, promotion, and tenure process must be its reliance upon student evaluations of faculty teaching ability.

More recently, in October 1972, Alan Shark, chairman of the CUNY Student Senate, continued the attack, arguing that under current economic conditions, union demands for a reduced teaching load and higher salaries could only be met "through increases in fees and tuition costs." He criticized union insistence on separate faculty "elevators, private dining facilities, as well as private lavatories . . . [suggesting that] it is quite demeaning to see locked faculty bathrooms; it depicts an uncomfortable polarizing class distinction." He pointed out that the Board of Higher Education had stated that "students should have a participation role in the academic decision-making process . . . [while the union] has continually rejected new governance plans that provide for a greater sharing of academic responsibility with students" (Shark, 1972, pages 552-558).

During the 1972-73 CUNY negotiations, the student senate sought permission to have observers present at bargaining sessions and to give testimony before the factfinders. The Board of Higher Education supported the student request, the union opposed it. "The student leaders came away from the rebuff openly skeptical of the union's slogan, 'Professors Want What Students Need.' The union's president, Professor Belle Zeller of Hunter College, retorted: 'All the students have to do is holler, and the administration quivers. We are fighting to preserve the power of the faculty . . .' " (Raskin, 1973).

In an editorial in the union newspaper, the PSC argued vigorously against the CUNY administration's proposal to allow students "to participate in college governance," contending that the students had been responsible for a major blunder, Open Admissions: "Three years ago, CUNY students petitioned for Open Admissions and won. But we see now that Open Admissions was an empty promise, effected without plan or understanding. As a result, CUNY now has the highest dropout rate in its history, and there is no sign that the rates will be arrested" (F. B., 1973, page 3).

At the State University of New York (SUNY), a comparable clash is in the making. Student representatives from the different SUNY campuses who met in Albany on February 6-7, 1972, to discuss the projected master plan for the university seemingly saw little good in the emergence of collective bargaining. A detailed report of that conference summarized their conclusions:

The formation of faculty and staff unions to further the self-interest of their members will inevitably clash with student interests. . . . The potential impact of these unions on university governance is particularly frightening. Negotiations between the University and the union on the terms and conditions of employment can and will cover every aspect of operation of the University. With students playing no role in these negotiations, the resulting contracts could nullify every gain which students have made in terms of increased participation in university governance . . . .

Unfortunately, faculty and staff unions are a reality in American higher education. Now all possible steps must be taken to ensure that unionization does not lock students out of university governance. . . . It is unacceptable for students as consumers and participants in the learning process to be locked out of decision making ["Proceedings of the Student Conference," 1972, pages 5-6].

As at CUNY, the student representatives opposed bargaining solely at the systemwide level, demanding some form of local campus negotiations. They also challenged the tendency toward "leveling," inherent, as they saw it, in "an across-the-board increase." They argued for some rewards "on the basis of individual merit" as an incentive to improve "the quality of teaching and scholarship" ("Proceedings of the Student Conference," 1972, page 6).

An explicit example of overt tension between a faculty union and students took place in the Chicago city college system. During an AFT strike in 1968, the union told students attending courses and planning to take exams that "grades and course credit which would be given without the certification of your teacher who is on strike would be invalid. *A college diploma issued to any of you on this basis will have no official standing*" (Finkin, 1971, page 148). The subsequent contract between the union and the college system contained a specific clause limiting the scope of participation by students within individual departments to "curricular matters" only, and provided that departments could only deal with "democratically elected student governing bodies," that is, not with activist organizations. The departments were also forbidden to make any agreement with students that might "abrogate faculty rights" in the contract (Finkin, 1971).

More recently, in the fall of 1972, students at two community colleges in Pennsylvania sought injunctions against faculty strikes. Both sides in the disputes agreed that student pressure helped force the settlements (Semas, 1973).

A report by a Central Michigan University faculty member of the background of the NEA victory there in September 1969 contends that the faculty were discontented with the new president's concern for students, at the expense of faculty interests. They supported collective bargaining as a way of restricting an overly pro-student administration (Hepler, 1971). The president, William Boyd, also emphasized as a cause of unionization "student demands for a share in decisions which were once the prerogative of faculties." And he noted the "danger . . . that contracts . . . may pay professors at the expense of students . . . . How ironic it is that, just as students were achieving a share of power in campus governance the locus of decision making should shift to a new location where they are unrepresented!" (Boyd, 1971, pages 308, 315-316).

Clearly, some professors view the growth of faculty unionism favorably for the same reasons that student leaders fear it, seeing in it a way for the professoriate to regain power given up to students during the activism of the late 1960's. Writing from experiences at SUNY, William McHugh suggests that "unionism may well appeal to . . . traditional elements of a faculty as a reaffirmation of the faculty guild concept in face of student pressures. Faculty unionism may result in a collision course with the newly emerging tripartite governance patterns . . ." (McHugh, 1973, pages 135-136). A report by a Michigan State professor, Robert Repas, on the 1972 bargaining election there maintains that many MSU faculty "supported collective bargaining because they looked upon it as a device to keep students out of the decision-making process" (Repas, personal correspondence, 1973). During the campaign, an article in the campus newspaper made the same point from the student side, arguing that "unionization could jeopardize student gains in academic governance, [since] the faculty generally would not be swayed by any concern for student input . . ." (Fox, 1972).

The shift in power—or at least in representation—that excludes students may be seen in the Rutgers experience. There it was anticipated that collective bargaining "would develop as a new base for faculty power . . . because the university senate included representatives of faculty, students, and administration, and the AAUP could claim to be the sole university-wide faculty body" (McCormick, 1973, page 280). A delegate assembly, with members elected by faculty from departments and campuses, has been set up by the Rutgers AAUP. On January 29, 1973, the assembly "moved to strengthen its function as the only university-wide body that exclusively represents and expresses faculty opinion." It passed a resolution "to petition for a University Assembly called for the purpose of disbanding the University Senate and recognizing the Delegate Assembly as the Faculty Senate" (Howard, 1973, page 6).

Conflict between students and unions already exists within the University of California. An official student lobby, created by the Associated Students of the University of California (ASUC), has offices in Sacramento. Interviews with AFT and student lobby officers indicate distrust between them. The student leaders argue the union is uninterested in student concerns and seeks to keep teaching loads low. The unionists report that the students complain to state officials about the "elitism" of the faculty, their emphasis on research rather than teaching, etc. A conflict also appears to be in the offing in the state of Washington, where student leaders contributed to the defeat of a collective bargaining bill in 1973 by demanding explicit student representation in the collective bargaining process (Semas, 1973).

The AFT, from New York to California, has sharply opposed student involvement in judging the quality of their teachers. Thus Allan Netick, the editor of *The UPC Advocate,* organ of the union for the California State University and Colleges System, objects to student evaluation of teaching as providing a means "whereby any chairman or dean, or PRT committee may judge a faculty member in comparison to other faculty members," thereby providing a supposedly objective basis for denying "tenure or promotion." After reviewing the spread of such evaluations around the country, he concludes: "Student evaluation has become an important tool of management" (Netick, 1973, page 10).

The exception that may prove the rule has occurred in Massachusetts. Both AFT and NEA units, which represent faculty at various state colleges, have endorsed new governance relationships that incorporate student representatives in the collective bargaining process (Walters, 1973). The explanation for the variation in reaction of Massachusetts faculty unionists from their colleagues elsewhere may be the deplorable conditions at the state colleges in a state known for the distinction of its private higher education. (Massachusetts ranks close to the bottom in its per capita support for higher education, and state college salaries have been unusually low.) Unlike students at the highly salaried CUNY, Massachusetts state college students could not help but sympathize with the plight of their faculty. It may also be relevant to note that state law, although allowing faculty unions, forbids the college system from bargaining on economic matters. Consequently, faculty have less reason to oppose student involvement in collective bargaining that cannot affect their salaries.

The conflict between the interests of professors and students, made evident with the growth of faculty unionism, has served to modify the image presented during the 1960's by campus activists that students were the exploited "under-class" of the university, the equivalent of the workers in the factory. In fact, the students are the "consumers," the buyers, the patrons of a product sold by the faculty through a middleman, the university system. In economic class terms, the relationship of student to teacher is that of buyer to seller, or of client to professional. In this context, the buyer or client seeks to get the most for his money at the lowest possible price. He prefers that an increased share of the payment to the institution should go for more direct benefits to him—teaching, student activities, better housing, and so forth. The faculty seller of services, on the other hand, is obviously interested in maximizing his income and working conditions. Lower teaching loads and greater research facilities are to his benefit. Tenure not only reduces the power of administrators over faculty, it protects teachers from consumer (student) power as well.

The conception of students as "consumers" is not simply an analytic one. It has been explicitly argued in these terms by student leaders at CUNY and SUNY. Conversely, the CUNY union has editorialized in objecting to the students' demand to participate in negotiations, saying: "Management and labor do not invite consumers to the bargaining table, though consumers, of course, have rights and recourse elsewhere in the business sector" (F. B., 1973, page 3).

Efforts, much more successful in Europe than in America, to give students a major role in university governance, serve to weaken faculty power. Student power reduces the faculty's freedom to choose their colleagues, to determine the curriculum, to select research topics, and to control their work schedules. It does not, however, affect the power of those who control the purse strings to determine how much shall be spent on higher education, and the ways it will be distributed among alternative sectors. Hence, even conservative politicians have been willing to support systems of student-faculty government in a number of European countries.

Student groups, of course, may ally with faculty factions for common extramural sociopolitical objectives. Given a similar political position—on racism or the Vietnam War, for example—they can work together against common opponents. Students may join with junior, nontenured faculty, close to students in age and style, in opposition to senior professors. Such alliances, too, often reflect similar ideological leanings in both strata. But where the issues are purely of the marketplace, where they revolve around the faculty's desire to maximize income and reduce the direct service (teaching) that they give to buyers (students), a conflict of interests exists that cannot be easily bridged. There may, in fact, often be a congruence of interests between the student buyers and the middlemen public authorities and administrators. The latter may also be more interested in optimizing the services rendered to the students than in the conditions of the faculty. Students, their parents, and alumni form a much larger voting bloc than do professors. Thus, in spite of the "anti-establishment" sympathies of most politically active students, tacit alliances between administrators and students against faculty may emerge.[11]

In the long run, it is likely that those who view faculty unionism as a way of enhancing faculty authority and reducing student power are right. Faculty unions, employing experienced permanent professional negotiators, public relations staff, etc., and allied with the labor movement, are at a considerable advantage in contests with student groups, which are dependent on a rotating leadership drawn from a highly transitory student population. The unions, once institutionalized, press on from year to year for "more." Student groups rise and fall, have little memory, and in the long run will be unable to best the faculty in any adversary relationship.

References

Accomplishments in Higher Education. Trenton: Association of New Jersey State College Faculties, 1972.

11. For a related discussion see Lipset (1972).

"Any Doubt Means No Tenure, Promotions?" *The Faculty Advocate* 1 (March 1971).

"Bargaining Brings Benefits." Washington, D.C.: NEA, 1972.

Benewitz, Maurice C. "Grievance and Arbitration Procedures in Higher Education Agreements: Extent, Nature, and Problem." New York: National Center for the Study of Collective Bargaining, Baruch College, 1973.

Blackburn, Robert T. "Unionization of Faculty Expected to Pick Up Speed Because of Tight Money and Ph.D.'s." *College Management* (September 1971).

"Bloustein Asks State to Make All 1973-74 Salary Increase 'Merit' Raises." *Rutgers AAUP Newsletter* 4 (December 1972).

Bonham, George W. "The New Class." *Change* 3 (Winter 1971-72).

Boyd, William. "Collective Bargaining in Academe: Causes and Consequences." *Liberal Education* 57 (October 1971).

Cantor, Arnold. "The Real Enemy." *LC Reporter* (March 27, 1972).

"CCUFA to Act; Duplicity Ends CSUC Salary Talks." *The California Professor* 7 (December 1972).

Cherniak, Jack. "Grievance Procedures Under Collective Bargaining." New Brunswick: Institute of Management and Labor Relations, Rutgers University, 1972.

Clark, Burton. "Faculty Authority." *AAUP Bulletin* 47 (Winter 1961).

Conant, James B. *My Several Lives.* Cambridge, Mass.: Harvard University Press, 1970.

DeMelas, Anthony. "The Need for Reasons." *Clarion* 2 (February 5, 1973).

"Dues Increase, Agreement Ratification Change Voted by Rutgers AAUP Members at Fall Meeting." *Rutgers AAUP Newsletter* 4 (December 1972).

"Editorial: Where the AFT Stands on Probation." *The Faculty Advocate* 1 (April 1971).

"Executive Board Asks for Open Files." *The Faculty Advocate* 1 (May 1971).

F. B. "Students: Why We Care." *Clarion* 2 (February 5, 1973).

Finkin, Matthew W. "Collective Bargaining and University Government." *AAUP Bulletin* 57 (Summer 1971).

Finkin, Matthew W. "Grievance Procedures." *Faculty Unions and Collective Bargaining,* edited by E. D. Duryea and Robert S. Fisk. San Francisco: Jossey-Bass, 1973.

Fox, Michael. "Wharton Taints Union Vote." *Michigan State News* (October 27, 1972).

Garbarino, Joseph W. "Faculty Unionism: From Theory to Practice." *Industrial Relations* 11 (February 1972).

Garbarino, Joseph W. "Creeping Unionism and The Faculty Labor Market." *Higher Education and the Labor Market,* edited by Margaret Gordon. New York: McGraw-Hill, 1973a.

Garbarino, Joseph W. "Emergence of Collective Bargaining." *Faculty Unions and Collective Bargaining,* edited by E. D. Duryea and Robert S. Fisk. San Francisco: Jossey-Bass, 1973b.

Glazer, Nathan. "City College." *Academic Transformations,* edited by David Riesman and Verne Stadtman. New York: McGraw-Hill, 1973.

Hepler, John C. "Timetable for a Take-over." *Journal of Higher Education* 42 (February 1971).

Hixson, Richard. "Unionbusting Disguised." *American Teacher* 57 (November 1972).

Howard, Daniel F. "Delegate Assembly Meets, Explores Possible Role as Faculty Senate." *Rutgers AAUP Newsletter* 4 (March 1973).

Hueppe, Frederick E. "Private University: St. John's." *Faculty Unions and Collective Bargaining*, edited by E. D. Duryea and Robert S. Fisk. San Francisco: Jossey-Bass, 1973.

"The Intellectuals' Buyer's Market." *The Faculty Advocate* 1 (March 1971).

Keck, Donald J. "The 1970s for the College Professor." *NSP Forum* 6 (October-November 1972).

Kerr, Clark. *The Uses of the University*. Cambridge, Mass.: Harvard University Press, 1963.

Kerr, David J. "Collective Bargaining in Public Institutions: The Process." *Faculty Power: Collective Bargaining on Campus*, edited by Terrence Tice. Ann Arbor: The Institute of Continuing Legal Education, 1972.

Kugler, Israel. "The Union Speaks for Itself." *Educational Record* 49 (Fall 1968).

Kugler, Israel. "Unionism: A New Instrument for Faculty Governance." *ISR Journal* 1 (Summer 1969).

Kugler, Israel. *Higher Education and Professional Unionism*. Washington, D.C.: American Federation of Teachers, n.d.

Lazarsfeld, Paul F., and Thielens, Wagner, Jr. *The Academic Mind*. Glencoe, Ill.: Free Press, 1958.

Lieberman, Myron. "Representation Systems in Higher Education." *Employment Relations in Higher Education*, edited by Stanley Elam and Michael H. Moskow. Bloomington, Ind.: Phi Delta Kappa, 1969.

Liberman, Myron. "Professors Unite!" *Harper's Magazine* 243 (October 1971).

Lipset, Seymour Martin. "The Political Process in Trade Unions." *Political Man*. Garden City: Doubleday Anchor, 1963.

Lipset, Seymour Martin. "White Collar Workers and Professionals—Their Attitudes and Behavior Towards Unions." *Readings in Industrial Sociology*, edited by William A. Faunce. New York: Appleton-Century-Crofts, 1967.

Lipset, Seymour Martin. *Rebellion in the University*. Boston: Little, Brown, 1972.

Margolin, Leo J. "Negotiated Increases put CUNY Professors at Top Pay." *The Christian Science Monitor* (October 22, 1969).

McConnell, T. R. *The Redistribution of Power in Higher Education: Changing Patterns of Internal Governance*. Berkeley: Center for Research and Development in Higher Education, University of California, 1971.

McConnell, T. R., and Mortimer, Kenneth P. *The Faculty in University Governance*. Berkeley: Center for Research and Development in Higher Education, University of California, 1971.

McCormick, Richard. "Rutgers." *Academic Transformations*, edited by David Riesman and Verne Stadtman. New York: McGraw-Hill, 1973.

McHugh, William F. "Collective Bargaining and the College Student." *Journal of Higher Education* 62 (March 1971).

McHugh, William F. "Faculty Unionism." *The Tenure Debate*, edited by Bardwell Smith. San Francisco: Jossey-Bass, 1973.

"Memorandum to the Faculty." *CUPA Voice of the Faculty* (January 4, 1973).

Merton, Robert K. *Social Theory and Social Structure*. New York: Free Press, 1968.

Mortimer, Kenneth P., and Lozier, G. Gregory. *Collective Bargaining: Implica-*

tions for Governance. University Park: Center for the Study of Higher Education, Pennsylvania State University, 1972.

Mortimer, Kenneth P., and Lozier, G. Gregory. "Contracts of Four-Year Institutions." *Faculty Unions and Collective Bargaining*, edited by E. D. Duryea and Robert S. Fisk. San Francisco: Jossey-Bass, 1973.

National Student Association. "Congress News, August 23, 1971." *Measure* (November 1971).

Netick, Allan. "The Student Grades the Prof." *The UPC Advocate* 3 (April 1973).

Oberer, Walter E. "Faculty Participation in Academic Decision Making: As to What Issue, By What Forms, Using What Means of Persuasion?" *Employment Relations in Higher Education*, edited by Stanley Elam and Michael H. Moskow. Bloomington, Ind.: Phi Delta Kappa, 1969.

"On Faculty Unionism." *Measure* (November 1971).

"On Implementation of New Academic Salary Structure." Testimony presented by United Professors of California before the Faculty and Staff Affairs Committee of the CSUC Trustees (December 8, 1972).

O'Neill, Robert M. "Tenure Under Attack." *The Tenure Debate*, edited by Bardwell Smith. San Francisco: Jossey-Bass, 1973.

"Organized University." *New York Times* (December 6, 1972).

"Pennsylvania Pact Approved by Profs." *CUPA Voice of the Faculty* (September 1972).

Perkin, H. J. *Key Profession: The History of the Association of University Teachers*. London: Routledge & Kegan Paul, 1969.

"A Position Paper on Tenure." Trenton: Council of New Jersey State College Locals AFT, 1972.

"PSC Contract Proposals." *Clarion* 2 (October 25, 1972).

"Proceedings of the Student Conference on the 1972 Master Plan." Albany: State University of New York, 1972.

Raskin, A. H. "Unionism and the Content of Education: What Are the Bounds?" *New York Times* (January 8, 1973).

Report of the Ad Hoc Committee on Collective Bargaining. East Lansing: Michigan State University, 1972.

Riesman, David. "Commentary and Epilogue." *Academic Transformations*, edited by David Riesman and Verne Stadtman. New York: McGraw-Hill, 1973.

Scully, Malcolm G., and Sievert, William A. "Collective Bargaining Gains Converts Among Teachers: Three National Organizations Vie to Represent Faculties." *The Chronicle of Higher Education* 5 (May 10, 1971).

Semas, Philip W. "Students Consider Own Bargaining Role as Faculty Units Dominate Key Issues." *Chronicle of Higher Education* 7 (April 30, 1973).

Shanker, Albert. "Double Standards at the *Times*." *New York Times* (December 17, 1972).

Shark, Alan. "A Student's Collective Thought on Bargaining." *The Journal of Higher Education* 43, no. 7 (October 1972).

Smith, Page. "Letters to my Colleagues." *University Guardian* 2 (January 1973).

"UC-AFT Brief on Faculty Tenure and Due Process at U.C." *University Guardian* 2 (October 1972).

"UPC-Labor-Demo Coalition Rolls Back Salary Scheme." *The UPC Advocate* 3 (February 1973).

Walters, Donald E. "Collective Bargaining in Higher Education." *AGB Reports* 17 (March 1973).

Wollett, Donald H. "The Status and Trends of Collective Negotiations for Faculty in Higher Education." *University of Wisconsin Law Review* 150, no. 1 (1971).

Wollett, Donald H. "Historical Development of Faculty Collective Bargaining and Current Extent." Paper presented to the First Annual National Conference of the National Center for the Study of Collective Bargaining in Higher Education, Baruch College (April 12, 1973).

Zeller, Belle. "Panel Discussion." *Faculty Power: Collective Bargaining on Campus*, edited by Terrence Tice. Ann Arbor: The Institute of Continuing Legal Education, 1972.

20

Academic Senates and Faculty Collective Bargaining

J. Victor Baldridge and Frank R. Kemerer

In late 1974 we sent a questionnaire to a random sample of college presidents, to every college president with a faculty union, and to every faculty member who was chairperson of a union in the United States. One of the questions was this: "Do you believe collective bargaining will increase the effectiveness of campus governance?" To say the least, there was a sharp difference of opinion: only 10 percent of the sample of presidents agreed, 20 percent of the presidents with unions agreed, and a stunning 77 percent of the union officials agreed!

At the very heart of the academic governance process—and at the heart of the controversy—are the academic senates. At their best faculty senates[1] are the arena where faculty and administrators meet as educational professionals to deliberate on matters of shared concern, providing the forums for the academic community's deliberations in curriculum matters, budgetary issues, and other professional activities. Although they are often criticized because their powers are largely advisory, senates have nevertheless played a valuable function in symbolizing the academic community's commitment to shared

Reprinted from *Journal of Higher Education* 47, no. 4 (July/August 1976), pp. 391-411. Copyright 1976 by The Ohio State University Press.

1. The term "senate" is widely used, but of course there are many different types of faculty deliberative bodies. However, to simplify matters we use the commonly used term "senate" to cover all such groups.

governance. With the advent of faculty unionization, however, there are serious questions about the relationship between senates and unions, and about the impact unions may have on shared governance. Some observers believe that collective bargaining may actually enhance and protect traditional academic governance procedures. Others, however, fear that collective bargaining is a substantial threat to collegial practices.

Starting in 1971, the Stanford Project in Academic Governance, a study funded by the National Institute for Education, undertook a major research effort to study the impact of faculty collective bargaining on governance and decision making in higher education.[2] The Stanford Project was conducted in two phases. For phase one, in 1971, we selected 240 institutions at which to study general issues of academic governance. In this phase, collective bargaining was only one issue among a larger set of concerns. We used a variety of research tools. Over 17,000 questionnaires were sent to faculty members and administrators, with a 53 percent return rate. Another questionnaire went to the presidents of the institutions, with 100 percent return after several series of coaxing letters and phone calls. In addition, information about the colleges was gathered from published sources, both governmental and private.

Phase two was conducted in 1974, and the prime focus was on collective bargaining. We resampled the original 240 institutions, but also added *all* the unionized schools in the United States. (At that time, the total was over 300, but several were eventually excluded because of their extremely specialized character.) In addition to providing longitudinal data, the two samples provide valuable contrast between a random sample of all colleges and universities and the specialized groups that had faculty unions. In phase two, we used two questionnaires on collective bargaining. One went to the presidents of the institutions, both the 1971 national sample and entire population of unionized institutions in 1974. The other went to the faculty chairpersons of the local campus bargaining units. Both questionnaires had response rates in excess of 65 percent. A complete discussion of the findings regarding faculty collective bargaining is found in Kemerer and Baldridge (1975).

The Weaknesses of Faculty Senates: A Cause of Unionization

At many institutions, weak faculty governance has been unable to safeguard faculty interests from the onslaught of economically re-

2. In addition to the authors, the principle investigators on the SPAG project were David Curtis (Governor's State University), George P. Ecker (Ohio State University), and Gary Riley (UCLA).

lated environmental pressures. The problems of senates can be seen in a few simple facts. Most campuses included in the 1974 SPAG study have senates, though less prestigious institutions, especially the unionized ones, are likely to have a faculty representative body. However, nearly 75 percent of the presidents at two-year institutions reported that their senate is eight years or less in age. Only 25 percent of the public and private multiversities reported such a recent senate formation. The absence of a strong tradition of faculty participation in governance may presage the growth of faculty collective bargaining, as evident at two-year and at less prestigious four-year public colleges.

The Stanford survey results showed that the faculty senate no longer represents only the faculty at a majority of institutions. Over 60 percent of the institutions have senates with administrative representation, nearly 50 percent have student representation, and almost a third have nonacademic staff represented. Our survey results also suggest that broad-based senates disperse much of their energy to deal with campuswide problems and faculty interests cease to be a primary concern.

The basic difference between faculty senates and unions is that senates operate on delegated authority and depend on institutional appropriations and staffing. Because faculty senates are dependent bodies, their power to affect decision making is granted by the grace of the governing board and the administration. Historically, elite private liberal arts institutions have encouraged faculty input in decision making and consequently are more likely to retain the influence of faculty senates. But younger senates may, under the influence of environmental pressures, find their role in shared governance reduced. A spokesman active in senate affairs at Central Michigan University has noted, "We became aware that we enjoyed the benefits of our hard-won battles purely at the pleasure of the Board of Trustees." Senates are therefore susceptible to being labelled "company unions." In addition, since administrators are often included in senate membership, senates are not really representative of the faculty qua faculty.

For these reasons, incidentally, a senate cannot normally convert to a recognized union. The NLRA states that it is an unfair labor practice for an employer "to dominate or interfere with the formation or administration of any labor organization or contribute financial or other support to it."

In 1974 the NLRB ruled in a critical decision that the Northeastern University senate could not gain status as the faculty bargaining agent. The NLRB stated:

The Employer [the university] contends that the Faculty Senate is a labor organization, the faculty handbook is the collective bargaining agreement, and a contract bar to the filing and processing of the instant petition exists. We find no merit in the Employer's contentions. . . . We find that the Faculty Senate functions as advisory committees and makes recommendations (which are totally different from bargaining demands that a union would make upon an employer during contract negotiations) to the president. Accordingly, we find that the Faculty Senate does not function as a labor organization within the meaning of the Act.

The Employer contends that the faculty handbook, coupled with existing practices in the academic setting of Northeastern University, is the equivalent of a collective bargaining agreement. The Employer argues this constitutes a contract bar under the Board's Rules and that the petition should therefore be dismissed. We find that the faculty handbook coupled with existing practices in the academic setting at Northeastern University, is not a collective bargaining agreement within the meaning of the Act. Moreover, the faculty handbook does not contain a termination date, which is a prerequisite for finding a contract to be a bar to an election. Therefore, we find no merit in the Employer's contention that a contract bar exists and that the petition should be dismissed [National Labor Relations Board, 218, no. 4, pages 3-5].

If a senate wished to convert into a full-fledged union, under most collective bargaining statutes it must first disband and reform into either an independent organization or sponsor a satellite group that overlaps senate membership. This option may not really be feasible. A senate that includes supervising employees, such as administrators, cannot function as a union nor create one with overlapping membership. In public systems, the tendency toward large, all-encompassing bargaining units eliminates the opportunity for faculty on a single campus to win representation with a union that is tied to a local campus senate. The expertise and money required for successful bargaining are so costly that affiliation with an outside agency will probably be necessary. Of the more than 300 unionized schools included in the SPAG 1974 survey, fewer than 30 had independent bargaining agents and most of these were special purpose institutions with small faculties, such as law schools.

A senate's ability to sponsor a viable union that wins election depends upon several factors. First, the personnel composition of the bargaining unit is critical. Bargaining units that include many professors who were excluded from the senate will undermine the chances of a senate-based union. Second, the strength of the senate is important. A recently formed or a weak senate will probably not attract many followers to the independent union it sponsors. Finally, senate-based unions face competition from other bargaining agents with the resources and expertise to campaign for members and fight at the bargaining table. Senate-based unions without outside affiliation are sadly underfinanced and understaffed.

To be successful even an independent senate-based organization would probably adopt the characteristics of a union. Of course, even a senate that performs the functions normally reserved to a union will be ultimately tested by its success at meeting employee needs. Serious liabilities are inherent and may be insurmountable. Since the senate functions outside of a legal framework, it lacks the legal backing to challenge the administration. In addition, since fiscal problems predominate today, experiments based on "shared governance" principles alone are unlikely to be successful, especially in institutions that had weak faculty senates. Therefore, the basic conclusion is that national trends and general conditions indicate that senates will be unlikely to assume successfully the role of a union on many campuses.

Let us turn now to the question of senate influence in academic governance. The 1974 Stanford survey asked presidents of nonunionized institutions to rate the influence of their senate on several issues. It must be emphasized that these ratings are based on the perceptions of campus presidents, who are likely to rate the senate influence higher than actually occurs. Hodgkinson, for example, concluded from his study of broadly representative senates that "administrators by and large are more euphoric about the performance and potential of campus senates than those who are directly involved in these bodies on a daily and weekly basis" (Hodgkinson, 1974, page 194). In any case, according to the perceptions of the respondents in our study, senates at nonunionized campuses are heavily involved in *academic* areas. The highest ratings presidents gave senates are over issues of degree requirements and curriculum. Issues of faculty promotion are also strongly influenced by senates at all types of institutions except at two-year colleges, which tend to follow the secondary school model of school administration. (A key role of secondary school administrators is the control of personnel policy.) In *economic* areas such as faculty salaries, department budgets, and faculty workload, senates were given far lower ratings. A similar pattern was evident for senates at institutions which are part of a state system of higher education.

For years the lack of real decision-making power by senates over economic issues in general and over personnel policy at public two-year institutions has caused many academicians to consider senates as ineffective. In 1969 the Carnegie survey asked respondents to indicate the effectiveness of their senates; 60 percent of the 60,000 respondents answered "fair" or "poor" (Bloustein, 1973b, pages 98-99). In Hodgkinson's study of 688 broad-based senates, campus presidents most frequently rated the influence of the senate in campus affairs as "advisory" and the second most frequent role as having "no responsibility at all." Hodgkinson also found that instead of "shared governance" the presidents stressed "the possibility of access" to decision-making channels (1974, pages 29, 136).

In many situations, then, senates seldom have any substantial impact on policy at institutions where boards and administrators opposed that influence. Because academics are seriously concerned about economic issues and job security, many faculties are interested in organizations that can effectively represent their interests as employees. Faculty union chairpersons indicated in the 1974 Stanford survey that along with economic concerns and job security, the weakness of existing campus governance mechanisms was a strong influence in bringing about collective bargaining on their campus.

These reservations particularly apply to the institutions where unionization has generally occurred—the community colleges, state colleges, and some less prestigious liberal arts institutions. Because these institutions rarely had effective faculty governance, it is difficult to determine how much unions have affected the process.

In light of these problems we frankly believe the importance of senates has been overstressed in the literature on academic governance. It is very doubtful indeed that at most institutions the senates deal effectively with matters of real substance. The critical issues are generally handled by the faculty at the departmental level (curriculum, student relations, faculty hiring, firing, and promoting), or by the administration at higher levels (budgets, overall staffing, physical plant, long-range planning). The average academic senate, we suspect, deals with relatively minor issues, and readily responds to administrative rather than faculty leadership.

Under these circumstances we can tell the effects of unions on weak senates, but we cannot predict what may happen to healthier senates in institutions with a long history of faculty governance. Therefore, we are cautious in projecting our conclusions much beyond the class of institutions where unionization has occurred. Entirely different consequences may occur if unionization comes to the prestigious colleges and universities. These words of caution are not meant to downgrade the importance of union-senate interaction but to be realistic; public discussions of senates and union impact on them have probably overstressed the issue. Nevertheless, it is an issue that deserves careful examination and in the following pages we will examine several matters.

Spheres of Activity for Unions and Senates

When a campus has both a senate and a union, what areas do each influence? What are the factors that promote or diminish conflict between unions and senates? The 1974 Stanford survey asked people on unionized campuses to rate union and senate influence over a broad spectrum of issues. Figure 20-1 suggests a number of conclusions.

Presidents and union chairpersons are basically similar in their influence ratings. They agree that unions strongly outperform senates in influencing economic issues, particularly faculty salaries, promotions, and working conditions. Meanwhile, senates retain influence over academic issues such as degree requirements and curriculum. Senates and unions share a joint area of influence over personnel issues such as faculty hiring, promotion, and tenure policy. Neither senates nor unions influence department budgets or long-range planning. It is interesting to note that there is little difference on all these issues between single-campus unions and multicampus unions or between two-year and four-year institutions (data not shown in Figure 20-1).

From our survey results it appears that both presidents and union chairpersons believe senates and unions have staked out fairly unique territories. The AAUP has argued that unions and senates should have separate areas of influence—the so-called "dual-track" approach. Both presidents and chairpersons react as the "dual-track" model predicts. That is, senates have their greatest influence in academic areas, while economic matters are the province of unions. Where the lines of demarcation are unclear, such as in faculty working conditions and long-range planning, the union and senate converge on degrees of influence.

Dual tracking assumes two mutually exclusive areas of influence for senates and unions. However, one qualification is needed, for much of the action occurs in the large area of overlapping concern between unions and senates. At one end of the continuum economic issues are under union jurisdiction. With their legal backing and their legal right to economic information, unions undoubtedly have more power than senates to gain economic benefits. On the other hand, senate jurisdiction over academic issues such as curriculum and degree requirements recognizes the need for a professional forum to resolve these matters. Between the two poles is a grey area where unions and senates share influence over department budgets, hiring policies, faculty promotion and tenure policies, faculty working conditions (student-teacher ratio, class load), and long-range planning. In

FIGURE 20-1
Influence Ratings of Senates and Unions on a Variety of Issues

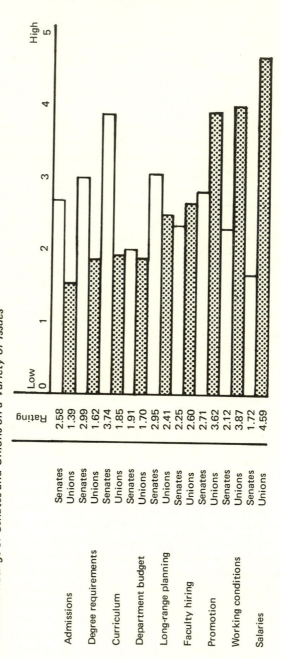

most cases the dual-track approach leaves *procedural* issues to the union but reserves policy affecting the *substance* of decisions to the senate, with academic departments actually responsible for decisions.

There are, however, a number of serious threats to the stability of the dual-track system. If the areas of senate and union influence remained stable, then the dual track would be a reality. Many factors cause a breakdown of the dual track, however, and encourage unions to expand into senate territory. Collective bargaining is a political process. In order to maintain membership support, union leaders will necessarily press to expand the scope of bargaining. Who is to decide which issues belong to the senate or to the union? Over a period of time the dilemma of drawing fine lines of distinction between issues suggests that the dual-track system is likely to become unstable.

There are many predictions about the future of traditional faculty governance in the face of union inroads. Some predictions are hopeful, but most are pessimistic. On the more hopeful side, Garbarino (1974, pages 108-115) tried to determine if the advent of unionization reduced faculty participation in governance through departments, committees, and senates. Using a study completed by the AAUP in 1971 he found that the participation rate in faculty governance for a number of institutions which unionized was actually higher than for the whole sample of institutions. Garbarino suggested that these faculty may have used collective bargaining to preserve governance influence in the face of threatened attacks. However, even in those institutions where unions had increased faculty participation, the relation to the administration was still categorized as "discussion" or "consultation." Neither union nor senate could claim joint participation with the administration in decision making, much less the right to resolve issues unilaterally. This was particularly true of economic and personnel issues.

Several other facts suggest that the breakdown in the dual-track system and the expansion of union influence is already occurring. First, the situation can be examined by studying contracts that have been negotiated. Research by John Andes (1974) shows that the contracts essentially deal with "working conditions"—workload, salaries, class size, and sometimes the selection of administrators. With each passing year, however, contracts are containing more items that were once the province of senates such as teaching load, governance issues, and matters related to faculty bylaws and policies. There is a "creeping expansion" of union areas of influence.

Similarly, in our survey the opinions of presidents and chairpersons predict a bleak future for senates and an expanding role for unions. We asked people to agree or disagree with this statement: "Where it occurs, faculty collective bargaining will undermine the influence of faculty senates or other established decision bodies." The presidents overwhelmingly agreed—74 percent of the presidents at nonunion colleges and 69 percent of the presidents at unionized colleges. By contrast, only 36 percent of the union chairpersons agreed with the statement.

Local Campus Unions and System Unions: Do They Affect Senates Differently?

Do systemwide unions affect senates differently from local-campus-only unions? Over half of our respondents said their union represents only the local campus. Few senates have disappeared at these institutions because of unions, but their future is clouded. Our survey showed that the majority of union chairpersons at two-year institutions believe the union has positively affected their senate, but the majority of union chairpersons at four-year schools believe unions have had little impact. Meanwhile, a majority of all presidents believe senate influence has *decreased* as a result of unionization (see Table 20-1).

Single-campus unions may be threatening to senates because these senates are recent and insecure creations. More than half of the four-year institutions and 72 percent of the two-year institutions reported that their senates were less than nine years old. A tradition of effective faculty participation in governance is crucial to maintaining viable dual-track bargaining. Apparently, recently established senates are jeopardized by unionization. Faculties expressing an interest in unionization are therefore expressing a lack of confidence in existing organizations, and unions offer the hope of gaining previously denied participation in governance.

How will multicampus unions affect senates? Of course, not every campus senate within a system will be affected the same because the campuses are usually quite diverse. This is particularly true of huge systems such as SUNY and CUNY. Thus, on campuses with little faculty involvement in governance, a multicampus union might fight to obtain governance rights. On other campuses where the faculty has long held governance power, a multicampus union contract might try to safeguard that tradition. The only way to assess accurately the impact of a master contract on faculty governance at a particular campus is to study that particular institution.

However, some general patterns do emerge. As Table 20-1 shows, on the whole presidents and chairpersons are pessimistic about the

TABLE 20-1
Impact of Unions on Senates

Single-campus unions	Number reporting	Influence of senate (percent)		
		Increased	About same	Decreased
Four-year institutions				
Presidents	17	6	35	59
Chairpersons	24	21	50	29
Two-year institutions				
Presidents	51	16	29	55
Chairpersons	49	45	27	29
Total				
Presidents	68	13	31	56
Chairpersons	73	37	34	29
Multicampus unions				
Four-year institutions				
Presidents	41	17	42	42
Chairpersons	32	9	44	47
Two-year institutions				
Presidents	22	14	27	59
Chairpersons	34	21	32	47
Total				
Presidents	63	16	37	48
Chairpersons	66	15	38	47

impact of multicampus unions on senates. About half of all respondents said unions had decreased senate influence. Compared to the single-campus situation, this was slightly less for presidents but nearly double for union chairpersons. Another third said unionism had made little difference; only about 15 percent said unionism had helped. Presidents at two-year campuses expressed negative attitudes, probably because their control would decrease substantially when unions encroached on their previously wide open field of presidential power.

As with single-campus senates and unions, an important factor in the decline of senate influence in multicampus systems is the lack of a strong tradition of faculty participation in governance. Sixty-seven percent of the senates at four-year campuses and 70 percent of the senates at two-year colleges were less than nine years of age.

More significantly, administrative centralization and multicampus bargaining pose a double threat to campus senates by shifting decision making off campus to central headquarters. It is not surprising that in multicampuses the SPAG survey showed 70 percent of presidents and 50 percent of union chairpersons agreeing that collective bargaining would undermine the senate's influence.

The Future of Senates in the Face of Unionization

Do all these facts about encroaching unionism mean that senates are doomed in the face of union pressure? Not necessarily, because most of the unionized campuses initially had a weak tradition of faculty participation in governance. It is no surprise, then, to find that unions have undercut impotent senates. In addition, other forces have threatened senates—especially institutional growth, centralization, and powerful economic pressures. When unions and senates coexist, the health or weakness of the senate depends upon many variables other than faculty unionization. Let us mention a few of the forces at play in the situation.

Our society has felt the impacts of cultural pluralism, conflicts of interest, and value differences in every area, but especially in our educational institutions. These differences have created a conflict on campuses about the proper mission of the academic profession. President Edward J. Bloustein of Rutgers concludes that collegiality is disappearing under the onslaught, but he does not blame unionism. Instead he believes unionism is a symptom, a result, of a deeper problem.

What has happened is that our faculties and our student bodies and our boards of governors have now discovered that their interests are adverse on occasion and that there is no single common overriding interest which can or should unite them on all issues [1973a, page 191].

Budget cuts and declining enrollments force latent conflicts of interest among campus constituencies out into the open and undermine the spirit of cooperative decision making. We believe such fundamental differences are becoming common on all campuses as the external economic and political climate for higher education worsens. Given the tendency of environmental pressures to exacerbate differences among campus constituencies, rapid institutional adaptation to changing times cannot be accomplished without great turmoil that directly threatens traditional modes of campus governance.

Growing dissent between administration and faculty, and within faculty ranks, makes consensus on principles less likely and dual tracking more difficult. In addition, the 1960's produced rising expectations that cannot be met in the 1970's. As a result, disillusioned academicians discovered the appeal of unions as a means of gaining their expected rewards. The breakdown in value and the sharp clash of vested interests are particularly threatening to the senate's continued health, for in many ways the senate represents the traditional professional viewpoints that are being challenged.

A second major factor determining the future of senates is the legal situation. Even a politically astute administration can do little to alter the effects of a multicampus unit determination that establishes a statewide union that undermines local campus senates, or a court decision upholding a union's involvement in governance. For example, the NLRA and most state laws outlaw company unions and establish the union as the exclusive employee representative. A company union charge by a competing union may challenge continued administrative support of the faculty senate. Once a union is voted in, it may force the administration to consider it the exclusive employee representative, thus curtailing the senate's and department committees' jurisdiction.

By placing few restrictions on the mandatory subject of bargaining, the law invites unions to move continually into new areas indirectly related to economic concerns. Some laws restrict the union by establishing "management prerogatives," activities essential to management's organizational control over which the union may not bargain. Management prerogatives are, however, at odds with shared governance and may be rendered ineffective by unions that bargain about issues irrespective of the law.

Administrative rulings by the NLRB or by the state PERBs become part of the legal context. Although their decisions interpreting the law to a given situation have not yet formed a distinct pattern, their decisions can be critical in shaping bargaining activities on a particular campus. Insofar as senates and unions are concerned, administrative rulings pertaining to the scope of bargaining may determine the fate of these organizations. For example, in 1975 a district NLRB official ruled that the AAUP union as a labor organization at St. John's University could not interfere with traditional senate areas of activity. The question was moot, however, since a settlement was reached before the decision was rendered.

Another legal question revolves around writing governance matters into the contract. Even where governance is not a mandatory subject of bargaining, an administration may agree to bargain about it. The opinions are divided on writing governance into the contract: it may strengthen formerly weak academic processes, or it may subject governance provisions to future negotiation. Both sides of the argument seem plausible and the trends are likely to be determined by local conditions on individual campuses.

A third variable that will help determine the future of senates is the style and degree of administrative support. Woodrow Wilson once likened democracy to living tissue: it must be carefully protected and nourished to thrive. Senates possessing little de jure authority are extremely fragile and, like a democratic government, they depend upon the willingness of individuals to work on their behalf. Unions can quickly replace ineffective senates if administrators refuse to recognize faculty discontent with them. Administrators who attempt to defeat a faculty union by negotiating with the senate on union matters are essentially also promoting unionization. Too often administrators pay lip service to the senate while condemning the union—forgetting that both are creations of the faculty. As a result unions grow more militant, senates become weaker, and faculties are torn by conflict. Administrators who support genuine, effective faculty participation in governance are, in fact, encouraging a strengthened senate.

In addition, administrators can be supportive of senates by acting to prevent union contracts from spreading into governance issues—by actively fighting for the dual-track idea. They can insist on the separation of the senate's right to control academic issues from the union's right to bargain over economic issues. In a sense, this is a matter of clarifying proper roles, of restraining different interest groups from encroaching on the proper influence area of others. This is a task made difficult by the multiple, overlapping decision bodies on a campus. It is not unusual for a single campus to have most of the following: (1) department, school, and division committees; (2) faculty senate; (3) student senate; (4) broad-based senate; (5) faculty union (sometimes more than one representing academic employees); and (6) administrative council.

Drawing the boundaries around the spheres of influence for each organization can be mind-boggling. Nevertheless, because of its unique position of authority on campus, the administration should take the lead in establishing a workable governance scheme. Where conflict of interest is great, however, the chances for a stable consensus are diminished. The administration has a central role to play in helping define proper spheres of action, and must take an active lead in that task.

To What Extent Should Unions Participate in Governance?

The definition of proper roles for union and senate, of course, involves many subtle value judgments and depends on many factors that are unique to each individual campus. In this section we want to speculate on the various responses administrators may take in dealing with unions in the governance arena. It is standard practice for most faculty unions to demand decision-making rights in areas other than just economic. Usually they begin by demanding influence over campus personnel decision making. This is not surprising since the quest for job security closely rivals the faculty's desire for higher wages and benefits as the leading cause of unionization. Virtually all faculty unions also eventually seek to expand their jurisdiction into areas traditionally considered the territory of senates, departments, and the administration. Because it has been repeatedly shown that contracts expand over time and because contractualized items rarely get eliminated in subsequent agreements, administrative reaction to union demands takes on added significance. Confronted with such demands, administrators are faced with a difficult decision: to what extent are governance rights a legitimate union concern?

At the extreme, two quite different views about collective bargaining have emerged. The first we can call the "union accommodation model." This approach assumes that improved employee relations and organizational functioning result when the scope of negotiation includes all matters of concern to either party and contracts contain provisions reflecting agreement on these matters. This model calls for few legal limitations on the scope of bargainable issues. Not only will unrestricted bargaining eliminate hiding places for incompetent administrators and union leaders, it will also give the parties the chance to discuss and resolve a variety of problems and concerns. Many proponents of this model argue that over time continued communication between employer and employee fosters a deepening relationship of understanding and mutual accommodation (Walker et al., 1976). Like a constitution or set of bylaws, the contract helps to set the boundaries of the relationship and through its grievance provisions helps to channel conflict to peaceful resolution. In a given situation the actual consequences of bargaining will be largely determined by the needs and bargaining strength of the parties. But in all instances, this model presumes that collective bargaining and the mechanisms it establishes help foster a working and living relationship between employer and employee.

Applied to higher education, this approach to collective bargaining will inevitably result in comprehensive agreements. Not only will the contract eventually contain provisions relating to campus personnel and governance policy, but provision may also be made for union-management consultation to occur during contract administration in order to study and resolve continuing issues of mutual concern, e.g., an affirmative action policy, a detailed retrenchment policy, and so on. Naturally, such comprehensive agreements will have the side effect of severely curtailing the influence of senates, unless, of course, such arguments include provisions supportive of senates. The early experience of the Massachusetts State System serves as a good example of the union accommodation model's approach to collective bargaining. Many key administrators in the system favored bargaining over governance when faculties at the eleven colleges began to organize. As Donald E. Walters, acting director of the Massachusetts System, has written,

If faculties are to prevent their reclassification as mere employees, if faculty professionalism and independence is to be preserved where it exists and sought after where it does not, if institutional autonomy is not to be eroded, and if college communities—faculty, student and administrators alike—are to emerge from the experience of unionization and collective bargaining as colleagues and not as adversaries, then campus governance must become a matter of collective bargaining; for properly negotiated it becomes a potent force for integration on campus [1972, page 18].

Until 1974 the Massachusetts State System's bargaining law prohibited bargaining over economic issues, a fact that may in part have elicited the positive administrative attitudes. The union jointly with the administration set up a tripartite governance system representing administrators, faculty, and students. While the union thus agreed to share some of its authority, it also acquired a formal role in the governance system. Without union concurrence, the system could never have been set up; without its continued support, the procedure probably could not continue to function.

Directly counter to the union accommodation model is the "union opposition model." This approach recognizes the tendency for union concerns to grow and contracts lengthen. It implicitly assumes that employers and employees have different interests and that the potential for management-union cooperation is limited, particularly when institutional resources are in decline. Thus according to the union opposition model, management must not simply rely on a restrictive legal framework or the good intentions of union officials to control the scope of bargaining. Management must exert an aggressive posture at the bargaining table and during contract administration to oppose union advances and to support the academic senate. In its purest form, this model seeks to limit management-union contact to as few economic issues of traditional union concern as possible, classifying all others as matters of management prerogative and senate influence. Those endorsing the union opposition model believe that a working relationship with unions is a contradiction in terms and thus are reluctant to consult with union representatives under any circumstances. "Consultation" to proponents of this model means bargaining by another name, not an amicable arrangement for communication and problem-solving during the term of a contract.

In higher education this approach is characteristic to some extent of the early administration-union relationship at Central Michigan University. In an address to the faculty in 1969, the former president of Central Michigan, William B. Boyd, warned of the evils of unions and thus set the theme his administration would take towards bargaining.

Increasingly, matters that ought to be reserved for the deliberation of faculties are transferred from the floor of the senate to a table-top pounded by adversaries engaged in something less than reasoned debate. Educational policy thus becomes the product of negotiation rather than deliberation. The exaggerated demands and counter-claims common to the bargaining process make a mockery out of scrupulous respect for truth and seem entirely alien to the scholarly processes. It is hard to believe the latter can be properly served by the former.

Administrators at Central Michigan have taken a very constricted interpretation of the scope of bargaining under the state bargaining law and have worked to keep the union from expanding its role.

Which of the two models is the more appropriate for higher education? The answer does not lie in the assumption that the collective bargaining process is less adversarial when used by academicians. While we hear much rhetoric to the contrary, there is little evidence that the collective bargaining process itself is any different when used by professors, symphony musicians, or the unskilled.

Rather, the answer largely depends on the characteristics of a particular institution, the characteristics of its faculty, and the force of pressures from the external environment. For example, consider the following: at institution A, a union is formed and quickly enrolls over 60 percent of the faculty in the face of drastic budget cuts and threatened dismissals. Traditional governance forms at this campus have always been weak with little real faculty input in decision making. The union demands that administrators negotiate with it over personnel decision making, class size, and a host of similar terms. Further, the union demands that periodic consultation sessions be set up during the contract to discuss and resolve matters of mutual concern. What response should the administration give? Clearly, management cannot afford to take an entrenched position towards the union because the union has become the primary voice for the majority of the faculty. To ensure organizational stability and even its own security, the administration must come to some accommodation with the union. While these same administrators may wish to establish a collegial governance system, such as the Massachusetts State System, they cannot do so without the cooperation of the union, which has become the exclusive representative of the employee. Bypassing the union will almost surely result in the union's filing an unfair labor practice suit against the administration. It still remains to be seen whether a working relationship can develop over the long run between management and union representatives at these institutions conducive to improving the quality of educational services.

Now consider institution B. Here departments play an important role in personnel decision making and the institutional senate is often consulted with regard to the development of academic policy. Union membership is low, with less than one-third of the faculty paying dues. The preponderance of union members are relatively young and untenured. The union at institution B is overly hostile to the administration in its literature and frequently files grievances accompanied by excessive publicity boasting of its actions in defense of faculty rights. The union demands that the administration consult it about any matter which relates to conditions of work. At institution B the administration rightly concludes that it should embrace the union opposition model and at the same time continue the policy of working closely with the academic senate and deferring as often as possible to departmental judgment in personnel issues. This administration concludes that the proliferation of grievances as well as the demands of frequent consultation are designed to increase exposure of the union. Consequently, they decide to avoid going out of their way to encourage management-union cooperation.

While it may seem an anomaly to suggest that the administration can determine what the union's legitimate interest should be, in many situations the administration is the *only* entity aside from the union itself in a position to do so. Faculty members are often apathetic and disorganized when it comes to governance; in our 1971 Stanford survey, only 21 percent of a broad sample of faculty members said they regularly got involved in campus governance. Likewise, only a handful take the time and energy to participate in establishing union policy. Often a union may be "captured" by the most discontented people who are not well established in their profession and do not subscribe to traditional academic values. The consequences of minority rule are well demonstrated by the Hawaiian and Central

Michigan experiences. At Hawaii, the Hawaiian Federation of College Teachers (HFCT), an AFT affiliate, negotiated a contract which, among other controversial features, compromised tenure. The majority of the bargaining unit (by law, all bargaining union members are eligible to vote in ratification elections) overwhelmingly rejected the contract. Eventually, the union itself was ousted and replaced by one jointly supported by the local NEA and AAUP chapters. During the years of turmoil, the real loser was the faculty which, in the words of one commentator, suffered "singular economic defeat" relative to the other unionized groups of public employees in Hawaii. At Central Michigan, the faculty union with only about a 30 percent dues-paying membership negotiated a contract in 1974 which included an agency shoplike provision (nonunion members must pay a fee to the union equal to union dues) and then reversed the previous practice by allowing only card-carrying members to vote in the ratification election. The contract was ratified.

Unlike faculty, administrators are relatively few in number and hold disproportionate control of institutional resources and power. They are in a unique position to control the role of a developing union where union membership is low, traditional governance mechanisms exist, and external pressures are not overly threatening. By dealing with unions fairly and carefully on economic matters but insisting that academic governance is the prerogative of senates, departments, and academic committees, administrators can help maintain valuable checks and balances. Of course, deeds speak louder than words. If environmental pressures tie the hands of administrators or if campus officials succeed only in demonstrating hypocrisy, union power will grow despite administrative opposition.

Conclusion

The increase in union power at the expense of the senates is often blamed on unsupportive administrators and on laws that arm the unions with legal weapons. But much of the future viability or failure of senates will be determined by the faculty themselves. Demands of teaching and research to satisfy the requirements for tenure probably preclude prolonged active participation by many junior faculty in campus governance. Many tenured faculty members find more satisfaction in their professional activities than in campus politics. Time and time again, the people interviewed in our case studies reported that senates were ineffective because faculty were not active participants.

If faculty do not become involved in both senate and union affairs, the ominous predictions about the demise of faculty governance may come true. Combined with other factors undermining
dual-track governance, faculty apathy can strike the final blow to traditional academic governance. On the other hand, faculty involvement, determination to preserve the best of traditional practices, and
an insistence on responsible union leadership may be the factors that
tip the scales toward a genuine dual-track system—with strong unions
and strong senates each doing what they can do best.

We really do not have enough experience to predict with great
accuracy the long-term impact that unionization will have on traditional faculty senates. This is especially true since, with only a few
exceptions, only institutions with weak senates have unionized, making it difficult to guess how unions might impact more developed
senates. However, with these reservations in mind, there are several
conclusions that can be drawn from the current situation.

First, the weaknesses of senates are a factor in promoting unionization in the first place. Moreover, senates are unlikely to convert
successfully to unions because laws hinder the change and senates
lack the support of national union affiliations. The opposite case is
also true, for where unions exist without a parallel senate they generally have *not* moved into the vacuum to tackle academic policy
issues.

Second, coexisting senates and unions appear to divide the responsibilities, with unions addressing economic issues and working conditions, and senates dealing with curriculum, degree requirements, and
admissions. Their joint responsibility covers personnel issues such as
hiring, promotion, and tenure. Finally, neither senates nor unions
have much control over budgets, selection of administrators, overall
staffing arrangements, physical plant, and long-range planning. In
these areas administrators remain in command.

Third, the dual tracks of influence may not remain stable, as the
union influence expands into traditional senate responsibilities. The
survey respondents, especially presidents and to some degree chairpersons, as well as the analysis of contracts, show expansion with
each passing year.

Fourth, how far the dual-track breakdown goes, however, will
depend on many factors, and unionism is only one. Conflicts of
interest, the leadership of administrators, the legal context, and faculty participation are all critical elements in the equation that will
determine the future viability of senates in the face of union challenges.

All in all, the evidence does not warrant the pessimistic view that senates will collapse with the arrival of collective bargaining, but serious problems definitely exist. Unions do curtail senate influence over economically related issues where senates and unions coexist, and to a varying extent unions also share concurrent jurisdiction with senates in areas such as personnel decision making. But unions alone cannot be held responsible for the problems of senates. Many impotent senates are also susceptible to other problems: faculty apathy, administrative interference, system-level power plays. Our primary conclusion is that the senates and other mechanisms of faculty governance are fragile, and, if not protected and supported, they will be destroyed by the political winds sweeping the campus.

References

Andes, John. "Developing Trends in Content of Collective Bargaining Contracts in Higher Education." Washington, D.C.: Academic Collective Bargaining Information Service, 1974.

Bloustein, Edward J. "Collective Bargaining in the Halls of Academe." *Liberal Education* 59 (May 1973a).

Bloustein, Edward J. *Governance of Higher Education: Six Priority Problems.* Berkeley: Carnegie Commission, 1973b.

Garbarino, Joseph W. *Faculty Bargaining: Change and Conflict.* New York: McGraw-Hill, 1974.

Hodgkinson, Harold L. *The Campus Senate: Experiment in Democracy.* Berkeley: Center for Research and Development in Higher Education, 1974.

Kemerer, Frank R., and Baldridge, J. Victor. *Unions on Campus.* San Francisco: Jossey-Bass, 1975.

Walker, D.; Feldman, David; and Stone, Greg. "Collegiality and Collective Bargaining: An Alternative Perspective." *Educational Record* (Spring 1976).

Walters, Donald E. "Collective Bargaining in Higher Education: Its Impact on Campus Life and Faculty Governance." *Academics at the Bargaining Table: Early Experience,* edited by James B. Begin. Eugene, Ore.: ERIC, 1972.